Since the fall of the Soviet Union in 199_ [P9-DZZ-378] the question of "whither Russia?" has been the source of ceaseless speculation both at home and abroad. In search of answers, twelve highly qualified scholars examine the complex interplay between continuity and change that has marked developments in Russia under the leadership first of Boris Yeltsin and now of Vladimir Putin. Analyzing the recent past, they also peer into the country's future. In his introduction to the volume, Peter Rutland asks whether we are witnessing the gradual entrenchment of parliamentary democracy, the slow return to autocracy, or mere political stagnation.

The Russian case appears in a relatively unflattering light when placed in the comparative context of post-communist transition studies (by authors Valerie Bunce, Alexander J. Motyl, and Anatoly M. Khazanov). On the other hand, a close look at the recent history of Ukraine by Ilya Prizel leads him to the implicit conclusion that the Russian state and society are, by comparison, well situated.

Marshall I. Goldman and Theodore H. Friedgut assess the massive upheavals that have transformed the Russian economy and society since 1991, and Vera Tolz traces the attempts made by politicians and intellectuals to define a new national identity for the Russian people. Politics – the parties, the electoral system and results, and the complexities of the federal system – are described and analyzed in detail by a number of prominent Russian scholars (Andrey Ryabov, Nikolai V. Petrov, and Oksana Oracheva), who add a Moscow-centered perspective to the volume. As for Russian foreign policy, Rajan Menon argues that the country's turn toward rapprochement with the United States is not tactical as often thought, but deeply rooted in a strategic reorientation.

Restructuring Post-Communist Russia poses the fundamental questions while providing the information and analysis needed to give the (at least, preliminary) answers.

Restructuring Post-Communist Russia

Since the fall of the Soviet Union in 1991, the question of "whither Russia?" has been the source of ceaseless speculation both at home and abroad. In search of answers, twelve highly qualified scholars examine the complex interplay between continuity and change that has marked developments in Russia under the leadership first of Boris Yeltsin and now of Vladimir Putin. Analyzing the recent past, they also peer into the country's future. In his introduction to the volume, Peter Rutland asks whether we are witnessing the gradual entrenchment of parliamentary democracy, the slow return to autocracy, or mere political stagnation.

The Russian case appears in a relatively unflattering light when placed in the comparative context of post-communist transition studies (by authors Valerie Bunce, Alexander J. Motyl, and Anatoly M. Khazanov). On the other hand, a close look at the recent history of Ukraine by Ilya Prizel leads him to the implicit conclusion that the Russian state and society are, by comparison, well situated.

Marshall I. Goldman and Theodore H. Friedgut assess the massive upheavals that have transformed the Russian economy and society since 1991, and Vera Tolz traces the attempts made by politicians and intellectuals to define a new national identity for the Russian people. Politics – the parties, the electoral system and results, and the complexities of the federal system – are described and analyzed in detail by a number of prominent Russian scholars (Andrey Ryabov, Nikolai V. Petrov, and Oksana Oracheva), who add a Moscow-centered perspective to the volume. As for Russian foreign policy, Rajan Menon argues that the country's turn toward rapprochement with the United States is not tactical as often thought, but deeply rooted in a strategic reorientation.

Restructuring Post-Communist Russia poses fundamental questions while providing the information and analysis needed to give the (at least, preliminary) answers.

Yitzhak Brudny is Senior Lecturer in Political Science and Russia Studies at the Hebrew University of Jerusalem. For the year 2003–4, he was Visiting Professor of Government at Wesleyan University. He is author of *Reinventing Russia: Russian Nationalism and the Soviet State* (1999), as well as of several journal articles and book chapters.

Jonathan Frankel is Professor of Russian and Contemporary Jewish Studies at the Hebrew University of Jerusalem. He has written and edited many books and articles, among them *Prophecy and Politics: Socialism, Nationalism and the Russian Jews, 1862–1917* (Cambridge University Press, 1981) and *The Damascus Affair: 'Ritual Murder,' Politics, and the Jews in 1840* (Cambridge University Press, 1997).

Stefani Hoffman is Director of the Mayrock Center for Russian, Eurasian, and East European Research at the Hebrew University of Jerusalem. She was editor of *The Commonwealth of Independent States and the Middle East* from 1983 to 1997. She is the author of several journal articles and chapters in edited volumes.

RESTRUCTURING
POST-COMMUNIST RUSSIA

Edited by

YITZHAK BRUDNY
Hebrew University of Jerusalem

JONATHAN FRANKEL
Hebrew University of Jerusalem

STEFANI HOFFMAN
Hebrew University of Jerusalem

CAMBRIDGE
UNIVERSITY PRESS

PUBLISHED BY THE PRESS SYNDICATE OF THE UNIVERSITY OF CAMBRIDGE
The Pitt Building, Trumpington Street, Cambridge, United Kingdom

CAMBRIDGE UNIVERSITY PRESS
The Edinburgh Building, Cambridge CB2 2RU, UK
40 West 20th Street, New York, NY 10011-4211, USA
477 Williamstown Road, Port Melbourne, VIC 3207, Australia
Ruiz de Alarcón 13, 28014 Madrid, Spain
Dock House, The Waterfront, Cape Town 8001, South Africa

http://www.cambridge.org

First published 2004

Printed in the United States of America

Typeface Palatino 10/12 pt.   *System* LATEX 2_ε [TB]

A catalog record for this book is available from the British Library.

Library of Congress Cataloging in Publication data
Reconstructing post-Communists Russia / edited by Yitzhak Brudny,
Jonathan Frankel, Stefani Hoffman
p.   cm.
Includes bibliographical references and index.
ISBN 0-521-84027-9
1. Russia (Federation) – Politics and government – 1991–
2. Post-communism – Russia (Federation).   I. Brudny, Yitzhak M.
II. Frankel, Jonathan.   III. Hoffman, Stefani.
DK510.763.R428   2004
320.947 – dc22   2003069685

ISBN 0 521 84027 9 hardback

To Theodore H. Friedgut
From his colleagues and friends

Contents

THE RUSSIAN POLITICAL SYSTEM: TOWARD STABILIZATION?

Contributors

Valerie Bunce holds the Aaron Binenkorb Chair of International Studies and chairs the Government Department at Cornell University. She is the author of *Subversive Institutions: The Design and the Destruction of Socialism and the State* (Cambridge University Press, 1999). From 2001 to 2002, she served as president of the American Association for the Advancement of Slavic Studies and vice-president of the American Political Science Association.

Theodore H. Friedgut is Professor Emeritus of Russian studies at the Hebrew University of Jerusalem. Among his books are *Political Participation in the USSR* (Princeton University Press, 1979) and *Iuzovka and Revolution*, 2 vols. (Princeton University Press, 1989 and 1995).

Marshall I. Goldman is the Kathryn Davis Professor of Russian Economics (Emeritus) at Wellesley College and Associate Director of the Davis Center for Russian and Eurasian Studies at Harvard University. His most recent book is *The Piratization of Russia: Russian Reform Goes Awry* (Routledge, 2003).

Anatoly M. Khazanov, FBA, is the Ernest Gellner Professor of Anthropology at the University of Wisconsin–Madison. Among his books are *Nomads and the Outside World* (Cambridge University Press, 1984) and *After the USSR. Ethnicity, Nationalism, and Politics in the Commonwealth of Independent States* (University of Wisconsin Press, 1995).

Rajan Menon is the Monroe J. Rathbone Professor of International Relations at Lehigh University. He was selected as a Carnegie Scholar for 2002–3 and served as senior Fellow at the Council on Foreign Relations. He is currently writing a book about Russia and Islam.

Alexander J. Motyl is Professor of Political Science and Deputy Director of the Center for Global Change and Governance at Rutgers University–Newark. He is the author of *Imperial Ends: The Decay, Collapse and Revival of Empires* (Columbia University Press, 2001) and *Revolutions, Nations, Empires: Conceptual Limits and Theoretical Possibilities* (Columbia University Press, 1999). He is an editor of the two-volume *Encyclopedia of Nationalism*.

Oksana Oracheva is Director of the International Fellowships Program (Russia) in the Moscow office of the Institute of International Education. She is Associate Professor of Political Science and Political Governance in the Russian Civil Service Academy attached to the office of the Russian president. Her recent publications include a number of articles in *Rossiia i Britaniia: v poiskakh dostoinogo pravleniia* (Perm, 2000).

Nikolai V. Petrov is a senior research associate at the Institute of Geography, the Russian Academy of Sciences, and head of the Center for Political Geographic Research in Moscow. From 1995 to 2000, he led the regional project at the Carnegie Endowment for International Peace Moscow Center, where his publications included the *Political Almanac of Russia* (1997) in three volumes and the annual supplements *Russian Regions* in 1999 and in 2000.

Ilya Prizel is Professor of Political Science and History at the University of Pittsburgh. His books include *Latin America through Soviet Eyes (1964–1982)* (Cambridge University Press, 1990) and *National Identity and Foreign Policy: Poland, Russia, Ukraine* (Cambridge University Press, 1998). He is editor of the quarterly, *East European Politics and Society*.

Peter Rutland is Professor of Political Science at Wesleyan University. Among his publications is *The Politics of Economic Stagnation in the Soviet Union: The Role of Local Political Organs in Economic Management* (Cambridge University Press, 1992).

Andrey Ryabov is a scholar in residence at the Carnegie Moscow Center, editor of *Mirovaiia ekonomika i sovremennye otnosheniia,* and author of *The "Party of Power" in the Contemporary Russian Political System* (Denmark, 2000; in Danish).

Vera Tolz is Professor of Russian History and Deputy Director of the European Studies Research Institute at the University of Salford, United Kingdom. Her publications include *The USSR's Emerging Multiparty System* (Praeger Publishers, 1990), *Russian Academicians and the Revolution* (Palgrave Macmillan, 1997), and *Russia: Inventing the Nation* (Edward Arnold, 2001).

Preface

In May 2001, the Marjorie Mayrock Center for Russian, Eurasian, and East European Research and the Department for Russian and Slavic Studies of the Hebrew University of Jerusalem held a conference titled "The Fall of Communism in Europe: Ten Years On." Most of the essays collected in this book were first presented in preliminary form at the conference. A few of the papers were solicited later to provide a more comprehensive overview of developments following the dissolution of the communist system in Europe. In this, its final form, updated through mid-2003, the book focuses primarily on the Russian Federation, although a number of its authors have adopted a strongly comparative approach. (Peter Rutland in his introductory essay briefly touches on events through the end of 2003).

The conference was organized as a tribute to Theodore (Ted) H. Friedgut, who had just retired from his professorial post in Russian history and Soviet/post-Soviet politics at the Hebrew University of Jerusalem. Ted received a B.A. in political science and economics at the Hebrew University in 1965 and went on to take courses in the newly formed Department of Russian and Slavic Studies, then jointly led by Michael Confino and Leah Goldberg. After receiving his M.A. from the University in 1967, he took graduate studies at Columbia University, where his advisor was Seweryn Bialer. Awarded his doctorate in 1972, he returned to Jerusalem to join the faculty of the Russian Studies Department.

Over the following 30 years, he became a pivotal figure in the department, which he chaired for a number of terms. Ted's fields of research turned out to be extremely varied, ranging from late tsarist and early Soviet history (particularly his two-volume book on the town of Yuzovka/Donetsk) via studies of post-Stalinist politics (his book on public organizations) and onto his many articles on contemporary Russian and Russian Jewish affairs. As a teacher and colleague, he was

xi

everything that could be asked for – a man of true integrity – dedicated, efficient, and loyal through good times and bad. It is our privilege to have had him as our friend and colleague.

We wish to take this opportunity to thank at least some of the many people who were involved in planning and running the conference: Leah Even, Laura Bandz, and Rita Kotik from the Marjorie Mayrock Center for Russian, Eurasian, and East European Research and Rita Blechman of the Department of Russian and Slavic Studies. We also want to thank Zvi Volk for his part in editing the manuscript. Special thanks go to Sergei Baranovski and, above all, to Anastasia Zolotareva (who has been a pillar of strength throughout this complex process) for their help in preparing the text and index.

Finally, we are grateful for the funding received from the Hebrew University that has made this project possible, specifically The Tamara and Saveli Grinberg Chair for Russian Studies, The Marjorie Mayrock Endowment, The Jay and Leonie Darwin Fund, The Committee for Conferences, and The Department of Economics.

Yitzhak Brudny
Jonathan Frankel
Stefani Hoffman

Restructuring Post-Communist Russia

Introduction

What comes after socialism?

PETER RUTLAND

THE essays in this volume originate from papers presented at a conference at the Hebrew University of Jerusalem in May 2001 to honor the
career of Theodore H. Friedgut, a scholar whose research on the Soviet
system was characterized by a scrupulous attention to detail and a willingness to treat Soviet citizens as real people with interests and views of
their own, still capable of making choices and exerting some human influence within the rigid and oppressive political system that entrapped
them. A concern with the human impact of politics and a willingness to
look beyond the facade to study the ways in which politics really works
are excellent principles with which to investigate the regimes that have
sprung up in the wake of the Soviet collapse.

The end of state socialism in the Soviet Union and Eastern Europe
was a defining moment of the twentieth century. The experience was
strikingly different in the various component regions of the Soviet bloc,
however. In Central and Eastern Europe the experience was, for the most
part, one of liberation. People were swept up by a surge of optimism
and a sense that the future would be better than the past – and better
than the present. In the former Yugoslavia, the situation degenerated
into violence and slaughter on a scale that few could have imagined.
In the countries that emerged from the former Soviet Union, the political breakdown produced a socioeconomic collapse with few parallels
in modern history. As Theodore H. Friedgut documents in his contribution to this volume, post-Soviet Russia has seen rising mortality rates,
declining birth rates, and an explosion of symptoms of societal breakdown – from a doubling in the murder rate to the return of previously
conquered infectious diseases such as syphilis and drug-resistant tuberculosis. Male life expectancy of 58 means that "a 20-year-old in Russia
stands only a 50 percent chance of reaching age 60." "The projected loss
of population for Russia in a single generation is thus between 10–20
million persons, a demographic shock reminiscent of the catastrophe of

3

World War II, from which Russia has never fully recovered, even after two generations."

Friedgut notes that the roots of these social strains lie deep in the Soviet era. The crash modernization program saw a surge in urban population from 64 million in 1960 to 110 million in 1991. This headlong growth outpaced the urban infrastructure of housing, communications, and real employment opportunities required to sustain this urban population for the long term (especially in the remote climes in which many of these new cities were located).

Echoing Friedgut, Marshall Goldman's contribution to this volume shows how the implosion of the planned economy produced an economic vacuum that will take a generation or more for market forces to rebuild. With only a dozen years passed since 1991, it is still too early to say how these profound social and economic effects, the "collateral damage" from the "End of History," will work their way into the political regimes, which will eventually stabilize in the countries of the region. But who would dare predict the future when the recent past has been so unpredictable?

The collapse of the Soviet Union came as a great surprise to the majority of social scientists, who had grown accustomed to the existence of the USSR as an integral part of the modern world as they understood it. Political theorists typically focused on the competition between liberalism and Marxism, with Soviet socialism being the dominant example of the latter. Students of international relations had taken the Cold War as a given for 40 years. Courses in comparative politics and comparative economic systems saw the Soviet-style, one-party system as a viable, even successful alternative path to modernity – one that was being taken, it seemed, by an increasing number of countries even as late as the 1970s, with the projection of Soviet influence into Africa under Leonid Brezhnev. Although many scholars had pointed to the inefficiencies of the Soviet system, and some were adamant that it was doomed to collapse, no one predicted the speed or manner of its demise.

It will not be easy to shake off these analytical frameworks and habits and it will probably take a generation or more for a lasting new perspective to emerge from the rubble of the Soviet collapse. The chapters in this book examine the developments since 1991 and represent a preliminary report based on the evidence currently available. The approach is inductive rather than deductive: the authors seek to establish facts, to extricate trends, and to look for patterns among the data that are now being gathered. It is too early to launch grand theories based on deductive categories. The main framework hitherto used for such efforts at generalization is of "transition" – the assumption that the political events of the past decade are best understood as a movement toward systems of liberal democracy and a market economy. Such a teleological approach is easy to grasp and comforting in its implicit assumption that current troubles are but stumbling blocks on the road to a brighter future. This approach, however, has triggered fierce objections from analysts who denied that events on the ground conformed to such a transition trajectory and who denied that we can know the parameters of the end-state toward which these countries are allegedly headed. Not least of the problems was the fact that half of the countries involved did not seem to be discernably in transition to the anticipated future: they are obstinately mired in an unattractive present, if not regressing toward an even less desirable state of affairs.

What, then, are the lessons of the post-Soviet period? The triumphalist rhetoric with which the collapse of Soviet socialism was greeted in the West has gradually given way to a weary acceptance that these societies are still somehow structurally different. Nevertheless, the developments of the 1990s are probably more positive than negative for most of the countries of the region. The scariest, worst-case scenarios failed to materialize. There was no return to communism in Russia. Irresponsible nationalists did not take power in Moscow, as feared by the "Weimar Russia" school.[1] There was no resurrection of the Soviet empire inside or beyond the boundaries of the former USSR. Few would have predicted, say, in 1989, that places such as Azerbaijan or Kyrgyzstan would emerge as sovereign nations within a few years. But so they did – and they have become, for all intents and purposes, permanent fixtures of the international landscape. Civil wars were confined to the flash points that erupted in 1988–92 and did not spread elsewhere. There was no significant leakage of nuclear weapons from the colossal Soviet stockpile, thanks in large part to the fact that they were removed from Ukraine, Kazakhstan, and Belarus.[2]

This book focuses on developments in Russia, both specifically and in comparative perspective, a choice that reflects Russia's size and importance relative to the other component parts of the Soviet Union. It also reflects a persisting bias in the way academics cover the region. It is easier to collate information from a single location, and the typical starting point for such research is inevitably Moscow. At the same time, a striking and most welcome development of the past decade has been the

---

[1] Stephen E. Hanson and Jeffrey S. Kopstein, "The Weimar/Russia Comparison," *Post-Soviet Affairs,* no. 13 (1997), pp. 252–83.

[2] This is cited as the major achievement of U.S. foreign policy in the decade by former Deputy Secretary of State Strobe Talbott, *The Russia Hand: A Memoir of Presidential Diplomacy* (New York: Random House, 2002).

emergence of a group of indigenous Russian scholars and observers who have gradually displaced Western commentators as the main source of information and analysis on developments inside Russia. Their grasp of the facts on the ground is matched by their analytical rigor and creativity, and – even more surprisingly – by their objectivity and ability to present their findings for a Western audience. A clutch of such scholars is represented in the pages of this volume.

Regrettably, equivalent teams of researchers have been slower to emerge in the other states of the former Soviet Union. This partly reflects the fact that the Soviet Union concentrated academic talent and resources in Moscow. It also indicates how tough life is for independent scholars in most of the non-Russian republics. Economic opportunities to sustain their work are few, and the political and personal costs of publishing material critical of the status quo can be severe. Scholarship in these countries has become heavily polarized between defenders and opponents of the incumbent regime, with precious few observers able to occupy the middle ground.

CONTINUITY AND CHANGE

The countries of the former Soviet Union have experienced a dramatic and disorienting political transformation over the past decade. Powerful institutions that had ruled people's lives for decades disappeared almost overnight – not only state structures such as the Communist Party of the Soviet Union and Gosplan, but also institutions that shaped social behavior down to its roots, such as the Young Pioneers or the practice of queuing for goods. Some feisty if unstable new institutions sprang up in their place: an elected parliament and president, a burgeoning capitalist class, markets, a free press, and even (perhaps) a free citizenry.

But not all the old institutions vanished. For all the debate about Russia as a fledgling democracy, it is important to bear in mind that two central pillars of the Soviet regime – the security services and the military – remain virtually unreconstructed as crucial pillars of the new political order.

The secret police (reborn in Russia as the Federal Security Service, or FSB) managed to preserve itself and carve out a niche in the new democratic market economy. Their information-gathering skills were handy in political campaigns and boardroom battles, and their access to legal (and not so legal) means of violence made them powerful competitors for mafia gangs in the burgeoning market for security services.[3]

[3] Federico Varese, *The Russian Mafia* (New York: Oxford University Press, 2001).

Especially since the accession to the presidency in December 1999 of Vladimir Putin, for 17 years a member of the State Security Committee (KGB), it has been even more obvious that the FSB is one of the main instruments of the new political regime in Russia.

Another Soviet legacy institution, the Russian army, saw its budget slashed and was forced to withdraw its troops from Eastern Europe. But the military slogs on, unreformed, as evidenced by the continuing horror of the two-year draft despite the repeated promises of Presidents Yeltsin and Putin to introduce a professional army. This unreformed military is another of the main pillars of the contemporary political regime. The army put Boris Yeltsin into power by refusing to back the August 1991 coup and kept him in power by agreeing to crush the parliamentary insurrection in October 1993. (Yeltsin "rewarded" the generals for their loyalty by turning a blind eye to their corruption and by allowing them to invade Chechnya in December 1994.) The army was unleashed against Chechnya for a second time in the fall of 1999, and this was the single most important factor ensuring Putin's accession to the presidency.

While political institutions were dying, adapting, or being created anew, a similar radical transformation was under way among the individual persons who made up the political and economic elite. It is difficult to calibrate whether the rate of social transition was faster or slower than the rate of institutional transformation. In Russia itself, the top stratum of the political elite was discredited by its involvement in the August 1991 coup and promptly left the political stage. (Most of them were anyway far past retirement age, given the gerontocratic structure of the Brezhnev era bureaucracies.) According to the careful calculations of David Lane and Cameron Ross, about one-third of the post-1991 Russian elite held some sort of position in pre-1991 elite institutions.[4] Is the glass of elite transformation half empty or half full? Is two-thirds turnover a lot or a little? Surely having two-thirds of elite posts held by newcomers represents a tremendous break from the closed, stagnant elite of Soviet times. On the other hand, it remains true that most of Russia's current leaders were raised, trained, and selected through the ranks of the Communist Party of the Soviet Union (CPSU) or organizations closely monitored by it, such as the Komsomol or the Academy of Sciences. The Soviet elite quickly learned the new rules of the electoral game (and rewrote some of them to their advantage). As Nikolai Petrov notes (this volume), "The results of the first (1989) and second

[4] They examined the biographical data on about 800 officials from the 1991–5 political and economic elite and interviewed 116 of them. David Lane and Cameron Ross, *The Transition from Communism to Capitalism: Ruling Elites from Gorbachev to Yeltsin* (New York: St. Martins Press, 1999).

(1990) elections profoundly affected the Soviet nomenklatura, leading, however, to its modification rather than its demise."

Comparable studies of elite turnover have not yet been done, to my knowledge, in the other ex-Soviet states. Looking at the presidential ranks in Central Asia and the Caucasus, one sees that in nearly all cases the incumbent in 2003 is the last top leader from the Soviet era. Armenia is the only exception in not having a post-independence president with a CPSU background. Azerbaijan and Georgia each had a brief (and disastrous) interregnum under a post-communist nationalist leader. Belarus certainly breaks the pattern, with a former collective farm chairman catapulted to the presidency, in the person of the erratic and dictatorial Alyaksandr Lukashenka. (This should serve to remind us that change is not necessarily a good thing.)

THE PHANTOM OF DEMOCRACY

Democracy has been the central organizing concept for the political evolution of the former socialist regimes – and the world in general – over the past decade. Yet it has proved to be maddeningly elastic and nuanced. As Alexander J. Motyl notes in his chapter "Communist Legacies and Post-Communist Trajectories," applying the Freedom House criteria of civil and political liberties produces three broad groupings of countries: those that are unequivocally democracies, those that are not, and those in the middle. Unfortunately, that middle group includes the largest countries in the region: Russia and Ukraine. These two states are five to ten times larger than their neighbors in the former Soviet Union, so the gravitational pull of their political, economic, and military policies on other countries of the region is considerable.

Is Russia a democracy? There is no simple answer to this question.[5] The consensus view in Washington is to duck the question: no one in U.S. government circles seems prepared to answer with an explicit yes or no. Thus, for example, Michael McFaul suggests that Russia as of 1996 was as democratic as it could reasonably be expected to be.[6] Tom Bjorkman, the former top Russia analyst at the Central Intelligence Agency, argues that Russia under Putin is ready for a new wave of democratic reforms

---

[5] Richard Rose and Neil Munro, *Elections without Order: Russia's Challenge to Vladimir Putin* (New York: Cambridge University Press, 2002); Timothy Colton, *Transitional Citizens: Voters and What Influences Them in the New Russia* (Cambridge: Harvard University Press, 2000).

[6] Michael McFaul, *Russia's Unfinished Revolution: Political Change from Gorbachev to Putin* (Ithaca, N.Y.: Cornell University Press, 2001).

to engage a population that Bjorkman claims is committed to democratic values.[7]

At one level, Russia has on paper met the formal criteria of democracy. Its president, parliament, and regional leaders are subject to popular elections involving more than one candidate and with results that are not a foregone conclusion. However, when one digs deeper, one realizes that the presidential elections of 1996 and 2000 involved the legitimation of an incumbent and not the freely contested selection of a leader from a range of alternatives. And the parliamentary elections, while regular, lively, and contested, do not really count because the parliament does not form the government and is limited in its capacity to hold the president and government accountable.

This leaves only the regional elections as a forum in which leaders with real power may be removed from office through the ballot box. Nikolai Petrov's exhaustive data on Russian electoral history reveal that, indeed, in the 1995–7 period, fully half of the incumbent governors who ran for reelection were defeated. However, in the 1999–2001 cycle, two-thirds of governors won reelection. Moreover, once in power, these regional bosses faced few constraints on their power from regional legislatures or elected municipal officials.

One important potential source of pluralism in Russia is the federal structure it inherited from the Soviet Union. However, Oksana Oracheva (this volume) shows that federalism has failed to serve as a buttress for nascent democracy in Russia. The reforms that Putin introduced soon after taking office in 2000, ostensibly aimed at creating a more rationally structured federalism, turned out to be more narrowly focused on boosting the power of the center. Putin backed off from challenging authoritarian leaders in the regions, a shift confirmed by the July 2002 Constitutional Court decision allowing regional leaders to run for more than two terms. With such leaders left in place and allowed to flout or undermine federal laws on their own turf, there is no point talking about a law-based division of powers between center and periphery. Equally depressing for democrats has been the ill-defined and constantly shifting structure and role of the Federation Council, the upper chamber of parliament that is supposed to represent the views of Russia's diverse regions. Under both Yeltsin and Putin, building democratic institutions took second place to political maneuverings aimed at consolidating the power of the president.

[7] Tom Bjorkman, *Russia's Road to Deeper Democracy* (Washington, D.C.: Brookings Institution, 2003).

At the national level, one wonders whether Russia really has competitive elections in any meaningful sense, if one adopts the minimalist, Schumpeterian definition of elections as a chance to change one's rulers. Russia's elections, even though they are formally competitive, serve to disempower and disenchant the electorate. Andrey Ryabov (this volume) goes a step further, provocatively suggesting that a "negative consensus" exists between elite and society around the principle of mutual noninterference. Ordinary citizens accept whatever leader the elite comes up with and agree not to disrupt or attempt to overthrow the political regime; in return, the state does not expect them to obey laws or pay taxes.

The party system – or lack thereof – adds to the confusion in society. Parties form and reform between elections, while individual deputies switch sides in a constant Brownian motion, leaving voters confused as to who stands for what. Russia does not have a party *system* as such despite having regular elections and formal freedoms of speech and association.

Ryabov sees the *potential* for a party system to emerge from the existence of three broad ideological positions among the Russian electorate: the friends of Western-style reform, the opponents of change, and a third bloc of "traditionalists" who reject both the first two alternatives. Putin has skillfully tapped into this third group, transcending the polarity of reformers versus reactionaries, which had been Yeltsin's main political gambit in 1996. The crucial problem, however, is that decisive power rests in the hands of the president, and neither Boris Yeltsin nor his anointed successor Vladimir Putin was willing to connect himself to a specific political party. Rather, they preferred to adopt the stance of a head of state who is "above politics." This was not an irrational whim on their part: both men feared that forming such a party might constrain their power and prevent them from achieving their personal agenda for Russia. For both men this agenda was broadly similar: forcing the country to take the tough steps necessary to remain a competitive state in the new post–Cold War world.

The situation is only slightly better in Ukraine. As Ilya Prizel shows in his essay "Ukraine's Hollow Decade," Ukraine had certain advantages back in 1991: no burden of foreign debt, no cities in the far north to be subsidized, and no violent ethnic conflict such as Chechnya. Yet an entrenched elite determined to cling to power has squandered the opportunity to build a new polity. Ukraine, like Russia, is ruled by a super-president, Leonid Kuchma, who puts himself above party politics, although unlike in Russia there was a competitive turnover of power in 1994. The Ukrainian party system is more robust, with nationalists as well as communists and Westernizers. The pro-reform bloc is more unified and has charismatic leaders (Yulia Timoshenko and Viktor Yushchenko) who have a reasonable chance of electoral victory in a fair contest. In the other post-Soviet countries, the quality of democracy is even more strained. In the Caucasus and Central Asia, civil society was even weaker than in Russia or Ukraine, and the economies of those regions post-1991 have been hit hard by warfare and geographic isolation.

The gap between the presence of competitive elections and the absence of real democracy is not unique to Russia. As Fareed Zakaria noted in his book *The Future of Freedom*,[8] an increasing number of countries around the world have introduced the formal institutions of democracy, such as periodic elections, without having created the political and social conditions that turn such institutions from a facade into a functioning reality. Why did this gap between superficial democracy and actual democracy open up in Russia and elsewhere? The answer, presumably, is that after the collapse of communism, countries around the world felt that recognition by the international community required at least the pretense of democratic elections. The problem – for liberal democrats and human rights activists – is that this is typically all the international community requires.

There may be other factors at work, beyond prevailing international norms, in encouraging rulers to adopt a facade of democracy. It is important to broaden the discussion beyond the decisions of the individual president (powerful though he is) to include the broader elite through which he governs and in which he is embedded. Perhaps phony democracy is the best vehicle for elites who want to cling to or rise to power. Elections may enable elites to identify and neutralize opposition leaders (by repression or cooptation) while fooling the masses with the illusion of involvement. If this cynical interpretation of democracy is correct, then the political advisers who crafted Russia's "managed democracy" may have learned their lessons a little too well.

Pseudo-democracy may also be useful for elites (national and global) that want to introduce a capitalist market economy. Anatoly Khazanov argues that in Russia the elite decided to abandon communism *before* the old regime was toppled by the events of late 1991 (this volume). He unearths a "virtually unnoticed" memorandum published in *Vek XX i mir* in 1990 that lays out a Pinochet-style agenda for the transition to capitalism.[9] Its authors included Anatolii Chubais, who went on to

---

[8] Fareed Zakaria, *The Future of Freedom: Illiberal Democracy at Home and Abroad* (New York: W. W. Norton, 2003).

[9] "Zhestkim kursom," *Vek XX i mir*, no. 6 (1990), pp. 15–19, cited in Khazanov's chapter, this volume, n. 24.

design and execute Yeltsin's controversial privatization program. Khazanov surmises, "It seems that at least some of the liberal economic reformers, even before their incorporation into the ruling elite, already had in mind an authoritarian scenario for their country."

Khazanov also notes that in democratic transitions in Latin America or southern Europe, opposition movements openly debated the relative merits of concessions versus confrontation as the best strategy for removing incumbent elites. The consensus was that it makes more sense to bribe them, not fight them out of office. A similar debate took place in Poland and Czechoslovakia, which focused on the question of "lustration" – banning former communist leaders from high office in the new democracy and organizing tribunals to name secret police collaborators. The debate was of much less practical importance than in Latin America, however, because the communist elites had abandoned political power so quickly during the chaotic years of 1989–91. In the countries of the former Soviet Union, no such debate took place. In contrast to Latin America or Central Europe, opposition movements were either too weak to be in a position to debate whether to confront or bribe the old political elite, or they were themselves members of that elite.

THE CONUNDRUM OF NATIONAL IDENTITY

Most of the countries that sprang from the Soviet Union had never before experienced sovereign statehood, and this challenge provided a goal and purpose for their new leaders and a framework through which they could appeal for popular and international support.

Valerie Bunce (this volume) reminds us that 22 out of 27 states in postsocialist Eurasia are new entities with no prior existence as sovereign states. Thus the dominant experience for most people of the region is one of the *fragmentation* of sovereignty and the fragility of new institutions. Yet given the exigencies of the international system, the region's rulers have to pretend that they are in charge of sovereign states, with full control over their territories and equipped with functioning institutions of rule. Bunce makes the intriguing point that one of the side effects of this fragmentation experience is that the erosion of central state sovereignty frees more liberal regions such as Moscow for more rapid socioeconomic transition. This widens the gap between successful and ailing regions and increases social inequality (which is bad). Yet, the emergence of dynamic regions like Moscow is one of the most important drivers of change in the post-socialist transition.

Ironically, it was Russia itself – the most powerful state in the region – that was also the one most troubled by the challenge of nation-building.

As Vera Tolz shows in her chapter, Russia's identity as a proto-nation was inextricably connected with and submerged beneath its identity as the leading force in the tsarist empire and subsequent Soviet state. With the successive disappearance of those two multinational polities, Russia is neither a civic nor an ethnic nation. Nor is it clear that its leaders, or its people, even want it to be one.

Tolz argues convincingly that Russia is still drifting between European and Eurasian identities, while trying to select from and blend its tsarist and Soviet legacies in constructing a new national identity. For his Western audiences, Putin has been emphatic in stressing Russia's core identity as a European country. Yet, when he was attending a meeting of Asia-Pacific leaders meeting in Brunei in November 2000, Putin embraced the language of the Eurasianists – a prolific intellectual current that insists Russia is a unique hybrid of European and Asian identities.[10] Russia's troubled quest for identity is also tied up with its ambivalent attitude toward the West – wanting to join yet also viewing it with suspicion and envy.

Tolz argues, with support from opinion surveys, that there is a real chance that some sort of Slavic Union, however improbable to Western eyes, might yet form the core of a new Russian nation-state. Russia's current policies toward Belarus, Ukraine, and the rest of the "near abroad" suggest that this is not an empty possibility. Russia continues to express concern over the status of the 20-million-strong ethnic Russian diaspora and seeks closer political, economic, and military ties with the former Soviet states, although this quest is now conducted through bilateral deals rather than through vapid multinational organizations such as the Commonwealth of Independent States.

Rajan Menon (this volume) shares Tolz's skepticism and challenges the complacent view that Russia has now taken its place in the Western family of nations. He argues that Russia is wounded but "not a spent force." "Russia cannot be counted on to become a partner – not because it is somehow untrustworthy, but because of its historical predicament" (that is, as the largest remnant of the Soviet empire). "Only by distorting the past and the present can one assume that Russia has chosen the West. In fact, Russia has always been ambivalent about the values that typify the West." It will take Russia many years yet to disentangle itself from the legacy of empire. In the process it faces threats of domestic instability, the risk of losing the Russian Far East to China, and the need to project power over Central Asia without getting entangled in other people's

[10] See the Putin text cited by Tolz, which appeared on www.strana.ru on November 13, 2000, "Russia always considered itself a Eurasian country."

wars. In geostrategic terms, the next half century will be dominated by the rise of China, so Menon suggests that we should not rule out the possibility of a balancing counterbloc of Russia, Japan, India, and maybe Vietnam.

IN CONCLUSION

Reflecting Russia's size and heft in the region that until recently it so strongly dominated, the essays in this volume, and the discussion in this introductory chapter, focus on the Russian case.

In the mid- to late 1990s, U.S. government officials were, in private, much taken with the discussion of what might happen if Russia "goes bad" – meaning what happens if a virulently anti-Western leader takes power, or if the country descends into civil war. Inside Russia, the debate started from a different premise – the "bad" things had already happened: the Soviet collapse, the economic disintegration. Now, perhaps, the two debates are converging. Russia is what it is, it will not "go bad," nor will it turn overnight into a Madisonian democracy. Viktor Chernomyrdin, Russian prime minister from 1992–8, is not among the more profound political thinkers of the twentieth century. But he came up with a pithy epithet that bears repeating: "We hoped for the best, but we ended up with the usual."

POSTSCRIPT

My chapter "What comes after socialism?" was written in the summer of 2003. Now, half a year on, two dramatic developments in Russia have severely undermined the hopes that Russia is in transition to a Western-style "market democracy." President Vladimir Putin ordered, or acquiesced in, the imprisonment of Russia's top businessman, Mikhail Khodorkovsky, and he used this popular move to reinforce the victory of the pro-presidential United Russia party in the elections to the State Duma on December 7.

These two events – the Yukos affair and the Duma elections – have arguably transformed the character of the Russian political landscape, leaving Putin the undisputed master of the field. They have made it clear that Putin is not merely a transitional figure, a place-holder for Boris Yeltsin's "Family," but a canny politician who has pursued a consistent policy of centralizing power while restoring Russia's international influence.

The Yukos affair began in June 2003 when the state launched a criminal investigation of the leaders of Russia's largest oil company. Initially, the accusations focused on an alleged fraud committed during a privatization deal in 1994, but they then widened to include money laundering and tax evasion to the tune of $5 billion. The head of Yukos, Mikhail Khodorkovsky, refused to concede defeat and flee the country, as did previous oligarchs who had fallen foul of the Kremlin. As a result, on 25 October, he was arrested, denied bail, and slapped with charges that could keep him behind bars for 10 years.

The arrest of Russia's richest man (Khodorkovsky's wealth at the time was estimated at $8 billion) attracted the attention of Western observers, who feared that Russia was turning its back on the market economy. For his part, Putin tried to assure Western investors that the Yukos case was not a prelude to a mass reversal of the privatization program of the 1990s.

Khodorkovsky was singled out for attack precisely because he was the most successful and ambitious of the oligarchs. His company had brought its accounting practices up to Western standards and was in the process of merging with Russia's fifth largest oil company, Sibneft. A subsequent merger with a Western oil major, probably Exxon, was also in the planning stage. Khodorkovsky was even promoting a new pipeline to China that would break the state-owned Transneft corporation's monopoly on Russia's oil exports. Finally, Khodorkovsky made no secret of his political ambitions. He was generously funding political parties across the political spectrum, from the liberal Yabloko to the communists. Experts speculated that Yukos could end up controlling one-third of the seats in the State Duma that was due to be elected in December 2003.

Putin decided to remove this political rival from the scene by unleashing an anticorruption campaign, which simultaneously provided a popular theme for the pro-presidential party, United Russia, in the Duma election campaign. To general surprise, United Russia swept the board. They received 37.6 percent of the popular vote and ended up with 300 seats in the 450-seat assembly. (They won 120 seats on the party list vote and 126 seats in single-mandate votes. After the election, 54 independents who had won in single-seat races joined United Russia.) This number not only provides United Russia a comfortable working majority, but also the two-third majority required to change the constitution – for example, to prolong Putin's presidency beyond a second term.

The election shattered the tripartite structure of Russia's political system (liberals, communists, and traditionalists) that Andrey Ryabov has described here. Rather than a "managed democracy" with a carefully constrained opposition, it could well be that the election has effectively transformed Russia into a one-party system.

The two liberal parties, Yabloko and the Union of Rightist Forces, each failed to clear the 5-percent threshold required to win seats in the party list half of the election, scoring 4.3 percent and 4.0 percent, respectively. Between them they won only seven seats in the single-mandate races, which provides them with their only presence in the new Duma, down from a total of 47 seats in the outgoing legislature. Prior to the election, the leader of Yabloko, Grigory Yavlinsky, petulantly rebuffed merger proposals from the Union of Rightist Forces, a step that would have guaranteed the liberals a significant representation in the Duma. Aside from the merger issue, the liberals had clearly lost their sense of direction under Putin. They were divided over whether to support or oppose the president, and their criticism of the Kremlin's anti-"oligarch" campaign lost them votes.

The communist opposition was also severely mauled, seeing its support halved from the 22 percent that it had won it 1999. In its place, one saw a resurgence of the nationalist Liberal Democratic Party of Russia headed by the veteran maverick, Vladimir Zhirinovskii, and a new party, Motherland, created by the Kremlin just three months before the elections. But both Zhirinovskii's party and Motherland (which won 11.5 and 9.0 percent of the vote, respectively) are more or less loyal to Putin. Their nationalist slogans serve to add spice for the benefit of the domestic audience but are not likely to determine the course of governmental policy.

The victory of United Russia was in large part due to its mobilization of the state's "administrative resources." They received generous coverage from the national television networks, with Putin having closed down the independent stations (NTV and TV6) in preceding years, and the last such station, TVS, in June 2003. Ironically, the "party of power" ran as the party of "antipolitics," disdaining to take part in the organized television debates with the representatives of the "minor" parties. United Russia persuaded nearly all the regional leaders to support its campaign, with 30 governors signing up as candidates on the United Russia party list. In return, the Kremlin toned down its criticism of wayward regional bosses. The Central Election Commission operated as an Orwellian "Ministry of Elections," imposing ridiculous limits on media coverage and striking down troublesome candidates for the most footling of reasons.

As of now, the elections appear to have left Russia with a reconstructed authoritarian political system. The best that Russians (and the West) can hope for is that it will prove to be an enlightened authoritarianism. There are, however, several reasons for doubting that this authoritarianism will be so benign. Most important is the fact that, in constructing his new system, Putin has relied heavily, as noted earlier, on cadres drawn from the security services. The *siloviki* ("men of power"), who make up at least one-quarter of the governmental apparatus, have only a shallow understanding of and commitment to the institutions of democracy and to a market economy. Whatever Putin's agenda for modernizing Russia, these men, on the contrary, have their own: the grim pursuit of the war in Chechnya, the projection of Russian power in the "near abroad," and – perhaps – a challenge to U.S. hegemony.

Second, there is the question of what happens in 2008. Putin's re-election as president in March 2004 was not in doubt. The constitution, however, bars a third term, and Putin has repeatedly stated that he does not want to alter the constitution. Yet, Putin's personality is vital to the stability of the political system that he has created. None of the other figures in his government or in the leadership of United Russia is capable of balancing the competing views of the economic managers and power ministries in the government while maintaining popular support. Thus most Russians – of the left and of the right – consider it all but inevitable that the constitution will be changed to lengthen Putin's term in office. The alternative would be a return to the feuding and instability of the early 1990s.

Are there, nonetheless, any grounds for optimism? Perhaps there are. First, beginning in 1999, the Russian economy has grown at 6 percent a year for five years in a row. This has transformed the face of the city of Moscow, and some of the wealth has trickled down into the provinces, in the form of low inflation and the prompt payment of wages and pensions.

Second, although Putin's democratic credentials are threadbare, his understanding of and commitment to market economics still appears to be relatively robust. He has introduced a series of legal and tax reforms that do, in principle at least, lay the foundations for a competitive market economy. With a compliant Duma, it is reasonable to suppose that the reform process will continue, especially with regard to the huge, and hugely troubled, utilities sector.

Finally, there are some signs that a civil society is gradually taking shape in Russia. Nongovernmental organizations, successful business-people, and new educational institutions are making their presence felt. For most of the 1990s, these developments took place outside, and in contempt, of state political institutions – wisely so, given that the Yukos affair has demonstrated what can happen when one of these social forces tries to enter the political realm. In the future, it is not unrealistic to expect a more fruitful and balanced interaction between the state and civil society. The alternative, a return to a Soviet-style crushing of civil society, is obviously not impossible, but it is far from inevitable.

Grounds for optimism on this score came from an unlikely source at the close of 2003. Georgia experienced civil war and economic collapse throughout the 1990s, but in November 2003, after a rigged parliamentary election, people took to the streets of Tbilisi and toppled the long-time incumbent president, Eduard Shevardnadze. This bloodless "revolution of roses" was the first display of "people power" in the former Soviet Union since 1991, and it sent a warning signal to dictators from Minsk to Tashkent.

The events of 2003 have almost certainly put paid to Western hopes that Russia is in the process of becoming a "normal" country with European-style institutions of government. Its deviations from the acceptable standards of democratic behavior can no longer be attributed to the birth pains of a new democratic society. Rather, it is becoming clear that the infant political system that was born some dozen years previously is congenitally deformed. What form that deformation will take over the coming years, how far it will go, and how dangerous it proves to be at home and abroad, only the future will tell.

The comparative dimension

What went wrong? Post-communist transformations in comparative perspective

ANATOLY M. KHAZANOV

> Whether we like it or not, the deadly angel who spells death to economic inefficiency is not always at the service of liberty.
> —Ernest Gellner

> Мы хотели, как лучше, а получилос , как всегда.
> (We hoped for the best, but we ended up with the usual.)
> —Viktor Chernomyrdin

In 1989–91, when communism was defeated in East Central and Southeastern European countries and in the Soviet Union, some scholars in the West tried to provide a kind of theoretical assurance that the transition to Western-type liberal democracy would be smooth and rapid, almost automatic, or at least inevitable. In this respect, the references to Fukuyama's hasty dictum about the end of history have already become commonplace.[1] Fukuyama, however, was not alone. Some scholars argued a basic similarity between the democratization processes in the former communist countries and the democratization witnessed in Southern Europe and Latin America. In their opinion, expressed implicitly or explicitly, not only the process but also the final outcomes should end up as similar.[2] A new branch of comparative political studies has even been

---

[1] Francis Fukuyama, "The End of History," *National Interest* (Summer 1989), pp. 3–18.

[2] See, for example, Russel Bova, "Political Dynamics of the Post-Communist Transition," *World Politics* 44 (October 1991), pp. 113–18; Philippe C. Schmitter, "Dangers and Dilemmas of Democracy," *Journal of Democracy*, no. 2 (1994), pp. 57–74; Philippe C. Schmitter and Terry Lynn Karl, "The Conceptual Travels of Transitologists and Consolidologists," *Slavic Review*, no. 1 (1994), pp. 173–85. For an opposing view, see Valerie Bunce, "Comparing East and West," *Journal of Democracy*, no. 3 (1995), pp. 87–100; Valerie Bunce, "Should Transitologists Be Grounded?" *Slavic Review*, no. 1 (1995), pp. 111–27; Anatoly M. Khazanov, "The Collapse of the Soviet Union," *Nationalities Papers*, no. 1 (1994), pp. 157–74; Anatoly M. Khazanov, *After the USSR* (Madison: University of Wisconsin Press, 1995).

21

born and christened "transitology." The problem of democratization in the former communist countries was reduced by transitologists to the bargaining and interaction within and between the political elites and counterelites. The difference in principle between authoritarian capitalism and totalitarian communism (or, if one prefers, state socialism)[3] that had been noticed by a number of scholars[4] was blurred again.

It is thus still worth noting that communism was markedly different from authoritarian capitalism not only in the degree of coercion but also in the measure of social control and mobilization. The main peculiarity of communism is an almost complete monopoly over the ideological, political, and economic spheres exercised by the party-state and, in practical terms, by the ruling elite, or, to use the Soviet parlance, by the nomenklatura.

Under authoritarian capitalism, ideologies are rather insignificant; to some extent, they remain a private domain. The state does not seriously attempt, nor is it strong enough, to control human minds and even less to brainwash them. It is enough if individuals refrain from voicing their opposition in public, but even this is not always the case. Often it is enough if they do not actively compete for political power. Under communism, Marxism became a secular religion, and deviations from its dogmas were persecuted more severely than the Inquisition had persecuted deviations from Catholicism. The communist culture was never context free. It was prescribed and ideologized, and all deviations from it were considered to be at least a form of hidden dissent. It was the party – and the party only – that had a monopoly on all decision making regarding what was right and correct, what was acceptable or at least tolerable, and what was incorrect and wrong.

Ernest Gellner was surprised that when communism collapsed, it turned out there were few true believers in the communist countries. As he aptly put it, "There is now only a void under the banner of Marxism from which men flee as if from a pest."[5] From the very beginning,

---

[3] Linz and Stepan call communist regimes of the post-Stalinist period "post-totalitarian." Nevertheless, they admit that even in that period those regimes had less political, social, economic, and ideological pluralism than noncommunist authoritarian ones. For these reasons, I prefer to call the former "late totalitarian." It seems, however, that my disagreement with the authors is more terminological than substantial. Juan J. Linz and Alfred Stepan, *Problems of Democratic Transition and Consolidation* (Baltimore and London: Johns Hopkins University Press, 1996), 42 ff.

[4] Carl J. Friedrich and Zbigniew Brzezinski, *Totalitarian Dictatorship and Autocracy* (Cambridge: Harvard University Press, 1956); Jean Kirkpatrick, "Dictatorship and Double Standards," *Commentary* (November 1979), pp. 34–45; Walter Laqueur, *The Dream That Failed: Reflections on the Soviet Union* (Oxford: Oxford University Press, 1994); Juan J. Linz and Alfred Stepan, *Problems of Democratic Transition and Consolidation*, 40 ff.

[5] Ernest Gellner, "Homeland of the Unrevolution," *Daedalus*, no. 3 (1993), p. 146.

however, the communist regimes relied on coercion and repression, or a threat of repression, much more than on persuasion and faith. The number of true believers should not be overestimated for any period in the history of communist countries. No wonder that quite early in their history (in the Soviet Union as early as the 1930s), the communist regimes began to supplement the Marxist faith with the demands for loyalty to the state in the name of a patriotism that often acquired a nationalistic accretion. True believers are dangerous because they are activists; if and when they are disappointed, they tend to become heretics. No wonder so many of them were exterminated during the numerous purges. The main goal of an ideological monopoly was to inspire not faith and enthusiasm, but compliance and conformity, as well as disorientation. Doublethink served this goal well. Doublethink was more reliable than faith because it did not give birth to dissent; it could bring forth only apathy and cynicism.

Another difference between authoritarian capitalism and communism lies in the different relations to civil society. Authoritarian capitalism has to tolerate, sometimes even engender, some forms of societal self-organization that in proper conditions can facilitate a transition to liberal democracy.[6] In contrast, communism aimed at the utter destruction of civil society. Under authoritarian capitalism, the government and administration do not abide by the rules of the democratic game. However, the economic sphere remains partially autonomous, and an autonomous economy is the nursery that provides the soil for pluralism and political freedom.[7] Thus, in Southern Europe and even in Latin America, the transition to liberal democracy has been connected mainly, although not exclusively, with a simple change in political regimes.[8] In the communist countries, everything was turned upside down. Without private property and a market-oriented economy, civil society is impossible, just as ideological pluralism and tolerance are impossible without a civil society.

Communist countries were collectivistic but extremely atomized, and any form of social cohesion was deliberately weakened. Civil society, as an independent and institutionalized sphere of citizens' activity, was destroyed or at least suppressed. (In countries like Russia, it had been weak even before the communists seized power.) A limited number

---

[6] Michael Mann, "The Autonomous Role of the State: Its Origins, Mechanisms, and Results," in John A. Hall, ed., *States in History* (London: Basil Blackwell, 1986), pp. 113.

[7] Milton Friedman and Rose Friedman, *Free to Choose* (New York: Harcourt Brace Jovanovich, 1980), 2ff.; Ernest Gellner, *Conditions of Liberty* (New York: The Penguin Press, 1994), p. 146.

[8] Robert Fishman, "Rethinking State and Regime: Southern Europe's Transition to Democracy," *World Politics* 42 (1990), pp. 422–40.

of nonpolitical voluntary organizations tolerated by the state were put under its strict control. In democratic countries, civil society counterbalances the state and protects citizens from abuse by the state, but it does not necessarily confront the state. In the late communist period, the reemergence of independent civic organizations such as Solidarity in Poland, Charter-77 in Czechoslovakia, or the Helsinki Watch Group in the Soviet Union involved a direct confrontation with the state.

Authoritarian capitalism may sometimes intervene in the economic sphere through populist, protectionist, or other measures. Still, the market system and private property remain basically intact. To a significant extent, the economy is not monopolized by the state, and political elites have to coexist with economic ones. Therefore, the transition from authoritarianism to liberal democracy requires, for the most part, changing the political order while retaining basically the same economic system. Simultaneous democratization and economic liberalization may sometimes be difficult even in authoritarian capitalist countries;[9] however, the initial degree of economic liberalism there is much higher than in communist countries. Under Soviet-style communism, the economic elites did not have an independent existence. The centralized state monopolized production and distribution, arbitrarily regulated prices and wages, and systematically distorted valuations, while imposing bureaucratic management and excessive planning. It thus negated the market and, therefore, lacked the built-in mechanisms that enable the economy to function more or less smoothly.

Although the egalitarian character of communism was a myth, this system was characterized by a unique social structure. Inasmuch as the state had a monopoly over the means of production, class divisions in communist societies were much more political and functional than economic. Social stratification was based on access to power and on privileges connected with this access. Everyone, or almost everyone, was, in some sense, an employee of the state. This was especially important with regard to what can tentatively be characterized as the middle class. Barrington Moore's dictum, "no bourgeois, no democracy,"[10] although formulated in somewhat archaic terms, is still valid. Modern liberal democracy needs the strong and numerous middle classes consisting of people whose incomes and livelihoods are not directly dependent on the state's whim and benevolence. This is not to imply that the middle class is always and everywhere a strong champion of democracy (suffice

[9] Leslie Elliot Armijo, Thomas J. Biersteker, and Abraham F. Lowenthal, "The Problems of Simultaneous Transitions," *Journal of Democracy*, no. 4 (1994), pp. 161–75.

[10] Barrington Moore, *The Social Origins of Dictatorship and Democracy* (Boston: Beacon Press, 1966), p. 418.

it to refer to the example of Germany from 1871–1945), but without the middle class, which is interested in the maintenance of the liberal democratic order and has a stake in it, the very existence or, at any rate, the stability of this order seems precarious. In the communist countries, the middle class existed mainly in terms of its functional role and income; in all other respects, it did not have an independent existence.

Another class, the peasantry, whether collectivized, as in the Soviet Union, or not, as in Poland, was, in terms of production, price controls, investments, ownership restrictions, and many other aspects, put under the strict economic and political control of the state. This process in no way produced modern farmers – agricultural market-oriented capitalist producers and landowners. As for the upper class, the nomenklatura, it also did not consist of individual property owners; it existed and functioned only as a corporate body. The body derived spoils, rent, profit, and wealth from the huge enterprise called the socialist state and distributed them among its members in accordance with their positions in the party and the state hierarchy.

Thus, to be successful, the transition from communism requires a much more drastic change in the social structure than does the transition from authoritarian capitalism. The middle class, the upper class, and, to a great extent, the farming sector have to be restructured or even created anew on a different economic foundation, drastically reducing their linkage to the state. In this situation, a new kind of social engineering seems unavoidable, despite all of its deficiencies and dangers. In fact, the transition from communism consists of two main processes that are far from completely intertwined: the transition from totalitarianism to liberal democracy and the transition from state socialism to the market economy. Many former communist countries face an additional problem – that of nation-state building. Thus, everything has to be rebuilt or even built anew from the bottom up: the economic system, the social organization, the political order, and ideology. The transition from communism, while resembling that from authoritarian capitalism with regard to the ultimate desired goal, faces a far greater challenge at the stage of initial conditions and transitional procedures.

A DIFFERENT STARTING POINT

There is another serious problem that should be taken into account. The transition from communist rule is a reversal of the historical processes that resulted in the modern Western order. The latter are based on four main underpinnings: liberal democracy, civil society, nation-state, and welfare capitalism. The main characteristics of contemporary

Western societies did not emerge simultaneously. Regional and other differences notwithstanding, usually economic freedom and civic rights were achieved first, then political rights were won, and nation-states were created (the latter two developments sometimes were more or less synchronous and sometimes sequential, but a certain correlation between the two can be traced in many cases). Only afterward, mainly in the twentieth century, was a "social contract" agreed on in accordance with which the state was obliged to provide its citizens with protective welfare.[11]

The communist countries provided the people with cradle-to-grave social welfare as well. Although it was much inferior to the safety net provided in Western Europe, it guaranteed the satisfaction of one's basic needs at a minimal level. However, the economic reforms that followed the collapse of communism dealt a devastating blow to that social security system. The resulting resentment has been even greater because expectations were inflated. The social and economic infantilism cultivated by the communist regimes has backfired. The communist "new man" was as prone to consumerism as his capitalist counterpart.[12] The only difference was that the consumerism of the former was for a long time denied or suppressed; hence, his fairy-tale vision of imaginary capitalism, which was supposed to be the opposite of everything that was so disappointing and wrong with communism. It was a Manichaean vision inspired primarily by the poor economic performance of communism; but, after all, Marxism itself is no stranger to the Manichaean type of dualism. Moreover, this imaginary capitalism can be called "cargo capitalism" because it assumed that all good things in life would be delivered by the state.

Last but not least, a remark about the nation-states in the communist countries. The Soviet Union was a multiethnic empire; thus, a process of nation-state building by its successors, including Russia, is still in its formative stage. However, even in many East Central and Southeastern European former communist states, it is far from complete. The communist regimes there attempted to replace, or reduce, loyalty to the nation with loyalty to the party-state. Yet, even in this respect, they were inconsistent and tried to harness ethnic nationalism as a means for the legitimization of their power.[13] As a result of this policy, as well as of

---

[11] Thomas S. Marshall, *Citizenship and Social Class* (Cambridge: Cambridge University Press, 1950).

[12] Yuri Levada, ed. *Sovetskii prostoi chelovek* (Moscow: Mirovoi okean, 1993); E. V. Sal'nikokova, *Estetika reklamy: kul'turnye korni i leitmotivy* (Moscow: GII MK RF, 2002), 191 ff.

[13] See, for example, Katherine Verdery, *National Ideology under Socialism* (Berkeley: University of California Press, 1991).

previous historical development, a notion of a civic multiethnic nation existed more on paper than in reality. When communism collapsed, a full-fledged ethnic nationalism complete with discrimination against ethnic minorities reemerged and became another impediment on the path to liberal democracy even in those countries that were considered the most advanced in this respect.

This problem remains acute in virtually all former Soviet countries, both those that granted citizenship to all their residents and those that tend to limit it to state-building (titular) nationalities. Thus, in Russia, the problem of a civic versus an ethnic Russian nation is far from resolved. At present, the Russians are seeking a new basis for their identity as a nationality and as a nation; hence, the ongoing debate about the character of the Russian Federation and about the status of ethnic minorities there.[14]

The defeat of the Soviet Union in the Cold War – which was an ideological as well as an economic one – passed a death sentence on communism. But this was only the immediate cause of its ignominious end. Communism collapsed because it failed to deliver all of its main initial promises: social emancipation, national liberation, and economic advantage. A few abortive experiments proved that because of its totalitarian nature, communism was inconsistent with even controlled political liberalization. In addition, in many European communist countries, popular yearnings for prosperity and liberty were combined with a striving for national liberation. Communism there was perceived as an antinational force by the very fact that it was imposed on them and was backed by Soviet tanks. Some scholars argued and still argue that political systems should be abrogated or changed slowly rather than abruptly. The collapse of communist rule did not follow this prescription. It was rapid and in no way evolutionary.[15]

The transition in Europe began with political emancipation, although communism there came to an end in different ways.[16] In Poland and Hungary, it was negotiated with the opposition. In the Deutsche Demokratische Republik, it became inevitable after so many of its

---

[14] Anatoly M. Khazanov, "Ethnic Nationalism in the Russian Federation," *Daedalus*, no. 3 (1997), pp. 121–58.

[15] The development in China and Vietnam is different from that in European countries. So far, their transformation has only confirmed the well-known fact that although it is impossible to have a liberal democracy without a market system, the market may still exist without an established democracy. Charles E. Lundblom, *Politics and Markets* (New York: Basic Books, 1977), 162 ff. However, even the economic liberalization in these countries should not be overestimated.

[16] Ivo Banac, *Eastern Europe in Revolution* (Ithaca: Cornell University Press, 1992); Milton F. Goldman, *Revolution and Change in Central and Eastern Europe* (Armonk, N.Y.: M. E. Sharpe, 1997).

subjects "voted with their feet" and, of course, after the destruction of the Berlin Wall. In Romania, it was initiated by a plot within the ruling elite and the army, which resulted in violence, and in Bulgaria, it involved a palace coup. In Czechoslovakia, it came through the protest demonstrations christened a "velvet revolution." In Albania, it was to a large extent caused by the domino effect. In the Soviet Union, it was a consequence of the disintegration of the empire, which was accelerated by Gorbachev's unsuccessful reforms and by the reallocation of power within the state structures and within the ruling elite. It proved Alexis de Tocqueville's statement that the most dangerous time for an authoritarian regime is when it begins to reform itself.

Nevertheless, there was one common feature shared by these various terminations. Few among the ruling elites were eager to fight for the continuation of communist rule. The great majority anticipated that they would not lose much and might even benefit from the change. Political scientists who studied the transitions from authoritarian capitalism used to stress the importance of pacts with the ruling elites to assure them that they would not suffer from the introduction of liberal democracy. In other words, it was assumed that it was better to bribe than to fight.[17] To a greater or lesser degree, this is just what happened in some communist countries, often in ways rather beneficial to the former nomenklatura. The consequences were often not as positive as some Western political scientists and reformers in the communist countries had expected, however.

The change in Europe was revolutionary, but it was not caused by political revolutions if the latter imply, at the very least, the replacement of the power elites and institutions of the ancien régime. To characterize the situation, Timothy Garton Ash has coined a new term – "refolution."[18] It is rather incredible that after the events of 1989–91, the former communists in so many countries have managed not only to acquire wealth but also to retain their membership in the dominant elites and even (in many cases) to restore their political standing. In retrospect, however, one may come to the conclusion that the resurgence of the communists and former communists, both in significant numbers in the power structures

---

[17] See, for example, G. O'Donnell, P. Schmitter, and L. Whitehead, eds., *Transitions from Authoritarian Rule* (Baltimore: Johns Hopkins University Press, 1986); Giuseppe Di Palma, *To Craft Democracies* (Berkeley: University of California Press, 1990); Terry Lynn Karl, "Dilemmas of Democratization in Latin America," *Comparative Politics* 23 (1990), pp. 1–22.

[18] Timothy Garton Ash, *The Uses of Adversity* (New York: Random House, 1989), p. 309.

and as one of the influential political forces in the would-be new order, was inevitable.

Apparently, a complete and clean break with the totalitarian past is possible only under conditions of occupation, when, as in post-Nazi Germany, structural changes are imposed by foreign powers and backed by a program like the Marshall Plan[19] or after a social revolution. However, social revolutions always bring terror and repression as their inescapable corollary. People in the communist countries, especially intellectuals, remembered this lesson well. Smolar aptly described the dilemma: "History has taught us the price of revolutions: blood, violence, dictatorship. The dissidents in communist-ruled Eastern and Central Europe always condemned and rejected any form of revolution."[20] His words are backed by Król: "You cannot have a revolution without terror. . . . We have not dealt definitely with the forces of the old regime or with the psychic and moral legacies of that regime. We have not done so because we wanted only reform and evolution rather than violence as our means."[21] In Russia, Yegor Gaidar expressed a similar attitude, insisting that the historical experience of the country had made it immune to the horrors of violent revolutions.[22]

Yet, everything has a price – not only revolutions but also their absence. Dealing with the past remains a painful and unsolved problem in virtually all former communist countries. Tina Rosenberg has grasped well its moral side: "Who is guilty in societies where almost everybody collaborated with the system in some way?"[23] Anyway, in many countries there was no clear break with the communist order. In Huntington's terms, the system was transformed rather than replaced.[24] Bastilles were not destroyed all at once; at best, they were gradually dismantled in some countries, while in others only their façades were changed. After a few years, it turned out that in many countries, power was taken away from communism more than from the communists. It also

---

[19] Peter H. Merkl, *The Origins of the West German Republic* (New York: Oxford University Press, 1963); R. E. Ward and Y. Sakamoto, eds., *Democratizing Japan* (Honolulu: University of Hawaii Press, 1987); Frank A. Ninkovich, *Germany and the United States* (Boston: Twayne, 1988); Noel Annan, *Changing Enemies* (New York: Harper Collins, 1995).

[20] Aleksander Smolar, "The Dissolution of Solidarity," *Journal of Democracy*, no. 1 (1994), p. 84.

[21] Marcin Król, "Poland's Longing for Paternalism," *Journal of Democracy*, no. 1 (1994), p. 92.

[22] Yegor Gaidar, *Gosudarstvo i evoliutsiia* (Moscow: Evraziia, 1995), pp. 135–6.

[23] Tina Rosenberg, *The Haunted Land: Facing Europe's Ghosts after Communism* (New York: Vintage Books, 1996), xxi.

[24] Samuel P. Huntington, *The Third Wave* (Norman: University of Oklahoma Press, 1992), 144 ff.

became evident that their new allegiance to capitalism did not make them champions of liberal democracy.

When former communists returned to power in Poland, Hungary, or Lithuania, many democrats there sounded the alarm, and people such as Adam Michnik complained about the "velvet restoration." Their anxiety, however, turned out to be unfounded. The reasons for this outcome, which were very indicative indeed, become clear if one compares the changes in these countries with those in the former Soviet Union. In the latter, the situation was, and still is, quite different. The anticommunist (and simultaneously nationalist) opposition came to power, sometimes just for a brief period, in only a few of the newly emerged countries. In others, like the ethno-authoritarian states of Central Asia, old communist elites retained power virtually unchanged. In still other states, such as the "decorative democracy" of Ukraine, pragmatically oriented members of the old nomenklatura discovered a new legitimacy in the ideology of (ethnic) nation-state building. They forged alliances with some leaders of the nationalistic counterelites and retained their leading positions in the new "parties of power."[25] In Belarus, the old communist elite has split up. Whereas some of its former members joined the opposition together with democrats and nationalists, many more support the dictatorship of President Lukashenka. Even in Russia, the continuity with the previous order exceeded some peoples' hopes and expectations, and I use this country to illustrate my point.

In 1990, the Russian journal *Vek XX i mir* published an interesting anonymous memorandum, which, unfortunately, remained virtually unnoticed both in Russia and in the West.[26] It was written by a group of Leningrad scholars and contained the political concept behind the radical economic reforms. (It later became known that one of the authors was Anatoly Chubais, who indirectly admitted his coauthorship, although he preferred not to go into details or to mention many of his proposals.[27]) Without any hesitation, the authors proposed building a democratic society and economy by undemocratic means. The latter implied the retention of power by the political leadership and the "unfair enrichment of specific social strata," even though this process would also require lower living standards for the majority of the population, mass unemployment, a ban on strikes, the dissolution of trade unions if they were to oppose the suggested economic policy, governmental control over information, and other similar measures. It seems that at least

[25] Volodymyr Polokhalo, *The Political Analysis of Post-Communism* (College Station: Texas A&M University Press, 1997), pp. 151–4, 158–9.
[26] "Zhestkim kursom," *Vek XX i mir*, no. 6 (1990), pp. 15–19.
[27] A. B. Chubais, ed., *Privatizatsiia po-rossiiski* (Moscow: Vagrius, 1999), p. 27.

some of the liberal economic reformers, even before their incorporation into the ruling elite, already had in mind an authoritarian scenario for the country.

In August 1991, the majority of Russians clearly opted in favor of democracy. However, the events that unfolded in the country in the aftermath of the failed putsch in no way constituted an anticommunist revolution. In countries such as Poland or Hungary, the collapse of communism was accomplished by a negotiated consensus between the political elites and counterelites in a situation in which the former had, for all intents and purposes, been defeated and understood the writing on the wall. This resulted in the emergence of stable democratic institutions based on a system of checks and balances and a clear division of powers.[28] There was also a fairly significant turnover among the personnel of the government and administration, accompanied by the dismantlement or reform of many institutions and agencies inherited from the previous regime. The political transformation, welcomed by the majority of people and confirmed by the new elections, provided legitimation for the subsequent economic reforms.

In Russia, the transition from communism was neither really forced nor negotiated. In many respects, it was a spontaneous process that just followed the events and reflected the infighting and the changing balance of power within the ruling elite. It is very indicative that, in late 1991 and early 1992, the Yeltsin leadership rejected such important institutional procedures as adopting a new constitution or holding new parliamentary elections, although had it been decided to accept these important political reforms, they would have had a good chance of success.[29] Many totalitarian structures were not dismantled, and the state institutions were insufficiently modified. Nothing was done to prevent the revival of the Communist Party and the emergence of fascist groups and organizations.[30]

Only the weakened part of the partocracy and of the all-union bureaucracy was removed from power and the state machinery, in many cases only temporarily; the remainder has survived, constituting much of the government and administrative personnel and of the ruling stratum in the post-totalitarian society. There was no real turnover of the political and administrative elite, let alone of the bureaucratic apparatus, except that the many middle-ranking members of the nomenklatura advanced

---

[28] Karen Dawisha, and Bruce Parrot, eds., *The Consolidation of Democracy in East Central Europe* (Cambridge: Cambridge University Press, 1997).

[29] Lilia Shevtsova, *Rezhim Borisa Eltsina* (Moscow: ROSSPEN, 1999), 41 ff.

[30] For a recent publication on the latter, see Stephen D. Shenfield, *Russian Fascism* (Armonk, N.Y. and London: M. E. Sharpe, 2001).

to its higher ranks.[31] The regional elites, in particular, have undergone little change.[32] Moreover, in 1996, deputy head of the presidential administration, and before that a high-ranking FSB (the successor to the KGB) officer, Evgenii Savostianov, publicly claimed that many former KGB secret agents and informers had become prominent members of the political and economic elites but continued to maintain their ties with the secret service.[33]

This state of affairs was admitted even by those who, at one time, tended to overestimate the level of democratization achieved in Russia.[34] All echelons of the bureaucracy, judiciary, and the repressive agencies inherited from the communist regime remain virtually the same. No serious attempts have been made to turn the Soviet-type omnipotent, politicized bureaucracy, which was not endowed with a strong sense of duty and in which career advancement depended largely on patronage, into a professionally competent and impartial civil service based on career meritocracy. Research by scholars at the Russian Academy of Sciences' Institute of Sociology revealed that by 1995, only 40 percent of the parliamentary deputies, 25.7 percent of the government officials, 25 percent of those in the president's inner circle, and 17.7 percent of the regional elites were people who in the recent past had never belonged to the nomenklatura.[35]

The picture is even more grim if one takes into account that many of those who managed to enter the ranks of the ruling elite in the post-Soviet period now adhere to the nomenklatura's own rules of the game. As Mikhail Kodin, one of the members of the communist nomenklatura in the Soviet period, remarked – and not without a degree of irony – the former crusaders for people's rights and social justice are now turning into grandees rapidly accepting traditions and acquiring, even extending, the privileges of the old elite.[36] Even in terms of organization and recruitment, there was no sharp break with Soviet

---

[31] Lilia Shevtsova, "The Two Sides of the New Russia," *Journal of Democracy*, no. 3 (1995), p. 59; Lilia Shevtsova, "Russia's Post-Communist Politics: Revolution or Continuity?" in Gail V. Lapidus, ed., *The New Russia* (Boulder, Colo.: Westview Press, 1995), 5 ff.

[32] D. V. Badovskii, "Transformatsiia politicheskoi elity v Rossii – 'ot organizatsii professional'nykh revoliutsionerov' k 'partii vlasti,'" *Politicheskie issledovaniia*, no. 6 (1994), p. 53.

[33] *Izvestiia*, October 17, 1996.

[34] Anders Åslund, *How Russia Became a Market Economy* (Washington, D.C.: Brookings Institute, 1995), p. 62.

[35] For a summary, see *Izvestiia*, May 18, 1996; also see N. C. Yershova, "Transformatsiia praviashchei elity Rossii v usloviiakh sotsial'nogo pereloma," in T. I. Zaslavskaia and U. A. Arutiunian, eds., *Kuda idet Rossiia? Al'ternativy obshchestvennogo razvitiia*, vol. 1. (Moscow: Interpraks, 1994), pp. 151–5; M. N. Afanas'ev, *Praviashchie elity i gosudarstvennost' posttotalitarnoi Rossii* (Moscow-Voronezh: NPO MODEK, 1996), 168 ff.

[36] M. I. Kodin, *Obshchestvenno-politicheskie ob"edineniia i formirovanie politicheskoi elity v Rossii (1990–1997)* (Moscow: PITs ISPI RAN, 1998), p. 84.

times. It is true that the Soviet political elite had been based on the principle of strict hierarchy with well-calibrated privileges, although this did not exclude patronage and cronyism, whereas its post-Soviet counterpart in the early 1990s was less consolidated, more open, and was structured mainly on the principles of clannishness and cliqueishness. At present, however, these differences are rapidly diminishing. The post-Soviet upper echelon is now demonstrating a growing desire to eschew public politics in favor of achieving the highest possible independence from society. Its statist orientation, which, incidentally, has deep roots in Russian political tradition, is detrimental to societal self-organization. No wonder that some Russian scholars characterize the post-Soviet political elite as "neonomenklatura."[37]

This alone makes the situation in Russia quite different from the situation in the countries that experienced the transition from authoritarian capitalism and even from that in some European ex-communist countries. Over the past decade, the former members of the Soviet ruling class have acquired wealth and property but without surrendering power. Indeed, communist rule had prevented the formation of an influential counterelite in the Soviet Union, where the dissident movement was weakened and disorganized by continuing repression and emigration. However, in the late 1980s and in the beginning of the 1990s, the counterelite emerged in Russia and began to enjoy significant mass support. In 1990, the "Democratic Russia" movement alone had at least 150,000 activists. In Moscow, it could bring up to half a million people into the streets to participate in protest demonstrations,[38] but the new counterelite consisted mainly of recent converts to democracy, people who had previously belonged to the privileged strata of the Soviet Union. Socially and professionally, most of them were connected with the nomenklatura and were influenced by its attitudes, lifestyle, and habits.[39] They changed their allegiance and became leaders of the opposition on the popular wave of the struggle against the Communist Party. Among those admitting to this change of allegiance was Yegor Gaidar, who belonged to this stratum.[40] As in other communist countries, these people were strongly against a revolution, arguing that "violence gives

[37] G. K. Ashin, "Rekrutirovanie elity," *Vlast'*, no. 5 (1997), p. 29.

[38] Mark R. Beissinger, *Nationalist Mobilization and the Collapse of the Soviet State* (Cambridge: Cambridge University Press, 2002).

[39] Lilia Shevtsova, *Rezhim Borisa Eltsina*, pp. 66–7. Even in 1999, Anatoly Chubais, with ill-concealed disdain, criticized the dissidents for their principled anti-Sovietism and unwillingness to work within permissible guidelines; see A. B. Chubais, ed., *Privatizatsiia*, p. 11.

[40] Yegor Gaidar, *Gosudarstvo*, p. 104. Gaidar's grandfather was a Bolshevik commander during the Civil War in Russia and later a famous writer much favored by the Soviet authorities; his father was a rear admiral. In the Soviet period, Gaidar always was a loyal and trusted member of the Communist Party and held high positions in the major

rise to violence" and that "one cannot build a civilized society on blood-shed." So far, so good.

However, in the aftermath of the failed August 1991 putsch, when the "democrats" were at the peak of their popularity and the ruling elite was in retreat, the former did not even attempt to negotiate fundamental political change or transitional compromise. They neither took advantage of broad public support for the building of democratic institutions, nor did they strive to attain such an outcome. Instead, they preferred to warn against a nonexistent "witch hunt" and to join the ranks of the elite. Those who had been ideological and political opponents of communism in Soviet times and who actually initiated the "revolution in human minds" were pushed aside,[41] and most of the leaders of the "new democrats" hurried to queue up for positions in the government.[42] Sworn atheists suddenly became bishops, without having lived a day as ordinary parishioners. In the long run, perhaps most detrimental to the country's democratic development was the reliance on personalism in politics at the expense of the rule of law and a system of checks and balances.

The "democrats" were co-opted into the basically unreconstructed power structure and state apparatus. It was argued that there was no need to forcibly pry Russia out of the grip of the nomenklatura because it was possible to ransom the country from them,[43] or because only the establishment could lead the transition.[44] A theoretical background for these views was provided by those social scientists who claimed that "combining radical economic reforms with the democratization of the country, which had neither democratic institutions nor, for some three generations, any experience of a market economy was impossible."[45] Whether the last statement is correct or not remains an academic question because it was never tested in practice in Russia.

As my late friend the great poet Joseph Brodsky once remarked, consequences seldom look on causes with approval. Complaints began to be heard only afterward, when most of the "democrats" had lost their governmental positions and had been defeated in the parliamentary elections. Thus, a chief ideologist of perestroika, Aleksandr Yakovlev, then expressed the regret that "bureaucracy misappropriated the August

ideological periodicals – the journal *Kommunist*, and subsequently at the newspaper *Pravda*.

[41] D. Lein, "Peremeny v Rossii: rol' politicheskoi elity," *Sotsiologicheskie issledovaniia* (1996), pp. 30–9.

[42] Lilia Shevtsova, *Rezhim Borisa Eltsina*, pp. 46–7.

[43] Yegor Gaidar, *Gosudarstvo*, p. 143.

[44] Gavriil Popov, *Snova v oppozitsii* (Moscow: Galaktika, 1994), 238 ff.

[45] Igor S. Kon, "Identity Crisis and Post-Communist Psychology," *Symbolic Interaction*, no. 4 (1993), p. 397.

victory."[46] Yegor Gaidar complained that the "Russian state cannot be considered a democratic one. . . . To a large extent, the nomenklatura remains the same. They only became a little more open for a while, but only a very little. They swallowed the 'best' democratic cadres and returned again to the point of departure."[47] Former mayor of Moscow Gavriil Popov admitted that "power remained in the hands of the nomenklatura."[48]

At present, the ruling elite and officialdom, hundreds of thousands of apparatchiks, the number of whom has significantly increased in comparison with the Soviet period, still hold power in Russia. In fact, the country lacks stable and well-defined mechanisms for the rotation of the elites. The "democratic" counterelite was absorbed by the nomenklatura or became compromised because of cooperation with it. The elite now represents an internally fragmented and squabbling collection of groups that has lost much grassroots support, lacks a clear political strategy, and is incapable of suggesting a convincing alternative to the ruling regime. In 1996, Yeltsin comprehended the situation well enough when he admitted during the presidential campaign that he would not cater to the democratic constituency; they would vote for him in any case simply because, in the runoff election, they would not have any other choice. In the 2000 presidential election, the former democratic constituency had an alternative (Grigorii Yavlinsky, leader of the Yabloko Party), but the majority preferred to vote for Putin, just as the leaders of the liberal Union of Rightist Forces (SPS) called on them to do.

The tragedy of Russian liberalism is that it never enjoyed broad and stable support of its own. Instead, many liberals tried in vain to win over to their side state officials and the ruling class. In this respect, little has changed since the prerevolutionary period. Just as in the past, contemporary Russian liberals are facing a hard choice: either collaborating with an illiberal government in the hope that at least some of their economic and other policies may be implemented or becoming an opposition without real political influence.[49] Just as in the past, one is now witnessing a split between liberal statists and liberal democrats. In a growing number of the post-communist countries in East Central and even Southeastern Europe, a bifurcation of the nationalist and statist discourse on one hand, and the liberal discourse on the other, is becoming evident. In Russia, on the contrary, one may observe the process of their partial merging.

---

[46] Aleksander Yakovlev, *Literaturnaia gazeta*, October 27, 1993.
[47] *Izvestiia*, January 20, 1994.
[48] Gavriil Popov, *Snova v oppozitsii*, p. 354.
[49] O. Yu. Malinova, *Liberalizm v politicheskom spektre Rossii* (Moscow: Pamiatniki istoricheskoi mysli, 1998), pp. 173–6, 181.

For a while after 1991, another political force in the country, namely, the communists, played the role of counterelite. At the moment, they are still fairly influential, but they are not strong enough to return to power, nor do they demonstrate a genuine desire to do so. The bipolar model of irreconcilable contradictions between the ruling class and the Communist Party is no more than camouflage. More and more often the communists are playing the role of loyal opposition to the ruling regime.

Since the events of 1989–91, the communist parties of the former Soviet bloc have undergone different metamorphoses. In Poland, Hungary, and Lithuania, they transformed into social democratic parties. In the Czech Republic and Latvia, where the social democratic political space was already occupied by other forces, they remain dogmatic and fossilized. In many countries of the Commonwealth of Independent States (CIS), such as Ukraine and Georgia, some former communist functionaries constituted the core of pro-presidential parties without clear ideological adherence, except a declared commitment to (ethno) nation-state building; others, especially those who were not in demand in the new power structures, reemerged in the old-new communist parties with populist slogans. Russian communists remain an antiliberal and antidemocratic force, which is hardly at the crossroads anymore.[50]

In fact, there are no good prospects for social democracy in Russia. Contemporary social democracy rejects the concept of a centralized and planned economy.[51] It advocates the partial redistribution to the weak of what had been earned in the market economy. In Russia today, there is little that can be redistributed. In the mid-1990s, the gross domestic product per capita was many times smaller in Russia than in developed Western countries.[52] Since then, the situation has not improved drastically. No wonder that, so far, numerous attempts to organize the social democratic or socialist parties in the country have failed. Even in other formerly communist countries where these attempts were more successful, the new social democratic parties resemble their Western European counterparts more in rhetoric than in practical policy, and this is one of the reasons for their frequent failures to build on their initial electoral successes.

---

[50] Joan Barth Urban and Valerii D. Solovei, *Russia's Communists at the Crossroads* (Boulder, Colo.: Westview Press, 1997).

[51] Seymour Martin Lipset, "No Third Way: A Comparative Perspective on the Left," in Daniel Chirot, ed., *The Crisis of Leninism and the Decline of the Left* (Seattle: University of Washington Press, 1991), pp. 183–232.

[52] Vladimir Mau, *Ekonomicheskaia reforma: skvoz' prizmy konstitutsii i politiki'* (Moscow: Ad Marginem, 1999), pp. 188–9.

In Russia, the communist leaders are mainly those who were losers in the first rounds of the power struggle that accompanied the collapse of the Soviet Union. They sloughed off a great deal of Marxist phraseology and ideology but only in favor of authoritarian nationalism. Communist leader Gennadii Ziuganov talks much more often like a Russian chauvinist than like a Marxist. Most of the rank-and-file communists in Russia do not care for ideological purity either. This is certainly not enough, however, to bring about their return to power, because the communists cannot offer their electorate anything that would be both attractive and feasible.

Many of those millions of people who voted for Ziuganov in the 1996 and 2000 presidential elections, and according to the most recent opinion polls are likely to vote for the communists once again in the 2003 parliamentary and 2004 presidential elections,[53] were not really voting for a restoration of the communist system. It was rather a protest vote against the political leadership and economic and social policy by those who were embittered by their wasted lives and vanished illusions. They became nostalgic about the times when, in a way, life was easier and simpler because the state prescribed for them what to do and what to think but, in turn, provided them with employment and a social security net. Those who think that they do not have a future are particularly resentful when the past is taken away from them.[54] Under certain conditions, such people are ready to accept authoritarianism.

Putin and his advisors understand well the widespread disenchantment with democratic ideals. His authoritarian policies and nationalistic and pro-Soviet rhetoric meet with wide public approval. The fact that a KGB man has become the most popular politician in Russia and lacks strong competitors is, at the moment, a very indicative symptom.

POST-TOTALITARIAN ECONOMICS AND POLITICS

The Western, especially West European, patterns of ideological and political orientation (conservatism, liberalism, and social democracy) are still not applicable to the CIS countries. There, the state continues to reign supreme, and the decision-making process to a large extent still

---

[53] *Monitoring obshchestvennogo mneniia,* no. 2, 2003: pp. 77, 82, 84, 89, 96.

[54] Actually, the problem derives not so much from historical amnesia but from the undeniable fact that, economically and even socially, many people fared better under the communist regimes than they do now. When a person does not have enough money to purchase any of the 20 or 30 kinds of sausage available in select shops, it does not matter much to him that under communism, he had to stand in lines to purchase any kind of sausage. What matters is that sausage, when available, was affordable.

has a closed and anonymous character. Different criteria and definitions
are needed to analyze their current character. Russia ceased to be a communist country but, at the moment, it is by no means a liberal country in
either economic or political respects. It has not yet even passed the test of
orderly power transfer based on a real political contest. At the moment,
I prefer tentatively to call Russia and many other formerly communist
countries "post-totalitarian."

There is an opinion that authoritarian regimes have some advantages
over new democracies in carrying out market-oriented reforms and even
in providing initial economic prosperity.[55] In this context, references are
usually made to a few Southeast Asian countries and to Chile. The more
numerous examples when authoritarian regimes have failed economically[56] are not taken into account. In the Soviet Union, proponents of
the authoritarian model were found as early as 1988. The aforemen-
tioned authors of the Leningrad Memorandum and others expressed
such views.[57] The fact that these views were advocated by individuals
who simultaneously claimed their allegiance to democracy made it almost beguiling. They considered enlightened authoritarianism to be the
best mode of transition from totalitarianism to democracy. They claimed
that benevolent autocrats would provide stability and become efficient
promoters of economic liberalization. Suddenly, General Pinochet became, and still remains, a popular figure in certain Moscow intellectual
and political circles. The only thing that has not been explained is why
the authoritarian regimes should be interested in democratization at
all. In this respect, the reference to Pinochet was certainly misleading.
Moreover, nobody considered another possibility, the appearance of a
Russian Perón.

Interestingly enough, these ideas were first expressed at a time when
the existing regime could best be characterized as an example of enlightened authoritarianism, by which I mean the perestroika period.
However, Gorbachev's reforms did not deliver economic liberalization
or real democracy; they just let the genie out of the bottle. The authoritarian experiment and its attempts at controlled liberalization failed in

---

[55] Leslie Elliot Armijo, Thomas J. Biersteker, and Abraham F. Lowenthal, "The Problems
of Simultaneous Transitions," *Journal of Democracy*, no. 4 (1994), p. 166; Giovanni Sartori,
"How Far Can Free Government Travel?" *Journal of Democracy*, no. 3 (1995), p. 107. For
the opposite opinion, see Larry Sirowy and Alex Inkeles, "The Effects of Democracy on
Economic Growth and Inequality: A Review," *Studies in Comparative International Development*, no. 1 (1990), pp. 126–57; José Maria Maravall, "The Myth of the Authoritarian
Advantage," *Journal of Democracy*, no. 4 (1994), pp. 17–31.

[56] Larry Diamond, "Democracy and Economic Reform," 118 ff.

[57] Lev Osterman, *Intelligentsiia i vlast' v Rossii (1985–1996 gg.)* (Moscow: Monolit, 2000),
p. 78.

the Soviet Union, and there is no reason to believe that the second attempt, if it takes place in Russia, will be more successful. The example of the Central Asian and Transcaucasian states of the CIS or of Belarus should be revealing in this respect.

The problem of authoritarian rule during the transition from totalitarianism is empirical as well as theoretical. Empirical observations prove that such formerly communist countries as the Czech Republic, Poland, Slovenia, and Hungary, or even the Baltic republics, which have escaped the authoritarian trap, are politically more stable and economically more advanced on the path to the market system than Serbia, Croatia, or Russia, not to mention the other CIS countries. The new-old nomenklatura is interested in economic reforms only on its own terms and only as far as these reforms are beneficial to them. In no way are they interested in promoting liberal democracy. In fact, the paths of economic reform and liberal democracy have already parted in Russia.

In several important respects, the transition to a market economy in the former communist countries is a political process at least as much as it is an economic one. The privatization of state property there was not a result of the expansion of a preexisting private sector. Therefore, economic reforms had to be accompanied (or, even better, preceded) by a drastic political restructuring of the state and the concentration of power in established democratic institutions. Without such a political transformation, how could a clear regulatory framework for privatization and other market-oriented transitions be established?[58] After all, in various degrees, all these countries experienced a conversion of power into property.[59] This fact should certainly be taken into account in the ongoing debate on the advantages and disadvantages of gradual economic reforms versus shock therapy, or, as some economists prefer to call it, "big bang reform."[60] There are many convincing arguments in favor of swift, comprehensive, and radical economic reform.[61]

---

[58] Juan J. Linz and Alfred Stepan, *Problems of Democratic Transition and Consolidation*, pp. 390–1, 435.

[59] Jadwiga Staniszkis, *The Dynamics of the Breakthrough in Eastern Europe* (Berkeley: University of California Press, 1991), p. 35; Ákos Rona-Tas, "The First Shall Be the Last? Entrepreneurship and the Communist Cadres in the Transition from Socialism," *American Journal of Sociology*, no. 1 (1994), pp. 40–69.

[60] Actually, the shock therapy method in its pure form was not implemented in any ex-communist country. Even Vaclav Klaus had not really been practicing the unfettered free-market reform that he preached. Carol Skalnik Leff, *The Czech and Slovak Republics* (Boulder, Colo.: Westview Press, 1997), p. 187.

[61] Leszek Balcerowicz, "Understanding Post-Communist Transitions," *Journal of Democracy*, no. 4 (1994), pp. 75–89; Grigorij Mesežnikov, "The Programs of Political Parties in Slovakia in Practice and Declarations," in Soňa Szomolányi and Grigorij Mesežnikov, eds., *The Slovak Path of Transition – to Democracy?* (Bratislava: Interlingua, 1994),

It is more humane to amputate a dog's tail with one stroke than to cut it off piece by piece. It is easier to persuade people to suffer for a while and to accept fiscal austerity when the state socialist economic system is totally discredited and the new post-communist governments are enjoying public trust. It is better to prevent as much as possible the negative influence of the old power structures and to shorten the period of economic uncertainty and political instability. The sooner the economic sphere is separated from the political one, the fewer opportunities the old elite has to mold the economic reforms in accordance with its own egoistic interests, including the creation of powerful lobbies and groups capable of undermining an emerging democratic system.[62]

Russia, however, experienced the shock of price liberalization without any real economic therapy and without the legal and institutional frameworks required for market-oriented reforms. In all other respects, its economic liberalization has been gradual, controversial, in some respects even reversible, and it is still far from complete. In some post-communist countries, such as Poland, Hungary, and the Czech Republic, a multiparty political system first became somewhat entrenched, then the economic reforms were introduced. In Russia, reforms were belatedly initiated in a situation in which the leadership relied on Yeltsin's personal authority more than on anything else and was not subject to any party or public control.[63]

As a result, the capitalism that has emerged in Russia is a state-apparatchik-oligarchic capitalism, in which organized crime was allowed a great deal of control. Following the bitter admission by Yegor Gaidar,[64] Russian capitalism may also be characterized as nomenklatura capitalism with a bureaucratic market. Contrary to Anders Åslund's claim,[65] Russia's economy has not yet been emancipated from politics. Independent entrepreneurship oriented toward free market competition

pp. 83–109; for the opposite opinion, see P. Murrell, "Evolution in Economics and in the Economic Reform of the Centrally Planned Economies," in C. Clague and G. Rauser, eds., *The Emergence of Market Economies in Eastern Europe* (Oxford: Basil Blackwell, 1992); Kazimierz Z. Poznanski, "Institutional Perspectives on Post-Communist Recession in Eastern Europe," in Kazimierz Z. Poznanski, ed., *The Evolutionary Transition to Capitalism* (Boulder, Colo.: Westview Press, 1995), pp. 3–30.

[62] Joseph C. Barada, "A Critique of the Evolutionary Approach to the Economic Transition from Communism to Capitalism," in Kazimierz Z. Poznanski, ed., *The Evolutionary Transition to Capitalism*, p. 203.

[63] Igor Kliamkin, Lilia Shevtsova, *Vnesistemnyi rezhim Borisa II* (Moscow: Moscow Carnegie Center, 1999).

[64] *Izvestiia*, April 7, 1995.

[65] Anders Åslund, *How Russia Became a Market Economy*, pp. 3, 273. For a much less optimistic account of Russian economic reforms and their results, see Michael McFaul, "State Power, Institutional Change, and the Politics of Privatization in Russia," *World Politics* 47 (1995), pp. 210–43.

is still weak. Economic reforms were tailored to fit the nomenklatura's desire to retain power and simultaneously to acquire wealth. The appropriation and privatization of state assets and property provided the nomenklatura and the managerial elite with disproportionate benefits.[66] The first Russian financiers were former party functionaries.[67] By the middle of the 1990s, 61 percent of Russia's wealthiest businessmen had belonged to the nomenklatura in Soviet times.[68] By 1997, around four-fifths of privatized Russian companies were owned by insiders, mainly directors.[69]

Under the old regime, wealth was mainly an appurtenance of power and had little independent existence. Nowadays, their fusion assumes new forms, and some degree of separation between the two has gradually been reached. Still, the state remains the principal agency of economic activities. The independence and influence of the Russian oligarchs turned out to be a myth that was undermined by the August 1998 financial crisis and was ultimately exposed by Putin's leadership. Vladimir Potanin, one of the most well-known oligarchs, bluntly acknowledged this when he stated the following: "The oligarchs are playing just the role that those in power want them to play. . . . The political authorities have the upper hand with regard to any business."[70]

The separation of financial and commercial groups from state structures is also insufficient and encounters many difficulties, especially in face of the strong resistance to change, both from the bureaucracy and also from the "political capitalists." The Russian economic reformers based their blueprints on the assumption that the emergence of every new capitalist was positive and that as soon as the members of the nomenklatura acquired property and became capitalists, they would have to enter open-market competition.[71] They did not. Just as in other CIS countries, the origins of the new property-owning class in the old nomenklatura and bureaucracy "make it far more comfortable doing business under the shadow of a corrupt, authoritarian state and in a semilegal atmosphere than in an open environment characterized by clearly defined rules of the game."[72]

---

[66] Alfred Kokh, *The Selling of the Soviet Empire* (New York: S.P.I. Books, 1998), pp. 29–30; A. B. Chubais, ed., *Privatizatsiia*, pp. 31–3, 53–6.

[67] Oleg Poptsov, *Khronika vremen "tsaria Borisa,"* (Moscow-Berlin: Edition Q Verlags-GmbH, 1995), p. 134.

[68] *Izvestiia,* January 10, 1996.

[69] *The Economist,* July 12, 1997, p. 12.

[70] *Kommersant-Daily,* March 9, 1999.

[71] Yegor Gaidar, *Gosudarstvo,* pp. 163–4.

[72] Lilia Shevtsova, "The Two Sides of the New Russia," *Journal of Democracy* 6, no. 3 (1995), p. 71.

Privatization of state property has resulted in the commercialization of state management. Retaining a degree of administrative and financial control over the economy, including nominally privatized enterprises and branches of the economy, provides the ruling elite and the bureaucracy with additional avenues of enrichment. In the current situation, positions in the government and administration open up almost unlimited possibilities for corruption and embezzlement, and, thus, in many ways remain more attractive than the risky endeavor of private ownership that is not insured against the vicissitudes of open market competition.

On the other hand, the transfer of state enterprises to holding companies has turned their managers into "red capitalists" with various possibilities to formalize their control over them, but without the obligation to make their enterprises profitable. In many important industrial and agrarian sectors of the national economy, the managerial elite successfully continues to protect its monopolistic positions and to solicit financial support from the state, despite its evident mismanagement and ineptitude. The government is prone to yield to pressures from the managers of large enterprises and the corps of agrarian directors, who often violate the principles of rational financial policy.[73] Their commitment to the market economy, and particularly their ability to adapt to it, is doubtful.[74] In this situation, Adam Smith's "invisible hand" is still not operative in the country.

The Russian economic reforms, coupled with high inflation and the financial crisis of August 1998, repeatedly destroyed the value of peoples' savings. Concomitantly, the middle and working classes were deprived of any real gains in the redistribution of state property. What was declared as an act of social justice was perceived by ordinary Russians as robbery. Together with profound economic hardships, it has significantly reduced the legitimacy of the capitalist transformation in their eyes. In all the former communist countries, the newly emerging capitalist class consists of many members of the former elite who have succeeded in exchanging *Das Kapital* for capital and private wealth and have successfully used such intangible assets as inside information, personal contacts and connections, and practical experience. However, the entire process of privatization, which is often called *prikhvatization* ("grabization") in Russia, brings into question more than the issue of social justice.

---

[73] Joseph R. Blasi, Maya Kroumova, and Douglas Kruse, *Kremlin Capitalism* (Ithaca and London: Cornell University Press, 1997), p. 180.
[74] A. B. Chubais, ed., *Privatizatsiia*, p. 56.

More than a dozen years after the transition from communism in Russia began, its social and economic stratification still does not correspond either to that of a postindustrial or even a developed industrial society. In the initial period of economic reforms, the Russian liberals had hoped to create their own support base, which would consist of a strong and numerous new middle class of private property holders with a vested interest in the democratic order. These goals have not been achieved, nor have they been consistently pursued in practice. Despite some claims to the contrary,[75] the reformers have had to admit their failure; moreover, they even admit that it was partly due to their own serious mistakes.[76] Instead, the Russian economic liberals and the political leadership prefer to ally themselves with the emerging class of the nouveaux riches. As for the middle class, it is conspicuous mainly by its absence on the Russian political scene. Many of the former middle-income groups are at the losing end. They are experiencing a relative status deprivation (the latter in relation to the rise of new social strata) and are still carrying an unequal burden with regard to economic reform.

True, despite all the difficulties, a new middle class is slowly emerging in the country. However, it is remarkably apolitical, and its political sympathies are far from always on the side of democracy.[77] At the moment, the middle strata consist of a heterogeneous group of individuals who are too atomized to perceive their common interests or to articulate corresponding political demands. It is worth noting that the percentage of office workers and state employees among the Russian middle strata is much larger than in developed countries, whereas the percentage of managers and businessmen is significantly smaller.[78]

The working class that used to be dependent on the state can also hardly be expected to be a champion of democracy at the moment, resentful as it is of the shrinking of social services and diminishing state support. At the same time, it is facing the threat of unemployment, the pressure of the market on inefficient enterprises, and many other problems. So far, the government has managed to maintain a rather high level of employment, but it is doing so by artificial measures that, among other things, produce very low wages, which is the opposite of what was intended.

---

[75] Alfred Kokh, *The Selling of the Soviet Empire*, p. 39.
[76] See interview with Chubais in *Kommersant-Daily*, October 28, 1997.
[77] O. A. Aleksandrova, "Sovremennyi ideinyi kontekst stanovleniia rossiiskogo srednego klassa," in I. A. Butenko, ed., *Rossiiskoe obshchestvo na rubezhe vekov: shtrikhi k portrety* (Moscow: MONF, 2000), pp. 61–76.
[78] M. K. Gorshkov, N. E. Tikhonova, and A. Yu. Chepurenko, eds., *Srednii klass v sovremennom rossiiskom obshchestve* (Moscow: RNISINP, 1999), pp. 234–5.

In the agricultural sector, privatization and other reforms were blocked at the initial stages. A class of independent farmers that might constitute another support base for economic liberalization has not yet been born. Just as with other economic sectors, Russian agrarian reform is, above all, about political power.[79] So far, the rural social structures have not undergone sufficient change. Private farmers are not numerous and hold only about 6 percent of agricultural land. Former Soviet state and collective farms remain basically intact as they transmute into joint stock farms or limited partnerships – or even retain their previous status. In addition, one should take into account cultural factors. Western type commercial farming and its concepts, such as individualism, competition, risk taking, and the flexible allocation of resources are alien to Russian rural areas. In this situation, it seems that the state and the "agrarian barons" (the former Soviet farm managers who retain their privileged positions and strongly resist the privatization of land) will remain the dominant forces in the agricultural sector for the foreseeable future.[80]

In sum, the transition from communism so far has produced different economic results in comparison with the transition in Southern Europe. Whereas in Spain and Portugal, income distribution has become more equal with democratization,[81] and all three recent democracies in Southern Europe have used their increased tax revenues to increase social welfare expenditures significantly,[82] the base for democratization in many formerly communist countries remains, at best, unstable. If the future of democracy hinges on its ability to achieve a reasonable degree of economic success,[83] its prospects in these countries do not seem very bright at the moment.

COMMUNISM'S LEGACY OF TRANSITION

Transitions to democracy consist not only of success stories but also of obituaries. Communism has left a very sorry legacy everywhere. Still, there are significant and growing differences between the various post-communist countries. At one end of the spectrum, there are the Czech

---

[79] Don Van Atta, ed., *The "Farmer Threat." The Political Economy of Agrarian Reform in Post-Soviet Russia* (Boulder, Colo.: Westview Press, 1993), p. 2.

[80] Stephen K. Wegren, *Agriculture and State in Soviet and Post-Soviet Russia* (Pittsburgh: University of Pittsburgh Press, 1998), 237 ff.

[81] José Maria Maravall, "The Myth of the Authoritarian Advantage," *Journal of Democracy*, no. 4 (1994), p. 27.

[82] Juan J. Linz and Alfred Stepan, *Problems of Democratic Transition and Consolidation*, p. 139.

[83] Bronislaw Geremek, "A Horizon of Hope and Fear," *Journal of Democracy*, no. 2 (1993), p. 102.

Republic, Poland, Hungary, Slovenia, Slovakia, and the Baltic countries. For historical, geopolitical, and other reasons, a certain disappointment among some strata and groups in the immediate results of economic reforms or in their pace and procedures in those countries was never accompanied by the mass rejection of their ultimate goal – to become a part of the Western political and security structures or of the liberal democratic order in general. Despite existing problems and difficulties, the post-communist transition in all of these countries seems already to be accomplished.

These countries are followed by Bulgaria, Romania, Croatia, and nowadays even by Serbia. Their political and economic performance is much less impressive, but at present they are trying to catch up with their more advanced neighbors. Perhaps it is still premature to call them working democracies, but they have a good chance to become such in the near future. Anyway, their pro-Western orientation, which enjoys the support of almost all the main political parties, and of at least a significant part (if not a majority) of their populations, may be an important factor in this regard.

At the opposite end are all CIS countries, which to varying degrees remain post-totalitarian. In these countries, democracy has not yet become "the only game in town."[84] Their progress toward a market economy is still insufficient, but different varieties of hard or soft authoritarianism have become even more noticeable than they were a few years ago.

Post-totalitarian countries are sometimes characterized as a combination of a weak state with a weak society.[85] This is an oversimplification. The fact of the matter is that a post-totalitarian state is weak where it should be strong (support of law and order by legal means or the management of a coherent, orderly, and effective privatization policy and market reforms), and it is strong where it should be weak (excessive control of the economy and a tendency to resort to extralegal measures). The immediate future of these countries seems more uncertain than that of those in the first group. The differences reside in many factors, including the historical past and its perception, political experience, the degree of public resistance to and resentment of communism, attitudes toward the West, and the character of the initial post-communist transformation.

First, one may conclude that the transition is easier when the rudiments of civil society survived or reemerged beneath totalitarian structures, or at least when they became embodied within various dissident

---

[84] Juan J. Linz and Alfred Stepan, *Problems of Democratic Transition and Consolidation*, p. 5.
[85] Ken Jowitt, *New World Disorder: The Leninist Extinction* (Berkeley: University of California Press, 1992).

movements.[86] Second, in the former communist countries, viable democracy cannot be guaranteed simply by the abolition of the party's monopoly of power or even by the introduction of formal democratic procedures such as more or less free elections. Although in principle, democracy can be created without a strong demand from the masses, it cannot be consolidated and remains fragile without their commitment.[87] At present, this commitment is weak at best in the post-totalitarian countries of the CIS. Third, beyond the expulsion from power of the Communist Party (the CPSU), the extent to which the former nomenklatura system was destroyed has proven important. Not only structures and strata, but also institutions and agencies matter, and sometimes they matter very much.[88]

Without an institutional break and a significant turnover of the ruling elites, nascent and weak democracies will remain in a state of permanent danger. In Hungary and Poland, those have-beens who remain in the power structure and bureaucracy or have returned to power were unable to operate anymore as representatives of the nomenklatura class because this class and its power base have to a large extent ceased to exist. In contrast, in countries such as Russia, the nomenklatura remains in power. Granted, it has incorporated some new members and changed the legitimization of its power, but it continues to exercise excessive and arbitrary control over the society and economy.

Fourth, the transition to the market economy needs a state dedicated to both democratic political and economic liberal reforms; moreover, such a state should be strong enough to carry them out. Successful transformation becomes dubious if economic reforms are not preceded by serious political reforms aimed at establishing and consolidating the democratic order. The more radical the political democratization and economic liberalization are, and the sooner they follow each other, the better they will be able to prevent a possible authoritarian backlash. The more gradual the transition, the more difficult it is to reach the point of no return. Last but not least, it is worth noting the importance of external factors, which in the past has been demonstrated by the German

---

[86] It is hardly accidental that while dissidents in East Central European countries (György Konrád, János Kis, Adam Michnik, Václav Havel, and others) revived the idea of a civil society capable of restraining the abusive state's power, their Soviet counterparts continued to call on the state to abide by its laws. The difference is significant. In the first case, it was assumed that a strong society was needed to control the state; in the second case, an appeal was made to the good will of the state and its willingness to curb its own excesses.

[87] Doh Chull Shin, "On the Third Wave of Democratization," *World Politics* 47 (1994), p. 154.

[88] Valerie Bunce, "Peaceful versus Violent State Dismemberment: A Comparison of the Soviet Union, Yugoslavia, and Czechoslovakia," *Politics and Society*, no. 2 (1999), p. 234.

example. Nowadays, the admission to NATO and to the European Union, or even the desire to be admitted to these organizations serves either as a guarantee of – or as an important stimulus for – a successful democratic transformation.[89] The economic adjustment of the countries admitted to the European Union cannot and will not be easy and may involve some social tension, but this should by no means threaten their already sufficiently entrenched democratic orders.

In 1999, Chubais[90] claimed that Russia was moving in the same direction as Poland or Hungary – although more slowly. Actually, there is little basis for such a triumphant statement. With regard to the democratization process, Russia is far ahead of the other CIS countries but well behind many of the former communist countries of East Central Europe. Suffice it to mention such characteristic Russian features as the insufficient separation of the economy from politics which, were it otherwise, could provide more political stability;[91] weak and unstable political parties; hyper-presidentialism (the situation in which executive power is much stronger than the legislature); the absence of a truly independent judiciary; and a government and administration that lack respect for the law and do not abide by democratic rules. Instead of constitutionally defined peaceful competition for the exercise of power, one witnesses a willingness to resort to extralegal measures. One may mention another important difference: market-oriented reforms are being carried out in Russia by essentially authoritarian methods. The problem consists not only in the tempo of ongoing reforms, but also in their direction and ultimate goals.

Although I am not pleased with playing the role of Cassandra, I can only repeat what I have claimed since 1991. The transition to liberal democracy is by no means secured in Russia or in many other former communist countries. Just at the time when one Latin American country after another is shedding its previous authoritarian experience, there is a serious danger that many of the former communist states are undergoing a process of "latinoamericanization." In this respect, my sad conclusion does not differ much from a growing number of similar pessimistic conclusions within and outside the country.[92] It is true that a

---

[89] Ronald D. Asmus, *Opening NATO's Door: How the Alliance Remade Itself for a New Era* (New York: Columbia University Press, 2002).

[90] A. B. Chubais, ed., *Privatizatsiia*, pp. 335–6.

[91] John A. Hall, *Coercion and Consent: Studies on the Modern State* (Cambridge: Polity Press, 1994), p. 47.

[92] See, for example, J. G. Merguior, "Thoughts on Liberalisation," in John A. Hall and I. C. Jarvie, eds., *Transition to Modernity* (Cambridge: Cambridge University Press, 1992), p. 337; Doh Chull Shin, "On the Third Wave of Democratization," *World Politics* 47 (1994), p. 170; L. A. Gordon, "Retrospektivy i perspektivy perekhodnogo vremeni," in

totalitarian restoration is hardly possible in Russia. The ruling elite and the bureaucracy are no longer interested in communist ideology and want to enjoy their power and wealth without hindrance. A return to totalitarianism is also difficult because of external factors. In the current international climate, few regimes would dare put themselves into political isolation with its probable economic consequences. However, different varieties of authoritarianism are at least as plausible as the democratic scenario.

Years after the disintegration of the Soviet Union, Russia remains suspended between totalitarianism and democracy. Its economy is still insufficiently reconstructed along modern lines, and its society remains in flux. The country is again bogged down in an essentially colonial war and is steeped in rampant corruption. The degree of social trust in Russia is very low, but the political exploitation of social frustration is tempting because the masses are apparently becoming more susceptible to all kinds of populism.

Perhaps the secret of Putin's popularity, which puzzles many observers in Russia and abroad, consists of the fact that Russian society is tired of the political and economic reforms, the unfulfilled promises, and the vanished expectations of the previous period and, at the moment, is striving for the stability personified in a strong leader much more than for a liberal democratic order.[93] The relative economic progress during the last few years, although rather precarious because it is mainly stimulated by oil and gas prices on the world markets, also contributes to the high ratings of the Russian president.

In Russia, disappointment in the post-communist transformation results in the calls for a search for a specific Russian path of development and for the rejection of Western patterns and values. To varying degrees, these views are propagated by certain political forces, which find a rather receptive audience. Putin's inconsistent but basically pro-Western foreign policy is dictated by pragmatic considerations much more than by his allegiance to democracy and is not matched by his domestic policy. The president and his allies in the power elite are well aware of (and, perhaps, share) the widespread feeling of humiliation connected with Russia's defeat in the Cold War, the loss of its superpower status, and the disintegration of the Soviet empire. Moreover, they are stirring up

T. I. Zaslavskaia and U. A. Arutiunian, eds., *Kuda idet Rossiia?* vol. 1. (Moscow: Interpraks, 1994), p. 306; Lilia Shevtsova, "Russia's Post-Communist Politics: Revolution or Continuity?" in Gail V. Lapidus, ed., *The New Russia* (Boulder, Colo.: Westview Press, 1995), pp. 33–4; T. I. Zaslavskaia, "Vstupitel'noe slovo" in T. I. Zaslavskaia and U. A. Arutiunian, eds., *Kuda idet Rossiia?* vol. 2. (Moscow: Aspekt Press, 1995), p. 5.

[93] Yuri Levada, "Ramki i varianty istoricheskogo vybora: neskol'ko soobrazhenii o khode rossiiskikh transformatsii," *Monitoring obshchestvennogo mneniia*, no. 1 (2003), pp. 8–12.

unrealistic hopes for a restoration of *derzhava* (a great power status) and, not infrequently, appealing even to ethnic Russian nationalism.

The collapse of the communist order has shaken the structure of society without creating a viable replacement. When the ruling elite and bureaucracy remain the most powerful strata in society while other strata are not yet organized politically, and the property is concentrated in the hands of financial-industrial groups, banks, and managers closely connected with the neonomenklatura, democratic consolidation cannot be achieved. Although Putin has waged a successful war against a number of the oligarchs (the country's wealthiest tycoons) inherited from Yeltsin's period and has proclaimed a policy of "equally distancing" them all from power, new oligarchs and gigantic corporations have emerged under the Kremlin's patronage.[94] They monopolize the lion's share of the national economy and are detrimental to the development of small and medium-sized enterprises. Under these circumstances, the social space for civil society is narrow, just as is the opportunity for developing the mechanisms required for the real public control of officialdom and the bureaucracy.[95] Stable political organizations with mass followings and specific social bases that provide democratic guarantees for political competition are, to a large extent, still absent.

All post-totalitarian countries face the possibility of the emergence of an authoritarian regime with a statist and nationalistic ideology but with only a few elements of a market economy. This outcome is clearly characteristic of the CIS countries. The willingness and ability of such regimes to accomplish economic liberalization seems rather dubious. Referring to the characteristics of authoritarian regimes that impede economic liberalization and development, Diamond[96] has pointed out that the typical authoritarian regime is consumed with rent seeking – manipulating import licenses, foreign exchange controls, subsidies, government jobs, and so on – by high officials, cronies, and clients of the regime and that such people are not inclined to pay more than polite international lip service to the structured adjustments that will damage their material interests. The situation is similar to that existing in the post-Soviet political space.

Actually, there is much evidence that Russia is moving away from the "soft," semiauthoritarian and patrimonial rule that it experienced

[94] David E. Hoffman, *The Oligarchs: Wealth and Power in the New Russia* (New York: Public Affairs, 2002).

[95] David Lempert, "Changing Russian Political Culture in the 1990s: Parasites, Paradigms, and Perestroika," *Comparative Studies in Society and History*, no. 3 (1993), pp. 628–46.

[96] Larry Diamond, "Democracy and Economic Reform: Tensions, Compatibilities, and Strategies for Reconciliation," in Edward P. Lazer, ed., *Economic Transition in Eastern Europe and Russia: Realities of Reform* (Stanford: Hoover Institution Press, 1995), p. 121.

during Yeltsin's years. Putin's leadership is, evidently, trying with some success to impose on the country a harder authoritarianism in the guise of a "controllable" or "managed" (*upravliaemoi*) democracy, characterized by the growing disjunction between appearance and reality.[97] The dictatorship of law proclaimed by the Russian president has turned out to be quite arbitrary in practice.

In this regard, the successful reining in, first of the freedom of television, of radio broadcasting, and then of print media; numerous violations of human rights and attacks on the remaining independent institutions; the reliance on administrative pressure; the growing influence of the FSB, the direct successor of the notorious KGB (which is reflected in a bitter joke about Putin's "capitalism with an FSB face"); the emerging cult of Putin, which sometimes acquires ridiculous forms; and some other developments, are quite alarming.

Ideologists and practitioners of "managed democracy," which is in itself an oxymoron, perceive it in the following way: the power elite rules the country by democratic procedures if and when these do not conflict with its interests. When this is impossible, it can resort to undemocratic means (for example, to achieve desirable results in local and national elections). In any case, the Russian parliament, in their view, should be fully dependent on the Kremlin.

Apparently, the political opposition will continue to be tolerated, on the condition that it never wins the elections and comes to power. So far, the fractional character of the ruling elite and its internal feuds and competition have done more than the still largely atomized society or the weak democratic institutions, some of which are deliberately undermined further by those in power, to prevent the establishment of a full-blown authoritarian regime in Russia. However, the ruling elite and the power structures now seem increasingly consolidated, and the possibility of a creeping "Thermidor" in the country has become quite real. In other words, Russia may become a virtual democracy for the convenience of those in the international community who want to be misled.

Overall, the transition from communism to liberal democracy constitutes one of the most complex and difficult types of social, political, and economic transformation. Contrary to Daniel Patrick Moynihan's optimistic claim,[98] the great trauma of totalitarianism has not yet ended.

---

[97] For the most recent publications on this issue, see Lilia Shevtsova, *Putin's Russia* (Washington, D.C.: Carnegie Endowment for International Peace, 2003); Aleksandr Verkhovsky, Yekaterina Mikhailovskaia, and Vladimir Pribylovsky, *Rossiia Putina. Pristrastnyi vzgliad* (Moscow: Panorama, 2003).

[98] Daniel Patrick Moynihan, *Pandaemonium* (Oxford: Oxford University Press, 1993), p. 15.

Its consequences will be felt for many years, if not for generations. At the moment, one can only hope, but in no way predict that, in many post-communist countries, the wandering in the wilderness between communism and the promised land of liberal democracy will not take the biblical forty years.

Communist legacies and new trajectories: Democracy and dictatorship in the former Soviet Union and East Central Europe

ALEXANDER J. MOTYL

For much of the 1990s the post-communist states fell into three geographically clustered groups of distinct types of regimes: market-oriented democracies in East Central Europe, dictatorships predominately in Central Asia, and parasitic authoritarian regimes in the vast area between East Central Europe and Central Asia. That third group may now be fracturing, with some middle-of-the-road authoritarianisms moving toward democracy and some toward dictatorship. This change of trajectory and the concomitant emergence of two camps are, like the emergence and persistence of the three clusters, for the most part the product of systemic forces inherited from the communist past. If so, overcoming these divisions will not be easy. Only a patient and steadfast commitment to targeted institutional change on the part of these countries and of the West – the United States and the European Union (EU) – may decelerate, deflect, or reverse the trend toward two camps in the medium to long term.[1] Whether such a commitment is likely in the aftermath of EU enlargement and the U.S.-led war on terrorism is, unfortunately, far from certain.

I

Table 1 groups the post-communist states according to their cumulative scores for a variety of indicators – relating to democracy, the market,

[1] This chapter draws on some of the arguments in Alexander J. Motyl, "Ten Years after the Soviet Collapse: Persistence of the Past and Prospects for the Future," in Adrian Karatnycky, Alexander J. Motyl, and Amanda Schnetzer, eds., *Nations in Transit, 2001* (New Brunswick, N.J.: Transaction, 2001), pp. 36–44.

Table 1. *Cumulative scores of the post-communist states, 1996–2001*

Year	1996	1998	1999	2000	2001
I. Most Advanced (Democratic Market-Oriented States), 10–19					
Poland	13	13	12	12	13
Estonia	17	16	16	16	15
Hungary	13	13	14	13	16
Slovenia	17	16	16	16	16
Czech Republic	13	14	15	16	17
Latvia	18	18	18	17	17
Lithuania	19	18	19	18	17
Slovakia	—	—	—	19	17
Mean	*16*	*15*	*16*	*16*	*16*
II. Middle (Parasitic Authoritarian States), 20–39					
A. Moving toward Democracy					
Slovakia	29	29	22	—	—
Bulgaria	36	30	28	26	25
Croatia	33	33	33	28	27
Romania	34	33	30	29	29
Mean	*33*	*31*	*28*	*28*	*27*
II. Middle					
B. No Change					
Albania	35	37	36	34	32
Georgia	36	35	31	32	33
Armenia	36	36	34	34	34
Moldova	32	33	32	32	34
Yugoslavia	—	—	—	—	34
Macedonia	34	34	32	33	35
Mean	*35*	*35*	*33*	*33*	*34*
II. Middle					
C. Moving toward Dictatorship					
Russia	30	32	34	36	36
Ukraine	33	36	36	36	37
Kyrgyzstan	34	35	36	38	38
Mean	*32*	*34*	*35*	*37*	*37*
III. Least Advanced (Dictatorial States), 40–55					
Yugoslavia	—	39	44	40	—
Azerbaijan	43	43	43	42	40
Kazakhstan	40	40	41	42	42
Tajikistan	49	48	47	44	44

(*cont.*)

Table 1. (*cont.*)

Year	1996	1998	1999	2000	2001
Uzbekistan	51	51	51	51	51
Belarus	48	50	51	52	52
Turkmenistan	53	54	54	54	54
Mean	*47*	*46*	*47*	*46*	*47*

Note: The *Nations in Transit* report, published annually by Freedom House since 1997, assigns scores of 1–7 (with 1 the highest score and 7 the lowest) to countries for the following categories: political process, civil society, independent media, governance and public administration, rule of law, privatization, macroeconomics, and microeconomics. Table 1 provides the sums of each country's scores, with 8 being the best possible and 56 the worst possible cumulative score. All figures were rounded out to the nearest whole number. Because the 1996 ratings had only one number for the economy, I multiplied it by 2 to make the ratings consistent with those for the other years. The table does not include Bosnia-Herzegovina, which is largely an international protectorate.

Source: Adrian Karatnycky, Alexander J. Motyl, and Boris Shor, eds., *Nations in Transit, 1997* (New Brunswick, N.J.: Transaction, 1997); Adrian Karatnycky, Alexander J. Motyl, and Charles Graybow, eds., *Nations in Transit, 1998* (New Brunswick, N.J.: Transaction, 1999); Adrian Karatnycky, Alexander J. Motyl, and Aili Piano, eds., *Nations in Transit, 1999–2000* (New Brunswick, N.J.: Transaction, 2000); Adrian Karatnycky, Alexander J. Motyl, and Amanda Schnetzer, eds., *Nations in Transit, 2001* (New Brunswick, N.J.: Transaction, 2001); Adrian Karatnycky, Alexander J. Motyl, and Amanda Schnetzer, eds., *Nations in Transit, 2002* (New Brunswick, N.J.: Transaction, 2002).

rule of law, and civil society – compiled and published by the U.S.-based Freedom House (in its reports on *Nations in Transit*). The *most advanced* category, the democratic market-oriented states (Czech Republic, Estonia, Hungary, Latvia, Lithuania, Poland, Slovenia), consists of countries that, by virtually any measure, most closely resemble functioning democracies with market economies, the rule of law, and civil societies. Not surprisingly, they also happen to be slated for accession to the European Union in 2004.[2] The *least advanced* category, the dictatorial states (Azerbaijan, Belarus, Kazakhstan, Tajikistan, Turkmenistan, Uzbekistan), is at the other end of the spectrum. They lack democracy, market economies, rule of law, and civil societies. The *middle category*, the parasitic authoritarian states (Albania, Armenia, Bulgaria, Croatia, Georgia, Kyrgyzstan, Macedonia, Moldova, Romania, Russia, Slovakia, Ukraine), possesses some elements of democracy, the market,

[2] See "Westward, Look, the Land Is Bright," *Economist*, October 26, 2002, pp. 24–6.

rule of law, and civil society on the one hand and venal elites and non-democratic power structures on the other. Yugoslavia (Serbia and Montenegro) moved from dictatorship to this intermediate group with the fall of Slobodan Milosevic.

As Table 1 shows, the most advanced countries are located in the 10–19 range, the least advanced are in the 40–55 range, and the middle-of-the-road regimes are in the 20–39 range.

Significantly, the clusters are not random. The most advanced group lies in a broad swathe running from the Baltic to the Adriatic Sea. The middle category – with Kyrgyzstan as the outer edge – occupies the huge landmass extending from Russia's eastern border to the Balkans. With the exception of Belarus and Yugoslavia, the least advanced category is confined to Central Asia and the littoral states of the Caspian Sea. As the mean scores indicate, the most and least advanced clusters have been stable since 1996 (with the exception of Yugoslavia). Although there may now be gradual movement toward the poles and thus a "shaking out" of the middle category, the central feature of the last decade is the relative impermeability of the boundaries between and among these three sets of countries.

II

The emergence and persistence of three geographically and systemically coherent groups of countries suggests that this division is not the product of wise policy choices. After all, why should political wisdom be greatest in East Central Europe and progressively less so toward the east? One answer might be cultural: the more "European" a country is, the more likely it is to get reform right.[3] But such an ethnocentric explanation fails for two reasons. It defines "Europeanness" ahistorically, as the epitome only of democracy and the market – and not, say, also of fascism, extreme nationalism, intolerance, and blind faith in planning.[4] It also rests on circular reasoning, whereby Europeanness is first defined in terms of democracy and the market, and progress toward democracy and the market are then explained in terms of Europeanness. Another answer might invoke the extent to which the EU has actively promoted

---

[3] Samuel Huntington is correct in highlighting the importance of culture – a factor that social scientists all too readily dismiss. He is incorrect in transforming the systems of symbolic meaning that constitute culture into almost primordial characteristics that doom peoples to certain political outcomes. See Samuel P. Huntington, *The Clash of Civilizations and the Remaking of World Order* (New York: Simon & Schuster, 1996).

[4] The fetishization of "Europe" and the demonization of "Russia" generally go together. See Milan Kundera, "The Tragedy of Central Europe," in Gale Stokes, ed., *From Stalinism to Pluralism: A Documentary History of Eastern Europe since 1945* (Oxford: Oxford University Press, 1996), pp. 217–23.

or inspired reform in the post-communist states. This explanation also fails. EU intervention may have made a difference in Slovakia, Albania, Bulgaria, Romania, and Macedonia, but most of the first-category countries on the EU's accession list arrived there because of changes they adopted and not because of changes the EU promoted.[5] And why would the benefits of EU membership inspire only some countries and not others?

If European culture and EU solicitude are inadequate explanations of policy wisdom, inquiry has to shift from policy choice to policy choosers – the post-communist elites. The apposite question, then, is why some elites have been consistently unwilling or unable to transform their societies. If the elites are unwilling, then their retrograde nature and puzzling resistance to policy wisdom must be explained. Such an inquiry would inevitably begin with the conditions that led to their formation in communist times. If the elites are unable, then the constraints on their behavior can be understood only in terms of the legacies of communist rule. Either way – and the answer involves both explanations – the institutional legacies of communism provide a simple and persuasive account of the division into and persistence of the three groups of geographically clustered regimes. As we shall see, institutional legacies also suggest – although not quite as simply and persuasively – why a fracturing of the middle-category countries should have occurred and which middle-of-the-roaders were more likely to move toward democracy and which toward dictatorship.[6]

Communist rule was both totalitarian and imperial. That is to say, all communist states were totalitarian – because the control they exerted was unchallengeable, if not quite total[7] – and the Soviet bloc was an empire, with Moscow as the metropole and the non-Russian republics and East Central European satellites as peripheries.[8] Communist legacies

[5] See Alexander Cooley, "Western Conditions and Domestic Choices: The Influence of External Actors on the Post-Communist Transition," in Adrian Karatnycky, Alexander J. Motyl, and Amanda Schnetzer, eds., *Nations in Transit, 2003* (Lanham, Md.: Rowman & Littlefield, 2003).

[6] No theory can possibly explain everything, and every theory is, by virtue of its being a humanly constructed theory, necessarily flawed. See Alexander J. Motyl, *Revolutions, Nations, Empires: Conceptual Limits and Theoretical Possibilities* (New York: Columbia University Press, 1999), pp. 10–17. See especially John Ziman, *Real Science* (Cambridge: Cambridge University Press, 2000).

[7] This point is made by Jan T. Gross, "Social Consequences of War: Preliminaries to the Study of Imposition of Communist Regimes in East Central Europe," *East European Politics and Societies* 3, no. 2 (spring 1989), pp. 208–10.

[8] For a more elaborate discussion of totalitarianism and empire, see Alexander J. Motyl, *Imperial Ends: The Decay, Collapse, and Revival of Empires* (New York: Columbia University Press, 2001), pp. 13–21, 46–53. The classic study of totalitarianism is, of course, Carl Friedrich and Zbigniew Brzezinski, *Totalitarian Dictatorship and Autocracy*, 2nd.

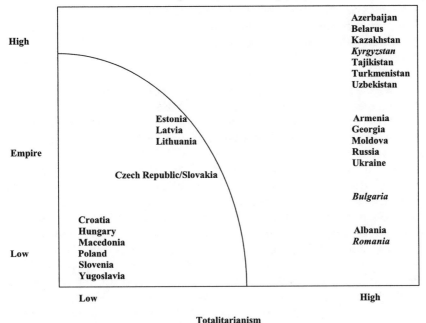

Figure 1. Totalitarian and imperial legacies.
Note: Countries within the arc are systemically more prone toward democracy;
those outside are systemically more prone to dictatorship. Countries marked in
italics are outliers.

may thus be usefully conceptualized in terms of totalitarian control and
Soviet imperial rule. The degree to which the state dominated political,
economic, cultural, and social life in a particular communist country determined the ease with which nontotalitarian institutions, such as those
instantiated in democracy, the market, rule of law, and civil society, could
emerge in post-totalitarian circumstances.[9] In turn, the degree to which
countries could act independently of Moscow's dictates determined the
kinds of states, governments, and elites (formless and unskilled or more
or less capable of decisive action) that countries possessed upon achieving independence.[10] Figure 1 places the Soviet republics and the East
Central European satellites within this matrix.

ed. (New York: Praeger, 1965). The best work on empires is Michael W. Doyle, *Empires*
(Ithaca, N.Y.: Cornell University Press, 1986).
[9] See Andreas Pickel and Helmut Wiesenthal, *The Grand Experiment* (Boulder, Colo.: Westview Press, 1997).
[10] I develop this argument in greater detail, both theoretically and empirically, in *Revolutions, Nations, Empires*, pp. 55–7.

As imperial ties burst and totalitarian controls were lifted in 1989–91, communist countries emerged from the rubble with varying degrees of nontotalitarian and nonimperial institutions in place. Insofar as totalitarianism primarily affected the nature of institutions and empire the nature of elites, the former weighed more heavily in the resultant mix of legacies and their impact on subsequent trajectories (as depicted by the area within the arc in Figure 1). Those countries that were least totalitarian and least imperial by and large joined the first category of advanced polities. With elements of democracy, the market, rule of law, and civil society already in place in 1989–91, they were best positioned to move toward full-fledged democracy and the market. Hungary and Poland, which evolved from goulash communism to market socialism to the free market, therefore epitomize East Central European development. Seen in this light, the "Big Bang" introduced by Polish Finance Minister Leszek Balcerowicz in 1990 was the logical next step in his country's decades-long movement away from communism. Yugoslavia is the big exception to this rule. It should, and presumably would, have been among the most advanced post-communist countries were it not for the intervention of Slobodan Milosevic's brutal nationalism.

Those countries that were most totalitarian and most imperial joined the third category, while those that were more or less totalitarian and more or less imperial belonged to the second. Like the second-category countries, the polities in the third category had almost no democratic institutions, market, rule of law, or civil society in place when they became independent. However, unlike the second-category countries, they had markedly underdeveloped states, governments, and elites. Not surprisingly, the least advanced countries generally developed highly personalized dictatorships – Alyaksandr Lukashenka of Belarus, Sapurmurat Niyazov of Turkmenistan, Heidar Aliev of Azerbaijan, Nursultan Nazarbaev of Kazakhstan, and Islam Karimov of Uzbekistan – that rested on continued administrative control of the largely unchanged Soviet economic system. The second-category countries adopted the veneer of democracy and the market on the one hand, while maintaining bureaucratic authoritarian regimes with official and unofficial elites engaged in untrammeled rent seeking and theft on the other. In a word, the middle-of-the-roaders, as hybrid regimes, rested on institutional contradictions.[11]

If the mix of totalitarian and imperial institutions accounted for the emergence of these three clusters, it is hardly surprising that it should

[11] On Russia as a hybrid regime, see Lilia Shevtsova, *Yeltsin's Russia: Myths and Reality* (Washington, D.C.: Carnegie Endowment for International Peace, 1999).

have contributed to their persistence after 1989–91.[12] It is in the nature of institutions – as the popularly accepted way of doing things[13] – to resist easy change, to persist, and thus to generate conditions of "path dependence."[14] At the end of the 1990s, the most and least advanced states were stable. That is to say, they possessed internally coherent systems capable of reproducing themselves and the conditions of their rule. The market-oriented democracies of East Central Europe enjoyed relatively high popular legitimacy and, no less important, could deliver the goods. The dictatorships of Central Asia, the Caucasus, and Belarus ruled by means of patronage, popular demobilization, and repression. Only the parasitic authoritarianisms of the largely Slavic middle were unable to attain such a degree of consistency precisely because, in contrast to the other two sets of countries, the institutions they inherited lacked internal coherence.[15]

The middle-of-the-roaders possessed features of formal democracy, formal markets, formal rule of law, and formal civil societies on the one hand and parasitic elites, authoritarian leaders, and corrupt bureaucracies on the other. Resting on contradictory institutional features, these hybrid regimes were inherently brittle. Formally democratic and market-oriented features enabled political oppositions and economic entrepreneurs to constrain elite rent seeking and bureaucratic malfeasance. At the same time, the elites and bureaucracies constrained the

---

[12] For alternative – more politically focused – explanations of these three clusters, see Valerie Bunce, "The Political Economy of Postsocialism," *Slavic Review* 58, no. 4 (Winter 1999), pp. 756–93; M. Steven Fish, "Democratization's Prerequisites," *Post-Soviet Affairs* 14, no. 3 (July–September 1998), pp. 212–47; M. Steven Fish, "The Determinants of Economic Reform in the Post-communist World," *East European Politics and Societies* 12, no. 2 (1998), pp. 31–78; Philip G. Roeder, "The Revolution of 1989: Post-communism and the Social Sciences," *Slavic Review* 58, no. 4 (winter 1999), pp. 743–55. Explanations that focus on parties, elections, and the like fail to explain why the clusters are not random, but geographically concentrated.

[13] On institutions, see Peter L. Berger and Thomas Luckmann, *The Social Construction of Reality* (New York: Anchor, 1966); John R. Searle, *The Construction of Social Reality* (New York: Free Press, 1995).

[14] For excellent discussions of path dependence, see David Stark, "Path Dependence and Privatization Strategies in East Central Europe," *East European Politics and Societies*, 6, no. 1 (Winter 1992), pp. 17–54; Paul D'Anieri, Robert Kravchuk, and Taras Kuzio, *Politics and Society in Ukraine* (Boulder, Colo.: Westview Press, 1999), pp. 90–140.

[15] As Cooley, "Western Conditions and Domestic Choices," argues,

"First, external actors have facilitated significant positive change in those regions that were independently committed to enacting substantial reforms at the outset of the transition. Western actors have had the most positive effects on the Central European and Baltic states.... However, the progress of most of these countries towards liberalization was predetermined by their existing civil societies, favorable geographies, and anti-Communist political cultures.... Conversely, external actors had far less impact on the Commonwealth of Independent States (CIS). Constrained by Soviet-era practices, extensive corrupt bureaucracies, and top-down patronage networks, the CIS countries have found it more difficult to extricate themselves from the Communist era." pp. 25–6.

oppositions and entrepreneurs.[16] The result was a provisional stalemate. As the next section argues, some of these regimes were more prone to develop democratically. Others were more inclined toward despotism. The most important contributing factor in both instances was the totalitarian and imperial legacy.

III

As noted previously, the middle-of-the-road category may be fracturing. Slovakia has already joined the most advanced category; Croatia, Bulgaria, and Romania are approaching it; whereas Russia, Ukraine, and Kyrgyzstan are on the verge of entering the least advanced category. Slovakia and Croatia embarked on reform once their ultra-nationalist leaders, Vladimir Meciar and Franjo Tudjman, left the scene. Accordingly, Slovakia's score declined from 29 in 1998 to 17 in 2001, while Croatia's went from 33 to 27 in the same period. Bulgaria (scoring 36 in 1996 and 25 in 2001) and Romania (with 34 in 1996 and 29 in 2001) have unexpectedly proceeded more or less steadily toward democracy and the market. Even Yugoslavia (Serbia and Montenegro), which was mired in the least advanced category for most of the 1990s, now appears set to overcome the Milosevic interregnum and adopt democratic and market-oriented reform. Its scores improved dramatically, falling from 44 in 1999 to 34 in 2001.

In contrast to these countries, Russia, Ukraine, and Kyrgyzstan have witnessed the emergence of more personalized forms of authoritarian rule by, respectively, Vladimir Putin, Leonid Kuchma, and Askar Akaev, as well as a marked growth in government efforts to curb the media, muzzle the opposition, enhance central authority, and bypass established institutional channels. Especially noteworthy are Putin's crackdown on the oligarchs, the Duma, the regional power holders, and the independent media; Kuchma's willingness to manipulate the constitution and tolerate extralegal means of dealing with the opposition; and Akaev's evident desire to extend his rule indefinitely. Although some of these measures may also be interpreted as means of building a stronger state – and a strong state is surely a necessary condition for a thriving market economy and democracy – the backgrounds, statements, and modes of operation of Putin, Kuchma, and Akaev do not inspire confidence in their democratic aspirations. As a result, between 1996 and

---

[16] See Thomas Graham, Alexander J. Motyl, and Blair Ruble, "The Challenge of Russian Reform at a Time of Uncertainty," *The Russia Initiative: Reports of the Four Task Forces* (New York: The Carnegie Corporation of New York, 2000), pp. 37–63.

2001, Russia's scores went from 30 to 36, Ukraine's from 33 to 37, and Kyrgyzstan's from 34 to 38.

Two reasons account for this emerging bipolarity. First, Slovakia, Croatia, and Yugoslavia experienced substantially lower degrees of totalitarian and imperial rule than Russia, Ukraine, and Kyrgyzstan (see Figure 1). The East Central European states were thus systemically more likely to resolve the institutional contradictions of second-category countries in favor of democracy and the market. Those states with longer totalitarian-imperial roots, such as Russia, Ukraine, and Kyrgyzstan, were by the same logic systemically more likely to move toward dictatorship. Bulgaria and Romania are the outliers in this scheme of things: the former was totalitarian and imperial, the latter was highly totalitarian and nonimperial. Their current progress, however welcome, is thus likely to stall – unless the EU swoops in and saves the day by incorporating them before they begin to backtrack. Of the remaining middle-category authoritarian states, minimally totalitarian and minimally imperial Macedonia should logically be more inclined to democracy, whereas highly totalitarian and highly imperial Georgia, Armenia, and Moldova and extremely totalitarian Albania should, according to this hypothesis, be more inclined to dictatorship. *Ceteris paribus*, of course: as Macedonia, Georgia, Armenia, and Moldova also face ethnic tensions and outside threats – something the totalitarianism-empire model has nothing to say about – their ability to adopt reform and indeed to survive is also a function of internal and external stability.

The second reason for the bipolarity involves the impact on elites of the contradiction between democracy and a market economy on the one hand and bureaucratic authoritarianism and elite parasitism on the other. Ironically, it is in these middle-of-the-road countries with especially complex institutional legacies where policy makers could have the impact usually attributed to their counterparts in the most advanced category. By "balancing" one another, these institutions expanded the political space available to leaders and thus, in the manner of Karl Marx's analysis of Napoleon III, enabled them to exert influence on a regime's trajectory.[17] Some leaders, such as Tudjman, Meciar, and Milosevic, deflected their countries from institutionally inclined upward trajectories. Others, such as Boris Yeltsin of Russia, Leonid Kravchuk of Ukraine, Eduard Shevardnadze of Georgia, and, for a time Akaev, decelerated their countries' downward drift. It may be that Emil Constantinescu of

---

[17] See Karl Marx, "The Eighteenth Brumaire of Louis Bonaparte," in Robert C. Tucker, ed., *The Marx-Engels Reader*, 2nd ed. (New York: Norton, 1978), pp. 594–617.

Romania and Simeon Saxecoburgottski of Bulgaria have played similarly positive roles.

Significantly, because such personal interventions represented deviations from, and not continuations of, institutional trajectories, their
impact as "intervening variables" perforce was temporary. Only if a
country was extremely lucky and managed against all odds to produce
a series of outstanding leaders in succession – a Hadrian, Trajan, and
Antoninus Pius – could their temporary interventions amount to systemic change. Such an eventuality is exceedingly unlikely in countries
burdened by the legacies of totalitarianism and empire.

IV

Although an institutional perspective leads one to expect the systemic
polarization described earlier, nondemocratic systems, whether parasitic authoritarian or dictatorial, can and sometimes do change for the
better – toward a greater opening of the polity or economy. Institutions
and institutional dynamics set certain parameters on change as well as
incline systems in certain directions. They do not predetermine the exact
trajectory that any country or set of countries will follow.[18] Indeed, authoritarian states can and do undergo greater or lesser degrees of change
for any of six reasons.[19]

First, and most obvious, crises can occur.[20] Crises may be external
interventions, such as those created by the world economy. Consider
the impact of Indonesia's financial collapse on President Suharto's rule.
They may also be internal convulsions, such as natural catastrophes.
Recall how the 1972 Nicaraguan earthquake helped delegitimize Anas-
tasio Somoza. Crises may also include humanly devised disturbances,
such as riots, strikes, attacks, and scandals. The Chechen seizure of a
theatre in Moscow in October 2002 comes to mind. If the timing, force,
and conditions are right, crises may actually force nondemocratic and
nonmarket elites to act against their own best interests and pursue or
tolerate reform.[21] For example, "Kuchmagate," which involved allega-
tions that Ukraine's president was directly involved in mastermind-
ing the disappearance (and presumed murder) of a critical journalist
in the summer of 2000, sparked the formation of a broad anti-Kuchma
coalition that, by late in 2002, actually managed to wrest some serious

---

[18] See Motyl, *Imperial Ends*, pp. 22–32.
[19] The entire transitions literature is concerned with just this question.
[20] On crises, see Motyl, *Imperial Ends*, pp. 77–81.
[21] See Gabriel Almond et al., eds., *Crisis, Choice, and Change: Historical Studies of Political Development* (Boston: Little, Brown, 1973).

verbal concessions from the president on the extent of parliamentary prerogatives.

Second, although stable authoritarian systems can survive for many years, their centralization of power and information generally produces a variety of systemic pathologies, resulting in growing ineffectiveness in the medium to long term.[22] Such decay makes authoritarian systems more prone to crises on the one hand and to antisystem pressure from below on the other. Disaffected elements within the elites, the population at large, or both may then rebel and compel governments to contemplate change. "People power" in the Philippines and popular mobilization against Indira Gandhi and the Shah of Iran are two such examples. Most impressive, perhaps, was the domino–like collapse of communism in East Central Europe, which showed that popular movements can succeed in both overthrowing delegitimized elites with peaceful means and ushering in positive reform.

Third, if parasitic authoritarian regimes manage to improve living standards for key sectors of the population, while refraining from opening their political systems, they may become prone to grassroots pressure by a middle class emboldened to engage in opposition politics. A variant of the modernization thesis, this view holds that political structures must, at least in the middle to long run, be compatible with economic structures for systems to remain stable.[23] Taiwan, South Korea, and Indonesia provide some evidence for the persuasiveness of this view. Ironically, this argument leads us, counterintuitively, to expect post-communist – authoritarian – regimes to become more vulnerable to instability as life improves, civil society emerges, and a middle class acquires sufficient resources to engage in effective opposition.

Fourth, authoritarian systems, not unlike the former communist states, are most susceptible to change during and immediately after intraelite power struggles, when policy initiatives serve to promote individual factions or clans in the clash for office, wealth, and influence.[24] Soviet and Chinese politics provided ample evidence of the validity of this argument; it was in the aftermath of the deaths of Vladimir Lenin, Joseph Stalin, Leonid Brezhnev, and Mao Zedong that power struggles

---

[22] See Joseph Tainter, *The Collapse of Complex Societies* (Cambridge: Cambridge University Press, 1988) and Karl Deutsch, "Cracks in the Monolith: Possibilities and Patterns of Disintegration in Totalitarian Systems," in Harry Eckstein and David E. Apter, eds., *Comparative Politics: A Reader* (New York: Free Press, 1963), pp. 497–508.

[23] The classic formulation is, still, Samuel Huntington's *Political Order in Changing Societies* (New Haven: Yale University Press, 1968). See also Chalmers Johnson, ed., *Change in Communist Systems* (Stanford: Stanford University Press, 1970).

[24] Seweryn Bialer made this argument well in *Stalin's Successors: Leadership, Stability, and Change in the Soviet Union* (Cambridge: Cambridge University Press, 1980).

between reformist and antireformist factions broke out and, despite the vicious opposition of the latter, usually resulted in significant reform. Even Leonid Brezhnev, who rolled back some of Nikita Khrushchev's changes, accepted others. Mikhail Gorbachev went so far beyond the stagnation ostensibly represented by Brezhnevism that he sparked the collapse of the USSR.

Fifth, genuinely charismatic leaders may exploit the power and resources associated with their office to attempt political and economic breakthroughs – either toward increased or decreased political and economic openness.[25] If they succeed in making improvements, then well and good. But even if they fail, their attempts can so rattle an authoritarian system as to permit popular mobilization, middle-class opposition, or elite initiatives to nudge the system in democratic and market-oriented directions. Here, too, Gorbachev is the emblematic example of a visionary leader who let things get out of control. A less-than-charismatic leader such as Putin could wreak similar havoc by pressing on with attempts to transform Russia's malfunctioning political system into a well-ordered state. History is rife with examples of the resistance of regional barons to the centralizing efforts of kings and the resulting instability.[26]

Sixth, outside actors – states, international institutions, and non-governmental organizations – can both force and induce authoritarian elites to adopt change. Saber rattling, threats of war, embargoes, foreign aid, subversion, declarations of outrage, promises, economic conditionalities, boycotts, and various acts of moral suasion are commonly accepted ways of external interference in the internal affairs of states. Even as brutal a despot as Saddam Hussein introduced a series of liberalizing measures in Iraq when faced with the threat in late 2002 of a U.S.-led invasion.

It is impossible to say with certainty, which, if any, of these scenarios will affect which post-communist countries. Crises are inherently unpredictable events, but we expect them to strike more often and with greater force the longer dysfunctional systems survive. In the long run, all post-communist despotisms and parasitic authoritarianisms will become increasingly vulnerable to externally and internally generated shocks. The capacity of civil society in general or revolutionary movements in particular to exert pressure is likely to be significant only in the long run as well. At present, the former is weak or minuscule (or both) in all post-communist authoritarian states, and the latter are nonexistent.

---

[25] See Sidney Hook, *The Hero in History* (Boston: Beacon, 1955).
[26] Charles Tilly, *Coercion, Capital, and European States, AD 990–1990* (Oxford: Blackwell, 1990).

Charismatic leaders or, more precisely, dictators with vision can emerge at any time. Russia's Putin may be just such an example. However, there is no way of predicting their emergence. Only intra-elite struggles are easily predictable. They are a permanent feature of parasitic authoritarian states even when succession struggles are not underway. As such, they should intensify at precisely those times when leaderships are in flux. Inasmuch as most post-communist states still retain the veneer of formal democracy, such struggles are likely to coincide with parliamentary and, especially, presidential elections, however unfree or unfair they may be. Outside pressure is about the only constant in this scheme of things.

V

This analysis has several implications for Western policy toward postcommunist states. Insofar as the first category of countries have "made it" and the third category may be hopelessly dictatorial, Western policy should concentrate on those second-category countries that, although for the most part are moving toward dictatorship, have experienced a dozen years of change and might be susceptible to outside influence. The West can decelerate or perhaps even halt their descent by focusing its policy efforts on the third and fourth scenarios. Because it makes little practical or moral sense to attempt to provoke crises, exacerbate inefficiencies, or search for charismatic leaders, a realistic strategy means promoting the development of a stable and strong civil society and middle class and supporting those factions in the elite that may be expected or induced, however ambivalent their attitude to democracy and the market, to use both as cudgels in their power struggles with opponents. Because developing a vigorous middle class and civil society takes generations, even in the best of circumstances, the West must be prepared for political engagement with less than fully democratic and marketoriented elites in ethically gray circumstances for many years to come.

Is the logic of these recommendations consistent with the strategic priorities of EU and NATO enlargement and the U.S.-led war on terrorism? Only minimally, if at all. The preference of the EU and of NATO for the most advanced countries effectively relegates the second and third clusters to a single category: the outsiders or, less generously, the losers.[27] Such a division is significant for two reasons. First, nonmembership in the EU or NATO is tantamount to exclusion from a political-economic

---

[27] For a forceful critique of NATO enlargement, see Michael Mandelbaum, *NATO Expansion: A Bridge to the Nineteenth Century* (Chevy Chase, Md.: Center for Political and Strategic Studies, 1997).

space that is undergoing dynamic institutional change. Second, non-membership means that the outsider countries will have no alternative to interacting more intensely with one another and, thus, reinforcing their already dysfunctional institutions.[28] It is hard to imagine how increased economic, political, social, and cultural cooperation – or, for that matter, competition – between and among Russia, Ukraine, Kyrgyzstan, and the other retrograde polities could possibly enhance their democratic and market profiles. What might mitigate this isolation is the possibility that the support provided by East Central Europe for the U.S.-led war in Iraq could serve to undermine intra-European solidarity and, thus, the cohesiveness of both the EU and NATO.

The implications of the war on terrorism are even more troubling. The emergence of a U.S.-Russian partnership and the stationing of American troops in Georgia, Uzbekistan, and Kyrgyzstan will have one positive consequence and several negative ones. On the one hand, Russia's integration into Western institutions can only be welcomed, especially as it is the largest and most important of the former Soviet states. On the other hand, the West's fixation on Russia has already translated into still greater neglect of those of its potentially reformable (middle-category) neighbors such as Ukraine, Romania, and Bulgaria with no obviously strategic role to play in the war on terrorism. (The war in Iraq and its aftermath, on the other hand, have provided some of these countries with the opportunity to establish closer security relations with the United States.) Even worse, the emergence of Central Asia as a strategic asset may lead the United States to prop up the very despotisms most allergic to democracy and the market.

Now more than ever, therefore, the future of democratic reform in the former Soviet empire depends on Russia. If the United States and the EU insist that Russia's strategic partnership with the West must involve the adoption by Moscow of democratic and market-oriented institutions, then Russia could set the example for its neighbors. If the United States and the EU fail to insist on this quid pro quo, then the evolving division of the second-category countries will continue and the ranks of the despotisms are likely to grow.

For better or for worse, the likelihood of the West's giving preference to policies designed to advance democracy in Russia, and other such middle-category states, is slim. The United States is, perhaps not unjustifiably, obsessed with the terrorist threat and less concerned with the democratic credentials of potential allies.[29] The European Union is,

---

[28] For a longer version of this argument, see *Imperial Ends*, pp. 105–8.

[29] Craig Kennedy and Marshall M. Bouton, "The Real Trans-Atlantic Gap," *Foreign Policy* (November/December 2002), pp. 66–74.

likewise understandably, obsessed with enlargement, a daunting task that, even if perfectly executed within the allotted timetable, will strain its policy-making institutions and make the EU even less capable of decisive action.[30] Last but not least, the war in Iraq has produced divisions both within Europe as well as between France and Germany on one hand and the United States on the other, thereby putting the very notion of a more or less coherent "West" in question. With the United States diverted, the EU indecisive, and the West possibly in tatters, Russia will have little reason to move vigorously toward democracy. And with Russia setting the tone, its neighbors – impoverished, authoritarian, and ignored by the West – will have even less incentive to embark on democratic projects. Indeed, prospects for democracy in the former Soviet space look decidedly bleak.

[30] See Jiri Sedivy, Pal Dunay, and Jacek Saryusz-Wolski, *Enlargement and European Defence after 11 September* (Paris: European Union Institute for Security Studies, June 2002), Chaillot Papers, no. 53.

Learning from post-socialism

VALERIE BUNCE

INTRODUCTION

The rise of new democracies throughout the world has produced a rich literature on the origins, forms, quality, and sustainability of democracy.[1] This literature has been based primarily on the experiences of two regions: Latin America and Southern Europe. The focus on these two areas in particular is understandable. The global – or "third" – wave of democratization began in Spain and Portugal and then moved to Latin America.[2] Moreover, specialists in these two regions were well positioned to compare democratization, given their earlier work on both democratization and democratic breakdown. Finally, these cases met many of the conditions that make for instructive comparisons. Latin America and Southern Europe contained a large number of cases and some variation in both the timing and modes of transition, yet they shared a similar culture in certain respects and the common political destination of democratic rule.

With the passage of time, however, what was once a broad geographic focus became an increasingly narrow one. By the 1990s, democratization had become a global phenomenon, extending from Latin America and Southern Europe to Africa, Asia, and Europe's eastern half. Indeed, for the first time in history, a majority of the world's population now live in democratic orders.[3] This diffusion of democratic politics introduces an obvious question. Once we include other new democracies in the empirical equation, does the literature on recent democratization – that

---

[1] The most influential work was the four volume series edited by Guillermo O'Donnell, Philippe C. Schmitter, and Laurence Whitehead, *Transitions from Authoritarian Rule* (Baltimore: Johns Hopkins University Press, 1986). Also see Juan Linz and Alfred Stepan, eds., *The Breakdown of Democratic Regimes* (Baltimore: Johns Hopkins University Press, 1978).

[2] See Samuel Huntington *The Third Wave* (Norman: University of Nebraska Press, 1991).

[3] Adrian Karatnycky, "Nations in Transit: Emerging Dynamics of Change," www.freedomhouse.org/ pdf_docs/research/nitransit/2001/ 02_nations.

is, the approaches, concepts and arguments that grew out of the Latin American and Southern European experiences – still hold?[4] This is a particularly important question, because new democracies have developed in such diverse economic, political, social, and cultural circumstances. For example, in many countries outside of Latin America and Southern Europe, regime transition has not involved a return to democratic rule, but, rather, the founding of genuinely new democratic orders. On the one hand, inexperience may mean that democracy is harder to sustain because the habits and practices of democracy are so foreign and because the historical absence of a democratic tradition implies the absence as well of what are commonly understood to be the preconditions for democratic rule. On the other hand, having ended democracy in the past, as in many Latin American countries, it may be easier to end democracy in the future.[5] This is particularly likely if there are negative memories of democratic politics and if the circumstances prompting the end of democratic rule are still in evidence – for example, public disorder, a powerful military, poor economic performance, and a social structure that undermines a class compromise supporting democratic politics.

Moreover, in direct contrast to the recent experiences of Latin America and Southern Europe, democracy in other contexts has shown itself to be a fragile enterprise. While the future of democracy is in some question today in Argentina, Columbia, and Venezuela and while scholars continue to debate the quality of Latin American democracy, two facts nonetheless remain. One is that democratic breakdowns have been far more common in Africa and post-communist Europe than in Latin America and Southern Europe. The other is that such breakdowns are hard to analyze from the perspective of the literature on recent democratization because this literature was based on the common political outcome of democratic governance. When combined, these two observations suggest a methodological, as well as an empirical, problem. We are unlikely to understand the origins and sustainability of new democracies if we limit our investigations to those cases in which democracy invariably followed dictatorship.[6]

---

[4] Also see M. Steven Fish, "Post-communist Subversion: Social Science and Democratization in East Europe and Eurasia," *Slavic Review* 58 (Winter 1999); Valerie Bunce, "Comparative Democratization: Big and Bounded Generalizations," *Comparative Political Studies* 33, no. 67 (August/September 2000), pp. 703–34.

[5] Adam Przeworski, Michael Alvarez, Jose Antonio Cheibub, and Fernando Limongi, "What Makes Democracies Endure?"*Journal of Democracy* 7 (January 1996), pp. 39–55.

[6] See, especially, Douglas Dion, "Evidence and Inference in the Comparative Case Study," *Comparative Politics* 30 (1998), pp. 127–46.

All of these problems suggest that the geographic limitations of the received wisdom about recent democratization may also constitute empirical and theoretical limitations. Until we expand our comparative horizons, we cannot be confident about the approaches, arguments, and generalizations that have emerged in the literature on recent democratization. Indeed, the addition of more cases may lead us to rethink our understanding of Latin America and Southern Europe. What seems to be at stake, therefore, is the validity of our definitions and concepts and the ability to make generalizations from our conclusions.

The purpose of this chapter is to begin this process of expanding our geographic and, therefore, empirical and theoretical horizons. I do so by highlighting some important patterns in the transitions from authoritarian rule in the 27 countries that make up post-communist Eurasia and assessing the extent to which these generalizations support or contest the received wisdom about recent democratization.[7] My goal, therefore, is to construct a dialogue between comparative studies of the "east" (the post-communist region) and the comparative literature on democratization in the "south" (Latin America and Southern Europe). In the course of this process, we shall discover a number of differences between these two sets of cases. These contrasts testify, most obviously, to comparative democratization as a regionally differentiated process. Less obviously, they carry two other implications. One is the methodological advantages of analyzing variation among states within regions, with the post-communist area particularly illustrative of this point. The other is to question, more generally, some core concepts and arguments in the literature – in particular, common definitions of democracy and common understandings of the preconditions for democratic rule.

GENERALIZATION ONE: POST-COMMUNIST DIVERSITY

Perhaps *the* defining feature of the Soviet Union and Eastern Europe during the communist era was the striking similarity among the countries that made up this region. In particular, they all shared the characteristics

---

[7] These are not the only generalizations that we can draw from such cross-regional comparisons. See, for example, Bunce, "Rethinking Recent Democratization: Lessons from the Post-communist Experience," *World Politics* 55 (January 2003); Valerie Bunce, "Comparative Democratization: Lessons from Russia and the Post-socialist World," in Michael McFaul and Kathryn Stoner-Weiss, eds., *Ten Years since the Collapse of the Soviet Union: Comparative Lessons and Perspectives* (New York: Cambridge University Press, forthcoming); Valerie Bunce, "Democratization and Economic Reform," in *Annual Review of Political Science* 4 (Palo Alto: Annual Reviews, 2001), pp. 43–65; Thomas Carothers, "The End of the Transition Paradigm," *Journal of Democracy* 13 (January 2002), pp. 5–21.

of state ownership of national wealth, central planning (although Yugoslavia deviated in this regard), rule by a single Leninist party, and an ideology committed to both rapid socioeconomic development and political and economic competition with the West. Indeed, their similarities, their isolation from the global capitalist system, and, in most cases, their integration with each other through the Soviet bloc and the Warsaw Pact, meant that this region was, more than most with a similar designation, precisely that: a region. Variance within the group was small, and the boundaries enclosing the group were hard.

With the collapse of state socialism from 1989–91, unity gave way to diversity and similarity to difference. Once an alternative world order, the post-communist area quickly became a political and economic microcosm of the larger and varied world within which these new regimes and states were embedded.

The sheer diversity of post-communist pathways can be seen, first, in the economic arena. To provide some brief examples of the extremes: in 2000, Slovenia's gross national income per capita was nearly eighteen times that of Uzbekistan, and during the 1990s, the percentage of the population falling below the national poverty line was 8 percent in Hungary and 68 percent in Azerbaijan. The contrasts in economic performance are equally sharp, although *all* of these countries' economies contracted in at least the first several years of the transition.[8] Thus, for example, from 1990–2000, the Polish economy grew by an average of 4.6 percent, whereas the Moldovan economy declined by 9.7 percent. For the war-torn economies of Bosnia, Serbia-Montenegro, Georgia, and Tajikistan, the decline was even greater. In these cases, the size of the current economy is roughly one-third of what it was at the time these states were formed in the wreckage of the Soviet Union and Yugoslavia.[9]

Another contrast is in economic reforms. The private sector share of the economy in the region ranges from about 15 percent in Azerbaijan, Tajikistan, and Turkmenistan to between 70 and 80 percent in the Czech Republic, Estonia, Poland, Hungary, and Croatia.[10]

---

[8] For example, in 1990 the regionwide decline in real gross domestic product was 5.0 percent; in 1991, 8.1; in 1992, 9.7; in 1993, 5.6; in 1994, 5.8; and in 1995, .3. It was only in 1996 that the economies of the region as a whole grew, and then only by .2 percent. See *Transition Report Update, April 2001* (London: European Bank for Reconstruction and Development, 2001), p. 15.

[9] See *World Development Report, 2002: Building Institutions for Markets* (Oxford: World Bank, 2002), pp. 233–7.

[10] These data are drawn from Valerie Bunce, "The Political Economy of Post-socialism," pp. 764–6, 770 (Tables 1–4); World Bank, *Knowledge for Development: World Development Report*, 1998–1999 (New York: Oxford University Press, 1998/1999), pp. 190–7.

Valerie Bunce

Political variations in post-communism are equally pronounced. One example concerns the age of the state. By the combined standards of sovereign statehood and the stability of borders, Bulgaria and Albania emerge as the oldest states in the region, with their present boundaries formed before World War I. By contrast, 22 of the 27 countries in the region are at most some dozen years old, having come into being through the dissolution of the Yugoslav, Soviet, and Czechoslovak states from 1991 to 1993. Regime transition in this part of the world, therefore, has gone hand in hand with the transformation of political boundaries. This is a familiar pattern in the eastern half of Europe, given similar changes after World War I and World War II. However, in the most recent round of state formation, the dynamic has been one of new states created from preexisting units within (at least theoretically) federal states rather than from unraveled empires. Moreover, in the great majority of cases, and contrary to most expectations, the boundaries of these new states have thus far proven to be durable. Nonetheless, secessionist pressures continue to be felt within the new, multinational and federal states of Russia and Moldova and, especially, Georgia, Azerbaijan, and Serbia and Montenegro.

A second political consideration is stability, which is a devilishly difficult term to define. Political stability is the capacity of the regime (or the organization of political power) and the state (or a political entity featuring a conjoined spatial and coercive monopoly) to provide political order. It implies such characteristics as relatively constant rules of the political game that are recognized by all and inform the behavior of all; the existence of a hegemonic regime (as opposed to competitive regimes); governments that function effectively; and physical boundaries that are clearly defined and uncontested. Instability, therefore, is indicated by high levels of social disorder; secessionist pressures; contestation over the legitimacy of the regime and government; high rates of governmental turnover; the failure of public officials to be *the* source of public policy; and governments that cannot decide, or, if deciding, cannot implement. In short, instability testifies to the failure of a regime or state to be hegemonic and to function effectively. It is both a question of "regimeness" and "stateness," with the two spheres of political activity often interactive and, thereby, mutually supportive or mutually subversive.[11]

---

[11] If there is any doubt about the interactive relationship between states and regimes, note what happens during revolutions – that is, the collapse of the coercive power of the state, the rise of secessionist movements, and the multiplication of regimes. The Bolshevik Revolution, in short, is typical and testifies to the interdependence between the strength of the regime and the strength of the state.

Once again, these indicators suggest considerable variations across the post-socialist area. The political stability of Slovenia and Hungary is in sharp contrast to the virtual states of Albania, Bosnia, Georgia, Tajikistan, and Serbia and Montenegro.[12] Russia can be added to this final group, given the continuing struggles to harmonize its legal system across space, establish a single economic and political regime within its borders, and meet its domestic and international financial obligations. However, all these difficulties have declined since Vladimir Putin became president.[13] The Russian case aside, however, it can be argued that a majority of the regimes and states within this region are unstable. Moreover, as the Slovenian versus Albanian examples cited earlier suggest, whether a state is new or old does not necessarily predict stability.

The final aspect of politics – one that has received the most attention from analysts – is regime type, or the simple contrast between democracy and dictatorship. Democracy, even according to minimal standards, constitutes the regional *exception*. This is evident from a glance at the Freedom House rankings, which measure civil liberties and political rights.[14] By their calculations, only 9 of 27 countries in the region are free.[15] However, recent political changes in Croatia, Serbia and Montenegro, and Slovakia, or elections that produced democracy-supporting governing coalitions, would make these three countries possible candidates to be added to this list in the future. At the other end of the continuum are those countries that are full-scale dictatorships: Azerbaijan, Belarus, Tajikistan, Turkmenistan, and Uzbekistan. The remaining regimes in the region are ranked as "partly free." They constitute the central tendency in the post-socialist era. Russia, as well as Ukraine, belong to this category, with Putin's curtailment of press freedoms and

---

[12] Charles King, "The Benefits of Ethnic War: Understanding Eurasia's Unrecognized States," *World Politics* 53 (2002), pp. 285–310.

[13] See, especially, Kathryn Stoner-Weiss, *Resisting the State: Reform and Retrenchment in Post-Soviet Russia* (New York: Cambridge University Press, forthcoming); Kathryn Stoner-Weiss, "The Russian Central State in Crisis: Center and Periphery in the Post-Soviet Era," in Zoltan Barany and Robert G. Moser, eds., *Russian Politics: Challenges of Democratization* (New York: Cambridge University Press, 2002), pp. 113–34; Thomas E. Graham, Jr., "Fragmentation of Russia," in Andrew Kuchins, ed., *Russia after the Fall* (Washington, D.C.: Carnegie Endowment, 2002), pp. 39–61; Lilia Shevtsova, *Putin's Russia* (Washinton, D.C.: Carnegie Endowment, 2003), Chs. 4–7.

[14] "The Comparative Survey of Freedom," *Freedom Review* 28 (1997), pp. 5–29. Also see Bunce, "The Political Economy" and M. Steven Fish, "Democratization's Prerequisites," *Post-Soviet Affairs* 14 (July–September 1998), pp. 212–47.

[15] These countries are Bulgaria, the Czech Republic, Estonia, Hungary, Latvia, Lithuania, Poland, Romania, and Slovenia. This list would be even shorter if exclusion of citizens from voting rights were to be taken into account. See Philip Roeder, "The Triumph of Authoritarianism in Post-Soviet Regimes," paper presented at the annual meeting of the American Political Science Association, Boston, September 3–6, 1998.

the autonomy of political and economic institutions, together with his centralization of power in the presidential office, casting some doubt on Russia's claims to being even partly free.[16]

Comparative Perspectives

The diverse character of the post-socialist region is even more striking once we introduce temporal and spatial considerations. Variations across countries in this region are joined by variations in the type of regime over time. For example, Belarus, Armenia, the Kyrgyz Republic, and Georgia have all de-democratized, just as Croatia, Slovakia, Serbia and Montenegro, Romania, and Bulgaria have recently become more democratic. At the same time, variations *within* countries are also substantial. These variations refer to the phenomena of microregimes and microstates. Thus, until the presidential and parliamentary elections in the fall and early winter of 2000, Serbia and Montenegro featured multiple regime types within its borders, ranging from the dictatorship in Serbia to a democratizing Montenegro. Secessionist dynamics within both Montenegro and Kosovo, together with growing demands for autonomy in Vojvodina, also challenge the notion of Serbia-Montenegro as a single state.[17]

A second example of "regimes within the regime" and "states within the state" is Russia. The sheer expanse of the Russian state, the weakness of the rule of law, the spatial fragmentation of the Russian economy, and local-level variations in both elite commitment to democracy and political practices have produced a patchwork of micropolitical and economic regimes within the Russian Federation.[18] The debates about Novgorod

---

[16] Shevtsova, *Putin's Russia*, Chs. 3–5; Vladimir Pastukhov, "Law under Administrative Pressure in Post-Soviet Russia," *East European Constitutional Review* 11, no. 3 (Summer 2002), pp. 15–22; and "Press Freedom Declines Worldwide," www.freedomhouse.org/media/pressrel/043003.htm. However, it is easy to forget that, for much of its history, the United States would be ranked partially free. For example, in New York and New Jersey, women had the vote until the beginning of the nineteenth century and were then excluded. Similarly, some blacks were enfranchised before the Civil War but lost those rights after it. Native Americans were not citizens until World War I and did not receive the right to vote until 1924. See Karen Dawisha and Stephen Deets, "The Divine Comedy of Post-communist Elections," Working Paper, Department of Government and the Center for the Study of Post-socialist Societies, the University of Maryland, 1999.

[17] See, especially, Tim Judah, "Goodbye to Yugoslavia?" *New York Review of Books*, no. 2. (February 8, 2001), pp. 44–7.

[18] See, especially, Kathryn Stoner-Weiss, *Local Heroes: The Political Economy of Russian Regional Governance* (Princeton: Princeton University Press, 1997); Kathryn Stoner-Weiss, "Central Weakness and Provincial Autonomy: Observations on the Devolution Process in Russia," *Post-Soviet Affairs* 15 (1999); Steven L. Solnick, "Russia on the Edge," *East European Constitutional Review* 7 (Fall 1998); Steven L. Solnick, "Putin and the Provinces,"

exceptionalism – which sometimes question the economic success of this region, while attributing economic performance, however evaluated, to either democratic or authoritarian politics – are a case in point.[19]

In this sense, the most useful historical analogy for contemporary Russia may not be other countries that have recently undergone a transition to democracy. Rather, the most instructive example may be Europe after the fall of the Roman empire. In both the contemporary Russian and the medieval European cases, economic disintegration and political fragmentation went hand in hand and produced widely disparate and relatively autonomous islands of political and economic activity. It was precisely this decentralization and "pluralization" of Western Europe so long ago that created the foundations for the eventual rise of both capitalism and democracy.[20] However, the many centuries separating these developments from the contemporary era have produced a major difference in at least one key aspect. Russia today exists after, not before, the Treaty of Westphalia. Russia exists, therefore, within an international system of states. As a result, Russia has – and must have – the pretensions of being a state, even if it is limited in its capacity to fulfill key functions associated with states, such as defending borders, designating the political community, integrating the economy, extracting resources, and enforcing the law.

There is yet a third comparative standard that can be applied. The political and the economic diversity of the region has grown dramatically since the collapse of state socialism. Of course, specialists on this region expected variation. Indeed, there have been few surprises with respect to where these new regimes are located in relationship to one another on the continuum anchored by dictatorship at one end and democracy at the other. What is surprising, however, is the sheer political distance separating the countries along this continuum. In particular, few specialists imagined that a little more than a decade after the disintegration of communist hegemony, the region would feature any, let alone nine, fully consolidated democratic orders. On the one hand, this development is puzzling because a democratic tradition in the region was negligible,

Program on New Approaches to Russian Security, *Policy Memo Series*, no. 115, Davis Center, Harvard University (May 2000); Steven L. Solnick, "Gubernatorial Elections in Russia, 1996–1997," *Post-Soviet Affairs* 14 (1998).

[19] Nikolai Petrov, "The Novgorod Region: A Russian Success Story," *Post-Soviet Affairs* 15 (1999), pp. 253–71 and Natalia Dinello, "Can Novgorod's Greatness Rub Off on Putin?" *Problems of Post-Communism* 38 (September–October 2002), pp. 15–32.

[20] See Jeno Szucs, "The Three Historical Regions of Europe." Also see Vladimir Shlapentokh, "Early Feudalism – the Best Parallel for Contemporary Russia," *Europe-Asia Studies* 48, no. 3 (1996), pp. 393–411 and Andrew Janos, *East-Central Europe in the Modern World: The Politics of the Borderlands from Pre- to Post-communism* (Stanford: Stanford University Press, 2000).

except in the Czech Republic. On the other hand, it is also puzzling be-cause state socialism, a political-economic system representing the polar opposite of democracy and capitalism in both design and function, was so all-pervasive for so long.

However, from several other vantage points, the political diversity of the region, including its consolidated democratic orders, should not be so surprising. While similar in form, state socialism was not so similar in the ways that it actually functioned, particularly during its last sev-eral decades.[21] Moreover, as Adam Przeworski reflected some time ago in response to the rise of the Solidarity movement in Poland, nothing disturbs politics as much as the sudden availability of alternatives.[22] This situation prevailed in 1989–90, particularly when two factors came together – a popular consensus against communism and the victory of the opposition forces in the first competitive election.[23]

Finally, at least some of the variance can be explained by the dis-solution of the Soviet, Yugoslav, and Czechoslovak federal states from mid-1991 to the end of 1992. It was this process that accentuated the eco-nomic and political extremes seen in the region today. State dismember-ment transformed what had been substantial interrepublican disparities within states with respect to economic development and commitment to economic reform and political liberalization into their interstate equivalents. In recasting interrepublican differences as differences among states, the range of political and economic variation within the region necessarily expanded considerably. This is most apparent at the democratic extreme, mainly because, with the foundations of democracy and capitalism largely in place by 1991, a mere decade of post-socialism was sufficient to allow for the quick consolidation of both.

The Implications of Diversity

These generalizations about the economic and political diversity of post-socialism have some important implications for the study of compara-tive democratization. We can begin this discussion by questioning some assumptions that have shaped the analysis of democratization as a con-sequence of the experiences of Latin America and Southern Europe.

[21] See Valerie Bunce, *Subversive Institutions: The Design and the Destruction of Socialism and the State* (Cambridge: Cambridge University Press, 1999); Grzegorz Ekiert, *State against Society: Political Crises and Their Aftermath in East Central Europe* (Princeton: Princeton University Press, 1996).

[22] "The Man of Iron and Men of Power in Poland," *Political Science* 15 (Winter 1982).

[23] In those new states formed in response to nationalist mobilization, a third factor became critical – when minorities first mobilized against the regime. See Bunce, "Rethinking Recent Democratization."

These assumptions include the tendency to presume that democratization is what follows authoritarian rule and to ignore, as a result, authoritarian forms of government as objects of study; that each state has a regime and that regimes are necessarily coterminous with the state; and that the liberalization of authoritarian rule necessarily leads to the collapse of formerly hegemonic authoritarian systems. The post-socialist experience questions all of these claims.

First, as noted previously, nearly one-third of the successor regimes in this part of the world are located on the authoritarian side of the political ledger.[24] Therefore, for the post-socialist world, there is no particular reason for studies to privilege democracy over dictatorship, or consequently, to frame investigations into regime change solely in terms of "progress" on the democratic front. This is an approach that is only partially helped by adding adjectives to the term "democracy."[25] At the same time, by narrowing the focus to democratization, the more encompassing and challenging question is often overlooked: Why does any type of regime endure or fail?[26] Put bluntly: Is Vladimir Putin being empirically correct or only politically correct when he observes that "history proves all dictatorships, all authoritarian forms of government are transient. Only democratic systems are lasting."[27]

Second, the events of 1989–91, widely coded as the collapse of communism, in many cases involved much less. Encapsulated in what was assumed to be a definitive and regionwide process was, in practice, a wide gamut of possibilities. These ranged from virtual continuity with the communist past (as in Turkmenistan, save for statehood), to a shift from monopolistic to oligopolistic politics, with the Communist Party remaining in power (as in Kazakhstan), and then to the only outcome

---

[24] Philip Roeder, "Varieties of Post-Soviet Authoritarian Regimes," *Post-Soviet Affairs* 10 (January–March 1994); Roeder, "The Triumph of Authoritarianism." Specialists in other regions of the world have also become very skeptical about the tendency to treat new regimes in their region as evidence of transitions to democracy. See, for example, Robert Fatton, Jr., "The Impairment of Democratization: Haiti in Comparative Perspective," *Comparative Politics* 31 (Fall 1999).

[25] See Guillermo O'Donnell, "Delegative Democracy," *Journal of Democracy* 5 (January 1994); Terry Lynn Karl, "The Hybrid Regimes of Central America," *Journal of Democracy* 6 (1995); David Collier and Steven Levitsky, "Democracy with Adjectives: Conceptual Innovation in Comparative Research," *World Politics* 49 (1997).

[26] For one exception, see Gerardo Munck, *Authoritarianism and Democratization: Soldiers and Workers in Argentina, 1976–1983* (University Park: Pennsylvania State University Press, 1998).

[27] Quoted by John Lloyd, former Moscow bureau chief for the *Financial Times*, 1991–6, writing in the *Globe and Mail*, June 28, 2000, and reprinted in *Johnson's Russia List*, no. 4387 (July 6, 2000). For discussions of this issue, see Philip G. Roeder, "The Rejection of Authoritarianism in the Soviet Successor States," in Richard D. Anderson, Jr., M. Steven Fish, Stephen E. Hanson, and Philip G. Roeder, eds., *Postcommunism and the Theory of Democracy* (Princeton: Princeton University Press, 2002).

that could be judged democratic: a fully deregulated polity. In short, the end of communism was uneven across space. Moreover, the political outcome of the process depended not on the mode of transition (whether pacting, mass mobilization, or reforms from above), as the democratization literature would have it, but, rather, on one factor in particular: whether the communists registered a decisive victory in the first "post-communist" election. Where they did, significant elements of the system remained, testifying in large measure to the relative weakness of the liberal opposition at the time when the Communist Party's monopoly was deregulated.

This, in turn, highlights some important considerations that have received scant attention in the literature on new democracies. One is that democracy and dictatorship are best understood not as dichotomous variables or as the two regime possibilities available in the world. Instead, democracy and dictatorship anchor the extremes of a political continuum, with the large space separating them consisting of hybrid systems that can remain precisely that for a long time or that could, under some circumstances, tip in one direction or the other. In other words, it may be a mistake to draw a thick line between dictatorship and democracy. This argument has also been made by some Latin American specialists.[28]

More fundamentally, the very notion of a regime, which is the central concept in all of these discussions, must also be understood as existing on a continuum. If there are degrees of stateness, then there are also degrees of regimeness. The term *regime* implies the spatial hegemony of a particular ideology and set of political arrangements, with different types of regimes (liberal and illiberal) having different sets of standards that they are supposed to meet if they are to be given the title of choice. Many "regimes" in the post-socialist world fail to meet either conceptual standard. They are hybrids in two ways: single states have multiple regimes within their borders, and single regimes combine elements of dictatorship and democracy.

One reason for the variations in the degree of regimeness and stateness and the reason that most regimes in this region are best understood as melded systems is that researchers have been misled by thinking of the point of departure as a matter of collapse. This is the term commonly used to describe what happened to state socialism and to the Soviet, Yugoslav, and Czechoslovak states. The key insight here is that

---

[28] See, especially, O'Donnell, "Delegative Democracy;" Guillermo O'Donnell, "Illusions about Consolidation," *Journal of Democracy* 7 (1996); Guillermo O'Donnell, "On the State, Democratization and Some Conceptual Problems," *World Development* 28 (1993), pp. 219–41.

"collapse" is often, indeed usually, an exaggeration, born of the scholarly preference for tidy descriptions over messy realities. Regimes, like institutions in general, continue to organize politics even when they seem to be unraveling. This is true even of revolutions.[29]

State Dissolution and State-Building

If some of the assumptions underlying the comparative study of recent democratization are questionable in light of the post-socialist experience, so are some of the arguments that have been made about the patterns of democratization. This is most evident with respect to the relationship among state dissolution, state-building, and democratization. On the basis of the patterns of post-socialism, one can argue that state dissolution can unexpectedly function as an investment in democratic politics. This is because, in some contexts, state dissolution has the effect of liberating the more liberal regions of the country, thereby freeing them from domination by those regions and their leaders that have less liberal or antiliberal political agendas.

Paradoxically, the notion of state dissolution as an agent of democratization meshes with a familiar argument about the effects of state integration into larger political units. The consolidation of postwar German democracy has been explained in part by Germany's inclusion in a larger Western European political and economic constellation, just as the more recent case of Spanish membership in the European Union has been understood as contributing in important ways not just to consolidation of that new democracy, but also to consolidation of the Spanish state. In similar fashion, the membership of the East Central European democracies in NATO and the European Union is widely seen as a critical investment in the sustainability of these new democracies and new capitalist economies. Depending on the circumstances, the dissolution into smaller units (or the multiplication of sovereignty in authoritarian political settings) and the integration into larger ones (or the shift of new democracies from sovereign to semisovereign politics[30]) can *both* contribute in powerful ways to the democratizing project. The particular relationship between changes in sovereignty and in borders on the one hand, and democratization on the other, seems to depend on intervening factors.[31]

---

[29] Bunce, *Subversive Institutions*.

[30] I have borrowed this term from Peter Katzenstein. See *Policy and Politics in West Germany: The Growth of a Semi-Sovereign State* (Philadelphia: Temple University Press, 1987).

[31] Indeed, in the German case after World War II, the loss of the East German lands, it has been suggested, contributed to the success of the German Federal Republic's

The relationship between state-building and democratization also needs to be reexamined. As noted previously, where the dissolution of states in the post-socialist world freed some new states to become democracies, democratization and state-building were simultaneous and mutually supportive. This is in direct contrast to the Western experience, where state-building preceded democratization – and for some very good reasons. State-building can be a bloody process, whereas democratization is based on the premise of peaceful resolution of conflicts. Moreover, if absolutism is the principle behind state-building and its consequences, liberalism captures the essence of democratization.[32] Finally, one goal of state-building is the provision of political order, a necessary condition for democratic governance.

From a variety of perspectives, then, state-building and democratization are often understood to be opposed to each other. Under ideal conditions, therefore, they are sequential processes. For precisely these reasons, in his seminal article published more than 30 years ago, Dankwart Rustow treated the settlement of state borders as a necessary, but not sufficient, condition for the transition from dictatorship to democracy.[33] Moreover, for precisely the same reasons, scholars now debate whether the Putin revolution – which is largely a process of state-building – supports or undermines the democratic project. On the one hand, firming borders, integrating the economy, streamlining political authority, building state capacity and increasing popular compliance with the regime and the state are all preconditions for democratic politics. On the other hand, Putin's approach to these tasks, like all state builders before him, is necessarily authoritarian. There is a tension, therefore, between constructing the coercive monopoly that defines and defends the state and using that monopoly to define and defend democratic politics.

How, then, can we reconcile the conflicts between state-building and democratization in the post-communist world? It is tempting to take the easy way out by arguing that the relationship between these two processes is unique in the post-socialist context and leave it at that. However, this begs the question. The existence of distinctive regions

democratization. See Michael Bernhard, "Democratization in Germany: A Reappraisal," *Comparative Politics* 33, no. 4 (2001).

[32] See Hector Schamis, *Re-forming the State: The Politics of Privatization in Latin America and Europe* (Ann Arbor: University of Michigan, 2002). For a helpful discussion of the failure to distinguish between regimes and states in authoritarian and other political contexts, and some implications for understanding issues of state-building and regime building, see Fernando Henrique Cardoso, "On the Characterization of Authoritarian Regimes in Latin America," in David Collier, ed., *The New Authoritarianism in Latin America* (Princeton: Princeton University Press, 1979), pp. 33–57.

[33] "Transitions to Democracy: Toward a Dynamic Model," *Comparative Politics* 2 (1970), pp. 337–63.

is no more a satisfactory explanation of political dynamics than the use of urban-rural distinctions to account for political behavior. In both cases, the key issue is *why* spatial factors assume political importance. The challenge for analysts is to identify the variables that, summarized through spatial considerations, produce variations in relationships – in our particular case, between democratization and state-building.

Three factors seem to be of particular relevance: whether there was a larger state in place, whether the structure of that state built proto-states within the state, and whether the political communities in these proto-states agreed on both the desirability of democracy and the necessity of having their own state to achieve that objective. In short, state dissolution is different from constructing new states. At the same time, existing states vary with regard to the creation of counterstates in their midst. This syndrome is surely the result of accident because no state (except in the theories of the young Marx) is committed to withering away. When such counterstates gain their independence, the most draconian aspects of state-building – precisely the ones that are most threatening, if not disallowing democratic governance – have in many, but not all cases already been resolved and thereby removed from the political agenda. Finally, if the dissolution of a state is also an exit from either an authoritarian regime or from a setting where future regime trajectories are hotly contested (or both, as in much of the post-socialist world by 1989–91) and if the former republic has a strong liberal opposition, then statehood, state-building, and democracy are fused projects and mutually supportive.

These are stiff and, therefore, unusual conditions. They certainly were not present in the West or, for that matter, in most of the colonialized world. As is evident from the post-socialist region, however, these conditions can materialize and, in the process, change the direction of the relationship between democratization and state-building. Even in this context, these conditions are exceptional, as evidenced by tensions throughout the area between constructing new states and constructing new regimes. The tensions reflect the absence of a popular consensus about state boundaries, membership in the political community, and the ideological and institutional foundations of the regime.

GENERALIZATION TWO: DEMOCRACY AS A THREE-PART PROPOSITION

It can be argued that there are as many definitions of democracy as there are democracies. Nevertheless, a rough consensus has emerged that has been strongly influenced by the parsimonious and procedural proclivities of the discipline. Thus, it has been argued that democracy is a political system distinguished from others by virtue of the existence of uncertain results – or institutionalized competition for political power.[34]

This definition, however, seems problematic once certain issues are taken into account – in particular, variations in regimeness and stateness in the post-socialist world and the large number of countries in this region that are "partly free" and thereby perched precariously between dictatorship and democracy. Once we recognize these considerations, two problems with the succinct definition of democracy emerge. The first is the failure to recognize that democracy is multidimensional. It includes not only competition but also freedom and certain procedures – or an institutional setting that secures both freedom and competition in an orderly and predictable fashion. The second problem is the presumption that the preconditions are in place that enable uncertain results to serve as an accurate summary of democratic political practices. Both problems converge to produce a definition that, because it is so concise and ignores so many prerequisites, generates a large number of false positives.

The definition of democracy can be refashioned by elaborating on what freedom, uncertain results, and certain procedures mean and what they require.[35] Freedom means that members of the political community, defined in ways that incorporate a very high percentage of long-term political residents within the boundaries of the state, have full, equal, and regular access to civil liberties and political rights. The second term, "uncertain political results," is based on a number of prior conditions: whether publics are fully enfranchised; whether the political system is competitive and the resulting competition is institutionalized through political parties that offer ideological choice and have the incentives and capacity to connect government and governed; whether free and fair elections are held regularly; whether those elections select the elites that actually make public policy; whether governing mandates are provisional; and whether, as a result of *all* these factors, politicians have the incentives and the institutional capacity to be fully accountable to the

---

[34] Robert Dahl, *Polyarchy* (New Haven: Yale University Press, 1971); Robert Dahl, *On Democracy* (New Haven: Yale University Press, 1998); Adam Przeworski, *Democracy and the Market* (Cambridge: Cambridge University Press, 1991); Adam Przeworski, *The Sustainability of Democracy* (Cambridge: Cambridge University Press, 1995). Also see Philippe C. Schmitter and Terry Lynn Karl, "What Democracy Is and Is Not," *Journal of Democracy* 2, no. 3 (Summer 1991), pp. 75–88; Valerie Bunce, "Elementy neopredelennosti v perekhodnyi period," *Politicheskie issledovaniia* 1 (1993).

[35] See Valerie Bunce, "Stalinism and the Management of Uncertainty," in Gyorgy Szoboszlai, ed., *The Transition to Democracy in Hungary* (Budapest: Institute of Political Science, 1991). Significantly, this trilogy of traits also describes capitalism and provides in the process equivalent analytical leverage.

electorate. The final dimension of democracy, "procedural certainty," refers to the rule of law, the control of elected officials over the bureaucracy, and a legal and administrative order that is hegemonic and transparent, commands compliance, and is relatively consistent in its operation across time, circumstances, and space. In this sense, procedural certainty underpins civil liberties, political rights, and political competition. As Stephen Holmes has eloquently argued, therefore, procedural certainty is central to the functioning of political accountability.[36]

Democracy can be defined by three straightforward conditions, but it must be emphasized that each of these conditions rests on a series of complex preconditions. Thus, the minimalist definition of democracy – the familiar emphasis on uncertain results, sometimes combined with civil liberties – is, in fact, too restricted and often misleading. However, it could be reframed as constituting a necessary, but not sufficient, condition for democratic governance. For example, one can imagine a situation in which there is genuine political competition, but without the usual characteristics that accompany such competition in well-established democratic orders. These include rich associational life; adequate information that comes from competitive media and well-defined parties that together allow voters to make informed choices and to monitor public officials; elected politicians who are primarily responsible for public policy; and the administrative capacity that gives elected officials the ability to make and implement decisions. Indeed, the gap between the formal and the substantive sides of democracy describes the situation in many of the post-socialist democracies. It is one reason that the expected consequences of democratic institutions, which are often assumed in minimalist definitions, fail to materialize.

These deficiencies can be boiled down to three issues: the weakness of civil society, the weakness of political parties, and the absence of procedural certainty.[37] All three jeopardize what more streamlined definitions assume to be the impact of political competition: the accountability of politicians. The first two problems are distinctive to the post-communist world and reflect the costs involved in the communist variant of dictatorship. With regard to civil society, state socialism destroyed the private realm, while expanding and controlling the public realm. Associational life, understood as membership in groups independent of the state, did

---

[36] "What Russia Teaches Us Now," *The American Prospect* 32 (July–August 1997), pp. 30–9.

[37] For a particularly helpful discussion of the rule of law with applications to economic reform, see Cheryl W. Gray and Kathryn Hendley, "Developing Commercial Law in Transition Economies: Examples from Hungary and Russia," in Jeffrey Sachs and Katharina Pistor, eds., *The Rule of Law: Economic Reform in Russia* (Boulder, Colo.: Westview Press, 1997), pp. 139–68; and Kathryn Hendley, "Legal Development in Post-Soviet Russia," *Post-Soviet Affairs* 13 (1997), pp. 228–51.

not exist, except in rare cases, such as Poland, where the Church, private agriculture, and constraints on Stalinization provided islands of autonomy.[38]

The weakness of political parties in the post-communist region reflects a host of factors, such as the very tainting of the word "party," given the earlier role of the Communist Party and the absence of a democratic tradition and, therefore, of precedents for institutionalized competition. Another factor is the way in which the transition has made it very difficult to determine economic interests at the individual level – the bulwark of most political ideologies that, in turn, anchor the party system – given the dramatic fluctuations in the distribution of income, in the ownership of property, in job security, and, more generally, in class structure. Borrowing from communist-era parlance, it is not accidental that the most well-defined party systems in the region are in those countries where economic reforms have gone the farthest.

If deficiencies in both civil society and party development are unique to the post-communist world, the problems concerning certainty of procedures are common to most new democracies, as recent studies of the limits of democracy in Latin America, Africa, and the post-socialist region have emphasized.[39] However, what is striking in the post-communist context is the interaction among deficiencies in associational life, political parties, and the rule of law. Once again, the Russian case is instructive. Russia is a competitive polity, but one that lacks those factors such as well-defined parties, respect for law, and the like that translate competition into a dynamic that enhances the dependence of government on the governed.[40] This disjuncture between political competition on one hand, and responsive and responsible government on the other, reminds us of the familiar costs for Russia and many of its neighbors of late developers, in this instance, late political developers. As the history of Eastern Europe over the past several centuries indicates, there has been a strong tendency for elites there to adopt the

---

[38] Marc Howard, *The Weakness of Civil Society in Post-communist Europe* (New York: Cambridge University Press, 2003).

[39] Mark Beissinger and Crawford Young, eds., *Beyond State Crisis: Postcolonial Africa and Post-Soviet Eurasia Compared* (Washington, D.C.: Woodrow Wilson Center; and Baltimore: Johns Hopkins University Press, 2002).

[40] On the weakness of civil society, see Grzegorz Ekiert and Jan Kubik, *Rebellious Civil Society* (Ann Arbor: University of Michigan Press, 1999); Howard, *The Weakness of Civil Society*; Valerie Sperling, *Organizing Women in Contemporary Russia: Engendering Transition* (Cambridge University Press, 1999). On the problems of political party development, see, especially, Robert Moser, *Unexpected Outcomes: Electoral Systems, Political Parties, and Representation in Russia* (Pittsburgh: University of Pittsburgh Press, 2001); "Russia's 1999 Parliamentary Elections: Party Consolidation and Fragmentation," *Demokratizatsiya* 8 (Winter 2000).

ideas and some of the institutions of the West, but without their usual foundations. In short, effects are imported when the politics of the moment enable or dictate, but without the causes.[41] Sequences also tend to be reversed, with political competition preceding the rule of law in the eastern half of the continent (the opposite has been true in the West); and, in the economic realm, with markets preceding property rights.

These are the familiar problems of revolutionary, as opposed to evolutionary, development, and top-down versus bottom-up processes of political change. The Leninist emphasis on the power of the superstructure to transform the base is an approach to policy making that can be used not only for illiberal ends but also for liberal ones and, as the debate on shock therapy indicates, for economics as well as politics.[42] In the process, of course, the very institutions being adopted change in form and especially in function. This dynamic is characteristic not only of democracy as it diffused from the Western core to the global periphery, but also of those other popular Western innovations that made the same trip: nationalism, capitalism, and the state.

The Centrality of The State

Implied in this revisionist definition of democracy is recognition of the importance of the state to democratization. This issue was addressed in abbreviated form earlier. Several recent observations can serve as a valuable point of departure for discussion. One is by Alfred Stepan, who has offered the stipulation: "no usable state, no democracy."[43] The other is by Stephen Holmes, who argues: "Today's Russia makes it excruciatingly plain that liberal values are threatened just as thoroughly by state incapacity as by despotic power" and that "the largest and most reliable human rights organization is the liberal state."[44]

Specialists in recent democratization have tended to overlook the issue of the state for a number of reasons. One has already been recognized – the use of a minimalist definition of democracy that presumed,

---

[41] An elegant and historically rich statement along these lines has been offered by Andrew Janos. See *East Central Europe*.

[42] Peter Murrell, "Conservative Political Philosophy and the Strategy of Economic Transition," *East European Politics and Societies* 6 (Winter 1992), pp. 3–16. But see Anders Äslund, *Building Capitalism: The Transformation of the Soviet Bloc* (New York: Cambridge University Press, 2002). On the costs of the state substituting for societal processes, see James C. Scott, *Seeing Like a State: How Certain Schemes to Improve the Human Condition Have Failed* (New Haven: Yale University Press, 1998).

[43] As observed in "Russia on the Brink: Democracy or Disaster?" *Newsletter of the Helen Kellogg Institute for International Studies* (Notre Dame) 31 (Fall 1998), p. 17.

[44] Both drawn from "What Russia Teaches," pp. 32–3.

among other things, that a capable state was in place. This assumption was all the easier to make, given the focus on democratization not only in long-established states, but also in longstanding capitalist economies. The latter perspective was critical because capitalism requires economic integration and secure property rights, and it is precisely the state that provides both preconditions. Finally, and perhaps most importantly, scholars tended to see democratic sustainability as a matter of ridding the system of authoritarian characteristics. As with much of the earlier thinking on economic reform, this meant, in practice, an emphasis on the importance of state subtraction.[45] It was thus assumed that in terms of economic efficiency, individual liberty, and, more generally, democracy, the less state, the better.

There are, however, two problems with this argument. First, we need to distinguish between the size of the state – or the propensity of the state to intervene in transactions – and state capacity – or the degree to which the state commands compliance and controls borders. Second, in the absence of a capable state, *none* of the preconditions for democracy can be met. Civil liberties cannot be guaranteed, political competition fails to produce accountability, and procedures are too irregular to produce effective, responsive, or responsible government. Moreover, without an effective state, the possibilities for democracy functioning as a hegemonic regime decline precipitously. States, therefore, have the important function of providing a single playing field within which regimes can function. Capable states define the boundaries of political as well as of economic activity. They also provide the possibility of consistent politics and economics within those boundaries, and they create many of the conditions necessary for efficient outcomes.

A related implication allows clarification of an earlier point – that democracy and dictatorship should not be treated as a dichotomy, but as situated along a continuum. It can now be suggested that incomplete democracies meet the first condition of freedom and perhaps the second

---

[45] For arguments recognizing the importance of the state as well as rule of law and the difficulties in creating a capable, legally based state in Russia (or "pravovoe gosudarstvo"), see, especially, Jeffrey Sachs and Katharina Pistor, "Introduction: Progress, Pitfalls, Scenarios and Lost Opportunities," in Sachs and Pistor, eds., *The Rule of Law and Economic Reform in Russia* (Boulder, Colo.: Westview Press, 1997), pp. 1–22. In 1997, the World Bank also did a turnaround, recognizing the importance of governance in its annual report on the state of the world's economies. See *World Development Report: The State in a Changing World* (Oxford: Oxford University Press, 1997). All of this would come as no surprise to Karl Polanyi. See *The Great Transformation: The Political and Economic Origins of our Time* (Boston: Beacon Press, 1944). For a study that makes good use of Polanyi and illuminates the connection between the state and the economy in Russia, see David Woodruff, *Money Unmade: Barter and the Fate of Russian Capitalism* (Ithaca: Cornell University Press, 2000).

condition of uncertain results, but certainly not the third condition of procedural certainty. By contrast, full-scale democracies meet all three conditions. Phrasing the question this way has several advantages. First, it reduces the problem of mislabeling regimes and the accompanying problem of comparing apples and oranges. Second, it enhances our ability to analyze what constitutes, perhaps, the largest category in the Latin American and the post-socialist region – hybrid democracies.

Finally, by arraying regimes on a continuum, a central problem in the democratization literature can be addressed. This is the theoretical and empirical sprawl attached to the concept "democratic consolidation." As Barry Weingast has suggested, "A complete theory of consolidation... requires an understanding of what makes democratic procedures self-enforcing."[46] The problem is that the conditions that define democracy have been streamlined with the result that meeting those conditions has become quite easy. This has been done to accommodate a wider range of regimes while conforming to the dictates of recent social science taste. To compensate for this easy entry into the democratic column, scholars have then identified a seemingly endless number of factors that are loosely theorized to indicate the stage that follows the initial democratic breakthrough: the consolidation of new democratic orders. While the standards set for democracy have become more minimalist and less demanding, explanations for democratic consolidation, and alternatively for breakdown, have grown more unwieldy.[47] These two processes are, of course, closely related. If democracy as a category is easily and quickly applied, then the variable forms and quality of the regimes that receive that title must be accommodated by other concepts and variables. We are left, therefore, with many transitions to democracy and few consolidated democracies, with a low threshold for becoming a democracy and an exceptionally high and cluttered threshold for democratic consolidation.

Defining democracies in terms of the three characteristics of freedom, competition, and administrative order also calls attention to another set of issues. Studies of recent democratization argue in virtual concert that democracy is easier than had been thought. The evidence for this

[46] "The Political Foundations of Democracy and the Rule of Law," *American Political Science Review* 91 (June 1997), pp. 245–63.

[47] On democratic consolidation, see Juan Linz and Alfred Stepan, *Problems of Democratic Transition and Consolidation* (Baltimore: Johns Hopkins University Press, 1996). For critical perspectives on democratic consolidation, see David Becker, "Beyond Democratic Consolidation," *Journal of Democracy* 10 (1999); Karen Remmer, "The Sustainability of Political Democracy: The Study of Latin American Democracy," *Comparative Political Studies* 29 (1996); Andreas Schedler, "What is Democratic Consolidation?" *Journal of Democracy* 9 (1998).

proposition comes from three sources: the sheer number of new democracies, the degree to which many of these new democracies have come into being despite "poor" historical preparation, and the extent to which it has proved possible to craft democracy quickly. However, some of this evidence is a definitional artifact because the minimalist definition of democracy is so forgiving that it embraces a very large number of cases. At the same time, the post-socialist experience brings into serious question the emphasis on democratization as a matter of crafting the "right" institutions.

Many of the post-socialist regimes that by some definitions might be termed democracies are, in actuality, facade democracies. The institutions appear to be democratic, and the politics are competitive, but real power and real politics operate elsewhere.[48] Indeed, many of the post-socialist cases suggest that older theories of democracy (not theories that account for recent democratization) may be quite relevant. Reference can be made, for example, to those analyses that emphasize the importance of social structure over that of formal political institutions in shaping the character and the quality of the regime.[49] In some ways, this is not surprising. Virtually all the post-socialist democracies represent a sharp break from an unusually long authoritarian past – a phenomenon that was a key concern to those older studies of democratization but not to those undertaken by the transitologists.[50]

In addition, it may very well be that certain aspects of democracy are easier to attain than others. In this respect, Latin America, the post-socialist region, and Africa speak with one voice: civil liberties and political rights are far more in evidence than genuine political competition, while procedural certainty is even less common. Therefore, there may be a hierarchy of democratic characteristics, running from the easier to the harder to attain. This in turn, testifies to differences in historical sequencing. Certain legal and administrative procedures were in large measure a gift of the Roman empire and, in some ways, of the Catholic Church. They preceded the emergence of capitalism and democracy, although they were, like the state, shaped by subsequent developments. Put another way, late democratizers have often to pay a high price for

---

[48] See, especially, Kathleen Collins, "Clans, Pacts, and Politics: Understanding Regime Transition in Central Asia," Ph.D. diss., Stanford University, December 1999.

[49] See, especially, Ralf Dahrendorf, *Society and Democracy in Germany* (Garden City, N.J.: Doubleday, 1967).

[50] The assumed contrasts between the rise of democracy in the West and recent democratization are challenged by Ruth Berins Collier. See *Paths Toward Democracy: The Working Class and Elites in Western Europe and Latin America*. (New York: Cambridge University Press, 1999). Also see Eva Bellin, "Contingent Democrats: Industrialists, Labor, and Democratization in Late Developing Countries," *World Politics* 52 (January 2000).

their need to place the cart before the horse. Political competition, at least in these contexts, seems to have been easier to import than the rule of law – not unlike the cases of consumption versus investment in the diffusion of capitalism from Europe's northwest quadrant to East Central Europe.[51]

GENERALIZATION THREE: DEMOCRATIZATION AND NATIONALISM

There is some consensus that democracy does not even enter into the zone of political choice until state borders are well defined and national identities well established. One only has to look back to the evolution of democracy in the West to see why these two factors constitute necessary conditions. If state borders are contested, politics is turbulent, interstate conflict often occurs, and the temptations of authoritarian government increase substantially. At the same time, the very notion of political rights in a democratic polity rests on an agreement regarding the composition of the political community.

With the demise of communism, the disintegration of three states in the region, and what seemed to be rising conflicts along national lines within the area and in other parts of the world, a consensus began to build around three assertions:

1. new states are poorly positioned to build democratic orders;
2. communism put the national question on hold and, with its departure, opened up these systems to considerable interethnic conflict; and,
3. as a result, democracy is highly problematic in the post-socialist world.

There are a variety of reasons to question these arguments – or what has often become, in practice, these assumptions. First, five of the nine well-established democracies in this region – Slovenia, the Czech Republic, Lithuania, Estonia, and Latvia – are new states, although three were states during the interwar years. Even if a more expansive definition of democracy is adopted, a strong correlation between the age of the state and democratic politics does not exist. Moreover, as already noted, state dissolution in some cases made a democratic trajectory both possible and desirable. Second, as a number of studies have suggested, nation-building was in fact part of the communist project, as was using national differences at certain times to mobilize political support,

---

[51] As argued by Janos, *East Central Europe.*

especially when regimes appeared fragile.[52] As a result, the deregulation of state socialism may be less a matter of unfreezing nations and
nationalism than the more familiar process of states having built nations
and nationalism in reaction to a weakening of the state and the struggles
surrounding regime transition. Spain is an instructive example.[53]

It is also the case that national identities are far from frozen. They
vary over time and in their relationship and importance to other types
of identity.[54] Just as national identity can become central under certain
circumstances, so it can recede in others. Indeed, the "cult of culture," as
Charles King has pointed out, can wear out.[55] Moving from nationalist
to other discourses is common; its analysis is not.

In addition, conflicts among nations, either within the same state or
across state borders, is the post-socialist exception, not the rule, as is the
case elsewhere in the world.[56] At the same time, disagreements among
nations and repeated rounds of bargaining among those who presume
to speak for them, do not always translate into interethnic conflict. One
has only to look at the peaceful dissolution of the Soviet Union and
Czechoslovakia to recognize the validity of this point. Violent conflict,
in particular, often requires that other factors come into play.[57]

Moreover, many conflicts that have been labeled "ethnic" are often
conflicts based on class, on divisions among elites, or on the tendency
of incumbent elites, jealous of their powers and fearful of more competitive politics, especially in authoritarian settings, to use the language of
national and territorial threats to demobilize liberal opposition forces.
For example, as Chip Gagnon has observed, the evidence for Serbian
nationalism is, in fact, quite thin, especially if the very high rates of

---

[52] Bunce, *Subversive Institutions*; Rogers Brubaker, *Nationalism Reframed: Nationhood and the National Question in the New Europe* (Cambridge: Cambridge University Press, 1996), esp. Ch. 1; Yuri Slezkine, "The USSR as a Communal Apartment, or how a Socialist State Promoted Ethnic Particularism," *Slavic Review* 53 (Summer 1994), pp. 414–52; Katherine Verdery, "Nationalism in Romania," *Slavic Review* 52 (Summer 1994), pp. 179–203.

[53] See, especially, Danielle Conversi, "Domino Effects or Internal Developments? The Influence of International Events and Political Ideologies on Basque and Catalan Na-tionalism," *Western European Politics* 16 (July 1993), pp. 245–70.

[54] See, in particular, Nicholas J. Miller, *Between Nation and State: Serbian Politics in Croa-tia before the First World War* (Pittsburgh: University of Pittsburgh Press, 1997); Loring Danforth, *The Macedonian Conflict: Ethnic Nationalism in a Transnational World* (Prince-ton: Princeton University Press, 1995); Charles King, *The Moldovans: Romania, Russia, and the Politics of Culture* (Stanford: Hoover/Stanford University Press, 2000); Mark Beissinger, *The Tides of Nationalism: Order, Event and the Collapse of the Soviet State* (Cam-bridge: Cambridge University Press, 2002).

[55] King, *The Moldovans*, p. 229.

[56] See James Fearon and David Laitin, "Explaining Inter-Ethnic Cooperation," *American Political Science Review* 90 (December 1996), pp. 715–35.

[57] Bunce, *Subversive Institutions*.

draft evasion, the absence of large-scale nationalist mobilization within Serbia, and Slobodan Milosevic's avoidance of deploying Serbian troops from Serbia in either the war in Croatia or in Bosnia are noted.[58] One can have nationalist rhetoric without having a nationalist movement. This is a generalization that applies to some other countries, including Moldova. Finally, while it is true that Western-style democracy is the exception in the post-socialist world, it is also true that national diversity does not go far in accounting for the shape of post-communist regimes. Other factors, such as the existence of antiregime protest during the socialist era and the timing of nationalist mobilization, seem to carry greater explanatory weight.

Comparing Nationalisms

The impact of nation and nationalism on democratization, therefore, is quite variable. The complexity of the questions involved can be revealed with three examples. The first comes from Poland, a country that has been rather successful in terms of democratization, economic reform, and overall economic performance. One reason Poland has excelled is the presence of a political consensus regarding liberal politics and economics. However, behind that consensus is another force that has been longer in the making: Polish nationalism, which was rooted in opposition to Soviet dominance and, before that, dominance by other empires, including, of course, the Russian empire.[59] In contrast to many other empires, the Soviet bloc was distinctive in both the character of the core – that is, authoritarian and not democratic, socialist and not capitalist – and the duplication of the core's defining political economy within each unit at the periphery. As a result, rebellion at the periphery was, simultaneously, against state socialism as a domestic system and against imperial domination. In this way, national independence and the establishment of liberal economic and political regimes – the polar opposites of the postwar status quo – were fused to become the national project.

[58] Valere P. Gagnon, *The Yugoslav Wars of the 1990s: A Critical Reexamination of Ethnic Conflict* (Ithaca, N.Y.: Cornell University Press, forthcoming).
[59] On the Soviet bloc as an empire, see Valerie Bunce, "The Empire Strikes Back: The Transformation of the Eastern Bloc from a Soviet Asset to a Soviet Liability," *International Organization* 39 (Winter 1984/85). On the role of the bloc in encouraging secessionist pressures in Eastern Europe, see Bunce, *Subversive Institutions*, Ch. 3. On the complexity of empire and the Soviet case, see Mark Beissinger, *Nationalist Mobilization and the Collapse of the Soviet State* (New York: Cambridge University Press, 2002); Alexander Motyl, *Revolutions, Nations, Empires: Conceptual Limits and Theoretical Possibilities* (New York: Columbia University Press, 1999); Mark Beissinger, "The Persisting Ambiguity of Empire," *Post-Soviet Affairs* 11 (April–June 1995), pp. 149–84.

However, for those socialist countries that were outside the bloc (Yugoslavia, Albania, and, in certain ways, Romania) or those that lacked a history of protest against Soviet domination or Communist Party rule, nationalism either stood alone without a liberal "partner" (as in Slovakia) or was less in evidence and did not produce a wholesale rejection of state socialism and an enthusiastic embrace of capitalist liberal democracy once communist and Soviet power were deregulated. Put simply, in Hungary, the Czech lands, East Germany, and Poland, along with the Baltic states as members of the "internal" Soviet empire, state socialism as a domestic and a regional system encouraged nationalism, partially because of the very design of the system. In these cases, moreover, nationalism was tied to a liberal project.[60]

Therefore, under certain circumstances, state socialism encouraged nationalism, and nationalism, in turn, functioned as a foundation for the eventual construction of liberal regimes. For example, Polish nationalism was crucial in beginning the processes that led to the regionwide deregulation of both state socialism and the bloc. Polish nationalism also provided the political honeymoon necessary to introduce macroeconomic stabilization and to engineer a rapid transition to capitalism. Nationalism, in short, can be an *investment* in democratic politics and even in capitalist economics – roles for nationalism that are often forgotten in the recent rush to condemn it but that are critical in historical accounts of the rise of the first democracies and the first capitalist economies. Central to both projects was the spatial integration of the polity and the economy leading to the formation of a political community. Moreover, when tied to liberal politics and economics, nationalism can lengthen political horizons. This is a valuable resource when new economic and political regimes are under construction and considerable economic costs and political uncertainty are attached.[61]

It can be countered that many of these examples are taken from unusually homogeneous national settings. However, homogeneity is no guarantee of liberal political and economic results, as can be seen from the recent trajectories of Albania and Armenia. What is crucial is whether nationalism is linked to a liberal or illiberal project. In the former case, it can serve as a vital political asset insofar as both democratization and economic reform are concerned.

[60] On the Baltic cases, see Rasma Karklins, *Ethnopolitics and Transition to Democracy: The USSR and Latvia* (Baltimore: Johns Hopkins University Press, 1993).
[61] See, especially, Rawi Abdelal, *Economic Nationalism after Empire: A Comparative Perspective on Nation, Economy and Security of Post-Soviet Russia* (Ithaca: Cornell University Press, 2001).

The second example is Russia. As Yitzhak Brudny has argued, Russian nationalism, while in evidence periodically, especially during periods of intraelite competition, reform and, more generally, weakened regimes, has never managed to consolidate itself in a way that generates a public consensus.[62] This phenomenon reflects a number of factors, all distinctive to the Russian case. For example, the active discouragement of a Russian identity and the related confusion between Soviet and Russian identities during Communist Party rule; the absence of an institutional base for Russian nationalism (as opposed to the titular nations of the other Soviet republics); and the problems involved in forging a coherent national identity in a context that has long featured a hybridized empire-state.

The way that the Russian Federation was formed in 1991 was also critical. It was less a product of internal demands for sovereignty than of the disintegration of the Soviet Union itself and of the power struggle between Gorbachev and Yeltsin that culminated in putting Mikhail Gorbachev, the president of the USSR, out of a job. Nationalism in Russia has become the preserve of political extremists who attract a lot of attention and some support, but who have failed to generate an effective nationalist movement. Nationalism in this context undermines democracy but is too fragmented and variable to consolidate authoritarian rule. This is one blessing of the weakness of the Russian state.

The final example comes from Croatia. As in Poland, Croatian nationalism developed over a long period and played a central role in periodic protests and intraelite conflict during the postwar era. However, while Croatian public opinion was, in fact, relatively liberal from the late 1970s onward, Croatian nationalism was not closely tied to a liberal project. In contrast to Poland during the communist era, where appeasement tended to be the regime's reaction to political protest and intraparty conflict, in Croatia, Tito took a much more repressive line. This was in part because Croatian nationalism was not disguised as having any goal aside from republican autonomy, and in part because any minority nationalism within multinational Yugoslavia simultaneously threatened both the regime and the state.

With the dissolution of Yugoslavia, Croatia became independent. However the dynamics of change in Slovenia were different. In Slovenia, a liberal opposition gained significant support during the second half of the 1980s and the leader of the League of Slovenian Communists,

[62] Yitzhak Brudny, *Reinventing Russia: Russian Nationalism and the Soviet State, 1953–1991* (Cambridge: Harvard University Press, 1998). Also see Veljko Vujacic, "Historical Legacies, Nationalist Mobilization and Political Outcomes in Russia and Serbia: A Weberian View," *Theory and Society* 25 (December 1996), pp. 763–801.

together with most of his followers, joined together with the liberal opposition, thereby creating a united front against the federal center and dictatorship. Meanwhile, given the crackdown on both liberalism and nationalism in Croatia, the liberal opposition there was much weaker than in Slovenia, and nationalism became the motive and the message of a new party opposed to communism, supportive of independence, and free of liberal commitments. As a result, in the Croatian setting, nationalism was antidemocratic, although tolerant of economic reform, especially when it benefited the party faithful. By 1999, with Franjo Tudjman's death, the disintegration of his party, the state issue settled, and the formation of a liberal coalition, Croatian nationalism was free to pursue a liberal agenda.

These three examples suggest that nationalism in and of itself is neither a force for or against democracy. Rather, what matters in authoritarian settings is a series of historical factors that shape whether national identity is well developed and whether there is a strong liberal opposition. When both are in place and regimes are in flux, nationalism supports democracy and, if the state is in flux as well, generates a positive interaction among nationalism, state-building, and democratization. This is precisely what happened in Slovenia, for example. However, where nationalism is weak, where nationalist leaders are present but lack followers, or where they are strong but the liberal opposition is weak, nationalism cannot contribute to democratization and may, in fact, undermine it.

The examples I have presented deal with a particular type of nationalism that has been given little attention – the nationalism of titular nations. What have we learned about the nationalism of minority populations? First, accommodation, albeit often with tension rather than overt conflict, has been the rule, not the exception. This summarizes interethnic relations, for example, in Ukraine, Latvia, Macedonia, Bulgaria, and Kazakhstan. Second, the most unstable situation is where minority populations are territorially concentrated, where democratic rights are least respected, and where minority populations are distributed across several adjacent states. Third, democracy is the best investment in international peace. Finally, while civic definitions of the nation are preferable to ethnic definitions, the former do not guarantee cooperation between national groupings. This is because civic definitions can support one of two very different policy objectives: autonomy or assimilation. Such is the message, for example, of the continuing conflict in Northern Ireland, where two understandings of civic identity are in conflict.[63]

---

[63] John McGarry and Brendan O'Leary, *Explaining Northern Ireland: Broken Images* (Oxford: Basil Blackwell, 1995).

CONCLUSION

The purpose of this chapter has been to use the post-socialist experience to question common understandings of the third wave of democratization. What has emerged in this discussion is, first, the need to reconsider some of the most basic assumptions that have informed the comparative study of democratization – for example, that the end of an authoritarian regime necessarily implies the rise of democracy, that democracy and dictatorship are usefully treated simply as dichotomies, and that state dissolution is harmful to the democratic project. We have also discovered a definitional problem. The minimalist definition of democracy that emphasizes political competition, sometimes in combination with civil liberties, in practice, specifies one necessary, but by no means sufficient, condition for democratic politics. Instead, as new democracies around the world remind us, democracy should be defined in terms of three characteristics, ordered with respect to ease and frequency of attainment: civil liberties, uncertain outcomes, and procedural certainties. In questioning the minimalist definition, I have also noted that it adds confusion to another conceptual staple of the literature: the familiar and formless concept, democratic consolidation. Finally, some arguments central to the study of recent democratization have been found wanting – in particular, that nationalism is necessarily harmful to the democratic project.

We can now step back from these specific points and address a methodological issue. Do these lessons drawn from the post-socialist experience mean that we need to rethink our approach toward recent democratization in general, or that we should treat the post-socialist experience as having a logic distinctive from that of Latin America and Southern Europe? I would argue that both theses are valid, depending on the question at hand. We do not have to choose, although we do have to compare. Thus, in terms of assumptions and definitions, the lessons drawn from post-socialist Europe can be generalized. They can enhance the study not only of Latin America and Southern Europe but are also relevant for the study of new democracies in Africa and Asia. Moreover, the observations about the relationship between nationalism and democratization appear to be just as applicable to other cases, particularly in Africa. In this sense, analyzing post-socialist developments has the benefit of alerting us to the limitations that have tended to characterize our approach to democratization, whatever the particular locale of our investigations.

Nonetheless, there are some aspects of the post-socialist world that seem to be distinctive. In particular, this is true of the significant political and economic diversification of the region over the past dozen years and the divergent ways in which state-building can, at times, serve the democratic project. Moreover, the weakness of both civil society and political parties in the post-communist region appear to be distinctive legacies of the unusually penetrative character of state socialist politics and economics.

To claim uniqueness, however, is merely to recognize that some causal factors need to be specified. When analyzing new democracies, we would do well to heed the impact of the past on the contemporary context. In this way, we do not have to choose, as is so often the case, between distant and proximate models of causation. Both are critical, with the former going far to explain the latter. Nor do we have to pose the question as one, simply, of whether post-socialist countries are different. Rather, the question is whether or not differences are consequential.

Ukraine's hollow decade

ILYA PRIZEL

ONE of the most unsettling experiences for anyone traveling in Ukraine nowadays is the sight of the country's cemeteries with many of the crosses and tombs stripped of their metal ornaments. Clearly, the poverty that has befallen the people of Ukraine has reached such a nadir that even stealing from the dead has become a strategy for survival. The purpose of this chapter is to assess Ukraine's experience as an independent state, to explore why Ukraine has ended up as the third poorest country in Europe,[1] and, finally, to ponder the future of Ukraine as it enters its second decade as an independent nation.

Upon attaining its independence in December 1991, Ukraine was almost universally conceived as potentially the most viable post-Soviet state. It did not have to start the process of nation-building from the same rudimentary level as most of the former Soviet republics did. Not only was Ukraine endowed with nearly a third of the world's black soil, which made it – along with Kazakhstan – one of the only two Soviet republics able to feed itself, but it also possessed some of the world's richest deposits of both iron ore and nonferrous metals. Ukraine's population numbering 52 million was thoroughly educated and literate, with many Soviet high-tech military and data-processing enterprises located on its territory, giving it a concentration of some of the best human capital anywhere on the territory of the former USSR. Furthermore, Ukraine did not have to deal with economically dysfunctional regions such as Russia's Far North. Finally, because of Russia's assumption of both the external assets and the liabilities of the USSR, Ukraine, unlike post-communist Poland and Hungary, was not burdened by a crushing foreign debt left behind by the old regime. In fact, Ukraine entered the

---

[1] In 1999, Ukraine with a gross domestic product per capita of $619, surpassed only Georgia and Armenia, both victims of armed political conflict; *Business Central Europe* (December 2000).

world arena in the enviable position of having neither an internal nor an external debt.

Ukraine's situation also appeared promising in the social sphere. Unlike Armenia or Azerbaijan, Ukraine did not inherit ethnic problems such as those of Nagorno-Karabakh. Ethnically, Ukraine's population was relatively homogeneous, in contrast to those of almost all other post-Soviet states. Although two languages were spoken (Ukrainian and Russian), the Russian-speaking portion of the population was thoroughly integrated politically and culturally, with virtually no visible tension between the two linguistic communities.

In terms of political legitimacy, Ukraine appeared to be far more secure than most other post-Soviet states. Not only was Ukraine's statehood endorsed by nearly 90 percent of its population in the referendum of December 1991, but it was also supported by one of the most organized and loyal diasporas lobbying on its behalf in world capitals. Furthermore, Ukraine's configuration as a political entity was far better established than that, for example, of most of the new states in Central Asia, a region where all the boundaries were a direct result of Stalin's nationality policies of the 1920s and 1930s, with little or no link to a collective memory or a "usable past." As one of the four founding republics of the USSR, as well as a founding member of the United Nations, Ukraine already had in place many of the institutional structures essential for a functioning state. In fact, from the psychological standpoint, its rebirth as a sovereign nation was far less traumatic than that of Russia, where the empire preceded the national state, resulting in a multifocused national identity and, thus, a very diffused polity. (Dean Acheson's characterization of Britain in 1962 as a state that "had lost an empire and had not found a role" could well apply to Russia after 1991.)

When independence was declared, the mood in Ukraine was euphoric. The country was on the dawn of a new "European" era that would enable it to become a Central European state in the mold of Poland, Hungary, or Czechoslovakia. Great hopes were expressed by the vast majority of Ukrainians who voted for independence. At the same time, a plethora of Western analysts, ranging from Germany's Deutsche Bank to the American weekly *U.S. News and World Report*, boldly predicted that Ukraine might well be the only success story to emerge from the debris of the Soviet Union. However, the euphoria of December 1991 soon turned to bitter disappointment.

In economic terms, the country has all but collapsed over the ensuing 10 years, with its 1999 gross domestic product (GDP) falling to a meager 37 percent of its level in 1989 (compared with 120 percent for

Poland and 58 percent for Russia).[2] By 2000, Ukraine found itself among the very poorest countries in Europe. With a per capita GDP in 1999 barely over $600,[3] income dipped below the equivalent figure for the Gaza Strip. The proportion of the population living below the international poverty line of 4 U.S. dollars per day (deflated for purchasing price parity, PPP) jumped from 2 percent of the population (about 1 million) in 1987 to 63 percent (about 32 million) in 1994.[4] The economic collapse in Ukraine had catastrophic effects in terms of the country's "human ecology." Thousands of university-educated Ukrainians chose to emigrate to Canada, the United States, Israel, and Russia, causing a profound and irreplaceable brain drain. Hundreds of thousands of other Ukrainians, often university-educated, sought menial seasonal work abroad from Poland to Portugal, leading to further degradation of the country's human capital. During much of the 1990s in Ukraine (as in Russia), millions of workers continued to work without monetary compensation, leading to the rebirth of both rural and urban serfdom.[5] The grinding poverty and the collapse of the state as a functioning entity have led to the criminalization of the society at many levels. Not only has the country had to endure scandals such as the sale of newborn infants from Lviv's maternity clinic, Ukraine has also become the world's largest exporter of women, and lately young boys, into the "white slavery" markets around the world. The country has also declined demographically. The population of Ukraine, which peaked at 52 million in 1985, is now less than 49 million.

To understand what has accounted for such a catastrophic performance by one of the world's most educated and richest countries, it is necessary to examine the dynamics of the process that led to Ukraine's independence following the demise of the Soviet Union. Although the world was mesmerized by Ukraine's peaceful exit from the Soviet empire, few observers noted the dark side of the transition. In East Central

---

[2] It should be noted that given the communist propensity to exaggerate economic performance and given the size of the unreported economy, the drop is most likely less precipitous; nevertheless, the decline of Ukraine's economy was the stiffest in all of Europe, save for war-torn Armenia and civil-war-ravaged Georgia.

[3] See *National Human Development Report*, United Nation Development Program, Kyiv, Ukraine, November 2001.

[4] Joan Nelson, Charles Tilly, and Lee Walker, eds., *Transforming Post-communist Economies* (Washington, D.C.: National Academy Press, 1997), p. 275.

[5] A serf is a person who is not compensated for his or her labor in legal tender and thus bound to a place of employment; it is often stated that the collectivization of the Soviet countryside by Stalin led to the rebirth of rural serfdom. The demonetarization of both the Ukrainian and Russian economies in the 1990s saw the birth of a new phenomenon, "urban serfdom."

Europe and Russia, the fall of communism led to the collapse of the Communist Party and to a substantive reorganization of the ruling elite. In countries of East Central Europe such as Poland, Czechoslovakia, and Hungary, the collapse of communism heralded a revolutionary transfer of power, in which genuine democrats such as Lech Walesa, Vaclav Havel, and Jozsef Antal replaced the old upper echelons of political leadership. In Russia, the ruling elite and the Communist Party of the Soviet Union (CPSU) were shattered by the long power struggle between Boris Yeltsin and Mikhail Gorbachev, which resulted in the collapse of the central authority and of the Communist Party as a coherent source of power.[6] In contrast, the independence of Ukraine did not result in either the replacement of the elite or the destruction of Ukraine's Communist Party (CPU) as a functioning institution of the ruling nomenklatura.

In a historic sense, the manner in which Ukraine and most other members of the Commonwealth of Independent States (CIS) attained their statehood is reminiscent of Brazil's struggle for independence in the early nineteenth century: the political center of the empire collapsed, and, thus, the local political elite mutated overnight from being an agent of the imperial power into an independent leadership without either the urge to change the existing order or a profound identification with the population in whose name independence was declared.[7]

In Ukraine, as in all the CIS states, independence was brought about in varying degrees by the same old nomenklatura which, following the collapse of the coup in Moscow in August 1991, repackaged itself as nationalist and seized power. Up until a few months before the collapse of communism, Leonid M. Kravchuk, the man who led Ukraine to independence, was the party secretary in charge of ideology. He was the man who used to denounce the use of the Ukrainian language as "bourgeoisie nationalism" and who "discovered" the great famine of 1932–3 only after Ukraine's independence. In the same vein, Evhen Marchuk, a former KGB chief in Kiev, and the man who had been appointed by the coup plotters in Moscow as their representative there,[8] was appointed prime minister of Ukraine shortly after the coup failed. Clearly neither of these personalities had any commitment to Ukraine's independence, let alone to any fundamental reforms.

---

[6] A Russian Communist Party (KPRF) did not emerge until 1990, and it never managed to recoup the institutional reach of the old CPSU.

[7] See Ilya Prizel, *National Identity and Foreign Policy: Nationalism and Leadership in Poland, Russia, and Ukraine* (Cambridge: Cambridge University Press, 1998), Ch. 9; also Andrew Wilson, *The Ukrainians: Unexpected Nation* (New Haven and London: Yale University Press, 2000), ch. 8.

[8] Ibid., p. 186.

Thus, the end of Ukraine's 337 years of subordination to Moscow did not yield a meaningful change in the makeup, structure, or modus operandi of the Ukrainian ruling elite. If anything, the quality of the country's governance visibly deteriorated. Although, in terms of education, background, and outlook, the members of the nomenklatura were no different from their counterparts elsewhere in the CIS, specific circumstances in Ukraine gave the "new-old" power elite leeway unknown in many other parts of the former Soviet Union. First, with the possible exception of the Leningrad oblast, Ukraine possessed the most ubiquitous and brutal KGB establishment in the USSR, prompting the dissident poet Ivan Drach to comment, "If they (the security organs) clip your nails in Moscow, they cut off your fingers in Ukraine."[9]

In Ukraine, decades of brutal repression by both foreign and domestic rulers created a remarkably isolated, atomized, and malleable[10] population. Ukraine in 1991 could fit Hannah Arendt's definition of a "flat" society even by Soviet standards. In addition, Ukraine's tragic history, the country's special economic role within the structure of the USSR, and the fact that Ukraine's independence was, de facto, the result of a preemptive coup by the existing elite, resulted in a quality of governance that was poor even by post-Soviet standards.[11]

Ukraine's heroic opposition, consisting of intellectuals and the political movement Rukh, was co-opted by the old elite in order to grace the new power with a patina of legitimacy. Having once consolidated its power, the nomenklatura elite marginalized and ultimately discarded its nationalist partners.

The elite of post-independence Ukraine took advantage of the unique political circumstances to consolidate its power without facing the pressure to reform. Ukraine's population was not psychologically prepared for major economic change for several reasons. First, the manner in which its economy collapsed was different from what happened in Poland, where the crisis created a psychological "teachable moment," making the population ready for, and accepting of, a painful restructuring. Second, the Ukrainian referendum for independence in December 1991 was presented as a choice between continued exploitation by

---

[9] See Bohdan Krawchenko, "Glasnost and Perestroika in the USSR," in Romana Bhary, ed., *Echoes of Glasnost in Soviet Ukraine* (York University, Ontario: Captus Press, 1989), Ch. 11.

[10] The malleability of the Ukrainian population was illustrated by the elites' ability to "deliver" 70 percent of the vote in March of 1991 in favor of retaining the Soviet Union and 90 percent in favor of independence in December of the same year.

[11] Note that Ukraine's place in the corruption chart is third from the bottom.

"Moscow" and instant prosperity that was bound to follow independence.[12]

It should be noted that no segment of the coalition that spearheaded
Ukraine's drive for independence was interested in economic reforms.
The nomenklatura elite's support for independence was based on its fear
of losing power and privilege as a result of the glasnost and perestroika
initiated by Moscow. Thus, the failure of the coup in Moscow in August
1991 left the party elite with no other option than to seek independence
as its only means of self-preservation. Similarly, a significant sector of
the population of eastern Ukraine, particularly miners and employees
of the huge military-industrial complex, the traditional "aristocracy" of
Soviet labor, supported independence for its own unique reasons. This
group saw independence as a means to thwart the economic reforms
advocated by the economists associated with the Novosibirsk institutes
that, among other things, called for the rationalization of the Soviet
economy, by – inter alia – closing the exhausted coal mines in eastern
Ukraine as well as trimming the military-industrial complex. Finally, the
intellectual nationalists clustered around Rukh were far more interested
in creating a national entity able to withstand the allegedly inevitable
Russian challenge to Ukraine's statehood than in dealing with the tem-
pest that would be unleashed by economic reforms.

DISASTROUS ECONOMIC MEASURES

The absence of a mandate for economic reform, the mind-set of the political elite, and the absence of an effective "loyal opposition" led to
the initiation of a series of disastrous economic measures that, within
a short period of time, led to a catastrophic collapse of the economy.
Because privatization had neither public support nor was it in the interest of the elite, Ukraine's political clans proceeded with a disastrous
policy that combined "rent seeking" and "asset stripping." Unwilling
to rationalize its economy, the elite continued to subsidize its industrial
behemoths through a variety of means. Initially taking advantage of
Yeltsin's reluctance to separate from Ukraine completely, the country's
industry continued to receive virtually free energy from Russia, much of
which was immediately resold on the world market with the elite pocketing the proceeds. Even more insidiously, relying on the old Soviet
structure, the Central Bank of Ukraine (CBU), continued to issue massive ruble-denominated credits, which were used by these enterprises

---

[12] See Anatol Lieven, *Ukraine and Russia: A Fraternal Rivalry* (Washington, D.C.: United
States Peace Institute, 1999), Ch. 2.

to sustain their existence, often despite the absence of economic viability. This fueled hyperinflation in Russia.[13]

This economic "strategy" was based on the assumption that Russian largess would continue indefinitely, despite Kiev's assertion of full political independence. However, within a year of the breakup of the Soviet Union, Russia realized that, as a result of the monetary policy pursued by Ukraine and other CIS states, it was suffering a hemorrhage of more than 10 percent of its GDP as well as fueling its own hyperinflation, and it brought this support to an abrupt halt. Thus, the "free rider" posture of the CBU, which enabled it to "create" 125 billion rubles in the short period between July and October 1992, was forced to change just as suddenly in September 1992, when the Central Bank of Russia started to refuse to honor the ruble-denominated checks of Ukrainian importers issued by the Central Bank of Ukraine, effectively ejecting Ukraine from the ruble zone.[14]

Simultaneously, the Russian energy sources that effectively had been providing Ukraine with about 6 billon dollars worth of free energy, started to raise their prices toward world levels: the price of a ton of oil went from 350 rubles to 80 dollars, and gas from 333 rubles to 45 dollars per 1,000 cubic meters.[15]

The response of the nomenklatura-dominated Rada was to force the CBU to issue massive subsidies to cover the budget deficits of both the government and the state industries, none of which were privatized. This time subsidies were denominated in the Ukrainian "temporary currency," the karbovanets. These actions, in turn, threw Ukraine into hyperinflation that reached 100 percent in December 1993 alone.[16] This resulted in an annual inflation rate of 10,115 percent.[17]

Once the CBU stopped engineering liquidity, inflation fell to 25 percent in January 1994 and to 5 percent by April of that year.[18] The result of Ukraine's policies was to create a distorted version of the Soviet economy. In contrast, Poland and Hungary, following the economic strategies of Balcerowicz and Bokros respectively, established emerging market economies, whereas Russia and the Czech Republic, following Gaidar's

---

[13] See M. Dabrowski and J. Rostowski, "What Went Wrong? The Reason for the Failure of Russia's Stabilization in 1992," *Case Paper*, May 1993.

[14] See Georges de Menil, "From Hyperinflation to Stagnation," in Anders Äslund and Georges De Menil, eds., *Economic Reform in Ukraine: The Unfinished Agenda* (Armonk, N.Y.: ME Sharpe Press, 2000).

[15] Ibid., p. 52.

[16] Ibid., p. 56.

[17] See Anders Äslund, "Why Has Ukraine Failed?" in Äslund and DeMenil, eds., *Economic Reform in Ukraine: The Unfinished Agenda*, p. 265.

[18] De Menil, "From Hyperinflation to Stagnation," p. 56.

reforms in Russia and Klaus's privatization in the Czech lands, created at least distorted market economies. In fact, in January 1993, when Russia opted to liberalize its economy by freeing prices and opening its economy to world competition, Ukraine's response was to reinforce Soviet-style administrative controls that further distorted the economy. Thus, Ukraine's independence ushered in neither privatization nor liberalization of the economy. Rather, it traumatized the population and exhausted the modest reservoir of confidence that the new state created.

Much as in the Soviet period, Ukrainian industrial enterprises continued to operate with no regard for economic rationale. Instead, the survival of each industry depended on its management's ability to acquire subsidies. In addition, prices on primary inputs remained controlled, which perpetuated all the irrational absurdities of the Soviet economy. However, even the Soviet state had exhibited a degree of economic discipline and demanded of management a degree of economic accountability. The economy of postindependence Ukraine exhibited neither of these virtues.[19]

A vast array of "all-union" enterprises, which before 1991 had been controlled by the ministries in Moscow, fell into the hands of the local elite. Members of the Kiev-based nomenklatura, no longer subject to outside supervision, with no political challenge from within, and with no pretense of ideological commitment, went on a binge of corruption and asset stripping of unprecedented proportions. This made Ukraine probably the most corrupt country in the CIS (except for Azerbaijan), and globally, behind Bolivia, Indonesia, Bangladesh, and Nigeria.[20]

The "rent" collected by the elite in 1992 reached a parity with the country's GDP.[21] Privatization was repeatedly delayed or carried out in a manner that created a class of enforcers of elite privilege rather than strong independent entrepreneurs. Because most of the enterprises remained either outright state assets or could survive only on the basis of state largess, the management's strategy continued to rely on two imperatives. The managers had to retain their positions as long as possible through providing "tribute" to officials in Kiev; and, given their realization that their stewardship as managers was temporary and could be withdrawn at any moment by a displeased "center," their goal became to enrich themselves as quickly as possible. As a result of this distorted Soviet economic model, left with all its vices and none of its virtues, the Ukrainian economy experienced one of the sharpest peacetime

[19] See Paul Hollander, *Political Will and Political Belief: The Decline and Fall of Soviet Communism* (New Haven and London: Yale University Press, 1999).

[20] See *Global Corruption Report* 2001, p. 236.

[21] Anders Äslund, "Why Has Ukraine Failed?" p. 264.

economic contractions on record. The rent seeking obstructionism of the political elite remained so deeply entrenched that, even as late as 1999, there were more than 1,600 major enterprises excluded from privatization, and those enterprises that actually had been privatized continued to function in such a distorted environment that private ownership did not result in any productivity improvement over state-owned enterprises.[22]

This crippling, distorted Soviet economic model afforded the new elite various opportunities to make stupendous fortunes. It could export metals, which in Ukraine's "controlled" internal market traded at 10 percent of the world level, pocketing hundreds of millions of dollars in profits. Energy, which was imported from Russia at subsidized prices or stolen outright from natural gas pipelines crossing Ukraine's territory, was immediately resold on the world markets, turning those in control of these transactions into millionaires overnight. Other members of the nomenklatura made substantial fortunes by borrowing monies from the state bank at 20 percent interest, at a time when inflation was soaring over the 10,000 percent level. The money they borrowed was often converted into a foreign currency, with the state bank being repaid only a minuscule fraction of the debt. Members of the nomenklatura involved in agriculture or coal mining, unlike those in the metal sector, had no opportunities for arbitrage between domestic and world prices. As a result, they relied on generous state subsidies that accounted for more than 10 percent of the GDP in 1994, again with much of these funds being siphoned off into private hands.[23]

The wholesale looting of state assets by the elite and its henchmen resulted in a new phenomenon, the birth of "urban serfdom." Large numbers of employees were not paid for extended periods of time and, thus, became de facto serfs because of their inability to leave their place of employment, which provided at least some benefits such as housing and the factory canteen. In this manner, a kind of contemporary feudalism was restored, and the exhausted population became further atomized.

The replication of a distorted Soviet model carried over to the country's political structure as well. Because the emergence of independent Ukraine did not result in either the replacement of the elite, as was the case in East Central Europe, or in an implosion of the state mechanism, as was the case in the Russian Federation, much of the political system in Ukraine continued to coast along as an ersatz version of the Soviet Union in miniature. As noted earlier, in the barren political landscape of

[22] Ibid., p. 257.
[23] Ibid.

late Soviet Ukraine, the only authentically democratic political grouping was that of the moderately nationalist intellectuals associated with Rukh, a group that had no governing agenda, other than independence, and no grassroots backing beyond the western fringe of the country and the city of Kiev.

Given the group's limited means of attaining independence, the Rukh leadership entered into a Faustian "grand bargain" with the communist elite whereby Rukh would support the national communists in exchange for the latter's commitment to independence. This joint front suited the communists in two ways: First, it afforded Leonid Kravchuk and his cohorts a popular legitimacy that they otherwise would not have had; second, in the early days of independence when the political rules of the game were being established, the new nomenklatura could start to govern without a credible opposition, paving the way for a kleptocratic regime with no countervailing political forces to provide any checks or balances. While the intellectuals within Rukh focused on developing a "national idea" for Ukraine, with some opting for "scientific nationalism" as a replacement for "scientific Marxism-Leninism,"[24] Kravchuk and the post-communist elites consolidated their control over the levers of power, thus contributing to Rukh's fragmentation and increased marginalization on Ukraine's political stage.

CONSTITUTIONAL ANOMALY

Within five years, Ukraine's political landscape evolved into three distinct groups: 1. on the right, increasingly nationalist and politically irrelevant splinters of the old Rukh; 2. in the center, a conglomeration of regional political clans and "red directors" involved in an orgy of "rent seeking"; and 3. on the left, a large yet unreformed bloc of communists, wallowing in nostalgia and dreaming of reunification with a "socialist Russia." However, none of these groups represented a liberal-democratic political force eager to transform Ukraine into a democratic state.

Because Ukraine did not adopt a new constitution until 1998, the country continued to rely on the old Soviet constitution of the Ukrainian SSR, which typically vested most of the political power in the legislature. This constitutional anomaly – although meaningless in Soviet times when real power resided in the Communist Party, which exercised tight

[24] See Yevhen Bystrtsky, "Nationalism and the Legitimization of Postcommunist Regimes," in Volodymyr Polokhalo, ed., *The Political Analysis of Postcommunism: Understanding Postcommunist Ukraine* (College Station, Tex.: A & M University Press, 1997).

control over all institutions – became a source of chronic political paralysis in many CIS countries. In Russia, the deadlock between the legislative and the executive branches nearly trigged a civil war between Yeltsin and the Russian Supreme Soviet in the autumn of 1993. Unlike the situation in Russia where the unworkable constitutional structure led to bloodshed and political violence, in Ukraine the ineffectiveness of the Verkhovna Rada created a political vacuum, allowing the essentially uncontrolled looting of the country and leading to the brazen criminalization of the state at all levels. Given the dysfunctionality of the legislature, the executive branch of the government expanded its powers, restoring most of the powers previously associated with the first secretary of the CPSU to the president of Ukraine. This presidential power of appointment resulted in a structure in which success in obtaining a governorship hinged on paying "tribute" (both financial and electoral) to the president, without regard for the interests or concerns of the local population.[25]

Now, more than a decade after attaining its independence, Ukraine still has to develop a balanced system. Under the current arrangements, Ukraine remains a hyper-presidential republic in which the president appoints the cabinet (the parliament only has to approve the candidacy of the prime minister), the heads of regional administrations, as well as the heads of the security, legal, and tax authorities, with no supervision by or accountability to the legislature. In reality, the president's power is even greater than the constitution seems to indicate because of the executive's habit of allowing members of the presidential administration to assume the responsibilities of various ministries. Without any clear division between the "government camp" and "loyal opposition," the legislature is a collection of ephemeral interest groups, all of which support the president and compete for presidential favor on one issue or another. Political parties that could be regarded as a challenge to the existing system are weak and have virtually no impact on the country's patronage politics.[26]

Much like the political and economic system, the legal system of Ukraine has continued to rely on some of the most odious holdovers of the Soviet system. The country has retained the office as well as the structure of the Soviet General Procuracy. This office, which can both issue arrest warrants and prosecute in court, retains all the characteristics

---

[25] In fact, excessive local popularity, which might be a harbinger for an independent power base, is far more likely to result in a dismissal by a jealous center than an incompetent yet "loyal" behavior toward the center.

[26] See Serhyi Makeev, "Desiatiletnii Krizis Legitimnosti Praviashchikh Elit," *Politychna Dumka*, no. 3 (2001).

of the Soviet political police, with a conviction rate of more than 97 percent[27] of those who are charged by the state. Thus, it has become a fearful tool of the presidency to silence opponents. The failure of Ukraine's judicial system to protect basic human rights has resulted in a scathing assessment from the London-based Amnesty International,[28] and in April 2001, the Parliamentary Assembly of the Council of Europe demanded the expulsion of Ukraine from the Council of Europe.

Another tool of intimidation that has remained firmly in the hands of the president is the control of the tax authority, which has repeatedly been unleashed on those who appear to have displeased the president.

The resulting political system in post-Soviet Ukraine has created, on the one hand, a fragmented legislature in which many members use the immunity granted by virtue of membership as a cover for brazenly illegal economic activity, and, on the other hand, a presidency with awesome powers of dismissal, intimidation, and persecution, creating a culture of political fear within the elite and of atomized passivity among the masses. As Anders Äslund has commented, "In Ukraine, however, there seems to be no line whatsoever between organized crime and leading economic-political groups, most of which consider racketeering to be one of their principal activities."[29]

Given the power of the president and the extent of repression and intimidation, Ukraine's media have been largely cowed into either silence about or a sycophantic posture toward the president. The few courageous journalists who have challenged the existing order have been arrested, beaten up, or murdered, possibly under direct presidential orders.[30] According to the Paris-based organization Reporters Sans Frontiers: "Ukraine has the worst record in Europe for violence against journalists."[31] At a conference in Washington, Yulia Mostovaia, the deputy editor of *Zerkolo Tyzhnia,* openly asserted that "there is no free press in Ukraine," and Vadym Rabinovich of the Media International Group (MIG) noted that in Ukraine the media are "a means to obtain power."[32]

---

[27] See Ilya Prizel, "Why Ukraine Is a Laggard," the Harriman Institute.

[28] See "Ukraine: Rights Still Being Violated," *AI Index EUR 50/002/2001,* no. 181. Available: http://web.amnesty.org/ai.

[29] See Ilya Prizel, *National Identity and Foreign Policy,* Ch. 9; also Andrew Wilson, *The Ukrainians: Unexpected Nation,* p. 268.

[30] The issue of the murder of journalists came to a head with the disappearance (and ultimately the apparent appearance of the decapitated body) of the editor of the Web-based publication *Ukrainska Pravda,* Heorhiy Honhadze. Although audiotapes implicating President Leonid Kuchma were leaked to the opposition, the regime weathered the crisis.

[31] "Nervous Times for Ukraine Journalists," *BBC World Monitoring: Media Reports,* July 17, 2001.

[32] See *Ukrainskii Vzgliad* (New York), no. 9 (October 2001).

Much of the electronic media continue to be dominated by state-owned Channel 1, which promulgates Soviet-style propaganda predicting a "happy future."

Given the trauma of Soviet rule and the continued repression in the post-Soviet era, Ukraine by now has one of the most passive and atomized populations in Europe, with fewer civic organizations than authoritarian Belarus.[33] In terms of political structure, Ukraine is rapidly slipping into what Alexander Motyl called "Zaireization" or "Pakistanization,"[34] a process in which a corrupt elite cannibalizes the society. A prerequisite for participation in the elite, as in any crime syndicate, is to partake in the criminal activity, so that no member is able to seek legitimacy on the basis of political integrity.[35]

Because of the enormous benefit that the Ukrainian elite is deriving from the political twilight of contemporary Ukraine, Volodymyr Polokhalo, one of the country's most prominent and independent political scientists, observed that in the case of Ukraine, "post-communism" has not become a transitory phase from Soviet Bolshevism to Western democracy. Rather, it has become a permanent condition, which continues to abort any notion of a birth of democratic civil society.[36] As a result of the continued survival of this "post-communist" political structure, Ukraine has become one of the worst-governed countries in Europe, which, according to one estimate, lags a full 75 percent behind Poland and Hungary in terms of the quality of governance.[37]

If the "old-new" elite of Ukraine has done little to lay a foundation for either democratic institutions or a viable market economy, it has expended a great deal of energy on devising a "national idea" for Ukraine and a foreign policy aimed at establishing a visible profile for the country as a major player in international affairs. Given the fact that Ukraine's independence was, in Andrew Wilson's words, "gifted" rather than attained as a result of a strong popular consensus, one of the most complex issues that confronted the newly independent state was the need to develop a "Ukrainian idea" that would provide a basis of legitimacy.

---

[33] Tadeusz A. Olszanski, "Ukrajina," *Osrodek Studi Wschodnich*, October 31, 2001. Available: http://www.osw.waw.pl.

[34] According to the *Global Corruption Index*, Ukraine, with its 83rd place in the world, was deemed to be the most corrupt polity in Europe and behind Pakistan and Tanzania, see *Global Corruption Report 2001*, p. 236.

[35] See Catherine Wanner, ed., *Burdens of Dreams: History and Identity in Post-Soviet Ukraine* (University Station: Pennsylvania State University Press, 1998), Ch. 7.

[36] See Volodymyr Polokhalo, *The Political Analysis of Post Communism: Understanding Post Communist Ukraine*.

[37] See *Ukraine Human Development Report 2001: The Power of Participation*, United Nations Development Program, Kyiv, (November 2001) Ch. 2, p. 2.

DIFFERENCES IN LANGUAGE AND RELIGION

The process of creating a Ukrainian national mythos was bound to be far more complex than in most post-communist states. Ukraine not only lacked a collective memory of prolonged, unified independence to serve as a legitimating "usable past," but it also had a population divided by language and religion. Although the number of Russophones and Ukrainophones was nearly even, the distribution of speakers of each tongue was very uneven, with the Russian speakers dominating the urban centers of eastern, southern, and central Ukraine, and Ukrainian speakers dominating the countryside and the urban and rural areas to the west. Even though the issue of language was not acute, as already noted, this situation clearly held potential dangers.

In terms of religion, while the overwhelming majority of the people of Ukraine are Orthodox, a minority of the population (about 10 percent) – mainly in western Ukraine – belongs to the Greek Catholic (Uniate) church, which, while following the Byzantine ritual, accepts the pope as its spiritual leader. Historically, the relationship between the two churches has not been amicable: the Orthodox community viewed the Greek Catholics as turncoats who accepted papal authority as a means of ingratiating themselves with the dominant Poles, whereas many Greek Catholics saw the Orthodox church in Ukraine as a tool of Russification and Russian hegemony. Since Ukraine gained its independence in 1991, a rift has developed in the Orthodox Church in Ukraine between those who continue to profess loyalty to the Moscow-based Orthodox Church and the new Kiev Patriarch, who has been seeking recognition of an autocephalous status within world Orthodox Christianity, on a par with the Russian, Greek, Serbian, Romanian, and other national churches that make up the Orthodox community. Thus, whereas some post-communist countries such as Armenia, Georgia, Poland, Serbia, or Croatia were able to rely on their respective religious institutions to buttress new "national solidarity," religion in Ukraine has remained a divisive issue that hinders rather than reinforces the birth of a national idea.

Another formidable obstacle to the creation of a coherent national idea in Ukraine is the absence of a common collective memory in relation to the nation's twentieth-century history. Different segments of the Ukrainian population retain conflicting memories of the country's experience during World War II, as well as during the period of Soviet rule. For the majority of Ukrainians, the war and Ukraine's participation in the Red Army's victory was, and remains, the defining event of this century. To this day, elderly Ukrainians proudly don their Soviet war medals for both official and personal celebrations.

In western Ukraine, however, World War II was perceived as a choice between two demonic tyrants, Hitler and Stalin. Given the vague hope that a German victory would ultimately yield independence, many young west Ukrainians joined Ukrainian SS units in the service of Nazi Germany. Thus, whereas in most of Ukraine, World War II ended in "our" victory, in western Ukraine, the end of the war was generally perceived as yet another enslavement of Ukraine by a brutal foreign occupation. Nothing demonstrates the split in Ukraine's collective memory more graphically than the contrast between Kiev, where a monument to Nikolai Vatutin, the Soviet general who "liberated" Kiev in 1943 stands in the town center, and western Ukraine, where there is a monument in honor of those Ukrainian nationalists who assassinated Vatutin in 1944. Thus, the absence of a common national narrative across Ukraine further complicates the effort of the elite to create a legitimating national idea.

Finally, with the Russian minority forming nearly a quarter of the population, a Russian-speaking population representing about half of the country's total, and the presence of other national minorities (Tatars, Romanians, Ruthenians, and Hungarians), the idea of building a "national state" was not a viable option for the political elite. Given the delicacy of this situation, it is remarkable that the Ukrainian political class has managed to avoid the ethnic strife that has typified most post-Soviet and some post-communist Central European states. For these reasons, Ukraine's declaration of statehood pointedly focused on the "People of Ukraine" rather than on the "Ukrainian People." On the issue of religion, whereas Leonid Kravchuk, Ukraine's first president, attempted to support the Autocephalous Kiev Patriarchate in its struggle with the Moscow-based church, the Kuchma administration opted to try to separate religious issues from politics despite the fact that the Russian Orthodox Church continues to control some of the most sacred properties in Ukraine and remains the largest single denomination in the country.

Similarly, while the government could not reconcile the contradictory collective memories resulting from World War II, the political class has managed to prevent the issue from gaining much political momentum by accepting the notion of a pluralist view of the country's past. Thus, while in the eastern city of Donetsk they continue to celebrate "Red Army Day," in Lviv and western Ukraine, the commemorations are held for the Ukrainian Rebel Army (UPA), which fought the Red Army.[38]

---

[38] See Klaus Bachman, "Nezavisimost' i svoboda ne odno i to zhe," *Novoe russkoe slovo* no. 11 (August 2001).

LINGUISTIC LEGITIMACY

Of all the obstacles impeding the molding of a Ukrainian polity, the language question may prove to be the hardest to overcome. Centuries of suppression of the Ukrainian language under the tsars, culminating in the Ems Decree, which "banned" the Ukrainian language (1876–1905), and decades of Soviet Russification reduced the Ukrainian language to a minority language, preponderant only in the countryside and western Ukraine, leaving Russian as the lingua franca of most of urban Ukraine. In its quest to find legitimacy, the ruling elite seized on the language issue, the political shibboleth of contemporary Ukrainian politics. Although there is certainly much merit in seeking the revival of the Ukrainian language, the Ukrainian regime, as in so many other spheres of its activities, has chosen to pursue a Soviet-style system of compulsion rather than follow a more enlightened approach. Unlike Finland which, while recognizing the bilingual structure of the society, chose a gradual, decades-long policy of assimilating its Swedish-speaking population, or Italy, which in 1960 abandoned the forced Italianization of German speakers in Tyrol, Ukraine has opted for policies that, while not requiring the adoption of Ukrainian as one's own language, has provoked a hostile response from many Russian speakers.

Despite the constitutional commitment to allow for the "free development, use, and protection of the Russian language" as well as the right to an education in Russian, since 1998 state policy has increasingly turned toward an enforced use of the Ukrainian language. On December 14, 1999, the constitutional court of Ukraine ruled that the Ukrainian language is "the obligatory language of instruction in all state institutions in the country . . . the obligatory means of communication on the entire territory of Ukraine for the state authorities and local self government bodies to exercise their powers, as well as in all other spheres of public life."[39]

This Soviet style of trampling on legal standards and the resorting to the politics of compulsion has led to a backlash. The Russian minority, which (apart from Crimea) previously viewed itself as an integral part of Ukraine, started to develop new political organizations such as the "Russian-Ukrainian Movement," the "Russian Movement of Ukraine," and the movement "For a Unified Rus'," which picketed the ministry of education, claiming that while "no less than half of the population (of

---

[39] See "Poland, Belarus, and Ukraine: A Survey of Developments," *RFE/RL*, February 7, 2000.

Ukraine) considers Russian to be its native language" only 10 percent of the country's education is conducted in Russian.[40]

The claims of the Russophones that the government's policies are "liquidating Russian-language education in Ukraine"[41] are overstated, to say the least, and there is little to indicate that, with the exception of the Lviv region, intercommunal tension between Russian and Ukrainian speakers is a significant issue. Nevertheless, there seems to be a growing Russian nationalist consciousness among the Russian speakers, which may, in the long run, threaten the integrity of the state.

Over the last 50 years, the Russian speakers, whether ethnically Russian or Ukrainian, have tended to conceive of themselves primarily as "Soviet." However, the current policies pursued by Ukraine seem, for the first time, to have awakened a distinct Russian identity among many Russophones in the eastern part of Ukraine. It is noteworthy that whereas in 1991 all of the regions of Ukraine, including Crimea, voted in favor of independence, by 2001 in some Russian-speaking regions of Ukraine, particularly in the Donetsk and Luhansk districts (as well as in Crimea), the people opposed to Ukraine's independence outnumbered those who favored it by a ratio of two to one. Although the reasons for rejecting Ukraine's independence are complex, there is a strong correlation between the proportion of Russian speakers and the share of the population taking this stand.[42]

POST–COLD WAR DYNAMICS OF WEALTH AND POWER

Interestingly, while Ukraine's political elite has inflicted poverty, deprivation, and discord on the country's long-suffering population, it has demonstrated a remarkable ability to retain power. The sources of the longevity of the power structure are threefold: 1. the demise of the USSR enabled the same political class to retain power as a coherent and unified entity, 2. the profound atomization and sheer exhaustion of Ukraine's population have made the sources of political resistance few and easily isolated, and 3. the elite has shown an unusual ability to attach itself to external powers, thus facilitating its grip on power at home. During the first decade of independence, Ukraine's political class managed to persuade the Clinton administration that Ukraine is the "keystone

---

[40] Paul Goble, "Ukraine Ponders Language Policy and National Integration," *RFE/RL*, September 19, 2001.

[41] Ibid.

[42] See Sergei Davydov, "Referendum ili desiat' let spustia," *Ukraina. RU*, December 1, 2001. Available: http://www.ukraine.ru.

in the arch," serving simultaneously to prevent the rebirth of Russian imperialism and to accelerate the democratization of both Russia and post-communist Central Europe.

Exploiting the notion of its alleged centrality to the stability of the post–Cold War order, Ukraine has managed, despite obvious corruption, mismanagement, and the crude expropriation of foreign assets, to become the third largest beneficiary of U.S. aid. This fact has resulted in the flow of billions of U.S. dollars into Ukraine and has enabled the elite to rely on a combined strategy of co-opting some domestic political forces while coercing others. Despite numerous corruption scandals at the highest level of the Ukrainian government, and despite clear links between high officials in Ukraine and Russian criminal gangs, the Clinton administration stubbornly continued to insist that Ukraine was making "progress" that warranted generous American aid.

While being a prime beneficiary of U.S. largess, Ukraine managed to extract generous benefits from its relationship with Russia as well. To lessen the political liability of being the man who destroyed the Soviet Union, Boris Yeltsin continued to cling to the fig leaf of the CIS as a confederate successor to the USSR. Given the importance that Yeltsin attached to Ukraine's participation in the structures of the CIS and given the symbiotic links between the elites in Russia and in Ukraine, he continued to allow Ukraine to build up a huge debt to Russia, knowing full well that the debt would, most likely, rapidly become a "nonperforming asset." Thus, between 1991 and 1998, taking advantage of the external environment, Ukraine's elite managed to leverage its situation and avoid making any decisions that would compromise its grip on either wealth or power.

The economic crisis that gripped Asia in 1997 and the Russian economic meltdown in the summer of 1998 had a profound impact on Ukraine's fortune. The economic fall of the "little tigers" of Asia followed by the dramatic Russian collapse of August 1998 finally convinced the United States that economic aid to a decaying corrupt elite not only does not facilitate reforms but also actually helps the existing power elites avoid the introduction of transparency, the rule of law, and the other essential ingredients of a modern market economy. As a consequence, U.S. economic aid, as well as private investment, sharply declined.

The fallout of the 1998 crisis in Russia was a generational change within the elite, which brought to the pinnacle of power Vladimir Putin, a man who was not associated with the collapse of the USSR and, thus, was immune to the political blackmail that the CIS's elites had been able to exert on his predecessor. President Kuchma observed the change in the Russian mind-set: "Mr. Putin pursues a very strict economic policy towards Ukraine, very strict, too pragmatic. With Yeltsin you could reach an agreement, but with Putin it's cash up front."[43] Thus, in the post-1998 era, the Russian elite had neither the means nor the motivation to continue to subsidize Russia's erstwhile empire.

REORIENTATION TOWARD RUSSIA

The sudden end of foreign economic support brought the Ukrainian elite face-to-face with a dilemma. Ukraine could reform its legal and economic structure to make the country attractive to foreign investment, which, given the country's physical and human capital, would have had a very good chance of refloating the economy. However, the cost of any meaningful political and economic reform was bound to threaten the elite's grip on power and privilege, a prospect that Ukraine's governing elite was not willing to contemplate. Alternatively, the Ukrainian elite could seek to reattach Ukraine to the Russian economy, relying on the competitiveness of a depreciated ruble, on high energy prices, and on the sense of stability engendered by Putin's restoration of a semblance of order in Russia.

Given the choice between loosing its grip on power or returning as a junior partner of Russia, the Ukrainian elite opted for the latter without hesitation. Since 1999, Russia has become by far the largest trading partner, investor, and creditor of Ukraine. Russian enterprises have acquired key sectors of Ukraine's metal and chemical industries, and Russia has undertaken the financing of the country's program of nuclear power plant construction. Whereas Moscow has taken a very accommodating position on the settling of Ukraine's debt issue, this Russian flexibility has been accompanied by a visible increase in Russian influence on Ukraine's political posture both in terms of economic and foreign policy.

It is true that segments of the nascent business community and others have increasingly voiced concern that Ukraine is dealing with what one analyst referred to as a "Trojan Friendship,"[44] and others have expressed concern that the deepening relationship between Russia, the United States, and NATO is bound to marginalize Ukraine's utility as a buffer state between Russia and NATO and push Ukraine ever deeper into the Russian orbit.[45] Yet, although Ukraine's drift back into Moscow's orbit has alarmed some analysts and intellectuals, it has had little resonance

---

[43] John McLaughlin, "One on One: Guest Ukraine's President Leonid Kuchma," December 7–9, 2001.

[44] See Tatiana Grebneva, "Troianskaia druzhba," *Kompan'on*, Kiev (November 31, 2001).

[45] See Oles' Ilchenko's analysis in *Kompan'on*, Kiev (November 30, 2001).

either among the political elite, which realizes that an alliance with the Kremlin is the best strategy for political self-preservation, or among the vast sectors of the population that increasingly associate the resumption of Ukraine's economic growth since 1999 with the closer links to Russia.

With the exception of those political groups whose power base lies on the western fringes of the country and of the nationalistically inclined population of Kiev, few groups have made a significant issue of the closer links to Moscow. Once again, much as in 1654, when the Cossack elite surrendered much of Ukraine's sovereignty to the Romanov dynasty by the Pereiaslav Agreement, or as in 1991, when the decision was made to adopt the Belovezhsk agreements to dissolve the USSR, so now it has been the interests of a narrow political class that have determined the economic and political direction of the country while the rest of the population has been confined to the role of bystander.

Ukraine's current reorientation toward Russia is a decision of the elite in power, designed to advance its own interests, with little or no thought being given to how such policies might affect the country's long-term prospects. In a way, the proclivity of the Ukrainian elite to swing from one foreign sponsor to another is also reminiscent of the policies conducted in 1918 by Pavlo Skoropadskyi on behalf of Ukraine, during the country's brief independence following the collapse of the tsarist empire, a policy that discredited the reliability of Ukraine and hastened its demise as an independent state.

Unlike the situation then, however, the current Ukrainian elite is the prime beneficiary of independence and, thus, will defend the sovereignty of Ukraine tenaciously. At the same time, post-Soviet Russia is emerging as a national state with little appetite for imperial expansion, especially when such expansion is bound to impoverish Russia's own rapacious elite. Finally, no independent state since Newfoundland in the 1930s has ever opted to return to the hegemony of its former overlord. While Ukraine's sovereignty is thus secure, for the country's 49 million citizens, the idea of a dignified democratic existence continues to be a dream deferred, reinforcing an atomized society where some 90 percent[46] of the population considers its government corrupt and, hence, not concerned with the well-being of the country's long-suffering people.

---

[46] Gary A. Ferguson, *Public Opinion in Ukraine 2000* (Washington, D.C.: International Foundation for Election Systems, 2000), p. 90.

Russia in free fall? Key challenges

The Russian transition to the market: Success or failure?

MARSHALL I. GOLDMAN

THE difficulties in the transition from communism to a market economy in Russia should not have come as a surprise. Many assumed that, given the opportunity, the Russians, like the Chinese and the Poles before them, would jump at the chance to switch to a competitive economy, and that, for their part, like crocuses in the spring, the institutions suited to the market economy would quickly reemerge from the frozen soil.

In retrospect, such hopes ignored how profoundly 70 years of communism battered not only those institutions but also the cultural behavior that gave rise to these institutions in the first place. After all, hardly anyone anticipated how quickly communism would collapse.[1] Because such disintegration seemed so unlikely, almost no one, either inside or outside the USSR, found the time to examine the challenge that would come with such a transition.[2] How badly suited Russia was for the transition is reflected in the near collapse of the economy. From 1990 to 1999, the gross domestic product (GDP) – at least according to official figures – shrank to between 50 to 60 percent of its pre-reform size (see Table 1).[3] This was sharper than anything experienced by the United States during the Great Depression.

If for no other reason, the fact that Russia's economy was so completely dedicated to the Cold War meant that any end to that confrontation, even a gradual one, would make both adjustments and civilian conversion difficult. Thus, Mikhail Gorbachev's decision to suspend

---

[1] See Marshall I. Goldman, *USSR in Crisis: The Failure of an Economic System* (New York: W. W. Norton, 1983).

[2] One of the few exceptions is Egon Neuberger, *Central Planning and Its Legacy* (Santa Monica: Rand Corporation, 1999), p. 6.

[3] Anders Äslund has argued, mistakenly, that the decline was nowhere near as steep. Admittedly, an impressive underground economy took shape rapidly, but a visit to the Russian provinces at the time illustrated how real the drop was. See "The Myth of Output Collapse after Communism," Working Paper 18, Carnegie Endowment, March 2001.

Table 1. *Annual percentage change in Russian gross domestic product (GDP)*[4]

	GDP as % of preceding year	Revised % change	Old GDP figure
1989	—	—	
1990*	97.6 to 95	−2.4 to −5	
1991	95	−5.0	
1992	85.5	−14.5	
1993	91.3	−8.7	
1994	87.3	−12.7	
1995	95.9	−4.1	
1996	96.4	−3.6	−3.4
1997	101.4	1.4	0.9
1998	94.7	−5.3	−4.9
1999	106.4	6.4	5.4
2000	110.0	10.0	9.0
2001	105.0	5.0	5.0
2002	104.1	4.1	4.3

* 1990 is for gross national product of USSR, Directorate of Intelligence, *Handbook of Economic. Statistics, 1991* (Washington, D.C.: Central Intelligence Agency, September 1991), p. 62.

the arms race meant that those working in the sector of the Russian economy involved in military production would suddenly become, to a great extent, unemployed. The size of military expenditures ranged from a minimum of 20 percent to significantly higher estimates.

As if the need to handle military conversion were not enough of a challenge, Gorbachev simultaneously sought to inject more initiative and flexibility into the Soviet planning system. He introduced the Enterprise Law, which gave factory directors increased autonomy. He also authorized the formation of cooperatives and even private businesses. Both changes undermined Gosplan, Gossnab, and the industrial ministries, while enhancing market-type activities.

The tampering set in motion the ultimate, albeit unintended, collapse of the planning system. There is good reason to believe that the Soviet system, if left alone, would have stumbled along for another decade or

[4] Goskomstat, *Rossiiskii statisticheskii ezhegodnik* (Ross Stat) (Moscow, 2000), p. 16, p. 559; Davis Center for Russian Studies, *Economic Newsletter*, Feb. 19, 2002, p. 1; June 2002, p. 1. *Moscow Times*, May 6, 2003, reports some major revisions in Russian GDP figures.

more. It would have been wasteful, and the shortcomings would have become increasingly evident, but the Soviet economy need not have collapsed as suddenly and precipitously as it did.

An analogy might help explain what happened. There once was a carnival act in which a motorcyclist inside a wooden cylinder built up his speed until he was riding perpendicular to the wall and parallel to the ground. As long as he maintained his speed, he could defy gravity and remain perpendicular. However, if he slowed down, the motorcycle would crash to the ground.

In many ways, the Soviet economy was like the motorcyclist. With its emphasis on heavy industry and ongoing military mobilization (in effect the Soviet economy operated as if it were at war from the 1930s until 1991), the system was dependent on the external stimuli of the Cold War. Were the Cold War ever to end, or the powers of the central planners to be trimmed, the driving force of the economy would also be undercut and the Soviet economy would, like the motorcyclist, come crashing down. Given the extraordinary reliance on military production, the end of the Cold War was particularly disruptive. Suddenly, there was no need for all the aluminum, aircraft, and tanks. Moreover, the conversion of the military industry to civilian production is difficult under the best of conditions, but it is particularly traumatic when the market system is brand new or when the conversion depends almost entirely on central planners who are also threatened. Thus, it is no wonder that the Russian GNP fell to as little as half of its former size.

The economic collapse was also a result of the faulty nature of the reforms that Boris Yeltsin's government attempted to implement – not that any far-reaching reform of the Soviet system would have been easy. After all, no one had ever attempted such a fundamental turnaround. There had been more modest and gradual reforms in communist Hungary and China. Closer to home, the Poles launched a program called "Shock Therapy" in January 1990, two years before Russia began its reforms on January 2, 1992. But as destructive as communism had been to market institutions in Eastern Europe, the system there had lasted only 45 years, and communism there had generally been imposed from the outside. No country other than Russia was faced with the task of undoing 70 years of homegrown communism. Moreover, a substantial segment of the Russian population preferred the status quo. This was very different from the situation in Poland, where the vast majority of the population agreed that Poland should switch from Eastern-style central planning to a Western market orientation.

The extra 25 years of communism in Russia made any reform more challenging. The purge of market institutions, codes, laws, and memory had been much more ruthless and effective in the Soviet Union than elsewhere. It was as if Soviet communist leaders had been determined to do all they could to burn their institutions behind them. They had assumed that the more thorough the destruction, the less likely the chance of ever restoring a free market. In effect, Soviet leaders had created a situation in which the options were either central planning or anarchy. Nothing else seemed viable. Since the 1930s, Gosplan and the industrial ministries superseded or destroyed the remnants of markets, both wholesale and retail, as well as formal and informal commercial and industrial codes and laws. Without instructions and orders from Gosplan and the ministries, factory directors and store managers were incapable of obtaining input or selling what they produced. To fill the void, in the late 1980s and early 1990s, local entrepreneurs created more than 300 so-called commodity or stock markets where individuals or groups with goods to sell could bargain with those who needed them. In fact, they did not deal in futures, but in actual products such as trucks, nails, soap, wheat, or cotton. This was one step above pure chaos, but no more than that. Further, the breakup of the Soviet Union into fifteen constituent republics in 1991 disrupted many established relationships between factories and their subcontractors, who suddenly found themselves in different countries.

The transition was also complicated by the fact that much of the infrastructure that had been put in place in the course of seventy years was intended for a socialist-communal, not a market-consumer society. Thus, factories were designed to produce massive quantities of uniform products. This provided economies of scale, but it necessitated unusually large assembly lines and made it all but impossible to produce small or varied batches of goods. Whether the factory produced 1,000 or 10,000 tractors, the workforce needed was almost the same. This made it extremely complicated to produce a limited output profitably.

This mentality that gave such priority to the large scale also affected the way cities, towns, and villages functioned. For example, to economize on the use of energy, the government ordered that heat and hot water must be supplied for large districts by a single central steam generating plant. Individual buildings were not allowed to have their own furnaces. This system worked reasonably well in the Soviet era and in large cities, even after the advent of the market. But in the less populated regions, the system generally proved cumbersome and unprofitable for private operators. This helps explain why so many regions now report a lack of heat as radiators and transmission pipes are allowed to freeze.

Such a communal system is simply not viable in most profit-oriented economies, and unfortunately for the less developed areas of the country, no other system can be quickly put in place.

The rejection of central planning and state ownership and the switch to the market were characterized by analysts such as Stephen Cohen as too much movement and by others, such as Anders Äslund, as too little.[5] In a sense, they were both right. This helps demonstrate why the reform process in Russia was all but doomed to fail, regardless of which remedies were adopted.

Because the transition came so quickly, it was inevitable that little could be done. Switching to a new system necessitated the introduction and adoption of a completely new set of institutions, including laws and codes, which meant discarding many of the most important existing institutions, laws, and codes. Under the best of circumstances, even if there had been a broad consensus as to the structure and direction of the proposed reforms, there would not have been enough time to design, implement, and absorb the extremely far-reaching changes that were needed. As a consequence, not enough of the new was implemented. There were no firmly established markets, commercial banks, or commercial codes, nor were there judges experienced in dealing with private business disputes. In addition, too much of the old that should have been abandoned actually remained – the residual state ownership of shares in privatized business, a central bank that was more Gosbank than commercial bank, and a president (Boris Yeltsin) who issued orders in the same manner as the tsars and party general secretaries of old.

Other shortcomings include the neglect, if not the outright obstruction, of new business startups. To open a business, a determined entrepreneur needed to spend a minimum of 3 months (the average is nine) to obtain the signatures of at least 250 bureaucrats, visit 20 to 30 government offices and obtain 50 to 90 clearances.[6] Instead, the emphasis was placed on privatizing large state businesses. This reflected the traditional Russian preference for working with massive enterprises.

Yegor Gaidar, the acting prime minister and architect of the reforms, also decided against a currency reform. Had there been such a reform, this would have allowed him to eliminate the ruble overhang. He feared that a currency reform would wipe out the earnings and savings of many honest businesspeople and consumers who, beginning in 1987,

---

[5] Anders Äslund, *How Russia Became a Market Economy* (Washington, D.C.: The Brookings Institution, 1995); Stephen F. Cohen, *Failed Crusade: America and the Tragedy of Post-Communist Russia* (New York: W. W. Norton, 2000).

[6] *Moscow Times*, March 26, 2001; *Johnson's Russia List*, March 24, 2001, no. 5168.

responded to the opportunity to go into business for themselves. Gaidar's failure to undertake such a reform precluded an across-the-board policy of price liberalization, however. Thus, he had no choice but to continue controls over oil and some food prices. He realized that without such controls, prices would increase dramatically, pushing the cost of energy beyond the reach of ordinary citizens and producing massive speculation and profiteering by oil producers.

In the end, however, the 26-fold inflation in 1992 wiped out almost everyone's savings anyway. Meanwhile, the failure to allow prices to reach world levels all but ensured that those with access to oil would eagerly seek to export it to avail themselves of the considerably higher prices abroad. To prevent such windfall profits from the export of oil at prices five or more times higher than those that were set for the domestic market, the government insisted that oil exporters must first obtain an oil export license from the government. It should have been anticipated in advance that this would make those who issued such licenses the recipients of very large bribes.

Simultaneously, some of the reformers were excessively zealous. In particular, they overindulged in privatization, notably of the country's larger enterprises. Initially, the government retained shares in some of the most lucrative properties and sometimes maintained complete control of them. However, in 1996, even many of these enterprises, or at least the shares in those still held by the state, were also put on the market.

The privatization of small business went reasonably well, and, for the most part, few seemed bothered by the manager and staff takeover of shops. Reflecting the same notion of entitlement, the management and staffs of the country's larger enterprises began to demand the same kind of access. Given their strong presence in the Supreme Soviet, the managers of large enterprises were able to win concessions from Anatoly Chubais, Gaidar's deputy director, who wanted to privatize as quickly as possible because he feared the country might revert to communism. He reasoned that by making the average citizen a stockholder, the public would resist any such temptation. Although he opposed the effort to make the staffs the outright owners of the larger enterprises, he nonetheless wanted to provide them with some equity because he felt that this would ensure opposition to any return to communism.

In the absence of an adequate system of controls designed to limit corruption and voucher manipulation, the privatization effort – which in every way was poorly designed – ended up with the massive theft of a substantial portion of the country's most lucrative assets. Some of these enterprises ended up in the hands of the former nomenklatura of the Soviet Union's Communist Party, including former industrial ministers, high-ranking officials, and factory directors. Their competitors in this takeover were a band of upstarts and outsiders, what in the Soviet days would have been considered traders, speculators, and black-market dealers. Prior to 1987 such activities were often treated as "economic crimes." The privatization frenzy that followed was made more intense by the fact that Russia was so rich and that there was so much to steal. Poland and China were spared similar problems on such a scale because they had fewer natural resources, and, consequently, there was less to grab.

Although some of the reformers were cognizant of these risks, they nonetheless supported instant privatization because they believed that without it, the state managers would strip their enterprises and divert assets to their own private holdings. Many reformers also believed that, by definition, private ownership would generate more effective operations than if the companies were left in state hands. It was assumed that privatization would encourage decision making based more on calculations of profit and loss than on political or personal interests. The state, however, continued to retain shares in most of the privatized companies and there was relatively little restructuring. As a result, many of these enterprises were thus often private in name only and remained inefficient while the managers, both state and private, stripped their assets. This development was very different from that in Poland, where there was relatively little asset stripping despite the fact that the privatization process there was launched only after a delay of some five years.[7]

Among the many negative factors was misguided advice from the International Monetary Fund (IMF). Based on earlier case studies, the IMF concluded that macroeconomic stabilization, especially the control of inflation, was one of the most important prerequisites for success. It reasoned that, as in other countries, once inflation in Russia was reduced to a tolerable level, economic growth could be expected to follow almost automatically. As a result, the IMF did all it could to lobby for a sharp tightening of credit and a balancing of the federal budget.

The IMF neglected to consider that the Russian economic and institutional situation was very different from that which had existed in those countries where this strategy was successful. For example, unlike

---

[7] Marshall I. Goldman, *The Piratization of Russia: Russian Reform Goes Awry* (London: Routledge, 2003), p. 195.

their counterparts in underdeveloped countries with established market economies, few Russian plant managers had much experience in borrowing from nonstate credit institutions. Previously, most of the funds for these state enterprises had come in the form of noncash clearing accounts from Gosbank. Thus, it was only natural that if they could not obtain credit from commercial banks, they would look to each other to recreate those clearing accounts. In other words, they began to rely increasingly on inter-enterprise barter and credit extensions. Often, this meant no more than that they stopped paying their bills to each other as well as their wages to the workers and their taxes to the state. Insisting on immediate payment would have meant even more widespread plant closings and unemployment. The end of the Cold War had already resulted in massive layoffs that the economy could not absorb, and more layoffs would have been politically explosive. The enterprises, therefore, played make-believe with each other.

Their unpaid bills and accounts payable and receivable reached record amounts, and their workers went without salaries for months at a time. Unable to collect taxes, the government began to borrow money in the form of ever larger quantities of GKOs (treasury bills) to pay even its minimal expenditures. First issued in moderate amounts by the Ministry of Finance on May 18, 1992, the number of GKOs rose astronomically. By the end of 1994, there were $3 billion of GKOs outstanding. One year later, there were $16.6 billion, and by May 1998, the total had reached $70 billion, or 17 percent of the country's GDP.[8] By then, all the proceeds had to be set aside to meet the interest payments on the already issued GKOs. In the West, this situation is referred to as a Ponzi game. This was clearly unsustainable.

These efforts at reform more often than not collided with Russia's cultural legacy. In an effort to speed up the process of legal transformation, the zealous reformers all too often transplanted, partially or completely, legal codes from other countries. Lacking an organic base within Russia, the transplanted laws often did not take root properly and were therefore either ignored – an old tsarist and Soviet tradition – distorted, or even perverted.

As if that were not bad enough, the inflation that soared in 1992 all but impoverished any honest civil servant who tried to rely solely on his official salary. It forced even honest officials to approve of, or even depend on, payoffs and graft. The traffic police, who openly began to extort bribes on the street, provided the most blatant example of such

---

[8] *The Moscow Times*, August 17, 1999.

behavior. In this climate, the rise of a mafia and the breakdown of law and order at all levels were inevitable.

Finally, the Russian transition was handicapped by some sociological factors that, at least in part, were unique to Russia. For example, because Russia was so richly endowed with raw materials and human talent, it was widely assumed that the Russian reforms would develop quickly and successfully. This belief led many investors, both foreign and domestic, to drop their guard and invest without the necessary due diligence. This seemed to be a get-rich-quick opportunity, and many did exactly that, at least until October 1997 (see Figure 1). Their early success attracted others, and the Russian stock market index soared 5 fold to a peak of 571 by October 1997. Investors bought Russian securities despite the 7-year drop in the Russian GDP and opaque corporate behavior. Lending by banks, private investors, and foreign governments to local and federal government bodies was similarly unrealistic.

The IMF and Wall Street investment bankers outdid each other in their eagerness to lend money to Russian provincial governments, which often had no notion about why they needed this money in the first place. Given so much natural wealth, it was assumed that the federal government was good for the loans and would stand by its provincial governors should there be temporary defaults. Furthermore, IMF lenders who normally insisted on rigid conditions, relaxed those controls because they feared that a rejection of a funding request from Russia might jeopardize Boris Yeltsin's political survival. This was of particular concern during the 1996 election campaign, when the Communist Party's return to power seemed a real possibility. Instead of exerting normal fiscal pressure, foreign investors stood by mutely while Yeltsin did as he pleased, the loans were squandered, and capital flight reached a billion dollars or more a month.

At the same time, oligarchs with political patrons in the Kremlin or regional centers gradually gained control of what had been state-owned assets. In many ways, it was a throwback to the way in which businesses had often operated during the prerevolutionary tsarist era. For that matter, this incestuous interaction between government patrons and plant managers was an important operating practice in the communist era as well. Whether under tsars or Soviets, whoever was in charge had to have a patron or friend in court – be it in St. Petersburg, Moscow, or Sverdlovsk – to protect the enterprise from government and private predators. Thus, the general secretary of the *obkom* and the enterprise manager had cooperated more or less as they pleased during the

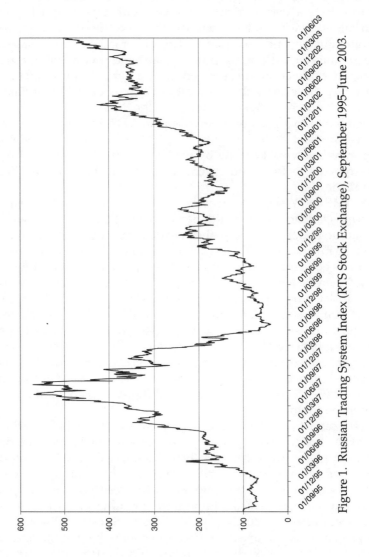

Figure 1. Russian Trading System Index (RTS Stock Exchange), September 1995–June 2003.

communist era, much as Tyumen Oil during the 1990s operated comfortably in Tyumen, where the governor also turned out to be the chairman of Tyumen Oil's board of directors.

Seen against this background, it should be clear why the entire edifice was doomed to collapse. The immediate cause was the spin-off from the financial crisis in Asia. However, given the corruption, the unrealistic prices being paid for the stock of companies that were losing money, the inability to absorb the cuts in the military-industrial complex, and the failure to pay taxes, not to mention the insistence by the IMF that Russia sustain, not devalue, the ruble – sooner or later the bubble was bound to burst. It finally did on Black Monday, August 17, 1998.

The impact was immediate. As investors and the public began the rush to convert their rubles into dollars, the government found itself without enough Western currency to redeem those rubles, and, therefore, had to abandon its support for the ruble. In a matter of days, the exchange rate fell from 6.5 rubles to the dollar to 24 rubles to the dollar. At the same time, the government defaulted on its GKOs while also declaring a moratorium on debt repayment on all foreign loans.

Of course not only the financial markets suffered. Industrial output also fell sharply. With no money available in the bank, consumers stopped buying and producers stopped producing. Table 2 shows that in September 1998, industrial output fell 15 percent immediately in the wake of the August financial collapse. In fact, industrial output had begun to decline in May 1998, in a sense anticipating the August crisis. This put an abrupt halt to the recovery that began in late 1997, the first time there had been such growth since Gorbachev's days.

Although Russia had previously survived a number of economic crises, it was hard to see how it would emerge from this one. The default on the redemption of GKOs had an enormous and unanticipated effect. Because they seemed so safe and yielded rates of return as high as 200 percent annually, investment in GKOs had seemed like a safe bet for commercial banks. Thus, with the exception of Alfa Bank and some provincial banks, most of Russia's banks, particularly the larger ones, suffered an enormous liquidity crisis. For example, the major Moscow banks had put an average of 40 percent of their assets into GKOs. With the default, these banks became insolvent and millions of depositors, both personal (including Mikhail Gorbachev himself) and organizational, lost their money. It was almost as if the Russian authorities had declared a bank holiday. Virtually overnight, many of the oligarchs discovered that their businesses inside Russia, particularly their banks, had ceased to function.

Table 2. *Changes in Russian Industrial Output*

Month	1998 as % of 1997	1999 as % of 1998	2000 as % of 1999	2001 as % of 2000
January	102.9	97.6	110.7	105.3
February	101.2	97.0	113.0	100.8
March	102.5	100.4	109.6	
April	101.1	100.6	105.5	
May	97.2	106.0	110.6	
June	97.1	109.0	109.8	
July	91.0	112.8	108.5	
August	88.4	116.0	110.2	
September	85.0	120.2	107.2	
October	88.3	110.3	110.4	
November	90.6	112.9	107.6	
December	93.3	111.1	102.5	

In a less dramatic fashion, foreign investors and businessmen also paid a heavy price. Some businesses, such as Pizza Hut, Phillips Electronics, Bankers Trust, Elf Aquitaine, Dunkin' Donuts, and ICN Pharmaceuticals simply packed up and left Russia. Others, such as Coca-Cola and Mars, found it necessary to write off hundreds of millions of dollars on their factories and inventories as the market for other than the most basic consumer goods simply dissolved. Responding to the moratorium on Russian debt, investment banks also found it necessary to write off hundreds of millions of dollars. For example, Credit Suisse First Boston alone wrote off $1 billion. All of this also almost brought down Long Term Capital Management, which lent money to many of those who had invested in Russia. For a time, Long Term Capital Management's collapse threatened the stability of the entire U.S. financial structure as well. As it was, out of fear that the collapse might not be contained, the Dow Jones index fell 20 percent.

The seriousness and depth of Russia's economic collapse made it difficult to envision a speedy recovery. There were few, if any, who predicted anything but prolonged economic agony. As Table 2 indicates, however, industrial production stabilized as early as March 1999 and began to improve steadily after that. What explains this unexpected and in many ways amazing turnaround, and why did it not occur earlier?

Surprisingly, there is general agreement about the reasons for the turnaround. One major factor was the sudden increase in the prices of raw materials, particularly oil and gas. Fortunately, in 1999, the Asian economy began to revive, and, as it did, Asian nations began to increase their demand for raw materials. This pushed up the price of oil, which rose from the 1998 level of $11 per barrel to as much as $35 a barrel in 2000. Because Russia is a major producer and exporter of petroleum and gas, this was a windfall. At the lower prices, some producers, often with support from creative accounting, complained that they could not earn a profit or pay taxes. Thus, despite being the largest supplier of gas to Europe, Gazprom reported a loss in 1998. Yet, even with the same questionable accounting procedures, once energy prices began to rise as much as they did, Russian producers could no longer complain of losses and finally began to pay some of their taxes. They also started paying their bills. Thus, the overdue debt of industrial enterprises fell from 64 percent of output in August 1998 to below 30 percent in mid-2000. Similarly, barter decreased from 52 percent to 26 percent.[9] Even the amount of wage arrears began to shrink.

An equally important factor, some say the most important for the Russian economy in the long run, was the devaluation of the ruble. The severely weakened ruble precipitated a drop in imports of almost 50 percent. Almost overnight, many Western goods disappeared from Russian shelves. This represented an enormous change because imports previously made up as much as 60 percent of Russia's retail trade. Even those Western companies that began to produce goods in Russia suffered because, for the most part, their products were intended for the top of the line, and high-priced goods were most adversely affected.

Although it was an unattractive market in all respects, the drop in imports of what were now overpriced Western brands provided Russian manufacturers with a golden opportunity because they generally produced lower-priced merchandise, even if it was also of lower quality. Because their costs in cheap rubles were so much lower than those of foreign producers, some were even able to increase their exports. Overall, export revenues increased approximately 50 percent in late 1999. The combined effect resulted in a trade surplus of almost $50 billion in 2000 and a swelling of Russian reserves from $11 billion in August 1999 to almost $60 billion in 2003. In retrospect, it would seem that the reformers inside and outside Russia (including the IMF), who had insisted on a strong ruble, balanced budgets, and restricted loans, would have done better to push for a weaker currency.

Given the apparently remarkable recovery of the Russian economy, why should there be concern for the future? Such a question stems partially from the nature of the current recovery, particularly because of

[9] Vladimir Popov, "Exchange Rate Policy after the Currency Crisis: Walking the Tightrope," in *Program on New Approaches to Russian Security: Policy Memo Series*, no. 174; *Russian Industry* (November 2000), pp. 158–9; *The Moscow Times*, December 19, 2000.

the apparent failure to deal with the legacies of the past, some of which were specified at the beginning of this chapter.

The irony of the post-1998 recovery is that the very nature of Russia's recent growth contains the seed of its future problems. For example, there is fear that oil prices will drop. As of this writing, at close to $20–25 per barrel, oil prices have already fallen far below the $35 a barrel paid in early 2000. But even at $20–25 per barrel, the revenue from oil exports has resulted in such an influx of dollars that it jeopardizes the cheap ruble. The impact of abundant oil and gas revenues is called "the Dutch disease," referring to the era when the Netherlands had the same problem. Dutch gas exports brought in large revenues to the Netherlands, which pushed up the value of the guilder. This priced Dutch manufactured goods out of export markets, thus leaving manufacturers in the Netherlands at the mercy of imports. As of this writing, the same thing is now happening to the ruble. Instead of losing value, it has actually strengthened relative to the dollar. This syndrome has also set off fears of increased inflation. There are now signs that imports are growing at an increasing rate, and while exports continue to rise, they consist primarily of raw material products, particularly petroleum and natural gas.

The more basic challenge, however, is for Russia to deal with its structural impediments. To his credit, President Vladimir Putin has pushed through legislation reducing and simplifying the tax burden and import tariffs. He has also recentralized many of the controls that Boris Yeltsin delegated to the country's approximately ninety governors. This measure will presumably reduce the extent of sheer chaos, but it has nonetheless been widely criticized. Although several of the governors have developed reputations for corruption and have taken action at the expense of the state and the country, the governors were, after all, elected. Emasculating their Council of the Federation, a constitutionally established parliamentary body, reflects negatively on the constitution and democratic procedures.

There are, however, even more serious complaints about Putin's record. He has done almost nothing to address the problem of the mafia and corruption. As the former head of the FSB (the successor to the KGB), it would have been natural and probably easy for him to crack down on any number of mafia groups. There is no doubt that he has the information as to who is doing what. Attacking the mafia, even a few selected groups, would have been a powerful symbol that he is a man with an agenda of integrity and reform. His hesitation to act may be a consequence of many factors, including that so many former KGB operatives are now working for, or are part of, the mafia. (It could be called the privatization of the KGB.) Indeed, there is good reason to believe that he has been hesitant to move against his former colleagues. In any case, the mafia, and along with it, widespread corruption, seem as ubiquitous as before.

Putin has, indeed, taken on some of the oligarchs, particularly Vladimir Gusinsky and Boris Berezovsky. Neither man would pass a Boy Scout honor code, but what most distinguished them from other oligarchs is that these two, particularly Gusinsky, ran television networks that were particularly outspoken in criticizing Putin. They were hard on his handling both of the war in Chechnya and the sinking of the submarine *Kursk*. While Putin, together with what he calls his "independent" prosecutor general, have hounded Gusinsky in Spain and Berezovsky in England, and called for Berezovsky's arrest and extradition to Moscow, he has seemingly embraced the other oligarchs, dropped legal charges against some insiders, and allowed them to create new aluminum and telecommunications empires, even though these concessions are often at the expense of already committed and operating investors.

The failure to reform corporate practices and protect minority stockholders has been a particular deterrent for foreign investors and a major reason why investment from abroad remains at such a low level. For example, foreign direct investment in 2002 was a mere \$4 billion.[10]

Foreign investors do not have to look far to find examples of shareholder abuse and corporate looting. The companies that have been charged with such practices encompass almost all of the leading businesses in Moscow. There is no doubt that the decision to invest in Russia does not come easily. For example, only a few months before it agreed to invest \$6.7 billion and join in a partnership with Tyumen Oil, BP Amoco was doing everything it could to sue Tyumen Oil. The reason was that BP Amoco had invested almost \$500 million in Sidanco, only to find that one of Sidanco's main producing subsidiaries had been seized by Tyumen Oil. In the meantime, Sidanco was restructured, further reducing the value of BP Amoco's shares. Despite efforts by Dart Industries to protect its holdings, Yukos Oil restructured in the same way. Norilsk Nickel and UES (the electric corporation) have attempted similar restructuring schemes.

In the meantime, Gazprom continues to spin or sell off some of its producing fields to Itera, a company headquartered in Jacksonville, Florida. As a result, Itera is now the main supplier of gas to Ukraine and many of the other former republics of the Soviet Union. What makes this noteworthy is that Itera is said to be owned by relatives of senior officials at

[10] *Moscow Times*, March 12, 2003.

Gazprom, which sold holdings worth hundreds of millions of dollars to Itera for about $2 million. Such abuse is not limited to traditional Soviet-era industries. Some Russian cellular telephone companies were suddenly told that their frequencies had been reassigned to other enterprises run by close friends of Putin and his new minister of communications.

Russia's corporate practices are marked by a lack of transparency, a misuse of transfer payments, tax evasion, and an abuse of the bankruptcy system to seize assets from otherwise legitimate companies. No wonder foreign investors are hesitant to invest in Russia. Those that have, including the European Bank for Reconstruction and Development, as often as not, have nothing but abuse to show for their efforts. As of 2000, of the $2.1 billion in loans the EBRD provided to Russian businesses, $500 million had been classified as nonperforming or bad debts.[11]

What most Russian businessmen disregard is that all of this is very costly, not only to the country as a whole, but to their own companies. Their short-run plunder comes at the expense of their long-term gain. As an illustration, almost everyone agrees that if foreign investors could invest freely in companies like Gazprom, and if Gazprom were operated according to Western methods and concern for investor rights, it would be worth considerably more than it is now. Few appreciate how much more, however. According to one estimate, the present capitalized value of all outstanding shares in Gazprom as of November 2000 amounted to about $4 billion.[12] However, if the oil and gas reserves that Gazprom owns were valued at the same rate as a firm with similar reserves in the West, the capitalized value of Gazprom would total about $2 trillion. This, as much as anything, is a measure of the failure to deal with Russia's legacy. By discouraging foreign investors in this way, they frighten away investment that Russia could use to ensure its basic economic resurgence.

To their credit, Vladimir Putin and his advisors have come to recognize that they have a problem. For that reason, in 2001 they began to push out some of the worst offenders among the oligarchs. While Putin's favorites have so far been allowed to remain, Rem Vyakhirev was replaced as CEO of Gazprom, and Viktor Gerashchenko was forced into early retirement from his post as chairman of the Russian Central Bank. At that time, some of the oligarchs who had thus far remained untouched, such as Mikhail Khodorkovsky of Yukos Oil, declared that they had turned

---

[11] *The Wall Street Journal*, January 13, 2000, p. A19.
[12] *The Financial Times*, November 21, 2000, p. 15.

over a new leaf and that henceforth they and their companies would be transformed into models of probity and transparency. Such declarations notwithstanding, there remains a long list of defrauded business partners, including some who have tangled with Yukos. Nonetheless, some of those burnt by earlier encounters such as BP Amoco believe this may indeed be a new day and they have returned to the market. This and higher prices for oil help explain why the RTS Index of Russian stocks hit 500 in June 2003 (see Figure 1).

There is no doubt that Russia has enormous economic potential. But whenever it looks as if the country is beginning to address its problems, something unexpected occurs. The Russians have an amazing knack for turning success into failure.

This is not to say that there are no outside influences. Just as a healthy world economy led to an increase in oil prices in 1999, so the subsequent cooling off in international growth could lead to a drop. At the same time, inflation in Russia will gradually erode the price advantage that initially came with the devaluation of the ruble. This in turn could produce a renewed decline in output, at least until Russia faces up to the structural reforms it has yet to make.

Reflecting this reluctance to make the necessary changes, the Russians tell a story about a meeting God had with President George W. Bush, Prime Minister Tony Blair, and President Vladimir Putin.

"Tell me, God," says President Bush, "Will the public ever come to believe that I really won the 2000 election?"

"Yes," God responds, "but it will take 25 years and you won't be around to see it."

Then Prime Minister Blair asks, "Will England adopt the euro and will Great Britain come to rule the waves again?"

"Yes," says God, "but it will take 50 years, and you won't be around to see it."

Finally, it's Putin's turn. "Tell me, God. Will the Russian economy ever recover and will honesty and the rule of law ever take hold in Russia?"

"Yes," answered God, "but I won't be around to see it."

Potholes on the road to a flourishing Russia: Structural problems in the second decade

THEODORE H. FRIEDGUT

To the casual visitor to Moscow's center, the claim that Russia has returned to the highroad of economic development would appear justified. The capital has returned to its finest, with new and impressive buildings, new monuments, clean and well-lighted streets – a city bustling with life. Beggars, the poor, and the homeless can still be seen, but in noticeably smaller numbers than in the nadir years of 1992 and 1993. Indeed, many of the indices of economic well-being showed improvement in 2002, and it would appear that the trauma of the August 1998 financial collapse has finally been overcome. President Putin informed his cabinet that gross domestic product (GDP) growth was 5 percent in 2001 and that the state's debt had been reduced by $10 billion without refinancing. Half a year earlier, Yegor Stroev, then speaker of the Federation Council, jubilantly announced to the St. Petersburg Economic Forum that President Putin's policies had put an end to Russia's new "Time of Troubles."[1] Yet, below the surface, the Russian polity and society face basic structural problems that put dark question marks on the country's horizon as it strives to make its second decade of independence one of growth. This chapter focuses on two of these problems, attempting to clarify the complexity of their roots and the broad ramifications of their consequences for Russia's future development.

The central problem to be considered is the demographic crisis that is facing Russia today. The complex nature of this phenomenon goes far beyond the simple decline in numbers that in 2000 reduced the population of the Russian Federation by 741,437 persons with an excess of 959,532 deaths over births mitigated by a positive migration balance of

---

[1] See Putin's statement of December 29, 2001, and the report of Stroev's speech in *Interfax*, June 13, 2001.

218,075,[2] mainly Russians from the neighboring republics of the former Soviet Union. Russia's demographic problems, it will be argued, are not simply a population cycle that may eventually stabilize and diminish in intensity. Rather, they are closely connected to problems of the economy, to politics, and to social ills – factors that intensify the chronic demographic imbalance that has existed over the past two generations and threaten to block the future growth of a healthy economy and society.

The second phenomenon discussed is widely referred to in the Russian press and social literature as "the infrastructure crisis." This chapter examines the physical, economic, and social facets of this question and the circumstances that have produced it. The connection between this crisis and the demographic one, as well as the reasons for and consequences of infrastructure neglect, are also examined.

Because many of the other chapters in this volume illuminate both the structural and procedural aspects of Russia's political system, this inquiry is limited to pointing out the connections between ineffective central government and the failure to solve the social and economic problems that threaten Russia's continuing recovery. By neither providing adequate resource allocations nor finding ways to ensure the proper use of those resources that are allotted for the social needs and infrastructure of the country, the government of Russia is undermining its own declared goals of economic and social development.[3]

THE DEMOGRAPHIC CRISIS

On January 1, 1991, the population of the Russian Soviet Federated Socialist Republic (RSFSR) stood at 148,543,000. Throughout the postwar period and until the dismantling of the USSR at the end of 1991, the population of the Russian Federation was increasing by 500,000–600,000 people annually. Nevertheless, the first signs of demographic problems had already appeared. During the 1980s, the rate of natural increase declined from 4.9 per thousand, to 2.2.[4] In addition, and perhaps even more important in terms of this discussion, adult mortality in almost every age group from 18 years up had been increasing from the late 1960s; at the same time, there had been a sharp upturn in infant

---

[2] *Demograficheskii ezhegodnik Rossii, 2001,* Moscow: Goskomstat R. F., p. 55, Table 2.1 for births and deaths shows a surplus of deaths over births since 1992, growing from 219,797 in that year to the figure cited above. Ibid., p. 314, Table 7.1 shows the net migration balance shrinking from 345,838 in 1993 to 218,075 in the year 2000.

[3] For a succinct exposition of the Putin regime's policy priorities, see his State of the Union address to the Federal Duma, reported May 20, 2003, at http://www.rambler.ru/db/news/msg.html.

[4] *Narodnoe khoziaistvo SSSR v 1990g.* (Moscow: Finansy i statistika, 1991), pp. 68–89.

mortality, which, although it was later reversed, wiped out twenty years of progress in that area, leaving the RSFSR well behind the standards of developed European countries. An additional warning statistic was the steady rise in suicide rates in Russia through the 1970s and into the 1980s. With the onset of perestroika, these dropped, only to rise again as the hopes and enthusiasm that Gorbachev had kindled faded away.[5] These worrisome statistics were in large measure the product of policy failures: economic stagnation, pollution, underinvestment in health and social facilities, and overall social malaise.[6]

The importance of this point is that a strong, perceptive government could reverse, or at least mitigate, the most pernicious effects of the demographic crisis through effective mobilization and distribution of resources. The governments of the Russian Federation through the first decade of independence did little or nothing in this sphere, and the current Putin regime is as yet far from proving itself greatly different in the collection of taxes, in stemming the outflow of capital – currently estimated at some $20 billion annually – and in everything connected to seeing that allotments for health, education, and social welfare actually reach the clientele for whom they are intended.[7]

Thus, as Russia goes into its second decade of independence, there is little or no sign that the worrisome symptoms of an ailing society have been diagnosed and dealt with. Indeed, the demographic crisis today is more glaring and urgent than it was a decade ago. According to the first results of the October 2002 Russian Federation census, the population stood at 145,287,400, a decline of more than 3 million in a decade.[8] In the 13 years between the last two censuses, the population decline has averaged 141,500 annually.[9] As we have already shown, the current annual decline is more than five times as great. Infant mortality,

---

[5] Ibid., p. 93. The low point in infant mortality in the Soviet period was reached in 1971, when it was 22.9 per 100,000. See Christopher Davis and Murray Feshbach, in *Rising Infant Mortality in the USSR in the 1970s* (Washington, D.C.: U.S. Department of Commerce, Bureau of the Census, 1980), p. 1.

[6] For a thorough discussion of the complex interface between social policies, economics and the upturn in infant mortality in the 1960s and 1970s, see Davis and Feshbach, *Rising Infant Mortality*.

[7] See the statement of Viktor Vasil'ev, director of the Moscow Office of the Federal Tax Police Service, who claimed that 60–80 percent of Russia's companies, enterprises, and institutions pay no taxes, with energy companies and financial institutions prominent among those he named. *RosBalt News Service*, January 8, 2002. See also President Putin's complaint to the cabinet that, despite declarations and decrees, no effective measures exist for the support and shelter of Russia's multitude of homeless children. *Izvestiia*, January 16, 2002.

[8] Available: http://www.gks.ru/PEREPIS/predv.htm (henceforth, gks.ru/PEREPIS).

[9] For the first October 2002 census results and the comparison to the January 1989 census, see gks.ru/PEREPIS.

always a good indicator of the effectiveness of medical services in a population, stands at 20.05 per thousand live births, very much the same level as in 1985, or indeed, in the early 1970s, although this index rose alarmingly in the 1970s and fell below its current level during the years of perestroika.[10] According to testimony by Health Minister Yurii Shevchenko, the figure for 2001 represents a rising trend over 1999 and 2000, when the index was 15.1 and 18.1, respectively.[11] As is the case in many countries, the uneven availability of good medical services leads to a geographic differential in infant mortality indices. In the case of the Russian Federation, this differential is extremely large, with the highest mortality rate (34.7 per 1,000) found in the Republic of Ingushetia and the lowest (10.1 per 1,000) in Samara oblast.[12]

Whereas in the early to mid-1990s the deficit in natural increase was partially covered by immigration from the neighboring republics of the former Soviet Union, these sources have now largely dried up, and today immigration compensates for less than one-quarter of the population loss. The 25-million-strong Russian diaspora in the neighboring republics has dwindled to less than 19 million, and less than one-half of those leaving have repatriated to Russia. According to the census of 2002, in the period between the last two censuses, 1989–2002, there was a total of 10,975,500 immigrants to Russia and 5,559,800 emigrants, a positive balance of more than 5.5 million. Today the propensity to leave the neighboring republics has diminished.[13] The largest concentrations of diaspora Russians, in the Baltics and in the Ukraine, have found a modus vivendi within the new societies forming there and, barring major upheavals, do not represent a reservoir of immigrants to Russia. Perhaps Kazakhstan, where a large number of Russians still live, can serve as such a reserve, but in recent years the repatriation from there to Russia has been small, and the great majority of Russians in that republic now live in a rather compact block in the northern provinces, where they are less affected by the Kazakh nationalism that drove half a million of their compatriots to leave the southern cities of the republic.

---

[10] Infant mortality is determined as the number of deaths during the first year of life per 1,000 live births, a live birth being defined as an infant surviving its first 24 hours. For an enlightening discussion of the complexities involved in the changes of this index, see Davis and Feshbach, *Rising Infant Mortality.*

[11] See Ministry of Health, Interfax press release of June 21, 2001.

[12] Ibid., January 6, 2001.

[13] For an analysis of the immigration balance from 1959 to 1998 and its effect on the size of Russia's population, see Julie DaVanzo and Clifford Grammich, *Dire Demographics: Population Trends in the Russian Federation* (Santa Monica, Calif.: Rand Corporation, 2001), pp. 13–14, particularly Fig. 2.5. Census data is from gsk.ru/PEREPIS.

The numerical decline itself has serious consequences for Russia. Even in the last years of the Soviet regime, the labor force in European Russia was diminishing absolutely. Today, the imbalance of population has serious consequences in many spheres. In 1998, the number of children and teenagers for the first time dropped below the number of pensioners. By January 1, 2000, the gap between these two groups passed the 1 million mark.[14] By the year 2015, the ratio of working to nonworking population may be four workers for every three nonworkers, with the nonworkers tending to be extremely aged.[15] The significance of this gap extends to several sectors. The scarcity of labor in the economy suggests the need for heavier capitalization of production, while the dwindling number of young males aggravates the shortage of manpower for defense requirements. The low ratio of workers to nonworkers also renders it difficult to provide the social infrastructure to support the large nonworking segment of the population. The demographic crisis of declining numbers is thus directly connected to the economy, to the level of industrial investment and to the lack of effective government.

The projections regarding the decline of Russia's population go well beyond the end of the current decade. The State Statistics Committee recently published a projection for the year 2015. Because all those who will be of childbearing age at that time are already in existence and caught up in current social and physical trends, this projection may be taken as highly accurate. Nevertheless, the committee cautiously gives three variants, the highest 138 million, and the lowest 128 million.[16] The projected loss of population for Russia in a single generation is thus between 10–20 million persons, a demographic shock reminiscent of the catastrophe of World War II, from which Russia has never fully recovered, even after two generations. A more recent projection depicts the decline as continuing to the middle of the twenty-first century, when Russia's population is expected to drop as low as 101.9 million people.[17]

There are two factors that are, perhaps, of even greater importance than the absolute decline in numbers. The first concerns those segments

---

[14] "Demographic Policy to 2015," *Rossiiskaia gazeta*, August 4, 2001.

[15] Murray Feshbach, "Demographic Trends," in National Intelligence Council (hereafter NIC) Seminar, *Russia's Physical and Social Infrastructure: Implications for Future Development* (Washington, D.C., December 2000, Internet edition http://www.fas.org/irp/nic/russia.html).

[16] See the announcement in Rossiiskoe Informatsionnoe Agentsro (*RIA*)-*Novosti*, February 28, 2002. An earlier projection made public by Labor Minister Aleksandr Pochinik on November 17, 2000, in a statement to the State Duma set the projection for 2015 at 138.4 million.

[17] Associated Press reporting a statement of Russia's State Statistical Committee, March 28, 2002. The projection gives a worst-case population of 77.2 million and a best-case number of 122.6 million.

of the population that are dying disproportionately, and the second, concerns the declining of quality of the population as a result of the social and demographic processes. The number of deaths of young women aged 15–19 increased from 2,236 in 1986 to 4,460 in 1998.[18] Increasing drug use, prostitution, and the spread of disease, particularly sexually transmitted diseases, were all named as contributing factors.[19] The rate of syphilis among girls aged 10–14 has grown by forty times, and as a result of such illnesses and poor medical care during abortions, as many as one-quarter of all women are sterile.[20] Undoubtedly, the 1 to 2 million homeless children wandering Russia today contribute substantially to this category.[21] A conference convened in Moscow by the Red Cross was told that one-third of the neglected children in Russia are alcoholics.[22] These statistics have great significance regarding the continuation, for at least another generation, of the extremely low fertility rate that is one of the cornerstones of Russia's population decline.

Among working-age men, a rise in mortality rates was first noted in the mid-1960s and has continued to this day. Alcohol, social stress, and crime have all contributed to the drop in male life expectancy, and although it has recovered slightly from its low of 57 years in 1994, it still stood at only 58.6 in 2001.[23] Most pertinent to this discussion is the tragic fact that a 20-year-old in Russia stands only a 50-percent chance of reaching age 60, compared with a 90-percent chance for his peers in

---

[18] For the 1986 figure, see *Naselenie SSSR*, 1987 (Moscow: Statistika, 1987). For the 1998 and 2000 figures, see *The Demographic Yearbook of Russia* (Moscow: Goskomstat, 2001), Table 5.1, p. 162. While the tenfold leap between 1995 and 1999 may well evoke some questions, it would appear to have been sufficiently well based for the Academy of Sciences of the Russian Federation to point to its existence. It is certainly consistent with the explosive growth of sexually transmitted diseases during the past decade.

[19] *Kommersant Daily*, June 20, 2001, writes that syphilis cases in Russia have increased by a factor of five in recent years and that there are now 1 million Russians with venereal diseases. In some regions, the incidence of syphilis is 1 per 500 population. Drug-resistant TB and HIV-AIDS are two additional diseases spreading rapidly through the 15- to 40-year age group. The rising incidence of both these diseases can be directly linked to economic and social breakdowns of Russia's society.

[20] Feshbach, "Demographic Trends."

[21] Not only has the government no effective plan for supporting or sheltering these children, but there is no agreement as to the dimensions of the problem. Although the official government estimate is of 1 million homeless children, the Prosecutor-General's Office puts the number at 2 million. See *Izvestiia*, January 16, 2002.

[22] Reported in RFE/RL Newsline, November 17, 2000.

[23] *Rossiia v tsifrakh, 2002*, Moscow: Goskomstat, 2002, Table 5.8, p. 73. Women's life expectancy at birth was 72.1 years. The huge gap between the life expectancies of men and women tends to perpetuate the social problem of an excess of women in the adult population that had its roots in the earliest years of twentieth-century Russian history. The census of October 2002 showed an excess of 10,157,400 women, increasing each year since 1999, and up more than a million over the previous year.

Great Britain or the United States.[24] Russia leads the world in the rates of accidents, homicides, and suicides, which cut deeply into this age cohort.[25] Among women, domestic violence has emerged as a major factor in premature deaths. Natalia Rimashevskaia, a sociologist, reported to a conference of officials and social workers in Moscow, that one in five Russian women suffers violence at the hands of her partner and that 14,000 women are murdered each year as a result of domestic violence.[26] In the first five months of 2001, there were 16,583 deaths from alcohol poisoning, most of which occurred in the male working-age group. For the first four months of 2003, an increase of 5.5 percent over the previous year was reported.[27] The annual number of alcohol poisonings is thus rather more than the number of deaths sustained by Soviet troops in Afghanistan during the ten years of war there. This reflects the increase in illegally produced alcohol that undergoes no inspection or quality controls.[28] The incidence of alcohol poisoning changes markedly from year to year, rising from 18 per 100,000 population in 1992 to 32 per 100,000 in 1995, and dropping back to 24 per 100,000 in 1998. This would appear to reflect erratic prices and even more erratic government inspection of alcohol, again an indication of ineffective government.

It is one of the peculiarities of Russia's socioeconomic situation that the adult population suffers not only from an increase in infectious and parasitic diseases typical of the Third World, such as malaria, hepatitis, and gastrointestinal diseases due to impure drinking water, but also from diseases typical of modern industrial society, such as cancer and stress-related cardiovascular ailments, at rates two and three times higher than in the United States.[29] In addition to HIV/AIDS, a disease that is spreading rapidly in Russia today, the problem of tuberculosis (TB)

[24] DaVanzo and Grammich, *Dire Demographics*, p. 41. To help the reader grasp the dynamics of the demographic crisis, we may note that ten years ago, the chances of a 16-year-old surviving to 60 were estimated at two to one in favor. See *Izvestiia*, March 3, 1993.

[25] According to Labor Minister Aleksandr Pochinik in an address to the Duma, the probability of accidental death in Russia is 4.5 times higher than in Europe as a whole; *RFE/RL Newsline*, November 20, 2000. General Vladimir Gordienko, commander of the Main Criminal Investigation Administration, noted that in 2001, the number of murders in Russia grew by 10 percent, putting Russia second only to South Africa in its per capita incidence of homicides.

[26] ITAR-TASS, May 13, 2003.

[27] For statistics of alcohol poisonings since 1992, see *Rossiia v tsifrakh, 2002,* Moscow: Goskomstat, 2002, Table 5.7, p. 173. For the 2003 figures, see the Goskomstat announcement at newsru.com, May 7, 2003.

[28] *Interfax*, June 9, 2001, citing the State Statistical Commission.

[29] For a full discussion of the extent and characteristics of this phenomenon, see Feshbach, "Demographic Trends." Also Julie DaVanzo and David Adamson, *Russia's Demographic Crisis, How Real Is It?"* (Santa Monica, Calif.: Rand, 1999). *Izvestiia,* July 17, 2001, reported a resurgence of malaria in parts of Russia due to the curtailing of antimosquito measures

looms large. Whereas there were 22,000 TB deaths in 1997, the annual rate reached 30,000 in 2001. The incidence of the disease, which appears today mainly in its virulent, multi-drug-resistant form, has jumped from 24 per 100,000 in 1990 to 83 per 100,000 in 1998. The incidence in Russia's prisons, where 980,000 persons are currently held (one of the world's largest per capita prison populations), is 20 percent. An estimated 2.2 million Russians are already infected with TB.[30]

Together with economic hardships and a widespread disintegration of society marked by a nearly 20 percent rise in divorce in 2000 compared to the previous year, all of these factors contributed to lowering the birth rate to an average of 1.3 children per woman of childbearing age in 1999 and 1.27 in 2001, a decline of more than 45 percent since 1992 and far below the 2.35 live births per woman needed to maintain the level of the population.[31] Abortion, long the bane of women's reproductive health in Russia, continues at a rate fifteen times higher than that of Western Europe. There are 192 abortions per 100 live births, 178 abortions for every 100 women between 15 and 44 years of age.[32]

Not only has the number of births declined sharply since 1991 but also only 20 percent of the children born are healthy. Chronic diseases have risen sharply, and mental illness has tripled in a decade, now affecting 4.5 percent of all children in Russia.[33] The health of children does not improve as they grow up, and the deputy minister of health noted that only 10 percent of Russia's children are healthy upon leaving school. They are underfed and overworked largely because the regional authorities fail to provide the food and funds needed by the schools to maintain their pupils' well-being.[34]

In the Kuzbass, almost 40 percent of the recruits called up in 2001 were found unfit for military service because of bad health. Because other parts of Russia are undergoing the same difficulties, it is not surprising that the Russian armed forces expect that by the middle of the current

---

that had been standard for many years. Other sources point to resurgences of diphtheria, botulism, and typhus.

[30] See *Rossiiskaia gazeta*, February 13, 1998, for an International Red Cross report cited in *RFE/RL Newsline*, November 27, 2001; Feshbach, "Demographic Trends." The incidence of TB in the United States in 1998 was 6.8 per 100,000. For the size and composition of Russia's prison population, see the *Press Conference of Russia's Minister of Justice*, January 8, 2002.

[31] See *Interfax*, September 2, 1999. For the 2001 figures, see "Russia: People," *World Factbook, 2001*, Internet edition http://www.outfo.org/almanac/world_factbook_01/geos/rs.html#People. In his 2003 'State of the Union' address, President Putin claimed that over the past three years, the birth rate has increased by 18 percent. At the date of this writing, census figures in this category had not yet been released.

[32] DaVanzo and Grammich, *Dire Demographics*, p. 31, Fig. 3.5.

[33] *Interfax*, August 2, 1999.

[34] Deputy Health Minister Gennadii Onishchenko, *Rossiiskaia gazeta*, August 24, 2001.

decade, the number of suitable recruits will decline to less than half of what the military considers necessary. In addition, the Russian military is faced with a problem of the mental state of its recruits. In recent years, fully 20 percent of deaths in the military have been suicides.[35] The army's solution to this problem is to suggest the cancellation of student deferments in order to fill the ranks.[36] This proposal, however, clashes with another social need made urgent by the demographic processes affecting Russia.

At present, the average age of a senior scientist in Russia (*Doktor nauk*) is 61 years. Fully one-half are already over pension age. The average age of working scientists with a Ph.D. (*Kandidat nauk*) is 52. By the year 2016, the average age of all scientists is expected to reach 59 – equaling life expectancy – and "science will disappear."[37] Not only is the median age of scientists and educators rising rapidly, but their work is negatively affected by exhaustion brought on by the need to hold down multiple jobs to make a decent living.[38] This situation is aggravated by the emigration of large numbers of specialists who are attracted by the good salaries offered in foreign countries and repelled by the rundown state of the laboratories and scientific facilities in Russia.[39] In 1992, there were 900,000 researchers in Russia. At present, there are formally 450,000, but only 100,000 actually conduct research. The remainder no longer have the funds and facilities for scientific work.[40]

In addition, there has been a massive "internal brain drain" that affects both science and education. Young teachers, particularly those with computer skills and knowledge of foreign languages, leave the universities and institutes for careers in private business.[41] These are, naturally, the younger and more talented of the skilled workers and scientific corps in Russia. In a recent discussion about the sorry state of Russia's scientific institutes, Vladislav Sherstiuk, first deputy secretary of the Russian government's Security Council, outlined a plan to reduce the number

---

[35] *Nezavisimaia gazeta, voennoe obozrenie,* April 24, 1998.

[36] See the discussion in *RIA-Novosti,* January 16, 2002.

[37] Deputy Minister of Education Boris Vinogradov in testimony before a Duma committee, reported in *RFE/RL Newsline,* August 2, 2001.

[38] Mark S. Johnson, "Russian Education and Politics," *NIC Seminar,* 2000. An acquaintance in Moscow, a senior academic figure in a prestigious institute, recently confided to the author that he lived well only because he could hold down three jobs, but having passed the age of 60, he felt his strength waning and wondered how his family would live should he become ill and have to limit his activity to his institute research and salary.

[39] *Vesti,* no. 108, cited in *RFE/RL Newsline,* September 26, 2001.

[40] Glenn Schweitzer, "The Impact of the Brain Drain," *NIC Seminar,* 2000. Schweitzer puts emigration at 1,000–2,000 scientists and engineers annually throughout the 1990s. This would appear to be an understatement, given the numbers that have come to Israel alone in the last decade.

[41] Mark S. Johnson, "Russian Education and Politics."

of institutes receiving government funding but to increase fivefold the funds available to science by the end of the coming decade. He named nine high-priority areas of research that would be funded, all of them security and technology oriented, none dealing with health, medicine, agriculture, or social welfare.[42]

Cannot the ranks of the scientists be filled from among Russia's youth? We have already seen the effects of the demographic crisis in diminishing both the numbers and the quality of the children growing up in Russia today. By the end of the current decade, the number of students in secondary schools in Russia is expected to decline from 20 million to 13 million. As for physical and mental quality, the Ministry of Education estimates that 40 percent of these students will need some form of therapy. By the middle of the decade, the number of annual graduates is expected to be only 1.3 million. At the same time, the institutions of higher education are planning on an enrollment of 1.7 million annually. Thus, even if every secondary school graduate were to pursue higher education, there would still be a need to recruit an additional 400,000 students annually.[43]

It has also been argued that without fundamental change, the Russian primary and secondary school system, structured in the 1930s, will not meet the country's needs for the new century. Only the top 20 percent, sent by affluent parents to new private schools, will receive an education appropriate to a modern technological power. Sixty percent will receive what is termed "an inadequate education," and the bottom fifth will be functional illiterates. Harley Balzer points out the strong link between economic and governmental reform and the possibility of modernizing the plant and curriculum of the schools.[44] In its current rundown and underfunded condition, Russia's school system cannot hope to meet the technological and educational challenges required to produce citizens who can compete among the leading nations of the world.[45] It would appear that a basic reorientation of policies and goals will be needed

---

[42] See the report in ITAR-TASS, March 20, 2002. Sherstiuk confirms a 50-percent drop in numbers of researchers and states that 200,000 scientists have emigrated.

[43] Education Minister Vladimir Fillipov in a statement on February 24, 2001.

[44] Harley Balzer, "Education Patterns in Today's Russia," *NIC Seminar*, 2000.

[45] Irina Khakamada, interviewed in *Nezavisimaia gazeta*, July 17, 2001, stated that the number of computers in Russia's schools is declining rather than increasing, that there is only one school computer for every 500 pupils, and that only 1.5 percent of the schools are linked to the Internet. Economics Minister German Gref was cited by ITAR-TASS, November 14, 2001 to the effect that there are only 1.5–2 Internet users per 100 population in Russia compared with 12 in Japan and 40–45 in the United States. Although Russia's lag in technology is nothing new historically, one remembers the days not so long ago when Gorbachev chaired a commission to place computers in every school in Russia.

if Russia is to improve or even maintain its place among the developed nations. Was it this situation that brought a Moscow newspaper to comment that in the coming generation Russia will rank with such states as Mexico and Brazil – but with a slightly lower infant mortality and a higher death rate in the working-age population?[46] Male life expectancy in Russia is already below that of Mexico, Iraq, Indonesia, and other less-developed countries.[47]

Russia as a whole suffers from these problems but, as already noted, they are particularly acute in some localities. In Perm, one of Russia's most polluted cities, the average male life expectancy in 2000 was 57.7 years, lower than the national average. In parts of the North, where the life expectancy is only 45 years and the unemployment rate is 60 percent, up to 40 percent of young people suffer from TB, over half have some sort of lung disorder, 96 percent suffer from infectious diseases, and 92 percent have dental problems. Evidently, health care is almost totally lacking for these peoples of the North, who make up 9 percent of Russia's total population and whose territory, rich in oil and gas, diamonds and gold, produces 20 percent of the federation's national income and generates more than half its foreign currency.[48]

The failure of the authorities to provide fuel, heat and a steady electrical supply to the eastern maritime regions has become a national scandal in the last two years. Given this region's climatic conditions, an interruption of heating means burst pipes, damage to homes and offices, suffering, illness, and even death to the residents. Worst of all is the fact that the entire crisis results from political infighting and governmental incompetence, with a substantial admixture of criminal activity that unashamedly diverts resources away from the designated beneficiaries.

The result in both the North and the Far East is a steadily growing stream of emigration. The North has lost 10 percent of its population, and the Magadan and Chukotka regions in the Far East have lost 50 percent. The majority of those leaving are young, male, skilled industrial workers.[49] This raises geopolitical anxieties among Moscow observers. Since the eighteenth century, Russia has been driving eastward. Throughout the Soviet period, increasing the population of the North and Far East and basing the exploitation of Siberian resources on such development

[46] *Vremya MN*, June 8, 2001.
[47] DaVanzo and Grammich, *Dire Demographics*, p. 38.
[48] For the Kuzbass recruits see *Interfax Eurasia*, October 17, 2001. For general health conditions in the Kuzbass at the end of the 1980s, see Theodore H. Friedgut, "Ecological Factors in the July 1989 Mine Strike," *Environmental Policy Review*, no. 1 (January 1990), p. 56. For the state of the northern peoples, see the declaration of the deputy minister for federation and nationality affairs, November 28, 2000, and *Nezavisimaia gazeta*, June 8, 2001.
[49] Timothy Heleniak, "Migration Trends in Russia During the 1990s," *NIC Seminar*, 2000.

projects as the Baikal-Amur Mainline Railway and the far northern city of Norilsk had been basic policy. Now that approach appears to be crumbling, and alarms are being raised regarding the number of Chinese coming into the Maritime Region, first as casual laborers, but later as settlers. In view of Russia's growing shortage of labor (even with the high unemployment rate), there have been those who have suggested relying on imported labor, including Chinese. Historically, Russia has been a country of emigration rather than immigration, and in the present state of society, with nationalist and xenophobic feelings running high, the introduction of any number of foreigners – particularly of "visible minorities" – would exacerbate already existing social tensions.

Writing in *The Russia Journal*, Andrei Piontkovskii pointed to demographic decline as the root cause of a process that could lead to Russia's leaving the Far East, and even Siberia, first de facto, and later de jure.[50] Another observer put the problem in broader and blunter historical terms. "Historically, societies that sustained population growth have conquered or otherwise absorbed their less-populous neighbors. East Siberia and the Far East have only two things between them and absorption by China: the Russian nuclear deterrent and their bad climate."[51] However far-fetched this may seem, the problem of the depopulation of these areas is real, as is the inability thus far of the Russian government, whether central or regional, to provide reasonable living conditions, including both an economic and social infrastructure for the citizens of these regions.[52] Lacking such policies, the danger of the "implosion of Russia," involving the potential loss of valuable resources and large territories, particularly under the pressure of Chinese immigration in the Far East, must become a very palpable anxiety for Russia's leaders. On this subject, the 2002 census figures are hardly comforting. Of the seven federal districts into which Russia is divided, only the central (11.6%) and the southern (0.2%) districts increased their populations in the years 1989–2002. All the rest suffered a shrinkage of population ranging as high as 15.9 percent.[53]

THE INFRASTRUCTURE CRISIS

As has been pointed out repeatedly in this discussion, the demographic crisis that has resulted from the havoc in Russian society today was

---

[50] *The Russian Journal*, August 24–30, 2001, cited in *RFE/RL*, August 27, 2001.
[51] Vladimir Kontorovich, "A Case Study: The Far East," *NIC Seminar*, 2000.
[52] For an additional discussion pointing to the Putin administration's lack of any coherent program in this respect see Otto Latsis, "Strategy and Demography," *The Russian Journal*, no. 46 (89) (November 2000).
[53] See Gks.ru/PEREPIS.

not inevitable, nor was it entirely part of a natural cycle of population change. Phenomena such as the increased mortality of women in the childbearing age group and of working-age men could be eliminated or greatly attenuated were the government to invest the resources, energy, and attention needed to fight their causes. Campaigns against the use of narcotics and alcohol as well as to fight the spread of TB and AIDS; a reduction of environmental pollution; a concerted effort to shelter, support, and educate Russia's homeless children – there are a dozen points at which population problems could be attacked and mortality and morbidity considerably reduced. There is no lack of groups advising the government about these needs, nor is it malevolent stupidity that prevents the launching of such programs, although a strong case may be made that venality is a prominent factor in obstructing structural reforms.

The central problem preventing the government from mounting a long-term multifaceted program to improve the demographics of Russia is the paucity of resources available when compared to the multitude and magnitude of demands on these resources. The point of departure for any such discussion has to be the government's failure both to curb capital flight and to collect from businesses the taxes due by law. Alexander Babichev, deputy head of Russia's Interagency Anti-Money Laundering Center, claims that the total of illegally exported capital held by Russians abroad is $250 billion, more than Russia's entire foreign and domestic debt, and several times greater than the annual state budget.[54] At the same time, investment in social and economic infrastructure has been put off and funds diverted to current consumption or private gain. But this process can continue for only so long before total collapse sets in.

In the first years of the twenty-first century, the phrase "the 2003 problem" (more cautious sources set the crisis date at 2005) came into common use in Russia's press.[55] This phrase refers to a complex set of circumstances: the falling due of large sums of foreign debt repayment ($17–18 billion annually) when Russia is already having trouble meeting debt repayments of $13–14 billion; the continued deterioration of the economic infrastructure carrying it below the minimal level needed for functioning; and the implosion of the social infrastructure. The payment due on Russia's foreign debt will be $14.9 billion in 2004 and $17.4 billion in 2005. Of the two-year total, $14.3 billion, 45 percent of the

---

[54] *RFE/RL Newsline,* March 29, 2001.
[55] See, for example *Vedomosti,* June 9, 2001. Also Fred Weir, "Alarms over Crumbling Infrastructure," *Christian Science Monitor,* February 15, 2001, citing Yurii Vorobev, Deputy Minister for Emergency Situations.

whole, is for interest and servicing.[56] This crisis has thus far been deferred by the high tide of oil and gas revenues that have been a windfall to the Russian government in recent years. As much as a billion dollars a month came into the treasury during the last two years, from 1999–2001 turning the budget deficit into a surplus that in 2001 amounted to $6.4 billion.[57] Nevertheless, it bears repeating that investment in the neglected structures of Russia's infrastructure must be based on a long-term policy decision, not on short-term windfalls. Up to this time, the Putin government has not yet come up with any such basic restructuring of priorities, although in his 2003 State of the Union address to the Federal Duma, Putin warned that too much of the improvement in the Russian economy was due to "fortuitous conjunctures" in the international economy and that Russia's economy was still essentially weak and unstable.

Let us consider the social infrastructure problem first: health, education, housing, and municipal services. A portion of the problem with these services is the great increase in the urban population from the start of the 1950s to the collapse of the Soviet Union. In 1960, the urban population of Russia numbered just under 64 million. By the start of 1991, it had peaked at nearly 110 million but has since declined throughout the post-Soviet period to 106.5 million at the beginning of 2000.[58] Thus, although the Yeltsin and Putin regimes inherited an overburdened system, the pressure of population on urban infrastructures has lessened slightly over the past decade. Investment in the health sector began to decline in the mid-1960s because of a stagnating economy and a growing defense burden. One of the weaknesses of Russia's health services is that this sector has, for budgeting purposes, always been regarded as residual, receiving its part of the budget only after all the high-priority sectors were funded. By the end of 1991, investment in the health sector had declined from about 6 percent of GDP to 2 percent.[59] Little was being done in terms of public health education or preventive medicine. It is no coincidence that at the same time, infant and male adult mortality rose. A decade later, there were severe shortages of even the most basic medicines, due in part to a lack of funds in hospitals and clinics, and in part to the undercapitalization of the pharmaceuticals industry. Moreover, hospitals and clinics were decaying. One in five hospitals had no running water, and 40 percent had no hot water.[60]

[56] RIA Novosti, April 29, 2003.
[57] *Rossiia v tsifrakh*, Moscow: Goskomstat, 2002, p. 292.
[58] *Demograficheskii ezhegodnik Rossii*, Moscow: Goskomstat, 2001, p. 20.
[59] Mark G. Field, "Trends in Russia's Health Situation and Establishment," *NIC Seminar*, 2000.
[60] *Delovye liudy*, no. 116 (2000).

In the post-Soviet period, Russia has changed from the provision of free medical services of the Soviet period to a contributory medical insurance scheme administered by regional and local governments, with deductions at source by the employers. Unfortunately, this level of government is the least reliable, both in terms of fulfilling its obligations and in terms of commanding the necessary resources. Monies collected for the health plan frequently end up elsewhere, and local government, responsible for paying the insurance fees of nonworking citizens, "routinely avoids doing so."[61] The result is that health workers, historically a low-paid sector, receive their pay late, if at all, and as a matter of survival demand direct payment from their patients. In the first quarter of 2002, 41 of 89 Russian Federation regions were in arrears in paying their health workers. The delays ranged from a few days to more than three months. After a long period in which the central authorities made the reduction of wage arrears to doctors and nurses (as well as to educational workers) a high priority, indebtedness is increasing again in seven regions.[62]

Housing, deeply subsidized throughout the Soviet period but poorly constructed and badly maintained, remains a large-scale problem for the Russian state today. Recent legislation provides for the transfer of the entire cost of purchasing and maintaining housing to the consumers by 2003. On May 8, 2003, President Putin indeed signed the housing reform bill.[63] However, it is estimated that 60 percent of the citizens do not have the means to pay for the homes or for their maintenance. One-third of all water pipes and one-sixth of all the sewage pipes serving residential housing in urban Russia are said to be in urgent need of replacement. According to this source, the leaks in the central heating systems are wasting no less than 80 million tons of fuel oil annually. The sum needed for immediate repairs to keep this housing habitable and serviced is $20 billion.[64] The cost of preventing breakdowns in winter heating due to overaged, leaking central heating steam and hot water pipes is by itself estimated at $500 million.[65] Moreover, this vast maintenance undertaking is the task of the regional and local governments, whose responsibility it is to administer this law. It remains to be seen whether and how such a law will come into force.

[61] Judith I. Twigg, "Challenges for Russia's Social Insurance," NIC Seminar, 2000.
[62] Cited in *RFE/RL Newsline*, March 11, 2002. Aleksandr Nemets and Thomas Torda, "Russia Suffers while Arming China," *Newsmax.com*, January 24, 2002 (Internet edition www.newsmax.com), note that arrears of industrial wages also increased by 10 percent in the last quarter of 2001.
[63] *Interfax*, May 8, 2003.
[64] Fred Weir, "Capitalism Hits Home in Russia," *Christian Science Monitor*, June 20, 2001.
[65] *Vremia novosti*, January 9, 2003.

Drinking water and wastewater are two interrelated problems that also require immediate, large-scale attention to prevent new ecological disasters from developing. Two-thirds of Russia's municipal drinking water comes from surface sources that are becoming more and more polluted by the discharge of untreated sewage and industrial waste. In 1997, only about 10 percent of wastewater was being treated by municipal authorities or industrial enterprises. The result is that substandard drinking water contributes 10 percent to gastrointestinal illness – hepatitis A and dysentery – costing the economy $13 billion annually. The cost of bringing Russia's drinking water up to European Union standards is estimated to be hundreds of billions of dollars.[66] Quite clearly this would have to be a long-term program, starting in metropolitan areas and gradually working out to the periphery. Reducing the incidence of illness could generate resources to pay a portion of the cost of upgrading. This is not the only economy that an effective government could introduce. Wastage of drinking water amounts to 50 percent of total usage through leaking pipes and faucets. Higher water tariffs could cut demand by 20–30 percent, reducing the excessive loads on treatment facilities and pipe networks. Combined with a nationwide educational program, it could help bring about substantial savings for both the public and the authorities.

However, the opposition to any such steps is widespread because subsidization of both housing and utilities, a holdover from the Soviet period, is popularly regarded as an entitlement that should not be eliminated. Moscow's residents pay 17 percent of the cost of housing and municipal services, half the percentage paid by Russians as a whole. As a result, 43 percent of the Moscow municipal budget is spent on subsidizing these services.[67] A first step toward reforming this situation has been announced by Mosvodokanal, Moscow's municipal water company. It claims that Muscovites use 320 liters of water per person per day – twice as much as Berliners – and that they pay a flat fee equal to $1.50 per month whatever the quantity used. The company

---

[66] D. J. Peterson, "Infrastructure and the Environment: The Case of Water and Sanitation," *NIC Seminar*, 2000.

[67] For a broad discussion of the extent of the repairs needed and the economic, social, and political problems involved in the privatization of Moscow's housing stock, see in Vyacheslav Glazychev, "Public Housing in Washington, D.C.: With Moscow in Mind," *Comparative Urban Studies Occasional Paper*, no. 28 (1999), pp. 1–9. *Pravda Forum in English* (Internet), November 19, 2001, reported a new law according to which, beginning in 2002, Moscow residents earning more than 8,500 rubles per month (a sum far above the average wage) would have to pay the full cost of housing and municipal services. The article noted that fewer than one-third of the population could afford to pay such a sum and that for the remaining two-thirds, the existing privileges and allowances would remain in place.

proposes to install 5,000 water meters and charge consumers for the quantity consumed.[68] Although the number of meters proposed is negligible for a city of some 3 million households, it is at least a first step in the right direction and indicates what an energetic and determined authority, in this case Mayor Yurii Luzhkov's Moscow administration, can do to gradually but consistently turn a disastrous situation around.

Other aspects of urban infrastructure are similarly in need of investment. Not only the pipes but also the power lines of Russia's cities are badly worn. There are, on average, seventy breaks per 100 kilometers of wires and pipes, compared with 15 to 20 in Russia in the early 1990s, and 10 in European countries.[69] The chronic interruption of water and electric services can cause untold harm. As noted earlier, in some cases it is caused by failure of the infrastructure. It has been estimated that if investment patterns in the power generating and distribution systems do not change quickly, close to one-third of electric capacity will fail by the year 2005.[70] During the winter of 2001–2002, close to 100,000 people in Arkangelsk oblast were left without water; in Leningrad oblast 11,000 were without heat for two days, as were 8,000 people in Irkutsk oblast; in a number of districts of Murmansk oblast, telephones were inoperative from the autumn to January. All these crises, like periodic power failures in numerous urban and rural areas of Russia, were caused by breakdowns in the system.

Another scenario exists that has become more frequent recently. In December 2001 and January 2002, when the Smolensk, Ulianovsk, and Ekaterinburg oblast regional governments could not or were unwilling to pay their electricity bills, both the residents and the industries of these regions saw their electric power cut in a series of brownouts and blackouts.[71] Cases of this kind are an expression of the failure of regional governments that have been unwilling or unable to break the vicious cycle of nonpayment of debt, disrupting administrative performance, industrial production, and the lives of the citizenry. This syndrome has led to electricity being cut off from television stations, governmental administrations, and even army bases.[72]

---

[68] *Moscow Times*, March 28, 2002.
[69] *Argumenty i fakty*, February 21, 2001.
[70] *Delovye liudi*, no. 116 (2000).
[71] RIA-Novosti, cited in *RFE/RL Newsline*, January 7, 2002. See also *Nezavisimaia gazeta*, June 20, 2001, and Aleksandr Nemets and Thomas Torda, "Russia Suffers while Arming China."
[72] For a description of such happenings, see *Pravda.ru*, March 14, 2002, cited in *RFE/RL Newsline*, March 15, 2002.

An estimated 80 percent of Moscow's streets are close to the end of their serviceable life, and it should be remembered that Moscow is several notches above other cities.[73] Moscow is in the throes of an automotive "population boom." In 2000, the city had 2.8 million registered vehicles, and the region had 2 million more. By 2004, the number of vehicles in the capital is expected to grow to 3.5 million, creating urgent problems of traffic congestion and air pollution.[74] In the preparations for the 300th anniversary of the founding of St. Petersburg, no less than $600 million had to be earmarked to bring the roads in and around the city up to standard, with loans from the European Investment Bank and the European Bank for Reconstruction and Development financing the repairs.[75]

The problems of Russia's roads have even more ancient roots than most of its infrastructure problems. Nicholas Karamzin, among the early modern observers of Russia, noted, "Russia has two misfortunes: its roads and its fools."[76] At the beginning of 1980, the Soviet regime was confronted by a mass exodus of its agricultural population due to an ill-conceived and even more poorly implemented rural modernization program.[77] The response was an attempt to increase road building to give all of Russia's isolated villages easy year-round access to district centers. This was not a simple task, given that, at that time, the entire Soviet Union possessed fewer paved roads than the state of Pennsylvania.[78] The USSR was unable to sustain the cost of such a plan then, nor can Russia today.

Yet, both the need and the plan remain. In the years 1995–2000, the construction of roads received only 48 percent of the planned financing, and only 59 percent of projected road construction was completed. Worst of all, Prime Minister Mikhail Kasianov has since stated that some 80 percent of roads are below par – limiting loads and slowing speed – and

---

[73] *Interfax*, July 19, 2001. Streets in the center of Rostov on the Don, seen by the author on a visit in the autumn of 2001, were so pitted with holes that cars falling into them risked serious damage.

[74] *Moscow Times*, September 21, 2000. See Tatiana Shaumian, *The Pioneer* (India), January 13, 2002, who writes that Moscow's traffic "is a creeping social, economic, and environmental catastrophe that threatens to engulf Russia's capital city and drag it under. It may also be a looming political problem." See also *The Russian Journal*, March 17, 2002, for a graphic description of Moscow's traffic jams. The subject becomes more and more salient.

[75] *Rosbalt*, January 9, 2003.

[76] Quoted by Shaumian, *The Pioneer* (India), January 13, 2002.

[77] For a discussion of this period see Theodore H. Friedgut, "The Persistence of the Peasant in Soviet Society," *Studies in Rural Development: Essays in Memory of Dov Weintraub, Scripta Hierosolymitana*, vol. XXXIV (Jerusalem: Magnes Press, 1993).

[78] See the editorial in *Pravda*, April 29, 1980.

that only 35 percent of planned maintenance and repair was carried out.[79] Despite this, in 2001 Kasianov announced a new ten-year plan for building 80,000 kilometers of new roads at a cost of $75 billion.[80] According to the deputy minister of transport, there were as yet 36,000 rural settlements without a road connection to the highway system. One of the goals of the Transport Modernization Program for Russia is to give one-third of these all-weather access to the overall road system by the end of the coming decade. Even this ambitious program is modest when compared with Russia's perceived current needs, which are estimated at almost 600,000 kilometers of new roads.[81]

The survey presented here, although far from complete, gives a picture of the vast and varied demands on the Russian government to maintain the country as a functioning modern society. It is also clear that urgent questions of clean water, decent housing, and properly equipped health facilities are directly linked to the most salient aspects of the demographic and social crises. Two elements are needed if Russia is eventually to correct the threatening deficiencies that are degrading its economy and society. First, there must be a government that can set social and economic priorities and translate these priority decisions into publicly relevant policy implementation. Up until now, the shadow economy, largely controlled by criminal elements whose interests are certainly not those of the public or of the government, has had a turnover larger than the government's budget. The public perceives this situation and regards governmental policy and activity as largely irrelevant to real life. Disdain for the government is not confined to the common man and broad masses of the ordinary public. Among the elites, the desire to protect their gains at any price spreads rapidly. Several of the larger Russian banks were recently found to have made payments abroad amounting to $5 billion for "marketing services," thus circumventing Central Bank restrictions on capital export. When the head of the Central Bank, Sergei Ignatev, declared that steps would be taken to render such transactions "disadvantageous," media observers noted that whatever barriers the Central Bank placed in their path, the oligarchs always found their way around them.[82] In a similar context, the international credit assessment

---

[79] Andrei Litvinov, "Ten Year Plan for Russia's Roads" (Internet). For Kasianov's statement at a conference on "Roads in the 21st Century," see ITAR-TASS, December 16, 2001.

[80] *Moscow Times*, June 29, 2001.

[81] See the statement of Deputy Transport Minister Oleg Skvortsov, cited in *RFE/RL Newsline*, June 15, 2001. Of Russia's existing 925,000 kilometers of roads, 416,000 belong to various industrial enterprises, 411,000 kilometers are gravel roads, and 201,000 are simple dirt roads, impassable for a large part of the year.

[82] RIA-Novosti, April 29, 2003.

company Standard and Poor's recently noted that up to one-half of all Russian bank loans may be considered dubious, that bank reform was paralyzed, and that in the entire banking system there were perhaps fifteen bona fide banking institutions, while the remainder served primarily as money-laundering conduits for various industrial and financial conglomerates.[83] This atmosphere has already brought one prominent observer to compare Putin and his government to the stagnation of the late Brezhnev era. The population looks on, first in bewilderment, then in irritation, and finally in disgust and even hatred.[84] Clearly, a major change in policy and in atmosphere is needed.

But policy cannot succeed without resources, and the key to successful implementation of any recovery program will be the ability of the government to generate wealth and to control its distribution, in keeping with the policy priorities adopted. This means adequate and effective taxation, with the revenues to be applied to social needs and economic development. It also requires the creation of an economic environment that will encourage both domestic and foreign investment in Russia.

Despite its recovery from the disastrous collapse of August 1998, the Russian economy is still some 40 percent smaller than it was in 1989.[85] In fact, a part of this decline represents the shutdown of many inefficient plants, but no modern productive sector in industry or technology has as yet appeared that can set Russia's economy on a new track of growth. The balance of payments and a significant portion of the GDP are dependent on oil and gas exports, with a smaller portion provided by mineral fertilizers and nonferrous metals. All of these have notoriously unstable prices, and as long as they, and not personal or corporate taxes, constitute the basis of the state budget, it is difficult for the government to make accurate long-range revenue projections.[86] The energy sector, particularly oil and gas exports, has been a source of enormous revenues for individuals as well as for the state, with three of Russia's four leading billionaires having significantly augmented their fortunes in the new century.[87] Because investment in extraction technologies has brought a steady increase in production, the coming decade will see a growing

---

[83] Michael Wines, "Putin's Sure Hand Abroad Belies Problems at Home," *New York Times,* May 28, 2003, p. A5.

[84] See *Nezavisimaia gazeta,* July 20, 2001; Boris Kagarlitsky, *Moscow Times,* July 20, 2001.

[85] Vladimir Mau, director of Economic Reform Center, cited by *Interfax,* July 30, 2001.

[86] See the discussion by First Deputy Energy Minister Ivan Matlashov in *Nezavisimaia gazeta,* July 19, 2001.

[87] See *Forbes Magazine,* March 1, 2002. The three are Mikhail Khodorkovsky, Roman Abramovich, and Vagit Alekperov.

need for the expansion and replacement of pipeline networks.[88] The average lifetime of a pipeline is 30 years, and the majority of Russia's pipelines were laid in the 1960s and 1970s. They are therefore coming due for mass replacement. Moreover, the structure of the oil industry has changed. In Soviet times, the main emphasis was on supplies to the domestic market. The combination of demand shrinkage at home and growth of more profitable export opportunities means that new export-oriented pipelines must be built to carry oil and gas abroad.[89] Yukos, one of Russia's larger oil firms, has new oil fields developing in Sakha and a contract to supply China with large quantities of oil. At present, the oil is trucked south for delivery. This is a slow and expensive procedure. The company must quickly plan and construct a new pipeline if the contract is to be profitably implemented.[90] Judging by recent performance, this may be one of the few bright spots in the entire spectrum of infrastructure maintenance and a hopeful point of departure for the rest of the economy.

Whatever the case regarding oil and gas may be, the long-term well-being of Russia's economy and its population rests on the recovery of the broader industrial sector. Oil and gas both employ relatively few workers, and their profits reach relatively few people. The manufacturing industry has a much broader impact, providing more of both direct and secondary employment.

Investment in industry has, for the most part, lagged sadly. In 1998, industrial capital formation was only a fifth of the 1990 level. The problem is less that of new capital investment than of the abysmally low utilization of existing capacities.[91] Even so, by Steven Rosefielde's estimates, while new gross capital formation is higher by half than that in the United States, the attrition of the industrial economy over the past decade means that the total capital stock of Russia is only between 36 and 44 percent of the U.S. level. Moreover, Russia's capacities are underutilized largely because of their obsolescence. If these capacities cannot be modernized, then perhaps as much as one-half of existing capital will have to be scrapped, and a massive new investment program will have to be mounted to replace the unusable capital stock that now exists. It may be true, as one critic writes, that the dismantling of the

---

[88] "Russian Oil Power," *New York Times*, Op-Ed section, November 30, 2001 (Internet edition www.nytimes.com).

[89] For a detailed discussion, see Matthew Sagers, "Energy Networks, Power Generation, and Associated Infrastructures," *NIC Seminar*, 2000.

[90] *Russian Regional Report* 7, no. 7 (March 20, 2002). http://www.isn.ethz.ch/researchpub/publihouse/rrr/.

[91] Steven Rosefielde, "The State of Russia's Capital Stock," *NIC Seminar*, 2000.

obsolete sectors of Russia's industrial economy is a positive development. Yet, it is also true that as long as these are not replaced by modern structures, no advantage has been created for the future producers.[92] Whole sectors of civilian industry will have to be built anew if Russia is to find a place in the world's markets for industrial goods, providing employment and a decent living for the country's underemployed and unemployed.

Although the majority of the investment, whether in automobile plants, furniture factories, electronics, or any other industrial line, will be largely private, the appropriate environment – legal, administrative, and financial – must be government-created. Organized crime that bleeds and strangles enterprises has not yet been effectively challenged. Despite all the work that has been done toward rationalizing and simplifying tax structures, the maze of local and federal taxation is a chronic deterrent to both domestic and foreign investors. While listing tax reform among the achievements of his government, Putin also noted that such reform has become a "permanent and unceasing process," confusing citizens, bureaucrats, and entrepreneurs alike.[93] This same speech made no claims as to growing efficiency of tax collection from businesses, which, as noted earlier, remains problematic in many sectors. The same is true of the traditional Russian bureaucracy that, as throughout much of its history, still proves to be slothfully inefficient at best and venally corrupt at worst. A recent observer, reacting to Putin's State of the Union address, noted that he omitted any reference to the worsening of corruption in government, claimed by the author to be a matter of $33 billion, 10 percent of GDP, paid each year by firms as bribes to government officials.[94] The combination of crime, bureaucracy, and uncertainty as to Russia's economic future brings Russian firms to invest considerable sums abroad. This is a swiftly growing trend. In 2001, Russian business invested $3 billion abroad. By the year 2005, Yukos alone will have invested $5 billion in Central European countries. Why? One source responds as follows: "Business in Russia is conducted at a Russian pace, on Russian equipment, with a high likelihood of the need to bribe officials."[95]

[92] For a sharply dissenting view of Russia's economic situation regarding everything from demography, through taxation, to infrastructure, see Anders Äslund, "Think Again: Russia," *Foreign Policy* (July–August 2001), pp. 20–5.

[93] See his speech to the Duma as reported May 20, 2003, at http://www.rambler.ru/db/news/msg.html.

[94] Yevgeniia Albats, "When Good Friends Make Bad Diplomacy," *New York Times*, May 28, 2003, p. A23.

[95] *Argumenty i fakty*, March 13, 2002.

CONCLUSION

Russia's government clearly faces a formidable task. The need to attack so many problems simultaneously is an overwhelming challenge to a government uncertain about its ideological path and lacking a deep-rooted civil service tradition that could lend stability to the system. But neither rulers nor citizens can doubt the need to set firm priorities and begin solving problems if Russia is to fulfill its aspirations as to its place in the world and to provide a worthy life for its citizens. The issue is not one of the disappearance or the disintegration of Russia as was the case with the USSR. Although such a possibility exists, the likelihood is low, given the predominance of Russians in most of the ethnic areas and the relative strength of the Russian government. Nor will science and education in Russia completely collapse even though some pessimistic observers think otherwise.

The primary question is one of arresting a progressive degeneration in the quality of the population and the quality of life. Population shrinkage by itself is not necessarily a phenomenon fatal to Russia. Rising death rates among the youth and among the working-age population are a different story, particularly when they are directly attributable to a breakdown of society and of social institutions. The deadly chain of widespread unemployment, crime, homelessness, alcohol, drugs, AIDS, and TB must be broken before it encompasses those parts of Russian society that are still comparatively normal. As this chapter has shown, this will require an enormous investment on the part of both the government and the private sector. Such investment is contingent on a clear framework of business law, effective law enforcement, a functioning tax system, a productive economy, and a level of business ethics totally unfamiliar to Russia (and elsewhere). What took more than two centuries to build in the United States (and it would appear that even today it is far from completely effective there) can hardly take root in two decades in Russia. Yet a start must be made, and for all his image as a tough and decisive statesman, Putin has neither initiated programs nor proposed them in all too many important spheres. His 2003 State of the Union address to Russia's Duma made no mention of the problem of organized crime, and while he castigated the civil service for its low efficiency, he did not level any charges of corruption, despite this apparently constituting an acute problem. He noted that poverty was declining all too slowly, but outlined no specific program for its elimination. His speech was notable for a lack of specificity of remedies for the ills he so graphically described. At the same time, the secretary of the President's Security Council, former Interior Minister Vladimir Rushailo, noted in a television discussion that crime fighting was inadequate; that the economy was more and more dependent on raw materials exports; that industry continued to decline. All this was alleged to be the fault of an inefficient bureaucracy. The remedy proposed by another discussant was to devolve decision making and more administrative powers to the regional governments – a reversal of the policy that Putin has followed and that he noted as one of his administration's successes.[96]

The social price for procrastination must be recognized. No "national idea" for the future or scapegoating of ghosts long gone can substitute for a coherent and energetic policy to shore up the foundations of a weakened, often demoralized Russian society. An effective policy must be adopted and implemented without delay, for as Yegor Stroev, then chair of the Council of the Federation, pointed out to the St. Petersburg Economic Forum, the future of Russia depends on whether new approaches and technologies are in place before the country's natural resources, the first among them being human resources, are exhausted.[97]

[96] ORT Television, May 20, 2003.
[97] Cited in *RFE/RL Newsline,* June 14, 2001.

The search for a national identity in the Russia of Yeltsin and Putin

VERA TOLZ

Scholars tend to view nations as a modern phenomenon, the consequence of the social organization of industrial society.[1] Such a society cannot function unless its members are bound by a common culture, created by its political and intellectual elites and transmitted through a universal system of education. In Western Europe, where modern nations were created in the course of the nineteenth century, strong states were already in existence. Their boundaries determined the membership of national communities. Nations were perceived as civic communities, whose members were all citizens of the state bound by loyalty to its political institutions. The elites in Eastern and Central Europe, where people lived in premodern empires, visualized nations as predominantly ethnic communities, bound by a common language, culture, and history.

In Russia, both the civic and ethnic elements of nationhood were weakened by the peculiar form of Russian state-building. Because Russia was a multiethnic empire, the development of a Russian ethnic identity was stunted. The development of a unifying civic identity within the borders of the state was stultified by the fact that the governments of Russia and the USSR were authoritarian and, moreover, poorly institutionalized compared with governments in Western Europe. Despite the fact that in the Soviet period, Russian ethnic identity was, sometimes unwittingly, advanced through government policies, the process of identity formation was still far from complete in 1991.[2]

At the time of the USSR's disintegration, the majority of citizens in the newly independent Russian Federation did not regard it as a

---

[1] Ernest Gellner, *Nations and Nationalism* (Oxford: Basil Blackwell, 1983) and Charles Taylor, "Nationalism and Modernity" in John A. Hall, ed., *The State of the Nation* (Cambridge: Cambridge University Press, 2000), pp. 191–218.

[2] These themes are explored in Geoffrey Hosking, *Russia and the Russians. A History* (London: Allen Lane, 2001).

160

legitimate national homeland. The debate about who belongs to the Russian nation and what are the "just borders" of the national homeland has dominated the agenda of politicians and intellectuals in post-communist Russia. The question is, indeed, central to Russia's future. The ways Russians define membership in their community and the territory of their national homeland will have major implications for Russia's domestic policies (the success of its democratic transition), its foreign policy toward the other former Soviet republics, and Russia's global role.

This chapter looks at how this central question of Russian identity was addressed in the 1990s and assesses the new turns that the search for national identity have taken under President Vladimir Putin.

THE RUSSIAN IDENTITY CRISIS IN THE 1990s

Following the disintegration of the USSR, the elites were divided in their views on Russia's future prospects. Some participants in this debate chose to regard Russia as an empire, while others saw it as a nation-state. The most outspoken advocates of defining Russians in terms of their imperial mission were the communists and those Russian nationalists who, in the 1990 republican parliamentary elections, created a joint Bloc of Public and Patriotic Movements with the goal of preserving the USSR. After December 1991, the communist and nationalist press was dominated by the belief that eventually the union would be re-created; otherwise the Russians would completely disappear as a distinct community. Even today, the communist-nationalist opposition in the Russian parliament views the rebuilding of the union as its program-maximum.

Throughout the 1990s, the view that Russians should preserve their union identity was expressed not only by the extreme right wing and the communists but also by some moderates. In May 1996, the Council for Foreign and Defence Policy, led by Sergei Karaganov and Oleg Kiselev, members of Yeltsin's Presidential Council, published a working paper arguing that a Russian national state could not be formed unless a fully fledged economic, political, and military union was revived on the territory of the defunct USSR.[3] The influence of this union or imperial identity could likewise be seen in the official position of the Russian government that there was no need to demarcate borders between the countries of the "fraternal" Commonwealth of Independent

---

[3] *Nezavisimaia gazeta*, May 23, 1996.

States (CIS) and in the government's insistence that Russia was entitled to play a special role on the territory of the former USSR.[4]

Traditional imperialism began to decline by late 1992 and early 1993, however. Even some former imperialists began to feel that Russians might have a better future within the framework of a nation-state. Various new ideas of a smaller Russia, with a different definition of its national community and different "just" state borders started to be articulated. These new ideas emphasized nation-building along either ethnic or civic lines.[5]

Above all, the emphasis on the ethnic Russian component predominated in the notions of "Russia" as an East Slavic union, and of "Russia" as a state of Russian speakers. These visions focused on the ethnic elements of statehood, such as cultural similarity and the alleged common historical origins of the East Slavs in the medieval state of Kievan Rus, with language as the main marker of identity. In both cases, Orthodox Christianity was also regarded as one of the major unifying forces.[6] Both concepts are potentially irredentist because their proponents often make territorial claims on Ukraine, Belarus, and those newly independent states that have sizeable Russian-speaking minorities. The most extreme representatives of this tendency deny that Ukrainians and Belarusians have an identity separate from that of the Russians.[7]

These visions of Russia had a direct impact on the policies of Yeltsin's government. The position that Russia should defend all Russian speakers on the territory of the defunct USSR reflected the view that Russian identity was characterized primarily by language. This approach strongly affected government policies between late 1992 and 1995.[8] The idea that Russians were an inseparable part of an East Slavic community reinforced the decision of the Russian government to enter into a union with Belarus, despite the negative economic implications

---

[4] See Yeltsin's decree of September 14, 1995, titled "The Establishment of the Strategic Course of the Russian Federation with Member States of the CIS" (FBIS-SOV-95-019, September 28, 1995).

[5] For a detailed analysis of these visions and their impact on government policies, see Vera Tolz, "Forging the Nation: National Identity and Nation Building in Post-Communist Russia," *Europe-Asia Studies* 50, no. 6 (September 1998), pp. 993–1022 and her "Conflicting 'Homeland Myths' and Nation-State Building in Post-Communist Russia," *Slavic Review* 57, no. 2 (Summer 1998), pp. 267–94.

[6] Andrei Andreev, "Kto est' kto v rossiiskoi politike," *Moskva*, no. 9 (1995), pp. 145–56; P. Kolstoe, *Russians in the Former Soviet Republics* (Bloomington: Indiana University Press, 1995), pp. 276–80.

[7] See the description of the views of the nationalist Russian politician, Sergei Baburin, in *Segodnia*, March 29, 1995.

[8] Igor Zevelev, "Russia and the Diaspora," *Post-Soviet Affairs* 12, no. 3 (1996), pp. 265–84.

of this move. This approach also delayed the signing of a bilateral treaty on friendship and cooperation with Ukraine until May 1997.

In the course of the 1990s, despite the nostalgia for the USSR, only a small minority of the general population favored reunification with the Transcaucasus, Central Asia, and the Baltics.[9] But attitudes toward Ukraine and Belarus were different. Opinion polls conducted by the Moscow-based Public Opinion Foundation in 1997 indicated that up to 64 percent of respondents supported the idea of merging Ukraine and Russia into one state and 75 percent endorsed a union with Belarus.[10] The polls showed that the majority of respondents regarded Ukrainians and Belarusians as part of the Russian nation. There was also sizeable support for the idea that Russian speakers in the "near abroad" were also part of the Russian nation. A poll conducted in 1995 by the Public Opinion Foundation found that a significant minority (33 percent) thought Russia should incorporate territories of other newly independent states where Russian speakers were living in compact majorities.[11]

The post-communist period also witnessed a proliferation of groups that defined Russians in exclusively racial terms by blood. Those advocating a racial definition of Russianness argued that to survive, Russians needed to safeguard themselves from the harmful influences of other "ethnoses." Whereas the ideologists of the early twentieth-century Black Hundreds had seen the Jews as the main "enemy" of the Russian people, contemporary extremists have added the peoples of Central Asia and the Caucasus.[12] When the Russian army began military operations in Chechnya in 1994, the mainstream Russian media began constructing an image of the peoples of the Caucasus, particularly the Chechens, as "treacherous" and "savage" enemies of the Russians. This image was also reflected in the political discourse.[13]

Popular support for such ultranationalist groups is limited. Yet, the anti-Chechen propaganda of the government and the media since the mid-1990s has contributed to the rise of anti-Muslim, racist feelings. Opinion polls in early 2000 indicated that up to 80 percent of the

---

[9] I. M. Kliamkin and V. V. Lapkin, "Russkii vopros v Rossii" (part I), *Polis*, no. 5 (1995), p. 80; and T. Kuskovets and I. Kliamkin, "Postsovetskii chelovek," *Informatsionno-analiticheskii biulleten'*, nos. 1–2 (Moscow, 1997).

[10] Igor' Kliamkin, "Russian Statehood, the CIS and the Problem of Security," in Leon Aron and Kenneth M. Jensen, eds., *The Emergence of Russian Foreign Policy* (Washington, D.C., 1994), pp. 11–12; *Argumenty i fakty*, no. 27 (July 1997).

[11] Kliamkin and Lapkin, "Russkii vopros v Rossii," pp. 94 and 96.

[12] Vladimir Pribylovsky, "A Survey of Radical Right-Wing Groups in Russia," *RFE/RL Research Report*, April 22, 1994, pp. 28–37.

[13] Aleksandr Iskandarian, *Chechenskii krizis: proval rossiiskoi politiki na Kavkaze* (Moscow: Carnegie Endowment for International Peace, 1995), p. 30.

respondents regarded Islam as a "bad thing," whereas in 1992, only 17 percent subscribed to such views.[14]

Others, who did not favor ethnocentric views of the Russian nation, promoted the idea of a civic *rossiiskaia* nation, to which all citizens of the Russian Federation belong, regardless of their ethnicity. This notion of a civic *rossiiskaia* nation within the borders of the Russian Federation, united not by ethnic ties but by loyalty to the state institutions and the constitution, was put forward at the time of the demise of the USSR first and foremost by Valerii Tishkov, a prominent Moscow ethnographer and former head of the State Committee on Nationalities.[15] He called on the Russian government to introduce state symbols and encourage the development of common values that would have meaning for all citizens of Russia, not only for ethnic Russians. Supporters of the concept of a civic nation of *rossiiane* reminded the government that, given that 18 percent of federation citizens were non-Russians, the only way to preserve the integrity of the state was to forge a compound civic identity.

These attempts to forge a civic identity among all the peoples of the federation informed government policies in 1991–2. No distinct Russian ethnic characteristics were specified in the 1991 Russian citizenship law, which did not even require a basic knowledge of the Russian language as a condition for obtaining citizenship.[16] Although in 1993–5, the government defined the Russian nation as a community of Russian speakers throughout the former USSR, the 1993 Russian Constitution described the civic Russian (*rossiiskaia*) nation as a multiethnic community of all citizens of the RF.

After Yeltsin's reelection as president in 1996, he resumed attempts at constructing a nation of *rossiiane* within the borders of the Russian Federation. Yeltsin's call to society to search for a new "Russian idea" in his first postelection address to the nation in July 1996 should be seen in this light. Liberal critics of Yeltsin's endeavor feared that the government was again trying to invent a new political ideology for Russia. In fact, it seems that Yeltsin's goal was far more modest – it was a desperate attempt to unify a polarized society by promoting a vision of a civic nation based on values that all its members could share.

Although there is widespread popular support for the concept of Russia as a "common home" for all nationalities of the federation, there are

---

[14] Paul Goble, "Idel-Ural and the Future of Russia," *RFE/RL NewsLine*, Part I, May 17, 2000.

[15] V. A. Tishkov, "O novykh podkhodakh v teorii i praktike mezhnatsional'nykh otnoshenii," *Sovetskaia etnografiia*, no. 1989; and Tishkov *Ethnicity, Nationalism and Conflict in and after the Soviet Union* (London: Sage, 1997), pp. 246–71.

[16] For the text of the law, see *Vedomosti Rossiiskoi Federatsii*, no. 6 (1992), pp. 308–20.

serious obstacles to realizing this idea.[17] The first such obstacle is the Soviet approach of equating nationality with ethnicity and the heritage of the ethnically based federation. It is not surprising that in the 1990s, the most vigorous "nation-building" in the Russian Federation took place in Russia's ethnic republics. On one hand, the elites of these republics define their entities as homelands for all the nationalities residing there, including ethnic Russians, who predominate in 15 of the 21 republics. On the other hand, whereas in republican laws these republics are described as multinational in form, these laws as well as the dominant political discourse define (in clear self-contradiction) only the titular nationalities as the indigenous and culturally and historically significant members of the communities. In some republics, particularly Tatarstan and Bashkortostan, school textbooks often fail to link the republican identity with that of the Russian Federation.[18]

As for the ordinary non-Russian citizens of the federation, the overwhelming majority of those who live outside their ethnic-autonomous areas view themselves primarily as *rossiiane* and direct their main loyalty to the Russian Federation, even though most do not deny their own cultural identities. (Sixty-seven percent of non-Russians in the federation live outside their ethnic-autonomous areas.)[19] At the same time, according to the polls conducted in 1993–5 by the Center for the Sociology of Interethnic Relations in the Institute of Socio-Political Studies (of the Russian Academy of Sciences), up to 50 percent of members of the titular nationalities in Bashkortostan, Sakha, and Yakutiia subscribed to the view that Russia was the territory of the Russian Federation with the exception of the non-Russian ethnic autonomous republics.[20]

Like the elites of the ethnic republics, even the advocates of a civic *rossiiskaia* nation among the federal elites have to some extent also confused the civic and ethnic discourses of nationhood. Those members of the federal government who rejected the idea of nation-state-building in the Russian Federation along ethnic lines often did not hesitate to use the Russian Orthodox Church to legitimize their power. Yeltsin's search for a new "Russian idea" was very indicative in this regard. It was presented as a call to all citizens of the federation, but, in fact, most

---

[17] According to a study, conducted in 1996 by the Independent Institute of Social and Nationalities Problems, 74 percent of those polled perceived Russia as a "common home" of all nationalities. Quoted in Astrid Tuminez, "Russian Nationalism and Vladimir Putin's Russia," *PONARS Policy Memo Series*, Memo 151, 2000.

[18] Katherine E. Graney, "Education Reform in Tatarstan and Bashkortostan: Sovereignty Project in Post-Soviet Russia," *Europe-Asia Studies* 51, no. 4 (1999), pp. 611–32.

[19] Tishkov, *Ethnicity, Nationalism and Conflict*, p. 266.

[20] V. N. Ivanov, I. V. Ladodo, and G. Yu. Semichin (eds.), *Rossiia: sotsial'naia situatsiia i mezhnatsional'nye otnosheniia* (Moscow: Akademia, 1996), p. 169.

proposals for such an idea published in the press came from ethnic Russians. Moreover, the word *russkaia,* which has an ethnic connotation, rather than *rossiiskaia,* which refers to civic affiliation, was used to define the new unifying idea.[21] The award-winning proposal by Gurii Sudakov, for instance, presented Orthodoxy as a symbol of Russianness and, on the whole, was strongly influenced by the views of the nineteenth century Russian Slavophiles.[22]

Moreover, by the late 1990s, the Russian Federation was not the sort of state within which a compound civic identity could develop. Scholars have persuasively argued that a modern civic identity develops within the parameters of a democratic polity.[23] In the 1990s, Russia continued to have a political system based on patron-client networks rather than on formal democratic institutions. Society was polarized and a major gap existed between the rich and the poor on the one hand, and between ordinary people and the elites on the other. Russian citizens lacked a state to which they could feel loyalty and that could, therefore, unite them as a nation. This situation was reflected in opinion polls. According to a poll conducted by Rossiiskoe obshchestvennoe mnenie i issledovanie rynka (ROMIR) in 115 cities and towns within 40 regions of the federation in September 2000, 75.9 percent agreed with the statement that the government was corrupt and only 30.3 percent believed that the gap between the political establishment and society had narrowed compared with the Soviet period.[24]

Last but not least, by the late 1990s, the question of Russia's position vis-à-vis its traditional constituent "other," the West, had still not been resolved.

Throughout the post-communist period, intellectuals and politicians have constantly raised the question of Russia's relations with the "West" when trying to define the affiliation of the Russian nation and develop a concept of the post-communist Russian homeland. This is hardly surprising. Ever since Russia's "modernization" began in the early eighteenth century, Western Europe and, from the nineteenth century onward, also the United States, have been Russia's "other," against which the Russian identity has been constructed. The famous nineteenth-century debate between Slavophiles and Westernizers was precisely about Russia's difference from, or similarity to, Europe.

---

[21] *Rossiiskaia gazeta,* July 19, 1996.

[22] *Rossiiskaia gazeta,* September 17, 1996, p. 4, and December 31, 1996, p. 1.

[23] Liah Greenfeld, *Nationalism: Five Roads to Modernity* (Cambridge: Harvard University Press, 1992), p. 10.

[24] Quoted in N. V. Laidinen, "Obraz Rossii v zerkale rossiiskogo obshchestvennogo mneniia," *Sotsiologicheskie issledovaniia,* no. 4 (2001), p. 29.

In the course of the nineteenth century, Russian intellectuals also raised the question of Russia's relationship to the East. After all, geographically the Russian empire was located partly in Asia, and many of the empire's subjects were non-European. In the late nineteenth century, a view emerged that Russia constituted a world of its own, a unique continental multiethnic civilization. The émigré intellectual movement of the 1920s known as Eurasianism (*Evraziistvo*) brought these ideas to a logical conclusion by completing the dissociation of Russia from Europe and declaring its affinity with Asia. This movement advocated a concept of "Russia-Eurasia" as a unique civilization of various peoples of Slavic, Finno-Ugric, Turkic, and Mongolian origins. It argued that this civilization stood in opposition to Western European, particularly Anglo-Saxon, civilization.[25]

In the Soviet period, Lenin's vision of the capitalist West as the main adversary, an antimodel in a political sense as well as a positive example of technological development, had by the mid-1930s been superseded by an overwhelmingly hostile attitude toward Western Europe and North America. This sharp division of the world was reconsidered in Mikhail Gorbachev's era, and it was replaced by the idea that the USSR/Russia was undoubtedly part of Europe and that isolation from Europe was harmful for Russia. In the early 1990s, this approach was enthusiastically taken up by Yeltsin and members of his government, who viewed Russia's integration into Western political, security, and economic structures as their primary goal.

The main opponents of this vision of Russia in the communist-nationalist camp used the ideas of the Eurasian movement to construct an alternative one. From the early 1990s there were several trends in Russian neo-Eurasianism. The ideology propagated on the pages of *Den'*/*Zavtra* by the "spiritual opposition" to Yeltsin's government identified Russia's national mission as preventing the harmful influences of the "Atlanticist, maritime powers"– above all the United States and Great Britain – from spreading around the world.[26]

At the same time, in the spring of 1992, Sergei Stankevich, the presidential advisor on foreign policy matters, offered a moderate version of Eurasianism as a middle ground between the radical Westernizers and the opposition. For Stankevich, Russia's history and its not exclusively European geography make it a unique continental civilization,

---

[25] For a good overview of the ideas of the Eurasians from the 1920s to the 1990s, see E. L. Moroz, "Nasledie Evraziitsev. Mezhdu istoriosofiei i politikoi," *Barér*, no. 1 (5) (St. Petersburg, 1999).

[26] For the summary of the views of neo-Eurasians, see A. Prokhanov in *Literaturnaia gazeta*, September 2, 1992.

with special interests in the CIS and the Baltic countries that the West must recognize. Stankevich's Eurasianism suggested that Russia's foreign policy should not be oriented exclusively toward forging strong ties with Western Europe and the United States but also should pursue Russian national interests in the CIS and in Asia.[27] By mid-1993, Yeltsin's government had modified the exclusively Western orientation in its foreign policy and adopted a position much closer to that of Stankevich. Meanwhile, opinion polls began to indicate a change in public attitudes, with a growing sentiment that Russia should promote its own "indigenous" values, which were never, in fact, clearly defined.

The change of opinion among ordinary people and the elites was connected with a feeling – shared by many liberals and conservatives alike – that, as Russia had lost its superpower status, the United States was trying unilaterally to set the terms of world politics, even in those areas that Russia had traditionally viewed as central to its national interests. The integration of Russia into European structures was also proceeding much more slowly than many liberals initially had anticipated. The increasing suspiciousness in popular attitudes toward the intentions of the United States vis-à-vis Russia was connected with the peoples' assessment of Yeltsin's economic policies.[28] Disillusionment with reforms was accompanied by growing criticism of the West.

At the same time, those who supported the idea that Russia was unquestionably (at least in the cultural sense) part of Europe – they constituted the majority among those who envisaged Russia as a civic nation-state – did not resolve the question of the place of the Muslim minority (almost 10 percent of the population) in this Russia that they imagined as exclusively European.

Not surprisingly, the contradictions in the thinking and policies of Yeltsin's era found their reflection in the political symbolism of the state. In the early 1990s, the State Duma, which was then dominated by forces antagonistic to Yeltsin, opposed the restoration of the old Russian imperial symbols – the two-headed eagle as the national emblem, the white-blue-red flag, and the national anthem with music from Mikhail Glinka's first Russian national opera *A Life for the Tsar* – by presidential decrees. (In January 1998, Duma deputies overwhelmingly voted against the anthem and the flag proposed by Yeltsin.) The communists in the Duma, in particular, supported reinstating the Soviet national anthem and the red flag. However, at the same time, even the communists favored viewing the Orthodox Church as a symbol of Russianness.

[27] Sergei Stankevich, "Derzhava v poiskakh sebia," *Nezavisimaia gazeta*, March 28, 1992, p. 4; "U Rossii est' svoe mesto v mire," *Rossiiskie vesti*, February 27, 1993.
[28] See I. Kliamkin in *Kuranty*, October 23, 1992.

State awards also reflected the conflict between prerevolutionary Russian and Soviet symbolism. The order of the Apostle Andrew the First Appointed, introduced by Peter the Great in 1699, coexisted with the title of the Hero of Russia (formerly the Hero of the USSR).

The new-old symbolism was not only transitional and contradictory. It was also insensitive toward the non-Russian nationalities of the Russian Federation. Imperial or ethnic Russian symbols could hardly have a resonance among them. Thus, at a roundtable discussion on the federation's new state ideology organized by *Svobodnaia mysl'* in 1999, T. S. Saidbaev, a journalist from Tatarstan, complained about the insensitivity of the federal government in its choice of symbols. He noted that the residents of the Muslim republic of Dagestan, who had fought on the Russian side against the Chechens, were awarded medals decorated with Russian Orthodox crosses.[29]

RUSSIAN NATION-STATE BUILDING UNDER PUTIN

At the time of Vladimir Putin's accession to power in December 1999, the Russian political elites recognized that the weakness of the state and the crisis of Russian identity were among the main problems facing the country. The concepts of Russianness outlined earlier still exert their impact. A union identity is still widely propagated by the proponents of messianic Eurasianism. This notion, along with a belief in an East Slavic union, influences the Foreign Ministry position on the demarcation of the border with Ukraine. The ministry has been opposed to demarcation on the grounds that the border between Russia and Ukraine "should be one of friendship, accord and communication, uniting rather than separating our two nations."[30] A union with Belarus was singled out as one of Russia's top priorities in the new Foreign Policy Concept that was adopted in June 2000. Displaying a belief that all Russian speakers throughout the former USSR belonged to the Russian nation, the Foreign Policy Concept paid more attention than its 1993 predecessor to "protecting the rights and interests of Russian citizens and Russian compatriots (*sootechestvenniki* [sic]) abroad."[31]

At the same time as it is being influenced by these conflicting and potentially irredentist visions of Russia, Putin's government also has the goal of consolidating a civic nation within the borders of the Russian Federation. The fact that, in contrast to Yeltsin, Putin is not held

[29] *Svobodnaia mysl'*, no. 12 (1999), p. 31.
[30] Taras Kuzio, "Russia Continues to Hold Up Border Demarcation with Ukraine," *RFE/RL Newsline*, Part II, October 30, 2001.
[31] *Izvestiia*, April 11, 2000.

responsible for the demise of the USSR by the Russian population has proved to have significant policy implications. The president has not felt under pressure to emphasize his commitment to maintaining special ties with Ukraine, to championing the Russian-Belarusian Union, or to CIS integration. His policies toward the newly independent states have, therefore, been more determined by economic than ideological considerations. His "ultimatum" to the Belarusian President Lukashenka in August 2002 that, in exchange for integration with Russia, the Belarusian elites would have to give up their country's sovereignty was interpreted by the liberal Russian media as Putin's admission that "the creation of a Russian-Belarusian Union state is impossible."[32] Similarly, the communist opposition condemned the president's proposal as a manifestation of the liberal reformers' attempt to "lay to rest the Union treaty" between the two countries.[33] Putin is thus better positioned than his predecessor to focus on the consolidation of a national community within the current borders of the Russian Federation. He made this commitment clear in his very first public statements as president.

In his first address to the Federal Assembly upon his election as president in March 2000, Putin put the task of consolidating society at the top of his political agenda and used strong words to describe the threats (particularly demographic trends) to the survival of Russians as a nation.[34] He also published a programmatic article titled "Russia at the Turn of the Millennium" in which he warned that in the 1990s, just as after October 1917, Russian society was in a state of schism (*raskol*).[35] It was essential to overcome this *raskol* by uniting people around one common *rossiiskaia* idea. By referring to a *rossiiskaia* rather than a *russkaia* idea (as Yeltsin had), Putin demonstrated a greater sensitivity than his predecessor toward ethnic minorities in the Russian Federation. Responding to the liberals' criticism of Yeltsin's search for the "Russian idea," Putin stressed that in no way did he envisage the introduction of a new state ideology. For Putin, the "Russian idea" is the combination of (unspecified) panhuman values and such traditional *rossiiskie* values as patriotism – a feeling of pride in one's country, its achievements and its history, *derzhavnost'* (Russia as a great power), and *gosudarstvennost'* (statism, a belief in a strong state that ensures order and is at the forefront of progressive reforms).[36]

[32] Dmitrii Furman, "Priglashenie k samoubiistvu," *Nezavisimaia gazeta*, August 20–6, 2002.
[33] *Sovetskaia Rossiia*, August 17, 2002.
[34] M. N. Rutkevich, "Konsolidatsiia obshchestva i sotsial'nye protivorechiia," *Sotsiologicheskie issledovaniia*, no. 1 (2001), p. 27.
[35] Putin, "Rossiia na rubezhe tysiacheletii." Available: http://www.panorama.ru.
[36] *Rossiiskaia gazeta*, July 11, 2000.

Putin has been making two key contributions to nation-building in the Russian Federation. These are his efforts at state-building and his attempts to identify Russia's place in the global community.

First, we shall examine the extent to which Putin's state-building policies are conducive to the consolidation of a civic nation within the borders of the Russian Federation and are able to unite different ethnic and social groups and reconcile state and society. In addressing this question, one should remember that a civic nation is a phenomenon closely connected with a democratic polity.

Thus far, it seems that Putin's "managed democracy" is gaining more support from the population than his predecessor's policies did. Putin has also decided to tackle one traditional feature of Russian political culture not conducive to modern nation-building – the lack of a clear distinction between public and private spheres, reflected in government ministers' habit of using their offices for private purposes. By trying to eradicate this habit, Putin could contribute to nation-building in Russia along civic lines.

Putin has already achieved some consolidation of society, if only at the symbolic level. In this area, he seems to have made an important breakthrough by offering a fairly sophisticated compromise between Russia's two pasts (pre-revolutionary and Soviet) and the present. On the one hand, a major concession was made to those who wanted to see the rehabilitation of some important symbols of the Soviet era. Sergei Mikhalkov, the author of the text of the Soviet national anthem, was asked to write new words, while the Soviet music was reinstated. Putin also suggested that the Soviet red flag become the official flag of the Russian armed forces.[37]

The return to the Soviet music in the national anthem provoked a wave of criticism among liberal intellectuals and politicians. However, from the point of view of the non-Russian minorities, it can be argued that the Soviet period offers more examples than pre-revolutionary imperial history of a "usable past," necessary for the consolidation of a common identity. The elites in non-Russian autonomous areas reject symbols associated with the tsarist era much more unequivocally than they do many aspects of Soviet history. On the other hand, Putin made a gesture toward those who wanted to stress ties between contemporary and pre-revolutionary Russia. The tricolor was finally accepted as Russia's state flag and the double-headed eagle as the national emblem. A new interpretation of the emblem was offered. Two small crowns over

---

[37] See Putin's comments on the new state symbols in *Komsomol'skaia pravda*, December 6, 2000.

the eagle's heads and a big one in the middle are now supposed to symbolize the sovereignty of the Russian Federation as well as its republics. A ribbon tying the crowns together reflects the unity of Russia and its constituent parts. The Russian parliament accepted these state symbols in December 2000, thus marking an important stage in the legitimization of the new Russian state.

Another important development in the sphere of civic nation-building within the borders of the Russian Federation is a new citizenship law, which was endorsed by the president and approved by the State Duma in the third reading in April 2002. The law does not give any special privileges to former Soviet citizens outside the federation in obtaining Russian citizenship, as had been the case in the 1991 law. Commenting on the new law, Oleg Kutafin, the chairman of the Presidential Commission on the Questions of Citizenship, argued that the new legislation was aimed at "finally stabilizing the situation inside the country (Russian Federation)." He pointed out that the hitherto loosely used word "compatriot" (*sootechestvennik*) should not be applied to any Russian speaker in the "near abroad" but only to the citizens of the federation who live outside its borders.[38] The new law is thus aimed against the widely held perception of the Russian nation as a community of Russian speakers, regardless of their current citizenship.

In other respects, however, the impact of Putin's domestic policies on nation-building is ambiguous. Policies aimed at curtailing the freedom of the media, a selective use of the law for potently political ends, and political centralization that tightens the vertical line of power are not conducive to democratization and, therefore, to nation-building along civic lines.

Putin's regional reforms serve as a good example of this ambiguity.[39] On the one hand, if the unity of the Russian Federation is to be maintained, there is a clear need, as Putin has demanded, to bring the legislation of the autonomous republics into line with federal law and to eliminate from republican laws provisions that are more appropriate for independent states than for administrative units of the federation. Those provisions in the republican laws that contradicted federal legislation often promoted local identities, which were in conflict with the idea of the overarching *rossiiskaia* identity.

On the other hand, the legal uniformity that Putin has tried to impose fails to take into account the ethnic complexity of the autonomies. In some instances, those republican laws that were not in line with the

---

[38] *Nezavisimaia gazeta*, November 20, 2001; *Rossiiskaia gazeta*, April 20, 2002.
[39] For an analysis of Putin's regional reforms, see Dmitrii Furman in *Obshchaia gazeta*, no. 22, June 1–7, 2000.

federal legislation helped to keep local ethnic tensions in check and thereby were conducive to ethnic and national integration within the borders of the Russian Federation. This was, for instance, the case with the electoral law in Dagestan, a republic comprising numerous small ethnic groups. The electoral law envisaged ethnic quotas in the republic's parliamentary elections. Such quotas ensured that all significant ethnic groups were represented in the republican legislature, thereby reducing ethnic tensions. This provision is now to be eliminated because quotas are not stipulated in the federal legislation. It is therefore likely that some ethnic communities will not be represented in the future Dagestani parliament, and this situation is likely to provoke ethnically motivated conflicts in the republic.

At the same time as he has been demanding the revision of republican legislation, Putin has not, however, unleashed a similar "war" against those policies of regional governors that, in violation of federal laws, promote interethnic strife in the provinces. Particularly since the beginning of the war in Chechnya in 1994, a number of governors have been pursuing policies that openly discriminate against people from the Caucasus even if they are citizens of the Russian Federation. If anything, the anti-Caucasian, and by implication anti-Muslim, rhetoric among federal and regional officials and in the federal media have intensified since Putin's accession to power and the renewal of military operations in Chechnya. A tough-worded law "On Countering Extremist Activity," adopted in July 2002, has not yet been applied to deal with the problem.

Putin himself portrayed Islam as a force threatening Russia when he claimed in an interview, published in the London *Times* on March 21, 2000, that if Chechen "extremists" were not stopped, "we will have the Islamization of Russia." The president expressed a similar sentiment during his visit to Brussels for a Russia–European Union (EU) summit in November 2002. Speaking to reporters, Putin stated that Chechens, together with their Muslim supporters from abroad, were trying to "establish a caliphate on the territory of the Russian Federation ... and ultimately throughout the world."[40]

PUTIN'S RUSSIA BETWEEN THE WEST AND THE EAST

President Putin's second contribution to the formation of a post-communist Russian identity lies in foreign policy. His foreign policy has been at the center of the debate within the Russian political and

[40] Quoted in *Kommersant*, November 12, 2002.

military establishment and the intellectual community about whether Russia is a European or a Eurasian country.

During Putin's first year in power, the representatives of messianic Eurasianism, led by the radical right-wing political analyst Aleksandr Dugin, became increasingly outspoken. Dugin has succeeded in drawing representatives of the Russian security forces, military and political establishment, the Russian Orthodox Church, and the Muslim community under the banner of his Eurasia movement, set up in April 2001. He has also become a political advisor to the Duma speaker, Gennadii Seleznev, and a member of the Council on Geopolitics affiliated with the presidential office. For Dugin and his followers, "Eurasia is based on the idea of a common enemy – the Atlanticist world," above all the United States and Britain. Russia, they argue, can withstand their damaging influence by creating a Eurasian Union (within the borders of the former USSR), in which its main allies will be Iran, India, China, and the Arab countries of the Middle East and North Africa.

For Dugin, the "Eurasian civilization" is distinctly non-European because it consistently rejects Europe's liberal values. In an article in *Krasnaia zvezda* on May 29, 2001, Dugin claimed that Eurasianism was on the way to becoming the common ideology of the entire political establishment. After the appearance in November 2000 of Putin's article, "Russia Always Considered Itself an Eurasian Country," Dugin proclaimed that Putin was firmly in the camp of the Eurasians. In this article, written in connection with the president's attendance at the forum of Asian-Pacific Cooperation in Brunei,[41] Putin talked about a "Eurasian common home" and about Russia as "a sort of integrating center, linking Asia, Europe and America." Commenting on the article, Dugin noted with disapproval that the inclusion of America on the list of the continents to which Russia should be linked reflected the influence of Anatolii Chubais.[42]

Some aspects of Russia's foreign policy in 2000 and the first half of 2001 seemed to indicate a certain affinity between Putin's actions and Dugin's geopolitical vision. For instance, Putin's visits to India and China, as well as increased links with Iran, were seen as signs of Dugin's influence.[43]

From the outset, however, in his foreign policy Putin has seemingly been a pragmatist for whom, in fact, Russia's integration into European structures is a more important goal than the exploration of Russia's opportunities in Asia. From the early days of his tenure in office, he has

[41] It appeared at the site strana.ru on November 13, 2000.
[42] See Dugin's comments on Putin's article at www.arctogaia.com/public/putin.html.
[43] Ilan Berman, "Slouching toward Eurasia?" *Perspective* (the Institute for the Study of Conflict, Ideology and Policy at Boston University) 12, no. 1 (September–October 2001).

also looked for ways of improving Russia's relations with the United States. Putin's statements about Russian identity have been determined by circumstances. When he was attending the forum of Asian-Pacific Cooperation, the president defined Russia as "a Eurasian country." On a number of other occasions, he has made it clear that Russia's key foreign policy priority is, in fact, closer integration into Europe. In his first interview with the foreign media, when he became acting president, Putin told the BBC that "Russia is a part of European culture, and I cannot conceive of our country isolated from Europe."[44]

The Foreign Policy Concept discussed earlier argued that the "relationship with the European states is a traditional priority of Russian foreign policy."[45] The president made the same argument in his first address to the nation on July 8, 2000. In an indication that, unlike many others in the Russian political establishment, Putin did not see globalization as a threat to Russian identity, he argued that "the country's democratic system and Russia's new openness to the world are not in conflict with our distinctiveness and patriotism."[46] On other relevant occasions, Putin has delivered a similar message. In his opening statement at the EU-Russian summit in May 2000, he reiterated that Russia "was, is and will be a European country by its location, its culture, and its attitude towards economic integration." Moreover, it would seem that Putin views Islam with suspicion, as indicated by his earlier-mentioned statements. He, therefore, does not fully share Dugin's vision of Russia as a "Eurasian civilization" in which Muslim influences are of major importance.

From the very beginning of his tenure in office, Putin has also been more sympathetic to Russia's close cooperation with NATO and less inclined than most members of Russia's political establishment to regard NATO's enlargement as a threat to Russian security. Finally, the president has been preoccupied with the need to improve Russia's relationship with the United States. None of Putin's speeches have been marked by the strong anti-Americanism clearly visible in the positions of such key figures in Russia's foreign policy and military establishment as Foreign Minister Igor Ivanov and Defense Minister Sergei Ivanov.

The difference between the ways in which Putin and Igor Ivanov interpreted the new Russian Foreign Policy Concept was telling. The Concept briefly observed that "the Russian Federation is willing to work to overcome the considerable differences that have arisen recently in relations with the United States." The criticism of the United States in

---

[44] *Izvestiia,* March 7, 2000.
[45] *Nezavisimaia gazeta,* July 11, 2000.
[46] *Rossiiskaia gazeta,* July 11, 2000.

the Concept was, in fact, brief and muted, and a hope for improvement was expressed. However, in presenting the Concept to the public and the media, Ivanov made the criticism of the United States his main focus, and he described resistance to American domination of the world politically and economically as Russia's main foreign policy goal.[47] At the very same time, in his address to the nation, Putin outlined his own vision of Russia's external threats, focusing on international terrorism. He did not directly criticize the United States at all, only vaguely mentioning that "Russia now confronts forces that are striving for the geopolitical restructuring of the world."[48]

Dugin's claims that Putin had been firmly recruited into the Eurasian camp were disproved by the president's attitude toward cooperation with the United States following the terrorist acts in the United States on September 11, 2001. Putin proclaimed Russia's close affinity with the Western world and described Islamic fundamentalism as the main threat to both the West and Russia. Putin's utilization of the situation following the September 11 events has indicated yet again that for him, Russia's integration into EU structures, an expression of Russia's orientation toward the West, was a priority. On October 10, 2001, an editorial in *Literaturnaia gazeta* optimistically concluded, "In the autumn of 2001, Russia, it seems, is making its final civilizational (*tsivilizatsionnyi*) choice. There is no 'special' or 'third' way. The choice is being made in favor of Europe, democracy and a market economy.... Obstacles in the way of Russian integration into Western political and state structures are primarily psychological.... Putin has overcome these complexes, the West should do the same."[49]

Putin's position remained unchanged during the U.S.-British military operation against Iraq in March–April 2003. Although the president condemned the war as being conducted "contrary to the principles and norms of international law,"[50] his criticism as well as that of other members of the Russian ruling elite has been restrained. Russia's foreign minister, ambassador to the United States, and other top government officials have stressed that a deterioration of relations with America was not in Russia's strategic interest.[51] Meanwhile, liberal observers have interpreted Russia's close cooperation with Germany and France in the opposition to the war in Iraq as potentially the "first step towards forging a greater European identity," "a greater Europe stretching from

[47] *Nezavisimaia gazeta*, July 11, 2000; and *Izvestiia*, July 11, 2000.
[48] *Rossiiskaia gazeta*, July 11, 2000.
[49] *Literaturnaia gazeta*, October 10–16, 2001.
[50] *Rossiiskaia gazeta*, March 21, 2003.
[51] *Kommersant*, March 19, 2003.

Reykjavik to Vladivostok," promised when the Cold War ended but so far not realized.[52]

However, there is strong opposition to Putin's cooperation with the United States, NATO, and the EU. Some Russian observers have drawn a comparison between the opposition that Putin's foreign policy encounters and the widespread opposition to Gorbachev's reforms on the part of the Communist Party establishment in the late 1980s.[53] Indeed, doubts that the United States and Russia can be genuine partners have been expressed by many politicians and military commanders, as well as by the media, including moderate and even liberal publications.[54]

Society at large has been split in its attitude toward the United States and Putin's pro-Western policies. During the U.S. bombing of Afghanistan, the opposition to its policies slightly outweighed the support. Commenting on this situation, *Izvestiia* observed on October 15, 2001, that Russians did not agree with Putin's support for the U.S. actions in Afghanistan "not because Russians are ignorant or supportive of terrorism, but because they do not trust the U.S. and believe that Washington will try to exploit the campaign for its own broader geopolitical and economic aims." The article noted that this attitude on the part of many Russians should not come as a surprise, because "the majority of Russians still have not decided whether Russia should be part of the West or pursue a special course with the East."[55] Similarly, during the war in Iraq, opinion polls indicated that an overwhelmingly positive view of the United States was still held by around 48 percent of the respondents, whereas 40 percent viewed the United States negatively. At the same time, more than 70 percent saw the United States as an "aggressor" and "the main threat to world peace."[56]

CONCLUSION

After the disintegration of the USSR and the emergence of an independent Russian Federation, the political and intellectual elites viewed the need to forge a new Russian (both *russkaia* and *rossiiskaia*) identity as a priority. The serious implications of this issue for Russia's domestic and foreign policies have been acknowledged. The elites are divided, some envisaging Russia as an imperial entity within the borders of the defunct

[52] *Nezavisimaia gazeta*, February 28, 2003.
[53] *Vremia novostei*, October 19, 2001, quoted in *RFE/RL NewsLine*, Part I, October 22, 2001.
[54] See, for instance, Gleb Pavlovskii and Sergei Karaganov in *Rossiiskaia gazeta*, March 21, 2003, and Konstantin Voronov in *Nezavisimaia gazeta*, February 19, 2003.
[55] Quoted in *RFE/RL Newsline*, Part 1, October 16, 2001.
[56] *Izvestiia*, March 15, 2003, reported the results of an opinion poll held by the All-Russian Centre for the Study of Public Opinion.

USSR and others envisaging a smaller Russia as a nation-state. Some of the projects for Russia as a nation-state (Russia as a state of all Russian speakers throughout the USSR and Russia as an East Slavic Union) are also irredentist, because their advocates make territorial claims on Ukraine, Belarus, and other newly independent states. Irredentist visions of a Russian nation-state as well as imperial concepts have been advocated particularly vigorously by the communist and nationalist opposition in parliament. Although the Russian population overall supports the idea of recreating a union with Ukraine and Belarus, and many view Russian speakers in the "near abroad" as part of the Russian nation, there is virtually no support among ordinary people for the use of force to achieve such goals.[57]

At the same time, this chapter has argued that the Yeltsin and Putin governments, in fact, have been more preoccupied with consolidating a national community within the borders of the Russian Federation and preserving the country's territorial integrity than with expanding beyond Russia's current borders. Both Yeltsin and Putin have been influenced by various ethnic concepts of Russianness based on language and the cultural similarities between all East Slavs, but at the same time they have shown a primary commitment to the formation of a civic Russian (*rossiiskaia*) nation on the territory of the Russian Federation. However, their policies in this area have been inconsistent and contradictory.

There are still formidable obstacles to the creation of a shared identity, able to unite all citizens of the Russian Federation regardless of their ethnicity. These obstacles include the weakness of the state, the economic polarization of society, a growing xenophobia in relations with the peoples of the North Caucasus and anti-Islamic feelings among ethnic Russians, the policies (particularly in the sphere of education) of the elites in the non-Russian ethnic republics that lead to the separation of local identities from the overarching civic *rossiiskaia* identity, and the still unsolved question of Russia's European or Eurasian orientation.

---

[57] Kliamkin and Lapkin, "Russkii vopros v Rossii," pp. 94 and 96.

The Russian political system:
Toward stabilization?

The dilemmas of federalism: Moscow and the regions in the Russian Federation

OKSANA ORACHEVA

THE principal idea of federalism is the diffusion of power from the center to the regions within a common political space. This entails the creation of two relatively autonomous levels of power and decision making – the center and the regions; the codification of their mutual rights and obligations in the form of a constitution, or some other mode of agreement between the constituent units and the center; the settlement of disputes by an arbitrator (a Constitutional Court, for instance); and the adoption of a system of checks and balances (the separation of powers, for example). In short, federalism is based on a power-sharing model of governance.

Therefore, in a narrow sense, a federal structure allows for the accommodation of demands for regional autonomy and self-determination within a common territorial framework. Furthermore, "federalism is also a way of decentralizing conflict and isolating continuous regional issues so that they do not bubble up to disrupt national policies."[1]

RELATIONS BETWEEN THE CENTER AND THE REGIONS IN POST-COMMUNIST RUSSIA

Relations between Moscow and the regions constitute a key element in the contemporary political system. One of the fundamental problems still confronting the Russian Federation is that of the extraordinary complexity of its administrative structure, which tries to accommodate both ethnic and regional diversity. The Russian Federation consists of twenty-one republics based on the ethnic principle; six krais and forty-nine oblasts that are purely territorial in character; ten ethnically based autonomous okrugs (districts); two federal cities, and one autonomous

---

[1] Peter C. Ordeshook and Olga Shvetsova, *Russia, Federalism and Political Stability* (Pasadena, Calif.: Social Science Research Council Working Paper, California Institute of Technology, 1995), p. 1.

oblast. This territorial structure (partially based on institutionalized ethnic nationhood[2]) is mostly inherited from the Soviet past.

The division of powers between the center and the regions is stipulated in the Russian Constitution (1993), which allocates powers to the center and to the federal units respectively as well as specific powers to be exercised concurrently (Articles 71, 72, and 73). Similar articles were later introduced into the republican constitutions and regional charters.

Especially in the area of the federal structure and center-periphery relations, the 1993 Russian Constitution was mostly a compromise between Moscow and the regions that resulted in the vague and sometimes unclear definitions of the interrelationship. Imprecise definitions regarding the Federation Council, presidential representatives, and the powers of joint jurisdiction enable the center to introduce changes in federal relations without changing the constitution.

The Federal Constitution contains a description of rights granted specifically to the ethnic republics – the existence of republican constitutions instead of regional charters and a state language other than Russian, for example (Article 5 and Chapter III). That gives the republics a chance to claim their unique and peculiar position within the federation. One can also argue that the ethnic republics did not miss the chance provided by the bilateral treaties signed between them and the center during the first years of the Yeltsin regime. These treaties were mostly the results of the regional leaders' ability to exert pressure on Moscow and to gain more power and privileges (in the areas of taxation and the management of natural resources, for example) than was stipulated by the Russian Constitution.

Treaties between the regions (not just the ethnic republics) and the center first mushroomed following President Boris Yeltsin's famous appeal of 1990 to the republics to "take as much sovereignty as they can swallow." Republics and autonomous okrugs that adopted declarations of sovereignty during the so-called parade of sovereignty (June 1990–December 1991) hoped to keep the powers thus gained even after the Federation Treaty was signed in 1992 and the new constitution was adopted in 1993. Therefore, they initiated the negotiation of new bilateral treaties with the center in the mid-1990s (not surprisingly, the first treaty was signed on February 15, 1994, with Tatarstan). However, once the krais and oblasts successfully joined the process of signing bilateral treaties (with the Sverdlovsk region in the lead), the nature of this institution began to change. Whereas the early treaties enshrined specific

---

[2] See R. Brubaker, *Nationalism Reframed* (New York: Cambridge University Press, 1996).

powers granted to the regions, later such documents mostly reconfirmed the power allocation stipulated in the constitution and therefore were of no real significance.

Under these circumstances, it is not surprising that, for the most part, the regions ceased to seek such treaties. Indeed, by 2002, no less than twenty-eight regional units had renounced their bilateral treaties with the center.[3] According to Chelyabinsk Governor Petr Sumin, such documents could readily be renounced because they were of no concrete benefit to the regions. However, the governor of the Sverdlovsk oblast, Eduard Rossel holds the opposite opinion, claiming that there is an on-going value in negotiating bilateral treaties between the center and the regions.[4]

While not disputing the legitimacy of the bilateral treaties, President Vladimir Putin sees their role differently. During the Yeltsin regime, bilateral treaties were concluded mainly as the result of personal negotiations between the two parties. In Putin's view, however, all bilateral treaties that might be adopted in the future to reflect the regional diversity of the Russian Federation "would have to be confirmed by a federal law"[5] and, therefore, would be a part of a single legal system. As he stated in his address to the Federal Assembly, the existence of bilateral treaties in their current form violates the principal of equity not only with regard to the different subjects of the federation but also with regard to the individual citizens of those regions. The Kozak Commission[6] suggested making the necessary changes in the appropriate laws. In the commission's view, bilateral treaties could exist only if they were justified by unique economic, geographic, or other circumstances in the region; each treaty should be confirmed by federal law.[7] However, this proposition could not put an end to the institution of bilateral treaties, which are justified by many regions as reflecting their unique character.

---

[3] V. V. Putin, *Poslanie presidenta Rossiiskoi Federatsii federal'nomy sobraniiu*, Moscow, July 8, 2002, p. 21.

[4] V. N. Rudenko, "Ural'skii federal'nyi okrug: pravovye aspekty federativnykh otnoshenii," *Sovet federatsii i konstitutsionnye protsessy v sovremennoi Rossii. Bulleten' Instituta prava i publichnoi politiki*, vyp. 0 (October 2001). Available: http://www.ilpp.ru/bulletin/oct2001. Accessed on December 6, 2001.

[5] *Poslanie presidenta*, p. 21.

[6] The commission headed by deputy director of the presidential administration Dmitry Kozak was established in 2001 for further harmonizing of federal and regional legislation and especially for the further redistribution of power among the federal center, the subjects of the federation, and the municipalities. As a result of its work, the commission proposed several thousand amendments to different federal laws.

[7] *Russian Regional Report* 5, no. 1 (January 13, 2003), p. 3.

The 1993 constitution gave all the federal units the right to adopt their own legislative norms in the form of regional charters and republican constitutions, regional and republican laws, decrees, and so forth. One can argue that the regions managed to make full use of this right during the 1990s, often implementing legislation that was clearly in conflict with federal law (for example, the claims to republican sovereignty, the assertion of the primacy of the regional over the federal legislature, and the limitations on the free movement of goods). The federal Ministry of Justice registered such contradictions between federal and regional legislation, but there was no enforcement mechanism to bring the latter into line with the former. Moreover, the Yeltsin regime did not view the contradictory nature of the regional legislation as a major problem if only because bilateral political negotiations, rather than the rule of law, were treated as being of primary importance.

Even though the 1993 constitution states that "the Russian Federation is a democratic federative state of the rule of law"[8] (Article 1) and that "the individual and his rights and freedoms are the supreme value" (Article 2), it takes no great effort to discern various types of undemocratic regimes in the regions.[9] As Bashkortostan President Murtaza Rakhimov proudly stated, democracy would come to his republic only in one or two hundred years.[10] The undemocratic nature of some regional regimes can be seen in the nationalistic discourse used by the local leaders, as well as in the adoption of legal norms that violate human rights. For example, the mayor of Moscow, Yurii Luzhkov, was among the first to introduce special restrictions on residence registration. Most of these restrictions were found unconstitutional by the Constitutional Court in decisions of 1996 and 1998 or were abrogated by the Supreme Court in 2000–2, but the Moscow government delayed the implementation of these decisions, leaving some of the restrictions still in place.[11] In reality, these rules primarily affect people of Transcaucasian and Central Asian origin, who are systematically discriminated against in Moscow. Similar restrictions were introduced in some southern Russian regions, the Krasnodar krai, for example.[12] These measures were adopted by

---

[8] I quote here the English translation of the Russian 1993 Constitution from the following volume: R. Sakwa, *Russian Politics and Society* (London: Routledge, 1996), pp. 395–429.

[9] See, for example, Vladimir Gel'man, Sergei Ryzhenkov, and Mikhael Brie (ed.) *Rossiia regionov: Transformatsiia politicheskikh rezhimov* (Moscow: Ves' mir, 2000).

[10] A. Rykhlin "Murtaza vsekh Bashkir," *Itogi*, February 22, 2000, p. 26.

[11] See L. Vakhnina, S. Gannushkina, A. Ossipov, V. Gefter, and O. Cherepova, *Diskriminatsiia po etnicheskomu priznaku i priznaku mesta zhitel'stva v Moskovskom regione. Avgust 1999–Dekabr' 2000 goda* (Moscow: "Zvenya," 2001).

[12] A. Ossipov, *Russian Experience of Ethnic Discrimination: Meskhetians in the Krasnodar Region* (Moscow: "Zvenya," 2000).

regional administrations starting from mid-1989 and are still in place. They include, for example, settlement limitations for newcomers, registration requirements for entrants from the near abroad, the right to deport foreign citizens, and special registration requirements for Russian citizens temporarily visiting the Krasnodar krai.

The economic crisis of August 1998 can be seen as the last significant chapter in center-regional relations during the Yeltsin regime. Even though the 1993 constitution clearly states that "the establishment of customs borders and the imposition of duties, levies, and any other hindrances to the free movement of goods, services, and financial assets is not permitted on the territory of the Russian Federation" (Article 74), within the first few months after the crisis, many regions adopted various measures that clearly undermined the integrity of the common economic space. Regional leaders used the chance to augment their power given the relative financial weakness of the center. It was clear enough what choice regional leaders made between joining the center in a common effort to weather the crisis or struggling on alone. Thus, the president of Yakutiia, Mikhail Nikolaev, decided to change the existing rules of distribution of mined gold between the republic and the center; the president of Kalmykia, Kirsan Iliumzhinov, claimed his republic's right to change its status unilaterally, and many regional leaders established barriers to the free movement of goods, food in particular, beyond the borders of their respective regions.

In 2000 alone, President Putin issued no less than eighteen decrees suspending regional legislation that restricted the free movement of goods, imposed local tariffs, and instituted the licensing of some services. Even though short-lived, these examples clearly demonstrate that regional leaders are ready to adopt extra powers whenever the center demonstrates its economic or political weaknesses.

PUTIN'S REFORMS OF THE RELATIONS BETWEEN THE CENTER AND THE REGIONS

One can argue that the transformation of the relationship between the federal and regional governments was among President Vladimir Putin's top priorities once he came to power. A number of reforms he initiated were directly or indirectly related to this issue. In this context, it is enough to mention the installation of the seven federal districts, the reformation of the Federation Council, and the new principles of budgetary allocations. These reforms initiated a new period in center-regional relations.

The Presidential Representatives and Seven Federal Districts

The introduction of presidential representatives goes back to 1991, when the first such appointments were made. The representatives were usually chosen from among the democratically oriented deputies of the Supreme Soviet who were loyal to President Yeltsin. While presidential representatives were easily appointed to the krais and oblasts, in many cases the republics resisted such initiatives. As a result, by the end of 1991, only sixty-two representatives had been appointed.

During the conflict between President Yeltsin and the Supreme Soviet in 1992–3, many presidential representatives found themselves in a difficult situation as they were forced to make a choice between loyalty to the president and to their former colleagues. Presidential representatives came under attack from different sides: by the State Duma that tried to send its own representatives to the regions and by regional authorities that tried to cut off their funding (presidential representatives were only partly funded by the center). Following the crisis of 1993, the appointment of presidential representatives in the regions was mostly negotiated between the presidential administration and the regions.

Under usual circumstances, presidential representatives played a rather limited role in federal and regional politics. One of the functions that they performed was to supply the presidential administration with information on the regional situation. However, with only meager administrative resources at their disposal, they were forced to rely on regional administrations in their daily work.

In 1997, the central government tried to augment the power of the presidential representatives, granting them the right to coordinate the activities of all federal agencies in the regions. In reality, little changed, if only because they remained largely dependent on regional budgets. While they received their salaries from the center, all other resources (office, technical support, etc.) came from the regions.

As a result, two tendencies could be clearly identified. On the one hand, some presidential representatives established a good working relationship with the local authorities and, in effect, became lobbyists for regional interests at different levels. On the other hand, when there was real competition for power between the presidential representative and the governor, the result was often to pit them against each other in gubernatorial elections.

The Russian Constitution of 1993 legitimates the existence of this political institution. According to Article 83, the president of the Russian Federation "appoints and removes [his] plenipotentiary representatives." However, the constitution does not specify in what particular form this institution exists, what functions presidential representatives perform, or how many representatives need to be appointed. The broad definition of this institution has allowed President Putin to reform it within the existing constitutional framework.

Within the concept of administrative reforms and the restoration of a hierarchical structure of executive authority, seven federal districts were created. Each district is headed by a presidential representative. According to the presidential decree of May 13, 2000, the representatives have a wide range of functions, including the following:

- the coordination of the activities of federal agencies in the regions;
- the coordination of activities between the federal authorities and the regional authorities;
- ensuring the implementation of federal law at the regional level; and
- evaluating the effectiveness of the law enforcement agencies in the regions.

However, it soon emerged that the text was not well prepared and that the decree has some obvious shortcomings. The city of Moscow, for example, was not listed in any of the seven districts. In addition, the presidential representatives were expected to coordinate the work of eight interregional economic associations, which had boundaries that did not correspond with those of the seven regions.[13]

The main goal of Putin's representatives during their first year in office was to restore the hierarchical structure of executive authority. Significantly, the majority had military backgrounds. Only two civilians were appointed: the former CIS minister Leonid Drachevskii (Siberia district) and the former prime minister Sergei Kirienko (Volga district). The latter, until the appointment of Valentina Matvienko as a representative in the Northwest District in 2003, was the only person among the seven representatives who was well known to the public, and he was, therefore, immediately chosen by the press as their unofficial spokesperson. On the basis of his first two years in office, it appears as though Kirienko was chosen to add a civic component to this new political institution. His federal district is often seen as an experimental one in which new political initiatives are launched.[14]

During their first year in office, the presidential representatives were expected to bring regional legislation into line with federal law, and in many cases they managed to do so successfully. According to the

[13] For a detailed analysis of the presidential decree see, for example, Leonid Smirniagin, "Velikolepnaia semerka," *Russian Regional Bulletin* 2, no. 10 (May 22, 2000) pp. 22–5.

[14] See, for example, "Presidentskaia Federatsiia" (May 13, 2002). Available: http://www.niiss.ru/polpred1.shtml. Accessed on May 15, 2002.

deputy director of the presidential administration, Dmitry Kozak, by October 2001, about 4,500 regional laws and decrees had been changed to bring them into line with federal legislation. However, at the same time, about 50,000 local pieces of legislation were still waiting to be changed.[15] Given the haste demanded of them, regional legislators could not fully harmonize regional with federal legislation but often had to make do with textual changes.[16] Beyond that, of course, there remains the fact that "good" laws are, for the most part, badly enforced.

Moreover, in the most difficult cases, such as the Republics of Tatarstan or Bashkortostan, even the process of changing regional legislation is not so easy. In 2000, the leaders of these two republics proposed their own way of harmonizing regional and federal legislation. Rather than making hasty changes, they suggested the formation of reconciliation commissions that would correct both republican and federal legislation. Both leaders managed to negotiate with the presidential representative in the Volga district, Sergei Kirienko, to establish such commissions. The commissions not only recommended changes to be made at the republican level but also summarized suggestions for improvement at the federal level. However, the proposals have been interpreted differently in different governmental institutions. For example, Kirienko strongly supported proposed changes to the Bashkortostan constitution,[17] but they were later contested by the public prosecutor's office of that republic. The president of Bashkortostan, Murtaza Rakhimov, subsequently negotiated with President Putin, reaching an agreement that the republican constitution would be changed by the end of 2002. Even though the necessary changes were finally introduced, the regime itself remains the same; it continuously violates federal legislation, especially in the sphere of the economy, and tries to avoid transparency of rule to the extent that is possible.[18]

The other related problem is that the rule of law is understood differently by federal representatives when it applies to regional legislation at odds with federal law and when it applies to the authoritarian practices adopted by regional leaders. While federal representatives tend to

---

[15] R. S. Boldyreva, "Parlamentskie slushaniia o kontseptsii razvitiia federativnykh otnoshenii," *Sovet Federatsii i konstitutsionnye protsessy v sovremennoi Rossii. Biulleten' Instituta prava i publichnoi politiki,'* vyp. 2 (December 2001). Available: http://www.ilpp.ru/bulletin/dec2001.

[16] Tatiana Vasil'eva, "Razreshenie pravovykh kollizii mezhdu Federatsiei i sub"ektami Federatsii" *Konstitutsionnoe pravo: Vostochnoevropeiskoe obozrenie*, no. 1 (2002), pp. 105–18.

[17] *Vremya novostei*, January 24, 2001.

[18] See, for example, *Russian Regional Report*, May 21, 2003. Available: http://www.isn.ethz.ch/researchpub/publihouse/rrr/docs/rrr030521.pdf. Accessed on May 24, 2003.

accept the need for some minimal compromise in the former area, they seem to ignore almost totally the latter problem. It would appear that some informal compromise was achieved between presidential representatives and regional leaders stipulating that if regional legislation were changed in accordance with federal demands, then interference in internal regional affairs would be kept to a minimum. Mikhail Afanas'ev has emphasized an interesting tendency. With the appointment of federal representatives whose main task is to enforce the rule of law in the regions, the authoritarian tendencies in the Russian regions actually have grown stronger rather than weaker.

This trend can be illustrated by an examination of the policies recently adopted by the regional regimes toward local self-government. According to the Russian Constitution (Article 12), local self-government is autonomous. Federal legislation grants urban and rural settlements the right to exercise a measure of self-rule in local affairs, but regional authorities have been encroaching on those principles. This authoritarian tendency was clearly affirmed by the Krasnodar governor, Aleksandr Tkachev, who claimed that the "hierarchical structure of executive authority should continue down to the level of local self-government."[19] The settlement-based model of local self-government has been abolished in the Krasnoiarsk krai and Tiumen oblast, and the governors of the Yakutiia, Kursk, and Riazan oblasts have appointed their representatives to supervise the raions, or subregional territorial units.[20]

The development of such authoritarian policies in the constituent units puts in doubt the possibility of creating a democratic federation as such. As Robert Dahl fairly points out, one of the requirements of a federal democratic system is that all units of the federation be democratic and the rights of individuals be respected.[21] However, political regimes in some Russian regions are still closer to one or another form of authoritarianism than to democracy.

The first reaction among regional political leaders to the establishment of the seven new federal districts was great uncertainty. There were many fears among regional elites that their power would be eroded, that the number of federal units would be reduced from eighty-nine to seven, and that the regional governors would be appointed by the

---

[19] "Vozmozhnosti federal'nogo tsentra sovsem neveliki," *Russian Regional Bulletin* 4, no 2 (January 28, 2002).

[20] Mikhail Afanas'ev, "Problemy Rossiiskogo federalisma i federativnaia politika vtorogo presidenta. Promezhutochnye itogi" (2002), p. 16. Available: www.ilpp.ru/projects/Laws/. Accessed on June 6, 2002.

[21] Robert A. Dahl, *Democracy, Liberty and Equality* (Oslo: Norwegian University Press, 1986), pp. 114–26.

center. Presidential representatives successfully exploited those fears at the early stages of their work.

One of the ways in which presidential representatives exert a measure of power over the regional elites has been to involve themselves in gubernatorial elections. To a certain extent, all seven representatives actively interfered in regional elections. In some cases, as in the Ingushetia presidential election of 2002, they managed to elect their candidate. However, this was not always the case. One of the best illustrations of the limited resources that the presidential representatives possess in determining regional election results comes from the Primorskii krai, where Gennadii Apanasenko, who was strongly supported by the office of the presidential representative for the Far East and by Konstantin Pulikovskii personally, lost the gubernatorial elections to Sergei Dar'kin', whose victory was unexpected.[22]

Indeed, the governors have set aside their fears, and presidential representatives need to use other means to achieve their goals. Because their financial resources remain rather limited, they have been left with no choice except to use all administrative resources to increase their power. One result has been the consolidation of the presidential administration – merging three departments, including that responsible for the regions. On the one hand, this move could be seen as an achievement for the presidential representatives because they not only managed to lobby successfully for important changes in the presidential administration but also gained some additional staff positions in their respective offices due to the restructuring of the head office. On the other hand, with this reorganization, their subordinate position has become more pronounced, and all presidential representatives find themselves directly responsible to the head of the presidential administration.

Even though the presidential representatives have by now become an integral part of Russian political life, the role of this institution as such remains unclear. Their functions are still uncertain, as the major document that regulates their work is the founding presidential decree which, as mentioned previously, contains contradictions and defines only basic functions. It would be difficult for this institution to continue for a long time in its present form. As many Russian politicians justly state, it should move in one direction or another: It should either be abolished, or its powers should be fully clarified. According to the head of the parliamentary group Regiony Rossii, Oleg Morozov, "Today the problem is to find further functions that the presidential representatives

---

[22] See, for example, Kirill Rogov, "Primorskii trend: Putinskaia gosudarstvennost' poterpela lokal'noe porazhenie" (2001). Available: http://www.polit.ru/documents/420154.html. Accessed on January 15, 2002.

could perform. The alternative is either clearly to define their functions (better by federal law than by presidential decree) or to leave this institution alone to start creating problems for itself."[23]

Relations between presidential representatives and the federal government do not always run smoothly if only because presidential representatives, whether on purpose or not, inevitably interfere in the regular functioning of the federal government. One of the areas in which the presidential representatives want to play a greater role is economics, and this aspiration is often aired quite openly. For example, the former presidential representative in the Northwest District, Viktor Cherkessov, asserts that "in the near future, the role of the presidential representatives in the economic processes will be to serve as anti-crisis managers – in the broad sense of this term."[24] The presidential representatives have quite often stated on different occasions that they want to play a greater role in interbudgetary relations.

The deputy head of the State Duma Budget and Taxation Committee, Mikhail Zadornov, has adopted a contrary position, insisting that the "participation of the federal districts in the distribution of the budgetary funds among federal units is contrary to the constitution, which stipulates that every level enjoys budgetary autonomy."[25]

Thus, there are not many options regarding the future direction of this institution. President Putin mentioned one of them as a task for the coming period: to perform some of the federal functions (including the supervision of financial outlays and federal appointments) at the regional level.[26] However, such a development would mean the further centralization of what is, at least formally, a federal state. Even this scenario would require a clear definition of functions and competencies.

Federal representatives tend to see their future in the further increase of their powers. For example, according to the report of the Center for Strategic Studies of the Volga Federal District, federal representatives should possess not only their current political and administrative resources, but should also enjoy the right to use different legal forms of coercion, that is, to have regional law enforcement agencies subordinate to them.[27] The demand for more power is typical of any political institution that does not have clearly stated functions. However, too much power allotted to the federal representatives could subvert the

[23] *Profil*, May 13, 2002.
[24] Ibid.
[25] Ibid.
[26] *Poslanie presidenta*, pp. 19–20.
[27] "Polnomochiia, funktsii i predmety vedeniia v strategicheskoi perspektive razvitiia gosudarstvennosti," *Doklad tsentra strategicheskikh isledovanii Privolzhskogo federal'nogo okruga*, Nizhnii Novgorod-Moskva, 2002, p. 36.

balance between the center and the regions and, in the end, might well weaken the federal center by again creating inflated regions with their own budgets, regulations, and law enforcement agencies.

The other option that still exists is that the president himself will liquidate this political institution, regarding it as a temporary arrangement to achieve concrete goals. This scenario seems the least likely to be implemented. Whereas after a year in office, Sergei Kirienko publicly stated that this political institution should be subject to radical reorganization once its initial goals were achieved, he now claims that the federal representatives should be seen as a permanent institution.

The last and most probable scenario is to maintain the formal status quo while allowing this institution gradually to lose much of its significance in center-regional relations.

The changes in regional legislation achieved in recent years are usually regarded as a measure of the success of the seven presidential representatives. Indeed, there is no doubt that many of the major contradictions between federal and regional legislation have become a thing of the past. The question remains, however, whether this is really the achievement of the presidential representatives or whether this is the result of the broader trends in center-regional relations. One cannot but agree with the deputy of the State Duma, Vladimir Ryzhkov, who has argued that the credit for bringing regional law into line with the federal legislation belongs not only to the presidential representatives but also to "the Public Prosecutors' Office and the Ministry of Justice and even more to the common fear that the new president inspired in the regional leaders."[28]

Even though President Putin stated that "from the organizational point of view the formation of the federal districts has been completed,"[29] one may argue that the institution of presidential representatives in its current form is no more than temporary. It has a growing bureaucratic apparatus that, in fact, constitutes an additional administrative level. But as this expanding apparatus inevitably tries to increase its power by putting claim to additional, primarily financial, resources, it will come into collision with the interests of a central government jealous of potential rivals. In such a clash of bureaucracies, the presidential representatives, lacking sufficient financial resources, would be at a disadvantage. Furthermore, while the administrative resources at their disposal are today not ineffective (elections are a different issue), once the institution of presidential representatives becomes subject to routine, regional leaders will also learn how to deal with it successfully.

[28] V. Ryzhkov, "Vsplytie pokazhet," *Profil*, May 13, 2002.
[29] *Poslanie presidenta*, p. 19.

In so far as their functions are not clearly defined (there is still no relevant federal law, leaving the presidential representatives to operate in accord with the presidential decree of May 13, 2000), there is huge diversity in the way that the presidential representatives interpret their mandate. Some practices even contradict one other. For example, Leonid Drachevskii tries to work closely with the interregional economic association "Sibirskoe soglashenie" (even though not all the geographic units in this association are within the Siberian federal district). In contrast, Petr Latyshev of the Ural federal district sees the interregional economic association Bolshoi Ural, headed by Sverdlovsk Governor Eduard Rossel, as a threat to his political power. There are many such illustrations of the fact that this political institution is too dependent on the individual office holders and therefore run not according to fixed legal norms. As a member of the Federation Council, Ramazan Abdulatipov, colorfully stated, "The presidential representatives are trying to deal with everything that moves, flies and crawls without really knowing very well where it is that they should be crawling, flying and moving – or why."[30]

While the center claims that the federal districts have brought it closer to the regions, the reality is more complicated. On the contrary, one could argue that the federal districts have given the center a chance to distance itself from the regions. The reasoning behind this argument is that all major decisions are still made in Moscow, while the regional component in these decisions has been decreasing dramatically as the "periphery" is now separated from Moscow by an additional layer of bureaucracy. One may agree with Mikhail Afanas'ev's view of the institution of presidential representatives as "a new bureaucratic level that has been established, but it is not a publicly recognized political institution."[31] According to Abdulatipov, the political institution of the seven federal districts has become very bulky and "has begun working for itself, forming a barrier between the president and the regional leaders."[32] The Kozak Commission, the aim of which is to provide for a new redistribution of power among various levels, almost ignored the federal districts as a specific level of power.[33]

Therefore, one may still ask the questions that were asked when the federal districts were first created: Is there a real justification for such a major reform from the cost-effective point of view? Could the same goals be attained differently – through the restoration of a hierarchical

---

[30] *Nasha vlast'. Dela i litsa*, no. 6, 2002, p. 13.
[31] Mikhail Afanas'ev, "Problemy rossiiskogo federalizma," p. 14.
[32] *Nasha vlast'*.
[33] *Nezavisimaia gazeta*, July 30, 2002.

structure of executive authority and the reinforcement of federal power at the center?

The Federation Council – A Party of the Regions?

The Federation Council (FC) – the upper chamber of the Russian parliament – is formed by "two representatives from each component of the Russian Federation": one from the local representative body and one from the local executive (Article 95). The FC plays a rather limited but important role in the policy-making process that is determined by the Russian Constitution. Whereas the lower chamber, the State Duma, makes laws, the concern of the Federation Council is only to examine the drafts already adopted by the State Duma and to approve or reject them (Articles 105 and 106). The Federation Council and its members ("senators") have the right of legislative initiative (Article 104), that is, to submit draft laws to the State Duma, but the FC does not participate in the later stages of the drafting process. Senators have only limited power in deciding issues of the federal budget, even though it is of such major importance for the development of the regions and for their relations with the center.

The initial idea in the early 1990s had been to elect two representatives to the Federation Council from each region. In the wake of the political crisis in 1993, it became clear that President Yeltsin would not support this idea. Whereas his famous decree No. 1400 (September 21, 1993) declared that the new State Duma should be elected, this principle was not applied to the upper chamber. It was then briefly assumed that the heads of the regional executive and legislative authorities would form the upper chamber. At that time, the heads of the regional executive power were presidential appointees. After the dissolution of the Supreme Soviet of the Russian Federation in October 1993, most but not all regional soviets were also dissolved. The idea of forming the upper chamber from appointed governors and from those heads of the regional soviets that had not been dissolved was unacceptable both to the federal center and to the public. It was therefore decided that for a transitional period the FC would be made up of two popularly elected representatives from each unit of the federation.[34]

After a long struggle between the presidential administration, the State Duma, the elected Federation Council and the regional leaders, a new federal law was adopted in 1995, "On the Procedure for Forming the

---

[34] See, for example, Mikhail Afanas'ev, "Izmeneniia v sisteme politicheskogo predstavitel'stva interesov sub"ektov federatsii." Available: http://www.ilpp.ru/projects/Laws/. Accessed on June 6, 2002.

Federation Council of the Federal Assembly of the Russian Federation." According to this law, the Federation Council was to be constituted from the heads of the regional executive and legislative authorities. Thus, members of the FC would have a dual mandate: first as heads of their respective regions and second as members of the upper chamber. In this form, it was assumed that the FC could possibly act as a counterweight to the State Duma, where President Yeltsin had less control. To ensure that the FC would not become too powerful, it was decided that its members should meet for only a few days a month.

In January 1996, the newly formed Federation Council started its first term of office. Since 1997 all heads of regional executive bodies have been elected and, therefore, are more independent of the center than their predecessors. The FC thus had a chance to change its role in the decision-making process and become a powerful and independent political institution.

However, until the crisis of August 17, 1998, the FC remained almost invisible to the population. Its activities were hardly covered by the national press, whereas those of the State Duma were always under scrutiny, and its deputies were involved in a variety of scandals. Because the FC met for only short periods, its bureaucratic apparatus played a key role in the decision-making process. Generally the senators themselves voted for or against a given issue in line with the recommendations of the apparatus. They often voted by mail because it was usually difficult to ensure a quorum. Its members regarded the upper chamber mostly as a tool for lobbying on behalf of regional interests. The under-use of legislative initiative by the members of the FC found graphic expression in the fact that only about 7 percent of draft laws initiated by the upper chamber and its members in 1994–8 were adopted as federal laws.[35]

With the deep economic and political crisis that followed in the wake of August 17, 1998, the center lost some of its power over the regional leaders. Deprived of sufficient financial resources, the center has difficulties in playing its traditional "carrot and stick" game. The relative weakness of the center almost immediately affected the position of the Federation Council. The FC thus considerably augmented its chances of becoming an independent political actor.

One of the first signs of its changing role in policy making was the new approach to the formulation of the federal budget. Previously, the

---

[35] V. M. Syrykh, "Sovershenstvovanie mekhanisma soglasovaniia interesov Rossiiskoi Federatsii i ee sub"ektov v protsesse podgotovki i priniatiia federal'nykh zakonov," *Zakonodatel'nye (predstavitel'nye) organy vlasty sub"ektov Rossiiskoi Federatsii. Praktika. Mneniia. Problemy,* vyp. 2 (1999), p. 7.

FC entered the budget discussions only after the draft budget law had passed all three readings in the State Duma. Starting with the 1999 budget, members of the FC began to work on the draft budget when it was still in the State Duma. For the 2000 budget, the reconciliation committee was formed even before the first reading in the State Duma, and since then this practice has become routine. Therefore, instead of approving or rejecting what the State Duma draws up, the FC takes part in the budget process almost from the beginning. It is still true, of course, that this aspect of the FC's activities is not typical; members generally continue to see themselves as responsible for their respective regions not as members of a unified political institution. Thus, the FC serves primarily as an increasingly strong lobby for local interests, something like a club of regional leaders. Nevertheless, the FC's activism in budgetary matters can be seen as a mark of its increasing influence as a coherent institution.

Another illustration of the rapidly changing role of the FC in the policy-making process was the so-called Skuratov case, in early April 1999, when it acted precisely as a unified political institution with its own political will. According to the Russian Constitution (Article 129), "the procurator-general of the Russian Federation is appointed to, and released from, that office by the Federation Council on the submission of the president of the Russian Federation." The approval or dismissal of the procurator-general by the FC has not usually involved an open confrontation with the president (even though the process of approval has never been an easy one). The Skuratov case was different. Three times the FC refused to ratify the president's request for Skuratov's dismissal. As several senators pointed out, their voting for Yurii Skuratov did not mean that they supported him as a person but that they wanted to reserve their constitutional right to make such an important decision (in the sphere of their competence) independently and without pressure.

However, such political actions have remained rather rare for the FC, which so far has not turned into a genuine regional force. One of the reasons has been the lack of effective political leadership in the FC. The governor of the Orel region, Yegor Stroev, who was the chairman of the FC from 1996 to 2001, did not see that institution as an actor that should involve itself as a collective body in open political battle. Rather, regional leaders sought to represent regional interests through other political institutions including so-called gubernatorial blocs. Participating in the electoral process, the governors sought to increase their representation at the federal level and especially in the main law-making institution, the State Duma.

The most recent illustration of the FC acting as a more or less unified political institution came in 2000 with its role in adopting Putin's FC reforms and his amendments to the laws, "On the General Principles of the Organization of Local Self-Government in the Russian Federation" and "On the General Principles of the Organization of the Legislative (Representative) and Executive Organs of the State Power in the Constituent Regions of the Russian Federation." President Putin suggested that in the future, the FC should be selected according to principles compatible with his attempts to restore a hierarchical structure of executive authority. Along with the introduction of the seven federal districts, this was one of the first reforms he initiated to strengthen the power structure and its manageability by the central government.

The major goal of his new legislation was to exclude the top-level regional leaders (primarily, the governors) from the FC and to man it with full-time, but subordinate, representatives from the regions. Henceforth, senators were to be nominated by the regional governors and legislators.

It is no surprise that regional leaders did not fully support the presidential initiatives as they sought to protect their own power, nor that they lobbied for some significant amendments. Acting as a unified political institution, the FC managed to negotiate some important compromises.[36] For example, the age requirement for members of the FC (at least thirty years old), which had been set aside by the State Duma, was restored; with the support of the State Duma, regional leaders were granted the right to recall their appointed representatives; the procedure to appoint the governors' representatives was settled by compromise (regional assemblies now need two-thirds of their members to vote down a governor's nominee). Moreover, in return for granting the president the right to dismiss the heads of regional executive bodies, the governors gained the same right vis-à-vis the heads of municipal units.

Despite their loss of status as FC members and despite the president's right to dismiss governors who systematically violate federal norms, regional leaders continue to lobby for their right to be reelected to executive office in their own regions. This right was limited by the federal law "On the General Principles of the Organization of the Legislative (Representative) and Executive Organs of the State Power in the Constituent Regions of the Russian Federation." According to this law, governors could not hold office for more than two consecutive terms. If this

---

[36] It is important to mention that the FC preferred not to use its right to veto the draft law but to use only reconciliation procedures.

law were to be fully applied, a vast majority of governors, including Tatarstan president Mintimer Shaimiev, Sverdlovsk governor Eduard Rossel, and Moscow mayor Yurii Luzhkov, could not be reelected. The governors' efforts enjoyed a measure of success when in February 2001, the State Duma adopted an amendment to the same law (popularly known as the "Boos amendment" because it was introduced by the pro-Luzhkov Duma deputy Georgii Boos). According to this amendment, the time served in office before October 1999 (when the federal law was adopted) was not to be counted, and the two terms in question were to be measured from the date when the law was adopted. Because of this amendment, sixty-nine regional leaders won the right to partici-pate in the elections and to hold office for a third and even for a fourth consecutive term.

The following spring, Deputy Boris Nadezhdin suggested another amendment that would have severely limited the number of governors with the right to be reelected for third and fourth terms, but the FC ve-toed the "Nadezhdin amendment." After the Yakutiia elections, when the Central Election Commission made a decision that former Yakutiia president Mikhail Nikolaev did not have the right to run again for the presidency of the region, this issue was brought before the Constitu-tional Court on appeal. The appeal was initiated by Yakutiia and later also supported by Tatarstan. Some of the State Duma deputies likewise insisted that the Boos amendment was unconstitutional in so far as it violated the principle of the ability to replace regional leaders.

It was clear from the beginning that the issue was political rather than legal and would be decided by power politics. It took the Constitu-tional Court three months to reach a decision because there was no unity among the judges. The court concurred with the opinion of President Putin, who stated that it should be up to the regional electorate to decide who should be the head of the region. On July 9, 2002, the Constitutional Court divided the constituent units of the federation into two groups: those where the regional charters and constitutions stipulate a two-term limit and those where there is no such stipulation. For the first group, it is up to regional legislatures to decide how to calculate the term limits; for the second group, all terms in office before October 1999 were to be ignored.

This was exactly the decision that regional leaders had been lobby-ing for since the adoption of the law. Freed of formal prohibition from the center, the regional leaders could manage the elections. It should be mentioned that the role of regional assemblies in dealing with the issue of term limits increased – it is with them that the governors need to negotiate charter (constitutional) changes. Some regional leaders have already done this, for example in the Bashkortostan and the Tomsk regional assemblies, where the current regional leaders won the right to run for reelection.[37]

Thus, one could agree with Sergei Markedonov that the Constitutional Court decision that allowed governors to run for a third term in office could be seen as a dividing line between two periods in the Putin era – "the period of strengthening [central] authority [*vertikal vlasti*] and the 'post-vertical' period."[38]

It can be argued that the governors' early fears, caused by Putin's reforms, including the changes in the FC, are gone, and they have managed to gain compensation for their withdrawal from the federal political arena. Some of them, such as Khabarovsk governor Viktor Ishaev, who has headed the region since 1991, but whose first term in office started officially only in 2000, has in effect, gained the right to be a governor for life. The luckiest of all seems to be Tomsk governor Viktor Kress, whose first term officially started only in 2003. This net result can be regarded as a real setback for the center, which initiated large-scale federal reforms but did not manage to see its own initiatives through to a successful conclusion.

Public opinion has split with regard to the presidential initiatives, especially those involving the composition of the FC. While there is agreement that the former process of selection was undemocratic, the new principle does not have such unified support for exactly the same reason. Its opponents, including the head of the State Duma Committee on Federal Issues and on Regional Policy, Leonid Ivanchenko, insist that the members of the Federation Council should be elected by public vote. This is the only way, he argues, to ensure that the members of the upper chamber have the legitimacy required if they are to play a key role in the policy-making process. As Mikhail Afanas'ev fairly pointed out, the new principle has three important negative consequences. First, there is a certain disparity between the constitutional role of the FC and the new mode of its selection. Second, the part played by the FC does not strengthen the Russian state as such. In particular, the appointment of members of the FC by the regional executive authorities without public elections, and possibly without public discussion, may broaden the basis for corruption and administrative influence. Third, the federal center

---

[37] See, for example, "Regional'nye elity v srochnom poriadke opredeliaiutsia so stavkami na gubernatorskikh vyborakh" (2002). Available: http://www.strana.ru/print/152322.html. Accessed on July 10, 2002.

[38] Sergei Markedonov, "Chechnya in the Context of Russian Federalism," *Russian Regional Report*, May 7, 2003. Available: http://www.isn.ethz.ch/researchpub/publihouse/rrr/docs/rrr030507.pdf. Accessed on May 24, 2003.

has too much influence on the appointment process, in many cases, simply imposing its own candidates.[39] One of the best illustrations of this process is the appointment of Yurii Volkov as senator from the Republic of Komi, representing former governor Yurii Spiridonov.[40] Volkov never lived in Komi and never worked with the republican authorities there.

Governors have secured for themselves the right to meet with the president on a regular basis by creating a new political institution – the State Council. It is, in fact, a club of regional leaders that has no place in the formal constitutional structure to control or even seriously influence the decision-making process. It can be seen as an advisory institution, some kind of moral compensation to regional leaders for their dismissal from the FC. The first meetings of the State Council and the agenda of its presidium meetings confirm this conclusion.[41]

Putin's initiatives in 2000 changed the entire image of the Federation Council and its members. Their relations with the regions they represent have become complicated. On the one hand, they should represent regional interests in the upper chamber, and regional authorities have a right to recall their respective representatives if their work contradicts regional interests. (However, this procedure is rather complicated and one can assume that it will not be used very often.[42]) On the other hand, the center now has greater administrative resources to influence the activities of the FC because its members are in many aspects more dependent than their predecessors on the center. (Work in the FC on a professional basis means having to find accommodation in Moscow, new jobs for family members, and so on.)

The collective portrait of the newly formed FC is rather interesting but not surprising. More than 50 percent of its members are people who are Moscow residents (about eighty deputies). St. Petersburg is also well represented (seven deputies were born in St. Petersburg; twenty graduated from St. Petersburg's institutions of higher learning; twelve formerly worked in St. Petersburg).[43] Former regional leaders are the single largest group among the non-Muscovites. For example, both former leaders of the Kaluga region (Viktor Kolesnikov and Vitalii Sydarenkov) have opted to hold on to their positions as senators rather than to seek local office. Some governors secured their seats in the FC by withdrawing their names from regional elections, throwing their support to favored candidates.

---

[39] Mikhail Afanas'ev, "Izmeneniia v sisteme," pp. 6–8.

[40] See, Yuri Shabaev "Novyi senator ot Komi – Peterburgskii chekist," *Russian Regional Bulletin* 3, no. 9 (May 7, 2001). pp. 4–5.

[41] See, for example, Mikhail Afanas'ev, "Izmeneniia v sisteme," pp. 8–11.

[42] Despite a very short term in the office, one of the newly appointed members of the FC was already dismissed on the governor's initiative.

[43] *Izvestiia*, January 30, 2002; *Vlast'*, February 26, 2002.

The internal structure of the FC has also changed. During the transition period a new group named "Federatsiia" (Federation) was formed. Its main goal is to support President Putin and his initiatives in the upper chamber. The very fact that such a group was created is ground breaking for the FC. The internal regulations of the upper chamber do not allow for the formation of factions. The FC is thus envisaged as a political institution that is above ideological disagreements. The new group eschews the status of a faction. As Valerii Goregliad, one of its founding fathers and now the first vice-speaker of the FC claims, one of its objectives is "to reconcile different ideological opponents, to prevent the formation of factions and groups."[44] In practice, however, this group plays a role similar to that characteristic of pro-presidential factions and groups in the State Duma. It can hardly be seen as a force for reconciliation because the group has, in fact, divided the upper chamber into two parts – those who are members of the Federatsiia (and support the president) and those who are not. Moreover, whereas the group originally included only thirty-five members of the upper chamber, within a mere two months it numbered 100, thus providing Federatsiia with a majority in the FC. If it adopts the principle of voting as a bloc, then this group, formed on the basis of personal loyalty to the president, will be able to dictate the law-making process in the upper chamber.

One of the first initiatives undertaken by the newly formed Federation Council, also initiated and supported by Federatsiia, was the adoption of new internal regulations. These changes involve the following very important areas: the selection procedures for the committees and commissions, the division of functions between these committees and commissions, the FC's rules of procedures, and the role of the upper chamber in the legislative process. As the new regulations also readopted the principle prohibiting factions in the upper chamber, one paradoxical result was to put an end to Federatsiia. According to Valerii Goregliad, the group has been transforming itself into a club of deputies with similar interests.[45] However, one may assume that the changes successfully made in the FC regulations were one of the new group's key tasks because without them the group as a whole or its individual members would have found it much more difficult to play the key role in the law-making process.[46]

[44] *Nezavisimaia gazeta,* April 27, 2001.

[45] Ye. V. Pershin and A. N. Dement'ev, "O nekotorykh novellakh tret'ei redaktsii reglamenta soveta federatsii," *Sovet federatsii i konstitutsionnye protsessy v sovremennoi Rossii. Bulleten' instituta prava i publichnoi politiki,'* vyp. 6 (April 2002). Available: http://www.ilpp.ru/bulletin/apr2002. Accessed on May 15, 2002.

[46] See, for example, Pavel Isaev, "Federatsiia opredelilas' s zakonodatel'nymi prioritetami," *Russian Regional Bulletin* 3, no. 7 (April 9, 2001). pp. 3–4.

The new regulations increased the number of committees (from eleven to sixteen) and the commissions working on a permanent basis (from one to seven).[47] As a result, about two-thirds of the senators hold membership in one or another of these bodies. However, to maintain a measure of equity, it was decided that only one of the two representatives of a given regional unit could be selected for such positions.[48] It was also decided that the FC should meet once a week. According to the speaker, Sergei Mironov, the time has come for the upper chamber to play a greater role in the law-making process.

No sooner had President Putin initiated the creation of the State Council manned by the governors, than the FC announced in May 2002 the formation of a new consultative organ: "The Council on Cooperation with the Legislative Organs of State Power in the Constituent Units of the Russian Federation," which provides a forum for the heads of regional legislatures. Some observers soon called this newly created institution the State Council II. The founding fathers of the new Council (Sergei Mironov, Aleksandr Torshin, and Valerii Goregliad) envisage it as playing a major role in the coordination of the law-making process; in assistance to the regional legislatures in their work on local laws; and in the harmonization of federal and regional legislation.[49]

The working of the newly created structures is still unclear. On the one hand, it is a positive sign that the influence of the FC's apparatus should now decrease. But it is also clear that all the new institutions have been initiated with a single goal in mind – to ensure that presidential initiatives win enough support to pass through the second chamber with only minor changes. If these goals are achieved, one can assume that the role of the FC would regress, serving merely as some kind of counterweight to the State Duma and to the regional elites with no unique and distinctive political face. It is important to stress that public opinion polls confirm this tendency: according to a January 20, 2002, survey, only 30 percent of the public knew what the FC was doing; only 30 percent concurred with the proposition that the FC was an influential political force; and only 10 percent knew how the FC was constituted.[50] The relatively influential role enjoyed at certain stages by the FC may now have become a thing of the past. At the moment, it is barely visible as a political institution that represents regional interests.

[47] However, in the beginning of 2003, Sergei Mironov suggested changing the FC's structure again by decreasing the number of commissions and committees to minimize duplication of their work (see, for example, *Nezavisimaia gazeta*, January 24, 2003).

[48] Ye. V. Pershin and A. N. Dement'ev, "O nekotorykh novellakh."

[49] Svetlana Mikhailova, "Pri verkhnei palate sozdan konsul'tativnyi organ dlia raboty s regionamy," *Russian Regional Bulletin* 4, no. 10 (May 27, 2002). pp. 3–5.

[50] *Profil*, February 4, 2002, p. 19.

Most of those tendencies in the development of the FC were clearly articulated at the international seminar held in the autumn of 2002, "The Constitutional Status of the Upper Chambers of the Parliaments": the highly important status of the upper chamber as against its limited authority; the senators' dependence on the regional authorities whom they represent ("the imperative mandate") as against their desire to become independent and influential political players on the federal level; the distinctive and clear role of the Federation Council in the law-making process as against its low-level commitment in actuality to this process.[51] Therefore, the reform of the FC has not managed to overcome the well-known shortcomings of this political institution.

THE ASYMMETRY OF RUSSIAN FEDERALISM

In a country with rich and strong internal diversity (cultural, ethnic, religious, and historical), it was always probable that an asymmetrical model of federation would be adopted. However, as the case of the Russian Federation illustrates, an asymmetrical federal structure does not remove the issue of cleavages between the center and the regions from the political agenda. Moreover, the less privileged constituent units (in the Russian case, the oblasts and krais) will always insist on the enhancement of their status, while the more privileged ones (the republics) will do their utmost to preserve their "special" position, defending it on ethnic or historical grounds. This was clarified, for example, by the president of the Republic of Tatarstan, Mintimer Shaimiev, in his article published in *Respublika Tatarstan* (February 1995). He argued that the lower-level "regions might and should have the same economic rights as those of the republics," but, at the same time, he argued that the latter had to retain their historical privileges.[52] Mordovia's president Nikolai Merkushkin shares such an approach, stressing that the asymmetrical nature of the federation is quite logical and, therefore, "full equalization of the status of the constituent units in the Russian case is unacceptable."[53]

There are different views on whether the formation of an asymmetrical federation in Russia was unavoidable. One could argue that such a structure was the only way to keep the country together. In other

---

[51] See, for example, Leonid Smirniagin, "Mezhdunarodnyi seminar 'Konstitutsionnyi status verkhnikh palat parlamentov,'" *Russian Regional Bulletin* 4, no. 20 (2002), pp. 19–22.

[52] M. Shaimiev, "Dogovor Tatarstana s Rossiei – na puti k podlinnoi federatsii," in *Suverennii Tatarstan* (Moskva: "INSAN,"1997), p. 60.

[53] "Asimmetrichnaia federatsiia – eto real'naia neobkhodimost'," *Russian Regional Bulletin* 1, no. 14 (1999), p. 15.

words, asymmetry was a forced response to the "parade of sovereignty" of the early 1990s. According to this argument, if President Yeltsin had not signed bilateral treaties with the various republics (especially with Tatarstan, where only one-third of the population supported the new Russian Constitution), the political scenario might have been completely different.

Opponents of this argument make some strong points. They insist that the asymmetrical federation was less a forced response than a tactic to achieve certain specific political goals. In 1990, it was Boris Yeltsin himself who encouraged the regions "to take as much sovereignty as they can swallow" and initiated the "parade of sovereignty." In yielding to the republics – primarily, Tatarstan, Bashkortostan, and Chechnya – Yeltsin was seeking their support in his power struggle with the Soviet government and personally with Mikhail Gorbachev. Once the Pandora's box was opened, it was impossible to close it again. Even the oblasts and krais then began to put forward claims to sovereignty and equal rights with the republics (Sverdlovsk region, for example, declared itself to be the Urals Republic in 1993). Thus, the asymmetrical federation resulted primarily from a chain of ad hoc decisions.

Moreover, the relations between the center and regions were developing within a very ill-defined framework – apart from the constitutional legacy from the Soviet period and a few presidential decrees, there were almost no established laws regulating federative issues. One of the basic documents to regulate federative relations – the federal law "On the General Principles of Organization of the Legislative (Representative) and Executive Organs of the State Power in the Constituent Regions of the Russian Federation" – was adopted in October 1999 after (not before) the regional elections were over and the executive and legislative power in the regions had already been institutionalized.

The asymmetrical principle supposes inequality not only in the institutional structure but also at the symbolic level. Thus, for example, according to Article 5 of the Russian Constitution, the republics are states with their own constitutions, whereas the status of the krais and oblasts is regulated by charters. The articles on republican sovereignty and the superiority of republican vis-à-vis federal legislation were removed from republican constitutions only after President Putin initiated his federal reforms and the Constitutional Court declared such principles unconstitutional.[54]

While the political elites in the republics enjoy great symbolic status (being presidents, prime ministers, ministers and so forth), the equivalent elites in the oblasts and krais have grounds for complaint, especially

---

[54] *Kommersant*, July 8, 2000.

when we compare territorially small and economically weak republics with large and economically well-established oblasts and krais. At another level, the loyalty of the regions toward the center depends on the restoration of its positive image among both the regional population at large and also among the regional elites. However, during their struggle with the center for greater power, the regional leaders systematically undermined that positive image. In their rhetoric, it was always the center that was responsible for the regional economic crisis and its social consequences.

Loyalty also supposes the establishment of some collective identity. The latter is not an easy task to achieve for a number of reasons, especially economic. Significantly higher transportation costs, for example, make it difficult for people from remote regions even to travel to their own capital. As a result, new generations are growing up having neither the experience nor even the opportunity of a visit to Moscow or to the European part of the Russian Federation. Federal representatives are trying to create an identity with and loyalty to Russia as a state and society. For this reason federal representatives have been establishing information agencies, newspapers, and television programs in the regions, but without any real success in achieving the goal of creating a common sociocultural space.

All in all, an asymmetrical federation involves endless complexities. While it allows for the accommodation of diverse interests especially in multicultural and deeply divided societies, it can also be seen as a temporary solution and merely a step toward further changes in the political and territorial structure of the state either toward confederation, toward the establishment of new state(s) by some of the constituent units, or toward a major renewal of centralization.

President Putin's federal reform seems to fit the latter scenario. Charles D. Tarlton appears to be correct in his conclusion that the possibility of conflict between the center and the regions would be greater when "the policies pursued and the conditions demanded by a single component state are importantly foreign to those of the overall system."[55]

CONCLUSION

The outcome of the federal reforms initiated by President Putin soon after his inauguration should be seen through the prism of the relations between the center and the regions developed during Yeltsin's presidency.

[55] Charles D. Tarlton, "Symmetry and Asymmetry as Elements of Federalism: A Theoretical Speculation," *Journal of Politics* 27 (1965), p. 71.

By the end of Yeltsin's tenure, the personal power of regional leaders was rapidly increasing; the rule of law on the entire territory of the Russian Federation was notable primarily by its absence, and the ability of the center to control the political and economic situation in the regions was considerably limited.

From the start, President Putin sought to strengthen the hierarchical principle and the central government, reducing the power of regional leaders who, at the time, were often called "regional barons." Although politicians and political analysts expected some changes after the new president came to power, they did not foresee the purposefulness of the reforms. The suddenness of the reform announcement took regional leaders by surprise. Speeding up the reforms (starting with the presidential decrees on legislative changes in some regions and republics, followed by the establishment of the seven federal districts, the reform of the Federation Council, and changes in the laws regarding the center-regional relations) allowed the center to mobilize its political and administrative resources in a concerted effort to push through the changes. The effect of suddenness combined with the relative weakness of the political institutions through which regional leaders could act collectively (the FC had then only just started working as a unified political institution) and the long tradition of negotiating with the center independently of each other did not give those leaders a real chance to unite effectively in opposition to the reforms. The strategy chosen by President Putin allowed him to achieve quick results.

The seven federal districts were created with limited opposition from the regional leaders. In some regions, the transformation of laws related to federal issues was initiated soon after the reforms started. Once the first shock was over, however, the regional leaders started their negotiations with the center in an effort to retain some of their power. One of the most important results they managed to achieve was the preservation of their right to be reelected for a third or even a fourth term of office.

The long-term results of the reforms are still uncertain. Regional leaders have found a way of dealing with the seven presidential representatives, and the latter are not guaranteed victory in cases of conflict. Regions are no longer showing any interest in the idea of being assigned to a different federal district. Similarly, the initial concern about the choice of the presidential representatives soon died down.

The restoration of the rule of law and the harmonization of regional and federal legislation is a complicated task. In the best tradition of the Soviet past, regional leaders and presidential representatives proved eager enough to report changes successfully made in regional law, but the new norms all too often are not actually enforced. Most changes are merely textual and do not affect established regional practices. Un-democratic methods and regional authoritarian regimes remain unre-constructed, leaving the impression that the presidential representatives do not see the establishment of democratic values and their enforcement as a priority. The campaign for the harmonization of federal and regional legislation only scratched the surface of the problem. Russian regions have not become more democratic.

The new mechanism for the selection of the FC allowed the removal of the regional leaders from the federal political arena. In theory, the FC is now able to stand on its own two feet. In reality, it appears that the FC prefers to remain invisible, conducting informal negotiations with both the State Duma and the presidential administration. One could argue that the role and authority of the FC as a political institution have been decreasing, even though its individual members actively participate in decision making.

The reform of the relations between the center and the regions is slow-ing down, removing the urgency of bargaining. The Kozak Commission could not use the effect of suddenness in proposing a new redistribu-tion of power between federal, regional, and local government. Con-sequently, different political actors are trying to use the results of the commission's work to strengthen their own power. For example, gover-nors easily supported proposed amendments according to which they could gain more power over mayors and, at the same time, they are trying to minimize changes that could effect their own position in the region. Experts on federal and regional issues insist that civil society should also be involved in discussions as proposed changes affect not only different power strata but almost every citizen in each region. Cur-rent trends suggest that the Federal Council will increasingly fall under the influence of the presidential authority, thereby losing much of its role as champion of regional interests. One way or another, then, it can be assumed that despite all the reforms, the center-regional relationship will not be removed from the political agenda.

The evolution of the multiparty system

ANDREY RYABOV

MORE than a dozen years have passed since the first political parties appeared in the former Soviet Union during the process of democratization undertaken by Mikhail Gorbachev. At first, the party founders tried to create a multiparty system patterned after that in the developed democratic states, with a similar range of political views (Liberals, Christian Democrats, and Social Democrats). This aim was not realized. During the period of the "August republic" (1991–3), all the political parties consolidated around two main centers of power: President Boris Yeltsin on the one hand, and the first post-Soviet parliament, the Supreme Soviet, on the other. The ideological and programmatic differences between the political parties proved to be of no great significance in the concrete political context of the time. Moreover, almost no "party-clientele" structures with their own leaders took root in Russian politics, even though such structures often emerge in countries making the transition from an autocratic regime to democracy. The only exception was the Liberal-Democratic Party of Vladimir Zhirinovskii.

After the creation of the "super-presidential republic" (December 1993), a new multiparty system began to take shape. Its structure and role in the political process developed under the strong influence of the new electoral legislation, which aimed at speeding up the creation of a strong system of party representation in the new federal parliament, the State Duma. This legislation was adopted because it seemed to President Boris Yeltsin at the time that it would be easier to control a parliament structured around parties than one like the former Supreme Soviet, consisting of free-floating "single mandate" delegates, who could be manipulated by Yeltsin's opponents. It should also be noted that the disparity of power between the presidency and the legislature, as well as the large degree to which the political elite is independent of society, then began to emerge as other specific features of Russia's political transformation greatly influencing the evolution of the political parties. Given these various factors, it is hardly surprising that the multiparty system has turned out to be highly complex.

WEAKNESSES OF THE MULTIPARTY SYSTEM

It is widely believed that the formation of a multiparty system in post-communist Russia has proved to be an unsuccessful experiment. At first glance, it seems difficult to refute this point of view. The current political parties really are weak and unstable, and they do not have strong and well-developed local branches. The effective activity of many of them is restricted to their administrative center in Moscow.

In academic discussions, proponents of this position generally present three basic arguments in some detail. The first argument is that political parties in post-communist Russia do not perform one of the main functions characteristic of parties in democratic political systems. They do not serve as agents for legitimizing the authority of the state, either on the federal or the local level. Consequently, the institutions of power in contemporary Russia strive to be independent of the political parties. During the past decade, only one attempt was made by Russian political parties to conclude an agreement with the presidency regarding cooperation on the basis of mutual obligations. This happened at the beginning of 1992, when President Yeltsin, having begun to implement radical market reforms, and fearing growing opposition on the part of procommunist forces, very much needed the support of the democratic political forces. Yeltsin promised to take into account the proposals and recommendations of the political parties when formulating his policies. In return, the parties undertook to support the president in his efforts to continue the course of reform. This was the era of "street politics," characterized by a high level of public political activism. Despite the presidency's apparent need for public support, in practice, this agreement was never carried out. Yeltsin preferred to maintain his freedom of action, and he was, indeed, able to preserve his complete independence from the political parties.

Thus, the elections for the presidency of the Russian Federation and for the heads of the regional governments within the federation take place without the exertion of significant influence by the parties. Of course, the parties take part in various preelection coalitions and groupings in support of the candidates, but they never play a key role. The same ineffectiveness of the parties makes itself felt in the formation of executive authority – both at the federal and local levels (in those places where local governments exist separately from the gubernatorial administrations).

There is only one exception to this tendency. The Communist Party of the Russian Federation (referred to by its Russian initials, as the KPRF) relies on its own organizational, informational, and financial resources, and it nominates its own candidates in the presidential – and often in the provincial – elections. In fact, the KPRF inherited most of its resources (especially organizational and political) from the Communist Party of the Soviet Union (CPSU), when it was a pampered state organization. Thus, it would be correct to state that, for the most part, the KPRF does not owe its power and influence to the development of a multiparty system in the past decade. Furthermore, even the so-called "red governors," elected as the official candidates of the KPRF, prefer to distance themselves from the communists and to be unshackled by any kind of "party" control and influence.

The second argument for the assertion that the formation of a multiparty system in post-communist Russia has proved to be an unsuccessful experiment is that the parties do not generate strategies for the development of society or policy priorities for the state. Only the executive power and the groups that control the bureaucratic resources of the state apparatus are engaged in this function. Such a situation follows logically from the fact that the executive authority enjoys such a high degree of independence from the political parties and legislatures.

The third argument is that the existing political parties do not represent the political interests of the large social groups present within Russian society. This is indeed the situation, and it can be explained by two main factors.

First, on account of Russian election laws, party representation in the legislatures is little dependent on the voters. Party bosses draw up the lists of party candidates for the elections. In contrast to Germany and some other countries that have voting systems based on party lists, in Russia, a candidate who obtains a place on such a list is not obligated at the same time to run in a specific district. Hence, party candidates feel themselves free of obligations to specific constituents. Parliamentary deputies elected according to this system are inclined, above all, to be loyal to their party bosses on whom they depend for reelection.

Second, the interests of the main social strata in Russian society are not yet adequately articulated. This fact inclines the parties to serve, primarily, the corporate interests of various elite groups. Quite often, of course, these interests do not coincide with those of the public at large. For example, in 2001, a majority of the State Duma supported the "Bill on the Burial of Nuclear Waste" proposed by the government. The implementation of this law promises to bring great profits to Russian companies during the next twenty years, but it was perceived very negatively by society. According to polls, from 80–90 percent of Russians opposed the law because of the likelihood that it would cause enormous damage to the environment.

WHY ARE THE POLITICAL PARTIES WEAK?

In trying to explain the weakness of the parties, then, many specialists argue that the political parties in contemporary Russia are weak because of the poorly articulated social interests. The parties are, thus, unable to play the role of mediator between the institutions of power and society. Although correct, this point of view needs to be defined more precisely.

During the past decade of transition, one factor in particular defined the character of the relationship between the institutions of power and society. It can be described as a "negative consensus" based on the tacit assumption that neither side would interfere with the other.[1] In the framework of this consensus, society renounced any efforts at control over the regime's activities, ignoring corruption, the theft of resources from the state budget, illegal privatization, and so forth. In practice, society even acquiesced in such an extreme a form of separation as the regime's nonfulfillment of one of its main obligations to the electorate – namely, the punctual payment of wages to workers on the state payroll. For their part, the authorities, in reality, renounced any active intervention in the realm of private interests. This included tacit acquiescence in a state of affairs whereby the overwhelming majority of the population did not pay taxes.

This situation is understandable. Not wanting to bear public responsibility, the authorities could not demand that society fulfill its obligations. The emergence of this phenomenon – the mutual unwillingness to interfere in each other's affairs – can readily be explained. Having dreamed for centuries about a time when they would be free from all dictates and pressures from the authoritarian and totalitarian state, Russians easily agreed to the "offer" of freedom, interpreted as freedom from any social obligations.

For their part, the post-Soviet elites, who retained power even after the "democratic revolution" of 1991, were striving to privatize former state-owned property as quickly as possible. Thus, they needed to be absolutely untrammeled by any form of public control. It was in the interest of the post-Soviet elites that the masses not participate in political life and that they remain socially inactive. Consequently, within this

---

[1] "Rossiiskoe obshchestvo i sovremennyi politicheskii protsess: opyt politologicheskogo i sotsiologicheskogo analiza," in *Obnovlenie Rossii: trudnyi poisk reshenii* (Moscow: Russian Independent Institute for Social and National Problems, 1998), p. 64.

framework of mutual noninterference, society had no need of a mediator between itself and the authorities. This state of affairs helps to explain why, during the past decade, there was no public demand for political parties to act as institutions representing and protecting the various social and political interests of the public within the power structures.

Another reason for the weakness of the political parties is related to contemporary Russia's "constitutional design." It is well known that in the Russian political system of a "super-presidential republic," the main centers of decision-making and political power are concentrated in the executive authority – in the institution of the presidency at the federal level and in the gubernatorial administrations at the regional level. The political and oversight functions of the legislatures are truly limited. Under such conditions, practically the only political power that the parties could acquire was control over the legislative process, but as a result of this fact, they came under the strong influence of various lobbies. Ultimately, this trend has served to weaken the role of the parties as political institutions.

Beyond the issue of the constitutional structure, it has to be remembered that during his entire presidential term, Boris Yeltsin conducted a policy of restraining the development of a multiparty system. In the provinces, the governors, no matter what the differences in their political regimes, basically maintained the same political line. This trend was made possible by certain specific features involved in the formation of the present political system, many aspects of which were determined by the political conditions existing at the end of 1993, when that system first took shape.

The split within the elite, which turned into a bloody conflict between the pro-presidential forces and the Supreme Soviet in October 1993, made a strong impression on Yeltsin. He was afraid lest such conflicts within the post-Soviet elite recur. Thus, he worked to consolidate his power and restrict the circle of politicians having access to the decision-making process.

Yeltsin also created a political mechanism that would guarantee him maximal independence from any form of interference. It is important to emphasize that he aimed to control not only society at large but also the elite. In this context, he could view the idea of organizing a "presidential party" as an attempt to create an instrument of control over the presidency. Yeltsin, therefore, repeatedly rejected proposals to establish a "presidential party" that he would head.

Striving to be absolutely free of any control, in practice Yeltsin adopted a complex decision-making structure and system of mutual relationships between the highest institutions of power. This arrangement was similar to the ones that existed in the constitutional frameworks of the Second Empire in Germany (1871–1918) and tsarist Russia (1907–17). In those states, the centers of decision making (the kaiser and the tsar) concentrated a large degree of power in their hands, without bearing any real political responsibility vis-à-vis the public. In fact, in those countries, the monarchy actually stood as an institution of power that was outside, and even above, the political system. This system enabled the decision-making center to initiate conflicts between the various institutions of power (between parliament and the government, between the lower and upper chambers of parliament, between the imperial chancellery and the ministers), enabling the monarch to play the role of political arbiter. Such a mechanism was ill-designed to further a strategy of development, but it ensured the political survival of the monarchies very effectively. Yeltsin used the key features of this system despite the fact that the Russian Federation is a republic.

It is clearly no accident that Russian analysts term Yeltsin's political system an "elected monarchy."[2] He turned the system of "checks and balances" into the institutional base of his power. In this framework, the president identifies himself not with a party but as the political leader of all the Russians. The pro-presidential party was left with only one role – that of supporting the president in the lower chamber of parliament and, to some extent, in the regional legislatures. Because the pro-presidential party was not officially led by Yeltsin or even identified with him, politicians and experts began to call it the "party of power." In reality, though, its participation in the decision-making process was limited even in the upper chamber (made up of regional leaders); the president preferred to reach agreements with the governors personally, without the participation of any party. Furthermore, if the president was dissatisfied with the activity of the "party of power," or if his new priorities in politics did not coincide with the political line of the party, he could create a new "party of power" before the next parliamentary elections. Thus, in 1995, Our Home Is Russia replaced Russia's Democratic Choice, and, in 1999, Unity replaced Our Home.

All these factors mean that the widely discussed plans for creating a multiparty system in contemporary Russia with one "dominant party" (like the Partido Revolucionario Institucional [PRI] in Mexico, which ruled for some 70 years), were unrealizable. The PRI's ability to serve as a "dominant party" stemmed from its character as the institutional center coordinating interests and not only from the fact that it was the

---

[2] Igor Kliamkin and Lilia Shevtsova, *Vnesistemnyi rezhim Borisa II: nekotorye osobennosti politicheskogo razvitiia v postsovetskoi Rossii* (Moscow: Carnegie Moscow Center, 1999), p. 12.

group that supported the president. Every seven years, the PRI, unlike the other parties, nominated its own candidate for the post of president.

Concluding our discussion of this question, it is necessary to emphasize that the strengthening of the parties as political institutions will remain impossible without changing Russia's "constitutional design" in the direction of broadening the authority and functions of the legislatures, thus transforming them into real decision-making centers. In 1993, the creation of a mixed electoral system in which half the deputies of the State Duma are elected by party lists enabled the leadership to select the candidates, depriving the rank-and-file within the party of the power to influence party policy. The system used to elect most of the regional legislatures chokes off the rank-and-file still more, rendering regional party structures and the representation of the parties in the local legislatures extremely weak.[3]

The influence of parties in local politics most probably will increase in the near future, however, as a result of Putin's policy oriented toward strengthening the multiparty system in Russia. First of all, we have in mind the political consequences of legal changes concerning the political parties at the regional level (within the "Subjects of the Federation"). Thus, the creation and activity of local political parties has been prohibited by the law "On Political Parties" adopted by the parliament in 2001. Since that time, the nationwide parties have received exclusive rights to function in the regions. In accordance with further amendments to the law on "On the General Principles of the Organization of the Legislative (Representative) and Executive Organs of the State Power in the Constituent Regions of the Russian Federation" (2002), no less than one-third of the seats in the local parliaments must be elected on the basis of party lists. Starting in 2005, legislatures in all the major regional units (Subjects of the Federation) must be formed according to the new principles. Thus, nationwide parties will be able to exert an active influence on local politics, relying on their factions in the regional assemblies.

REAL CHANGES: DESPITE PROBLEMS, THE MULTIPARTY SYSTEM BECOMES STRONGER

While noting the weakness of Russia's multiparty system, at the same time we must acknowledge that during the past decade it did become an important element in the political process.[4] Since 1993, Russia has

---

[3] *Politicheskii protsess v Rossiiskikh regionakh* (Moscow: Center for Political Technologies, 1998), pp. 224–31.

[4] Igor Bunin and Boris Makarenko, *Politicheskie partii: Ispytanie vyborami*, in *Formirovanie partiino-politicheskoi sistemy v Rossii* (Moscow: Carnegie Moscow Center, 1998).

had three national campaigns for the election of Duma deputies. Voting for parties has become a routine, and people have become used to expressing their ideological preferences in this way. Likewise, the Russian experience confirms the well-known political science thesis that the introduction of a mixed electoral system leads to the formation of a party system that fosters many parties. The voters have learned to distinguish the difference in significance between parliamentary and presidential elections. Presidential elections define who holds real power in Russia, whereas parliamentary elections express the population's political and ideological preferences. The voters consider parliamentary elections to be a kind of public opinion poll that reveals the political sympathies of the various social groups. It has already been noted that Russia's political parties do not express the real political interests to be found in society and that all the attempts to create a multiparty system similar to those existing in Western Europe have been unsuccessful. None of the efforts to shape a political spectrum made up of Social-Democratic, Conservative (populist), and Liberal parties have yielded real results.

From the beginning of their existence, the political parties in Russia have defined their place on the political spectrum in accordance with other principles. The first principle concerns the party's attitude toward the problem of reform in post-communist Russia. In spite of all the differences in their political and ideological platforms, all the parties supporting reform and the dismantling of the old Soviet state can be viewed as located in the democratic sector of the political spectrum. Counterbalancing them are all the parties that oppose reform and constitute the procommunist (in fact, conservative) section of that political spectrum. They use various arguments in calling for caution in reforming the foundations of the preexisting socioeconomic system and state apparatus.

A second defining issue is rooted in the age-old question of whether the country should follow a universal (that is, a Western) or, rather, a specifically Russian path of development. This division tends to reinforce that produced by the first principle. Supporters of the universal, or pro-Western, orientation can be viewed as located in the democratic section of the political spectrum, whereas the champions of a "Russian way," despite the differences between the communists and the nationalists, together constitute the opposite camp in the political arena. From the start, the formation of these two stable electoral focal points, in fact, created a bipolar foundation for Russia's multiparty system. This split reflects the great cultural schism in Russian society that first appeared at the beginning of the eighteenth century, in the course of Peter the Great's reforms and has lasted throughout all subsequent Russian history.

Ideological disputes between "Westerners" (*Zapadniki*) and supporters of a specific "Russian way" (Slavophiles or traditionalists) took place in serious literary journals even in the 1970s and 1980s, despite the official dominance of communist ideology. When Mikhail Gorbachev began his reforms, these ideological clashes were transformed into an open political struggle.

The "bipolar" character of the Russian electoral structure helps explain two important features of the multiparty system during the earlier period of its existence (1990–5). It was absolutely impossible to create a strong centrist party in such an electoral, social, and cultural context. Every attempt to do so proved to be unsuccessful, including such initiatives undertaken by influential groups within the post-Soviet elite, both democratic and communist, as the Civic Union in 1992–3, and the Union of Labor in 1995. The configuration of the political spectrum in Russia was thus anomalous when compared with that characteristic of the Western democracies. In Russia, the socialists, liberals, and conservatives represented one political trend, and the communists and nationalists represented another.

After the establishment of the "super-presidential republic" (1993) and the stabilization of the political system (1995), the ruling elite preferred to distance itself from the political forces that favored Western models of social and economic reform. This trend was encouraged partly by the failure of the various reforms to improve radically the social and economic situation of most Russians. With the aim of preserving social and political stability and the dominance of the new ruling elite, the presidential administration created a new political organization – the "party of power," which, while remaining reform-oriented, was supposed to take a more moderate position in social and economic policy than the democratic parties, which supported far-reaching liberal change. From that moment, the "party of power" became one of the main participants in the multiparty system. The nonideological and "nonparty" character of the post-Soviet elite made possible the emergence of this phenomenon.[5] The ruling elite needed room for political maneuver. It did not want to identify itself with any one ideology and preferred to combine adherence to some kind of reform with the use of moderately paternalistic methods for its implementation, while paying respect to the "distinctive features of Russia's national character."

The "party of power" does not depend on a centrist electorate but rather on two groups. The first is made up of voters with a traditional

[5] Grigory Golosov and Alla Likhtenshtein, "'Parties of Power' and Russian Institutional Design: Theoretical Analysis," *Polis*, no. 1 (2001).

mentality. These are mainly older and middle-aged voters who assume that those in authority are always right. They prefer to support the political forces currently in power. One of this group's specific features is an "elastic" type of political mentality, meaning that they are easily able to adapt to political changes and have almost no capacity for political protest. They do not want to return to a communist political order, but, on the other hand, they prefer to avoid radical change on the way to the creation of a market economy and a pluralistic democracy, which are the goals formulated by the current regime. The second group is made up of government employees and persons from the business circles. Their support for the "party of power" is based on rational motives because their careers and businesses depend directly on their proximity to the institutions of government.

Today, the structure of Russia's multiparty system is defined mainly by these three electoral and political subcultures (pro-democratic, pro-communist, and pro-"party of power"). Each has its own political myth. During the past decade, only those political parties that won the competition for voters from these "electoral pools" were able to gain leading positions and receive stable representation in the federal parliament. The factor of "rational voting" – a preference for the strongest parties – also helped to stabilize the multiparty system. Thus, in the 1995 parliamentary elections, it was still common for voters holding similar views to distribute their votes among several parties belonging to one section of the political spectrum. By the next elections, their behavior became more rational and predictable. As a group, they preferred to vote for the strongest among several ideologically proximate parties in the hope that it would be able to overcome the 5-percent threshold needed for election.

The myth that a "golden age" of Russian history existed during the period of Leonid Brezhnev's rule serves as a key element in the self-definition of the "procommunist" electorate. According to this myth, in Brezhnev's time, Russia (the Soviet Union) was a superpower, and all the people had firm social guarantees and enjoyed a ramified system of social welfare. No more than 10 percent of this electoral group supports the traditional communist values – social equality, the October Revolution, and so forth. It would be more correct, therefore, to call this subculture "social-traditionalist" rather than "social-communist"; it tends to favor paternalistic social policies carried out by the state, and "traditionalist" thinking because its social ideal is focused on the previous epoch.

These voters usually support the Communist Party of the Russian Federation (KPRF) in that they associate it with the myth of the lost past. At a time when all the other political parties were participating in the destruction of the previous social order, only the communists tried to preserve it. Boris Kapustin was absolutely correct when he characterized the KPRF as a "left-conservative" party:[6] "left" because it occupies a position on the left of the contemporary Russian political spectrum and "conservative" because it does not have a "project for the future" of Russia.

The "pro-communist" electorate limits its real protest activity to voting for the KPRF and participating in official demonstrations and meetings organized by the communist leaders. The local KPRF organizations do not take part in radical social protest actions, however, such as strikes or worker takeovers of enterprises. In its political course, the KPRF reproduces the contradictory behavior of its voters. The KPRF is radical in its political rhetoric, but very moderate and loyal to the government in its activity in the State Duma. For instance, in the second Duma (1995–9), in which the KPRF and its allies possessed a shaky majority, the KPRF always supported the state budget as proposed by the government, even though in their speeches the communists consistently criticized it as being "against the people." The total electorate supporting the "procommunist" subculture amounts to 25–30 percent of Russian voters.

The myth of a pluralistic democracy and a free market economy ("the end of history," as Francis Fukuyama put it) serves as the main element in the self-definition of the "pro-democratic" electorate and political subculture. The total electorate supporting the "pro-democratic" subculture amounts to 20–25 percent of Russian voters, and it, too, is made up of two groups. The first includes large-scale and medium-sized entrepreneurs, managers of private companies, and people in the creative professions, all of whom have achieved success during the period of reforms. Political pragmatism and the protection of property rights are the outstanding features of their political consciousness. These voters prefer political parties that actively promote thorough economic (market economy) reforms, often regardless of whether such measures are accompanied by deterioration in the welfare of a significant part of the population. In the earlier period, this electorate supported the Russia's Democratic Choice Party. Now they support the Union of Rightist Forces (referred to by its Russian initials as SPS [*Soiuz Pravykh Sil*]). Prior to the parliamentary elections of 1999, the SPS was formed as an electoral bloc of various parties and political groups. In 2001, it was transformed into a political party.

---

[6] *Nezavisimaia gazeta*, March 5, 1996.

In contrast, the second bloc of voters supporting the ideals of Western democracy includes various groups of people who have not necessarily achieved any notable success during the period of post-communist reforms. This conglomerate includes the "democratic intelligentsia," for instance, and modestly situated businesspeople. Its political priorities include the demand for consistent adherence to democratic procedures and the protection of human rights and liberties. Since 1993, it has formed the electoral core of the Yabloko Party. These voters believe that the post-communist reforms should be characterized by consistent social, economic, and political changes, taking place strictly within the framework of the law and democratic procedures. For them, in contrast to what SPS voters often seem to think, economic effectiveness should not override all other considerations. Logically enough, the attitude of Yabloko voters to Yeltsin's reforms was mainly negative because these reforms were often accomplished by authoritarian and bureaucratic methods in violation of the law. In other words, for the supporters of Yabloko, the reforms are of value as a process, in contrast to the view taken by the electorate that supports the SPS. The latter consider the most important value to be the final result, the achievement of social and economic goals, the construction of a market, a derivative of which will be democracy. These different approaches reflect cultural, political, and social distinctions within the "democratic" electorate.

In sum, the three political subcultures ("social-traditionalist," "pro-democratic," and the "party of power") will determine the framework within which the multiparty system will develop in contemporary Russia. Each of the subcultures has its representatives at the highest level of the multiparty system – among the parties represented in the parliament.

Sometimes Russian experts add to these three subcultures two others – the "centrists" and the "nationalists." In my opinion, this hypothesis is mistaken because neither the "centrists" nor the "nationalists" have their own positive political myths that can serve as a firm base for a distinct political consciousness.

The "centrists" do not accept the extremes of democratic or communist radicalism, but because they lack their own political priorities, they often waver between supporting the "party of power" and the communists. At the same time, although the "party of power" may be described as occupying a position in the center of the contemporary Russian political spectrum, between the "democratic" parties and the KPRF, this is only a "geographic," or "geometric," not a political, center. Its location is fixed by the unwillingness of the ruling elite to associate itself with either the idea of radical reforms or a return to the communist order.

The "nationalists," who are supported by approximately 12–15 percent of Russian voters, are trying to define their identity on the Russian political scene. Their rallying point is the rejection of Western models for the reform of Russia and the rejection of the leadership's pro-Western course in international relations. Exploiting these political positions, Vladimir Zhirinovskii and his Liberal Democratic Party of Russia (LDPR) received 24 percent of the votes in the parliamentary elections of 1993, and General Aleksandr Lebed took third place in the presidential elections of 1996. In other cases, however the nationalists, lacking their own positive political ideal, became a pool from which votes were siphoned off to other political blocs, mainly the "party of power" or the KPRF. For example, in the parliamentary elections of 1999, most "nationalists" voted for the "party of power" – that is, Unity – which used the slogan "Save Russia!" to exploit fear of international Islamic terrorism. Despite their weakness, the "nationalists" (in the form of the LDPR faction) have nevertheless managed to maintain their representation in all the Russian parliaments over the past decade. This has happened mainly as a result of the colorful and eccentric figure cut by the leader of the LDPR – Vladimir Zhirinovskii. If the "nationalists" do not put forward a positive project for the future of Russia, they will lose any chance of becoming a strong and influential force in the multiparty system.

It should be noted that at present the parties in Russia give expression mainly to the political views characteristic of the electoral subcultures that have emerged since 1991. The parties are only just beginning to take on new political functions – namely, representing and expressing widespread social and political interests. To the degree that these interests find articulation within the framework of the political parties, the multiparty system will advance in the direction typical of developed democracies. There, Conservative parties largely express the interests of the economically independent groups, while the Social-Democratic parties tend to represent the interests of those who are economically weak and dependent on state assistance.

FUTURE PROSPECTS FOR RUSSIA'S MULTIPARTY SYSTEM

In the post-Yeltsin era, the consolidation of a new ruling class has become the main tendency of the Russian political process. Having obtained power and property, the post-Soviet elites, would like to consolidate their dominance. The best way to achieve this aim might be to limit competition everywhere – in the economy, in politics, and in the media; to create a hierarchy of political groupings; and to subordinate all elements and institutions of civil society to the authority of the state. These factors are clearly involved in the efforts of the presidential administration to bring "order" into the multiparty system and to impose effective control over the political parties.

In 2000, the Central Electoral Commission of the Russian Federation formulated a new "Law on Political Parties." Its main aim was to decrease the number of parties and make the results of parliamentary elections absolutely predictable. The Russian parliament, as noted earlier, passed this law in 2001. It makes the procedure for registering parties more stringent. They must now have at least 10,000 members to be registered. Collective membership is forbidden. The ban on creating local parties serves the interests of the Kremlin administration, which would like to see the nationwide parties limit the power of regional leaders.

In 2001, when this law was being discussed in the parliament, many experts supposed that only parties that were either well known to Russian voters or supported by the presidential regime and the government would be able to survive. According to a prognosis that was widespread at that time, no more than perhaps ten of fifteen parties would be able to overcome the registration barrier, and only four or five would have a real chance of being represented in the federal parliament for a lengthy period of time.

Later, in 2003, it became obvious that the strict requirements of the law have not impeded most political parties from successfully completing the registration procedure. Only two parties were refused registration on political grounds. One was Liberal Russia headed by Boris Berezovsky, an uncompromising opponent of Vladimir Putin and his policies. Another was the National Great Power Party, well known as an ultra-nationalist and anti-Semitic political group. As a matter of fact, at the same time, the presidential administration tried to limit the number of small centrist parties that were permitted to participate in the Duma elections because of fears that those parties would win part of the electorate away from the "party of power." The Kremlin pressure on the Ministry of Justice did not yield appreciable results, however.

The Law on Political Parties represents a compromise between the political groups controlling the executive authority on the one hand, and the party political establishment on the other. The law guarantees the present party establishment that it will continue to dominate the legislative branch for a long time to come without having to fear possible rivals. In return, the parties represented in the parliament will be expected to be more loyal to the executive branch. The latter, for its part, basing itself on the new law, will have numerous ways to create problems for any party that shows disloyalty. For example, the executive authority could have the financial activity of the parties and their election funding investigated and accuse them of violating the law. In a country like Russia, with a vast "gray" economy, this would not be difficult.

The plans of the executive authority to reorder the multiparty system are not limited to the adoption of this law. The Kremlin also would like to have the "party of power" not as a temporary preelectoral political construction but as a stable institution constituting the pro-presidential majority in the State Duma. This is now a realistic goal because of Putin's immense popularity. The Kremlin administration, therefore, decided to combine the most influential pro-presidential political parties and groups (Unity, Fatherland, All-Russia) and to create on their base the new "party of power." It was officially founded in December 2001 and called "United Russia."

On the basis of a strong "party of power," the executive authority intends to redistribute power among the parties in a way that better suits the interests of the post-Soviet ruling class. This means that any party that tries to preserve its independence from the presidency will be removed from the decision-making centers in the State Duma or from the parliament altogether. Pursuing this approach in 2001, the presidential administration worked out two possible courses open to it.

In the first scenario, the executive could work toward the creation of a three-party system. Once this is achieved, an alliance could be formed between the "party of power" and the "Union of Rightist Forces" (SPS) that would represent the interests of the new ruling elite. The Communist Party would then give expression to the views of the electoral groups in opposition opposed to the president and the government. This plan posits the incorporation of the SPS, as a party of pragmatists, into the sphere of influence of the executive authority. In return for its loyalty, the SPS would be granted the opportunity to participate in the formulation of the government's economic and social strategies.

Alternatively, the executive could also aim to have the party spectrum dominated by two "parties of power" – a "right-centrist" and a "left-centrist" (social-democratic) party. Such a strategy would seek to marginalize both.

Since then (2002–3), however, these approaches have been modified. At one point, the presidential administration inclined toward creating a bipartisan system consisting of United Russia and the KPRF. In accord with this plan, some members of the State Duma proposed increasing the threshold for parties in the Duma elections from 5 to 12 percent. In that case only two parties – United Russia and KPRF – would have had realistic chances of winning seats in the State Duma. This proposal was not supported in the lower Chamber, and the deputies voted for a 7 percent barrier only. This legal norm will be applied starting with the next parliamentary elections in 2007.

After the failure of the bipolar plan, the Kremlin began to develop another strategy. The presidential administration decided to form the majority in the next Duma on the basis of three pro-presidential parties (United Russia, the Peoples Party, and the Party of Life) that rely on the support of various influential groups in Putin's milieu. Nevertheless, United Russia is still considered as the key party in this coalition. According to this plan, the liberal parties (SPS and Yabloko) and the "nationalists" (LDPR) are also needed in the parliament to allow the executive authority the space for political maneuvers. We can thus suggest that the Kremlin will not impede the electoral campaigns of these parties.

The future of Russia's multiparty system thus depends on the interaction between two tendencies. First, there is the natural development of the multiparty system that is dependent on the internal evolution of the main political subcultures. Second, there is the drive of the ruling elite to create a new system using the Law on Political Parties and plans worked out in the Kremlin.

In my view, there are objective limits to such administrative interference in the development of the multiparty system. For instance, it is hard to believe that the SPS can be completely incorporated into the political framework of the executive authority because it is a party that represents a genuine element of civil society in contemporary Russia. The voters would not agree to the party's becoming a mere appendix of the state's administrative apparatus. If, for some reason, the SPS does become integrated into the executive sphere of influence, then its voters will defect, preferring to support some other party that is able to express and defend their interests and views.

It is also difficult to imagine that the KPRF can be marginalized under pressure from the presidential administration and other institutions of the executive power. Many experts now acknowledge that the communists will retain their stable electorate for a long period.

The idea of creating two "parties of power" has no chance for success either. According to the traditionalist mentality of the people who tend to vote for the "party of power," state power can have only one face, only one party, and only one representative within the multiparty system. The electorate of the "party of power" does not understand who the social democrats are. If the social democrats support the president, then why at the same time do they criticize his policies? This question usually does not receive any persuasive answer. My assumption that the social-democratic project has little chance for success is supported by what happened in the 1995 parliamentary elections. At that time, the Kremlin initiated the creation of two "parties of power": Our Home Is Russia (right-centrist) and the Ivan Rybkin Bloc (left-centrist). The former party, received 11 percent of the votes whereas the latter received only 1 percent.

In present-day Russia, there is no electoral niche for a social democratic party. Voters who support the regime prefer to vote directly for the party identified with the president and the government. Voters who view themselves as in opposition to the regime prefer the communists. There is not yet a class of salaried employees in Russia who could provide the social democratic party with a base of voters who are, at the same time, both oriented toward social partnerships with their employers and also able to defend their interests through the use of unions and other civil initiatives.

The expansion of the "party of power" as a group that supports the executive authority in the legislatures can be successful only if a majority of the party's members have the possibility of obtaining positions in the state apparatus or in semi-state-owned businesses. Otherwise, the influence of corporate interests on the party's members will become predominant, and the presidential administration will lose control of the party.

A genuinely multiparty system can be realized by the gradual transformation of the contemporary "super-presidential" political system into a mixed presidential-parliamentary system. This idea is becoming popular, especially among the political and business elite in contemporary Russia. The new elite has become so strong economically and politically that it would like to have the mechanisms of decision making more adapted to the defense of their interests than is possible in the hierarchical system of the "super-presidential" republic. Indeed, the elite would like to have some means of actually controlling the centers of decision making. Some interest groups (such as the biggest oil company, Yukos) have therefore begun to work out a plan for creating a government that would be responsible to the Duma and be formed on the basis of a parliamentary majority. If approved, this plan would strengthen the role and leverage of the political parties. In accordance with such an approach, the government would be allocated a part of the presidential power especially with regard to economic and social policy. The concept of a government responsible to the legislature and the redistribution of power from the president to the government is conceived as a first step toward a mixed presidential-parliamentary republic. In May 2003, President Putin unexpectedly supported the idea of a government based on a parliamentary majority. Perhaps Putin also understands the need for far-reaching changes in the "constitutional design" of the Russian political system. It is difficult, however, to determine how far he is going to move because, at the same time, the logic of his own aspiration to be reelected and to retain the political initiative in the Kremlin cannot but work against any significant redistribution of presidential power in favor of the government and the parliament.

This analysis, then, suggests that the natural development of the multiparty system in Russia will not be hindered radically by the attempts of the administration to intervene in the process. To the extent that they are undertaken, such efforts can only delay the formation of new parties, and then, only until the moment when the civil and political activity of the population expands to such an extent that the state is left with no choice but to recognize the parties as an influential political force. New parties will be able to count on early success if they can compete in the struggle for influence over one or another of the three political subcultures described in this chapter. Outside the framework of those dominant political subcultures, new parties would have almost no prospect of long-term success.

The elections since 1989:
The end of the chapter?

NIKOLAI V. PETROV

A dozen years of elections is, perhaps, the major positive result of late Soviet and post-Soviet transformation in Russia. Because of these elections, it is now possible to discuss Russia's transition toward democracy, perhaps electoral democracy.

Since March 1989, when relatively free and fair elections to the Congress of People's Deputies of the USSR took place, Russian citizens have been coming to polling stations at least once a year. There have been five national parliamentary elections (1989, 1990, 1993, 1995, 1999), three presidential elections (1991, 1996, 2000), four national referenda (two in 1991, two in 1993); four rounds of elections for regional legislatures (1990, 1993–4, 1996–7, 2000–1); and two rounds of gubernatorial elections (1996–7, 2000–1).

The country passed through two complete electoral cycles (1995–7 and 1999–2001), when elections to all elective offices took place; and through two incomplete cycles, simultaneous elections to Soviets of all levels in 1990, and elections for both houses of the Federal Assembly and regional legislatures in 1993–4.

The number of elections and elective offices in Russia, however, is relatively small. There are approximately 3,000 elections once in four years[1] and about 20,000 elective offices.

The total number of officials and personnel taking part in the administration of elections is much larger: about 45,000 officials at the level

---

[1] There are about 2,500 elections of top executives at three levels: national, regional, and local (in some regions, such as Tatarstan, Moscow, Bashkiriia, there still exists the system of appointments of local level heads of administration) and 500 elections for legislatures at the same three levels (at the local level, legislative bodies exist in cities only). Some experts have suggested that there are too few elective offices in Russia now and that an essential increase in their number could promote both democracy and federalism. See Peter C. Ordeshook, "Russia's Party System: Is Russian Federalism Viable?" *PSA*, no.12 (1996), pp. 195–217.

of the federal, regional, district (in large regions), and territorial election commissions, and several hundred thousand more at the level of 96,000 precincts, plus several hundred thousand ordinary members of precinct commissions composed of teachers, trade union activists, and other grassroots citizens. Taking into account observers participating in the work of electoral commissions as well as campaign staffers and the candidates themselves, the total of those directly involved in elections comes to at least 1 million more.

Elections shape a society, especially during periods of upheaval when they play the role of a catalyst for change. They also reflect the politics of the society at a particular moment. Russian elections have attracted a lot of attention both in Russia and abroad. There are numerous publications on each of the national campaigns,[2] including three fundamental comparative studies on all Russian national elections.[3] However, the last electoral cycle of 1999–2001 added much to both electoral development

[2] See Vladimir Kolosov, Nikolai Petrov, and Leonid Smirniagin, eds., *Vesna 89: Geografiia i anatomiia parlamentskikh vyborov.* (Moscow: Progress, 1990); Michael Urban, "Boris Eltsin, Democratic Russia, and the Campaign for the Russian Presidency," *Soviet Studies* 2 (1992); Marie Mendras, "Le trois Russie. Analyse du referendum du 25 avril 1993," *Revue française de science politique* 43, no. 6 (December 1993), pp. 897–939; Timothy Colton and Jerry Hough, eds., *Growing Pains: Russian Democracy and the Election of 1993* (Washington, D.C.: The Brookings Institution Press, 1998); Ralph Clem and Peter Craumer, "A Rayon-Level Analysis of the Russian Election and Constitution Plebiscite of December 1993," *Post-Soviet Geography*, no. 8 (October 1993), pp. 459–75; Ralph Clem and Peter Craumer, "The Geography of the Russian 1995 Parliamentary Election," *Post-Soviet Geography*, no. 10 (December 1995), pp. 587–616; Ralph Clem and Peter Craumer, "Urban-Rural Voting Differences in Russian Elections, 1995–1996: A Rayon-Level Analysis," *Post-Soviet Geography and Economics* (henceforth: *PSG&E*), no. 10 (December 1997), pp. 379–95; Ralph Clem and Peter Craumer, "Regional Patterns of Political Preference in Russia: The December 1999 Duma Elections," *PSG&E*, no. 1 (2000), pp. 1–29; Laura Belin and Robert W. Orttung, *The Russian Parliamentary Elections of 1995* (Armonk, N.Y.: M. E. Sharpe, 1997); Jerry Hough, Evelyn Davidheiser, and Susan Goodrich Lehman, *The 1996 Russian Presidential Election*, Brookings Occasional Papers (Washington, D.C.: The Brookings Institution, 1996); Yitzhak Brudny, "In Pursuit of the Russian Presidency: Why and How Yeltsin Won the 1996 Presidential Election," *Communist and Post-communist Studies*, no. 3 (1997); Michael McFaul, *Russia between Elections: What the 1995 Parliamentary Elections Really Mean* (Washington, D.C.: Carnegie Endowment for International Peace, 1996); Michael McFaul, *The Russian 1996 Presidential Election: The End of Polarized Politics* (Stanford: Hoover Institution Press, 1997); Michael McFaul, Nikolai Petrov, and Andrei Riabov, eds., *Rossiia v izbiratel'nom tsykle 1999–2000 godov* (Moscow: Gendalph, 2000); Nikolai Petrov, *Analiz vyborov 1995 goda v Gosudarstvennuiu Dumu po regionam i okrugam* (Moscow: Carnegie Moscow Center, 1996), pp. 7–57.

[3] Stephen White, Richard Rose, and Ian McAllister, *How Russia Votes* (Chatham, N.J.: Chatham House, 1997); Michael McFaul and Nikolai Petrov, eds., *Politicheskii al'manakh Rossii 1997* (Moscow: Carnegie Moscow Center, 1998), vol. 1; Vladimir Gel'man, Grigory Golosov, and Yelena Meleshkina, eds., *Pervyi elektoralnyi tsikl v Rossii, 1993–1996* (Moscow: Ves' Mir, 2000); Vladimir Gel'man, Grigory Golosov, and Yelena Meleshkina, eds., *Vtoroi elektoralnyi tsikl v Rossii, 1993–1996* (Moscow: Ves' Mir, 2002).

in Russia and to the knowledge of its development. It is thus worthwhile reviewing the entire set of Russian elections to assess the general trends of their evolution.

MARCH 26, 1989–MARCH 26, 2000

The March 26, 2000 election completed an 11-year period of transformation from the Soviet decorative democracy into a Russian manipulative-delegative one, with preprogrammed election results and the approval of appointed officials by voting. The beginning of the election cycle of 1999–2001 was marked by a brutal collision of elite clans during the parliamentary campaigning, by the mobilization of the electorate orchestrated by the Kremlin, by the more effective exploitation of the war in Chechnya than in the 1995–6 elections, and by the preterm resignation of the former president and appointment of his official successor to provide maximum advantage to the latter. The result of the campaign was that the political class managed to avoid any real transfer of power. Power was bequeathed internally, while elections legitimized it externally. This blueprint has been observed throughout most of the post-Soviet period. One can hardly expect anything different in Russia, at least in the near future.

The presidential election of 2000 was similar to the previous elections in that it was again about preserving power, rather than transferring it. In maintaining the status quo, the Kremlin has significant advantages stemming from its substantial administrative resources and from the peculiarities of existing legislation. The law allows the denial of registration, as well as de-registration, of any candidate who provides imprecise information about him- or herself or members of his or her family or who exceeds the maximum campaign financing limit. The last election was rather inexpensive, but, because of the overall commercialization, candidates barely managed to comply with the requirements specified by this law. The sword of Damocles hangs over any candidate who is a potential threat to the Kremlin. It did not account for the disqualification of any candidate in this election, but the future remains perilous for any of the contenders for power.

ELECTORAL TRANSITION

The evolution of the elections reflects the general development of society. Increasing stabilization has become the major feature of the sociopolitical background influencing elections. Elections are held regularly and by the same rules. Since 1993, there have been three consecutive elections to the State Duma according to almost identical laws.[4] Once the initial social activism in the period from the late 1980s to the early 1990s declined, the unstable balance among elite groups enabled elections to be more or less free and fair.[5] Stabilization has thus resulted in an increase of administrative control over elections.

Another important point is the changing role of elections in providing connections between the regime and society. In the case of legislative elections in a state that invests an inordinate amount of power in the president, the process becomes more important than the result. In gubernatorial and especially presidential elections, the result is important, but an increasing number of voters feel that the results are predetermined and nothing depends on them as individual voters.

Recent electoral developments in Russia can be divided into four distinct periods:

1. March 1989–April 1993, the founding elections of 1989–90 and a plebiscitarian pseudodemocracy;
2. December 1993–April 1994, transitional elections;
3. December 1995–April 1997, hopeful second elections; and
4. December 1999–April 2001, the third elections amid the loss of hope.

THE FIRST CYCLE: 1989–93

The first period was characterized by great expectations and the highest level of social activism. The Soviet political elites were shocked by the first real elections, and it took several years for them to recover and adjust, building a kind of manageable electoral democracy. New elements intruded themselves into politics. Many referenda have been held at the national, regional, and local levels since the first one in Soviet history in March 1991. The main subjects included the state and political institutions, ecology, and the restoration of pre-Soviet geographic names.

---

[4] On the evolution of electoral rules see, Vladimir Gel'man, "The Institutional Design: Establishing the Rules of the Game," in Vladimir Gel'man, Grigory Golosov, and Yelena Meleshkina, eds., *Pervyi elektoralnyi tsikl v Rossii, 1993–1996* and Thomas Remington and Sarah Smith, "Political Goals, Institutional Context, and the Choice of an Electoral System: The Russian Parliamentary Election Law," *American Journal of Political Science*, no. 2 (1998).

[5] The voting in the 1991 all-Union and Russian referenda can serve as good examples of how the power struggle can promote electoral democracy. Because two separate commissions were acting at each of the polling stations, none of them could take a risk of cheating, and this system is considered to be the most fair.

None of these was launched by popular initiative. Rather, they were used by various elites to enforce their positions in the political struggle.

THE SECOND CYCLE: 1993–4

During the elections of 1993 and 1994, there was a trend away from ad hoc and leader-centered politics to more stable party and program-centered politics. The events of September–October 1993 have been described as the victory of one wing of Bolsheviks over another wing of Bolsheviks. The fight between two major branches of power was completed, and the elite consolidated its position. To reinforce and legalize the new political balance and to implement the transition from Soviet to post-Soviet political institutions, the adoption of a new constitution and legislative elections at all levels were required. At this stage, the voters, not the elites, were shocked by what was happening, and different forms of protest, including absenteeism, negativism, and voting for parties regarded as outside of the system such as the Liberal Democratic Party of Russia or the Women of Russia party reached their maximum. Because the central government was self-absorbed, it did not intervene in regional elections. This left room for a variety of new regional legislatures to be formed.

THE THIRD CYCLE: 1995–7

Political stability, the maturity of the political system, and the rationality of voters' behavior defined the entire third electoral cycle, from 1995–7. For the first time in contemporary history, elections took place on time and by the same rules as previous ones. These rules were now determined by law, not by presidential decree. Natural selection operated with regard to political parties, and only those with distinct platforms and strong representation in the regions reached the Duma. The growing political professionalism, commercialization, and inaccessibility of higher politics accompanied the general stabilization. Most important, presidential elections took place despite all fears, and the communists failed to bring the system down. This was a real achievement, and various deviations from normal democracy – the huge financial advantage of the leading candidate, the absence of pluralism in the media, the utilization of administrative privilege – were considered to be inevitable. In gubernatorial elections, which took place on a mass scale for the first time, nearly half of the incumbents lost, creating an impression of democracy triumphant.

THE FOURTH CYCLE: 1999–2001

With real power at stake, the situation changed radically. The fourth electoral cycle (December 1999–April 2001) is more reminiscent of the first cycle than of the second and third cycles of elections. The growth of political uncertainty brought back ephemeral political parties, an absence of programs, and so forth. The dirtiest political technologies now flourished, including the use of war in Chechnya for the negative consolidation of society. Instead of promoting democracy in the regions, the federal authority resorted to political tricks that were to be expected in many areas anyway.

Manipulation likewise manifested itself in the timing of the elections, in the establishment of the party of power on the eve of elections, and in the failure of its presidential candidate to campaign or even present a platform. All this led to elections with predetermined results. Blackmail was widely used by the Kremlin to promote its goals in parliamentary, presidential, and gubernatorial elections. In this cycle, the incumbent governors were much more successful except in those cases when they were forced out of the race by the Kremlin.[6]

Since April 1995, with the end of the transitional period, the voter turnout in national elections has stabilized at the "ordinary" level of between 60 and 70 percent. Obviously, during the Soviet period, the turnout figures of 99.9 percent signified something other than the highest social and political activism. Indeed, in the late Soviet period, absenteeism (the failure to turn out for the election) was an indicator of social protest. The December 1993 elections can also be seen as "abnormal," following so shortly after the bloody October events in Moscow. They were marked both by a drop in turnout and also by the phenomenon of protest voting.

THE BASIC PARAMETERS OF THE RUSSIAN ELECTIONS, 1989–2001

Table 1 presents the basic parameters of Russian elections from 1989 to 2001. These include voter turnout, competitiveness, the winners' electoral base and margin of victory, the percentages of the vote won by incumbents and challengers as well as by Muscovites and women, the

---

[6] These successful efforts to retain power can be explained by a number of factors, including the lessons learned from the first elections, the consolidation of regional elites, the increased control over legislatures by the governors, and the more convenient election rules (the general adoption of one-round elections giving the incumbent a decisive advantage).

Table 1. *Basic parameters of electoral behavior, 1991–2002*

	1989	1990	1991 Ref.	1991 Pres.	April 1993 Ref.	Dec. 1993 Ref.	1993 Duma	1993 CF	1995 Duma	1996-I	1996-II	1995-7 Gub.	1995-7 Reg.	1999 Duma	2000 Pres.	1999–2002 Gub.
Turnout	86.9	76.8	75.4	74.7	64.0	54.4	54.8	54.1	64.4	69.7	68.8	53.8	42.8	61.9	68.7	53.3
Candidates per mandate	2.0	6.3	—	6.0	—	—	6.8	2.7	11.7	10.0	2.0	5.0	5.9	10.4	11.0	6.2
Winner's base	…	…	73.0	57.3	58.3	57.1	27.0	52.3	28.6	35.5	53.8	60.8	…	33.9	52.9	61.7
Winner's margin	…	…	—	40.4	—	9.9	9.9	—	12.7	3.3	13.5	31.2	…	15.7	23.7	40.2
Share of Muscovites*	20.4	9.1	—	66.6	—	—	36.9	3.4	24.4	80.0	100.0	5.1	…	29.0	81.8	4.8
Share of women*	8.5	2.9	—	—	—	—	13.6	4.5	10.2	—	—	1.3	9.7	9.3	9.1	2.5
Share of party nominees*	85	86	—	—	—	—	40.6	…	65.8	18.2	—	13.7	18.6	50.5	16.7	4.8
Newcomers**	…	97.0	—	—	—	—	75.0	63.1	49.3	—	—	55.3	…	54.7	—	35.0
Incumbents in races	…	…	—	—	—	—	…	—	78.2	100.0	—	100.0	…	69.6	100.0	89.9
Invalid ballots	2.6	6.9	2.3	2.2	2.8	2.4	7.3	4.8	2.3	1.4	1.1	2.1	…	2.0	0.9	…

Negativism	9.2	14.5	27.0	1.9	8.5	40.6	14.8	12.4	9.6	1.5	4.8	5.8	…	3.3	1.9	7.4
Number of effective candidates***	…	—	2.7	—	—	…	9.1	…	11.1	3.9	2.2	2.9	…	6.8	2.7	3.0
Expenses ($ U.S. million dollars)	…	…	…	…	…	…	…	…	~200	…	~1000	~300	~400	~300	~100	~500
"Administrative resource"*****	…	…	3	4.5	7.5	10	10	15	13	6.5	9.5	~15	~10	~15	~7	~15

FC = *Federation Council*; Gov. = gubernatorial; Pres = presidential; Reg. = regional legislatives; Ref. = national referenda.

* Estimated as a share of candidates for presidential elections and as a share of winners for other elections (Communist Party of the Soviet Union members for 1989 and 1990).

** Estimated as continuity with the USSR Congress of Peoples Deputies for 1990 and with the RSFSR Congress of peoples deputies for 1993 (State Duma).

*** Number of effective parties in case of Duma elections.

**** Estimated as deviation from free and fair voting results in percentage points.

Regional legislatures: Calculated 72 campaigns in 1995–7 and 50 campaigns in 1998–2000 on a base of official Central Electoral Commission's reference books.

party nominees, invalid ballots, voting against all candidates, fraud, and money spent.

Absenteeism or the failure to turn out is one of the most universal indicators of electoral behavior in Russia. In stable democracies, it reflects the level of political passivity. However, transitional democracies, including Russia in 1989–2001, are very different. In the first post-totalitarian elections, absenteeism was *active* rather than *passive,* reflecting the progress society had made since the 99.9 percent turnout of the Soviet era. Until April 1993, when the turnout first reached its equilibrium level, the more active the region was politically, the greater the level of absenteeism. Not voting was seen as a way of demonstrating the break with the Soviet past. Cities, and especially capitals – which were the leaders in societal transformation – manifested the highest absenteeism.

Once the electoral transition is over, the failure to turn out reflects differences in political culture, including the degree to which administrative resources are used to control the elections.[7] Absenteeism is higher in a number of ethnic republics and rural regions and is lower in urban regions and in the north. Different elections attract different degrees of participation. The turnout has been the lowest in the regional legislative elections (30–40 percent), higher in gubernatorial elections (50–60 percent) and in national parliamentary elections (60–65 percent), and highest in presidential elections (65–70 percent).

The competitiveness of elections can be evaluated by various indicators. Taking *the average number of candidates per seat* in the Duma, it reached the rather high level of 6.3 in the second elections (1990), and it remained approximately the same until the 1995 Duma elections, when it almost doubled, reaching its maximum (11.7 candidates per seat). The 1999 Duma elections showed a slight decrease in the number of candidates (10.4).

Examining the *winners' margins* produces a different picture. It has been growing by a quarter in each Duma election. On average, the second candidate in 1999 received only about half the winner's votes. Taking the proportional part of the mixed electoral system, the *number of effective parties* can serve as a measure of competitiveness. In 1993, it was 9.5, it increased by one-third in 1995, and then dropped to 7.7 in 1999. In short, after an initial period of real competition, the competitiveness of elections is now in decline.

Negativism: in the elections of 1989 and 1990, the Soviet/Stalinist ballot was still used. Voters had to strike off the names of all candidates for

---

[7] The reported turnout there can easily reach 93 percent, as in Ingushetiia in the 2000 presidential election, and can be even higher in the case of regional elections.

whom they did not want to vote.[8] At the time, the size of the negative vote (the rejection of all candidates) could be counted by subtracting the total number of votes obtained by all the candidates from the overall number of ballots. In 1993, a new ballot was introduced, which had the option of voting "against all candidates." However, at that time and in the following parliamentary elections, negative voting did not count when determining the winner. In 1989–90 and again since 1999, it has counted. To a certain degree, negativism and absenteeism are interchangeable. If, for example, potential voters are disappointed with the lack of choice, they can protest by taking either the more passive form of absenteeism or the more active form of negativism. This is clearly seen in the case of simultaneous elections when voters who otherwise would have stayed away are drawn to cast their vote against all candidates in an election of major importance. [9]

The so-called *administrative factor* plays an important role in all Russian elections. Candidates and parties backed by the party of power are placed in a privileged position in various ways. These include the establishment of "convenient" rules and timing (especially in the case of regional elections); the use of state resources controlled by bureaucrats (primarily money and the mass media); and the mobilization of businesses dependent on the regime. They also include the use of courts and election commissions to put pressure on, or even to exclude, opponents. Finally there is *direct fraud*. The lack of transparency and of public control over elections makes it hardly possible to speak about proven fraud on a national scale. It is possible, however, to evaluate the extent of fraud in regions in a broad sense (a deviation from the freely expressed will of the voters) using mathematical-statistical methods[10] and specific cases.

---

[8] This form was designed for Soviet elections to make it easier both to vote (because there was only one name on the ballot, a voter only had to take the ballot and put it into a box without making any marks) and to control voting (it made it possible to define anybody who was marking a ballot paper as suspect).

[9] The December 1993 elections to the Moscow city duma can serve as a good example. They took place at the same time as elections to the State Duma and the voting on the constitution. Thus, the turnout was much higher than in other regional elections that took place later, but one-third of all votes were cast against all candidates.

[10] These methods have been developed over a long period of time by the analytical group led by Aleksandr Sobianin and Vladislav Sukhovol'skii. Results of their studies of 1991–3 elections were summarized in the book *Democracy Limited by Fraud*. Aleksandr Sobianin and Vladislav Sukhovolskii, *Demokratiia, ogranichennaia fal'sifikatsiiami: vybory i referendumy v Rossii v 1991–1993 gg.* (Moscow: Project Group on Human Rights, 1995).

The essence of these methods is easy. Any falsification of results if not uniform throughout the entire country, leads in certain places to a sharp increase in the number of votes obtained by a given candidate or a party while the average support for other parties and candidates remains stable. Thus, having vast information on election results by precincts, territorial commissions, and districts, we can determine with a certain degree of confidence the extent of the fraud and which candidate is favored. (p. 2)

Despite the numbers, which look similar to those of the 1995–7 cycle, the role of the administrative factor in the fourth cycle of elections increased significantly for several reasons. The most important of these are 1. the consolidation of the elites at different levels, and the growth of central control with its potential to augment administrative influence at both regional and federal levels; and 2. the active employment of election commissions, courts, and coercive structures simply to exclude undesirable candidates (rendering hidden forms of fraud superfluous). The declining number of incumbents participating in the races is a clear indication of this point. Gerrymandering as a form of electoral engineering is not particularly widespread in national elections. [11] However, in regional elections, it is common for the urban, less controllable population to be underrepresented.[12] This sometimes takes the extreme form of so-called administrative-territorial districts, in which a small rural *raion* (district) may receive the same representation as a larger regional center.

The *percentage of women among deputies* is indicative not only of women's position in society but also – as an analysis of the 1989 elections showed – the extent to which the nomenklatura controls elections.[13] Women constituted 8.5 percent of the members in the Congress of People's Deputies. As the table indicates, the women's showing in the second round of elections in 1990 was about one-third of that in the first one. There was a rise in 1993, when the Women of Russia movement received almost 9 percent of the votes. In 1995, the percentage of women dropped, and it has now returned to the 1989 level.[14] In individual

[11] See, however, *Riabomandra,* named after the former Central Election commission chair Nikolai Riabov, in Michael McFaul and Nikolai Petrov, eds., *Politicheskii al'manakh Rossii, 1997* vol. 1, p. 194.

[12] The resulting phenomenon of political life in Russia was illustrated and analyzed in full in material of the 1993–5 legislative elections (Nikolai Petrov, "Vybory organov predstavitelnoi vlasti v regionakh *FBIS-SOV-95-111-S* (Translation of the article "Elections of Organs of Representative Power," *Mirovaiia ekonomika i mezhdunarodnye otnosheniia,* no. 3, 4 (March/April 1995).

[13] It is worth recalling that the Supreme Soviet had perfectly balanced gender and occupational structures. In 1989, regional authorities in some cases tried to repeat the same practice choosing "representative" candidates. The greater the percentage of women among candidates, the more the nomenklatura interfered in elections (Kolosov, Petrov, and Smirniagin, eds., *Vesna 89*).

[14] The drop in women's representation in comparison with previous communist parliaments is typical of the post-communist transition (Steven Saxonberg, "Women in East European Parliaments," *Journal of Democracy,* no. 2 [April 2000], pp. 145–58), but in the majority of cases, unlike Russia, the drop in the first post-communist election was followed by a steady increase in the later elections. Russia would conform to the universal scheme much better if one considers the 1989 election as the first post-communist one.

rather than mass elections to executive offices, the percentage of women candidates is even lower.

The *percentage of Muscovites* among Russian parliamentary deputies is several times higher than the percentage of Muscovites in the Russian population as a whole. This is not surprising given the high level of centralization and the concentration of the intelligentsia in the capital city. The representation of Muscovites was smallest of all in the Russian Congress of 1990, but in the Duma elections of 1993 they constituted nearly 40 percent of the elected members. In 1995, the number of Muscovites decreased to one-quarter, but it is now increasing again. The national elections work like a pump, with only a few deputies from the regions leaving the capital after the expiration of their term. An opposite process, although incomparably smaller in scale, is the participation of Muscovites in regional elections. There are now a dozen governors and republican presidents who came from or through Moscow.[15]

The participation of regional leaders in elections during the decade has changed greatly in terms of both scale and success. In 1989, it was obligatory for first secretaries of the Communist Party regional committees to take part in elections. One-third of them failed.[16] This eventually led to vociferous scandals and quiet replacements. In 1990, many regional bosses participated in elections to the Russian Congress. Twenty of them won, including some who had failed a year earlier. None of the 1989 winners took part in these elections because it was impossible to hold a mandate in both the Congress of People's Deputies and in a republic-level legislature, and all regional bosses opted to take their places in the regional councils. The elections of 1993 to the Federal Council constituted the last national campaign in which regional leaders participated. It was a special, "deluxe" campaign that was very different from elections to the lower house. Seven of every eight governors thus managed to win that time. Since 1993, the regional leadership, even the highest, has not participated in national elections.

The results of the first (1989) and second (1990) elections profoundly affected the Soviet nomenklatura, leading, however, to its modification

---

[15] They are Ruslan Aushev (1993, Ingushetiia); Kirsan Iliumzhinov (1993, Kalmykiia); Nikolai Fedorov (1993, Chuvashiia); Yevgenii Savchenko (1993, Belgorod oblast); Yegor Stroiev (1993, Orel oblast); Yevgenii Mikhailov (1996, Pskov oblast); Viacheslav Liubimov (1996, Riazan oblast); Aleksei Lebed (1996, Khakasiia); the late Aleksandr Lebed (1998, Krasnoiarsk krai); Aleksandr Dzasokhov (1998, North Ossetiia); Nikolai Semenov (1999, Karachai-Cherkessiia); Boris Gromov (2000, Moscow oblast); Roman Abramovich (2001, Chukotka); Boris Zolotarev (2001, Evenki); Aleksandr Khloponin (2001, Taimyr district and 2002 Krasnoiarsk krai).

[16] It happened mainly in urban industrial regions to the north of Moscow.

rather than its demise. The nomenklatura, which became Russian in December 1991, recuperated quickly from the shock caused by the first elections and was, more or less, prepared for further changes by early 1993. In 1993, special elections "for bosses" were organized, and starting in 1995, there were individual elections in each region, where, to a significant extent, it was possible for regional leaders to establish their own rules of the game and avoid strict control from above or below. In the first of two series of gubernatorial elections that took place in 1995–7, about half of the incumbents won a subsequent term; in the second series, in 1999–2001, they lost only one-third of the contests.

There are two factors affecting *turnover:* extent and frequency. Neither of the first Congresses – the Union and the Russian – lasted its whole term, and the three first parliamentary elections – in 1989, 1990, and 1993 – were held under different rules and with different constituencies. In the second (1995) and the third elections to the State Duma (1999), about one-half of the deputies were replaced. The percentage of newcomers was rather high. Looking at 225 single-mandate districts, the continuity is even less pronounced: 176 incumbents sought reelection in 1995, and 68 (36.1 percent) of them succeeded. In 1999, 76 incumbents won of 156 contestants (48.7 percent). As many as one-third of the incumbents did not seek reelection in their constituencies. [17] Among those who did, the percentage of losers is at least as large as that of winners.

Governors are different. In 1995–7, all of them ran for reelection, but half lost. In 1999–2001, the incumbents' chances of winning became much higher, but because of pressure from the Kremlin, several did not run for reelection, or, as in the case of Aleksandr Rutskoi, were prevented from doing so by the courts. In regional legislative elections, the percentage of incumbents reelected did not exceed more than one-quarter to one-third.

Expenses: the first Russian elections were relatively inexpensive. With sociopolitical and economic stabilization, elections have become routine. Social enthusiasm has been declining and is increasingly replaced by professionalism. The 1995 elections to the Duma marked the start of real commercialization, when the cost of a serious campaign was measured in six-digit dollar figures. According to various estimates, the cost of Yeltsin's 1996 presidential campaign reached between $.5 billion to

---

[17] There are two basic reasons that incumbents are not trying to defend their mandates. The first is related to the loss of support of either regional authorities or sponsors, and the second has to do with the jobs they could find in the government during the four years of their term (this is why, in 1999, four years after the previous elections, the number of incumbents in races was less than in 1995, when only two years had passed since the 1993 elections). It shows, in any case, that the deputies' connections with the voters between elections are rather weak.

$1.5 billion. Putin's presidential election was less costly (if one does not add the cost of the renewed war in Chechnya, which was a necessary element in Putin's victory). A more or less serious gubernatorial campaign can cost the candidate up to $20 million.

There are two major obstacles when trying to estimate the financial cost of the elections. The first is connected to the huge gap between official and real expenditures, with the latter liable to exceed the former by a factor of 100. The second problem is connected to the transitional nature of the Russian economy, which retains the characteristics of a communal economy along with market characteristics. Costs for the same service can differ greatly, with incumbent governors and presidents receiving many services for free.

Partisanship: the percentage of candidates nominated by political parties is increasing, but the growth is slow. Elections in Russia are still personal, which leads to widespread populism and a lack of responsibility by elected officials. In 1999, there was a "departisanization" of the elections, with party candidates winning in half the districts, in comparison with two-thirds of the districts four years earlier. Even communist candidates – incumbents and regional party activists – were registered in some cases as "independents." Moreover, candidates who came into the Duma on a party ticket can easily leave a faction. Where they exist, factions in regional parliaments are organized not by parties, but by professional groups and, above all, by elite clans. In elections for executive offices, the percentage of party nominees is much lower. Overall, the personal factor is still strong in elections in Russia. This enables candidates to resort to populism and allows elected officials to evade responsibility and supervision.

THE CENTRAL ELECTORAL COMMISSION

Stalin's cynical formula: "It doesn't matter how they vote, it matters who counts the results," still retains its importance at both the national and regional levels. At the national level, the timing of elections is directly connected to the formation and operation of the Central Electoral Commission (CEC). Until the autumn of 1993, the CEC was under the leadership of Vasilii Kazakov, an old-fashioned Soviet-style official. In September 1993, when "old specialists" were unable to guarantee the organization of elections on very short notice, Yeltsin appointed a new commission under the leadership of Nikolai Riabov, who had served as deputy speaker of the Duma. His prior experience was limited to a small provincial technical college in the south. The CEC consisted mainly of bureaucrats from the former Supreme Soviet, and it produced the desired results for the authorities. Numerous complaints were filed, however, including those from newly elected Duma deputies whom the CEC did not manage to provide with detailed electoral statistics. Since 1993, the CEC has transformed itself from a technical service to an influential and powerful body. It has become "the ministry of elections," with the head of the CEC considered among the country's top-ten politicians. Soon after the 1993 elections, Riabov was appointed ambassador to the Czech Republic, and a new period began for the CEC under Aleksandr Ivanchenko, Riabov's former deputy.

Whereas the first post-Soviet CEC was merely appointed by Yeltsin, the next one was formed in 1995 under a new law. This law specified that five CEC members were appointed by the Duma, five by the Federal Council, and five by the president. Ivanchenko managed to keep his position in 1995, but not in 1999, when the ten names proposed by the Duma and the Federal Council differed from those favored by the CEC leadership, and when Yeltsin did not even include Ivanchenko in his list of five. Moreover, the Kremlin candidate failed, and Aleksandr Veshniakov, the former secretary and then deputy CEC chair was elected to be the new head of the Central Electoral Commission. He seemed close to leftists and thus, for the first time since 1993, the CEC looked as though it would not be directly controlled by the Kremlin.[18]

The CEC consists not only of 15 commissioners but also of a huge apparatus that is directly controlled by three leading CEC members: the chairman, his deputy, and the secretary. According to Soviet tradition, the person who controls the apparatus controls the entire mechanism. Ordinary CEC members did not play any important role in 1993 and were not even allowed to enter the rooms where voting results were counted.

Regional election commissions are supervised by the CEC, but they are not directly subordinate to it. Half of their members are appointed by the governor, the other half by the regional legislature. In the majority of regions, they are totally controlled by the local administration.[19]

In addition to the pyramid of election commissions, a whole election industry has emerged in Russia – the only industry to develop rapidly during the decade of Russia's "great depression." It encompasses consulting, public relations, image making, and mass media

[18] The last CEC rotation, which took place in 2003, retained eight "old" CEC members including Veshniakov, elected the chair for the next term. The seven new CEC members came either from its apparatus or from regional commissions.

[19] Since 2003, a kind of supervision if not subordination of the CEC over regional election commissions was introduced with the CEC naming two commission members – the one of the governor's half, the other of the legislature and commission chair.

businesses, with a turnover measured in billions of dollars. There are well-established "players" in the field,[20] but the electoral business is diversifying intensively with more and more companies springing up.

Russia has easily achieved a market economy in the electoral sphere. Given the weakness of political parties, this means that the results serve the interests not of major social groups but rather of the elite clans that dominate politics and business. Interestingly, instead of sending their representatives to elective offices, tycoons themselves are now starting to become deputies and even governors.[21]

THE REFORM OF ELECTORAL LEGISLATION

A large-scale reform of Russia's electoral legislation was launched early in Putin's presidency. According to the head of the CEC, Aleksandr Veshniakov, such a systemic review of the legislation had "not been undertaken in the last eight years."[22] The reform strategy was formulated in the CEC report of 2000 "On the Improvement and Development of the Electoral Legislation." Changes it recommended were subsequently incorporated into the law on "On Political Parties" and in the amendments to the preexisting law "On the Basic Guarantees Providing Citizens of the Russian Federation with the Right to Vote and to Participate in Referenda." The reforms have left a particular mark on the regions (much more so, for example, than at the center). Among the most important changes so far have been the introduction of a mixed proportional-majoritarian system in elections to the legislatures; the weakening of the control exercised by the regional authorities over electoral commissions; and the appearance of an "electoral vertical" leading toward tighter central control over elections in regions.

The new version of the law "On the Elections of the Deputies to the State Duma" contains a significant number of innovations. These include a tightening of control in some areas and a relaxation of control in others. To the first group belongs the introduction of a single fixed date for elections (the second Sunday of December), a mandatory reduction of the period allowed for campaigns, a sharp increase in the maximal

---

[20] They are 'Nikkolo-M' (Yekaterina Yegorova and Igor Mintusov), 'Image-Contact'(Aleksei Sitnikov), 'Novokom' (Aleksei Koshmarov), Polity (Viacheslav Nikonov), 'The Center for Political Technologies' (Igor Bunin), The Institute of Regional Problems (Maksim Dianov), Russkii Proekt (Mikhail Maliutin), et al.

[21] There were three such cases in 2001 in remote autonomous districts with rich resources and a sparse population: Aleksandr Khloponin in the Taimyr district, Roman Abramovich in Chukotka, and Boris Zolotarev in the Evenki district.

[22] "Centralization Is Needed for Protection of Democracy." Veshniakov's interview in *Vlast'* (in Russian). *Vlast'*, no. 325, July 2, 2002, pp. 26–27.

permissible campaign expenditures, [23] and, finally, more stringent regulation and enforcement of registration rules for candidates. The reverse is true of the new law's broader definition of "electoral agitation," permitting a looser and more benign regulation of the mass media. However, on the whole the defining element of the new version of the law is tougher control by the state – through the restriction of unsanctioned grassroots public activism (voters' groups lose the right to nominate candidates, with that right reserved for political parties and for independent candidates), and through the consolidation of the existing political parties, which, according to the law "On Political Parties," will be placed under strong administrative control.

Changes to the laws governing elections to the State Duma started to appear by the end of 2002 and continued into 2003, when the final amendments to the banking, the mass media, and civil as well as criminal law codes were passed. Changes in regional laws are to follow.

NATIONAL, REGIONAL, AND LOCAL ELECTIONS

Elites and Citizens in the Elections

Both reflecting and reinforcing the lack of interest in local elections, democratization operates less as it moves from the top down. The lower the level of elections, the more severe are the various violations. In fact, in many regions (e.g., Moscow, Tatarstan, Bashkortostan, Voronezh, Krasnodar, and Novosibirsk) in violation of the federal law, there are no elections at all to choose the heads of administration.[24]

Voter decision making operates according to various patterns: more personal in the national elections, partisan-personal in the regional contests, and professional-personal at the local level. National elections are about politics, regional elections are about economics, and local elections are about being "good guys." Implementing the same set of rules at different levels can produce very different results. For example, there are only six regions where the mixed system is used to form the regional legislature. In these cases, political parties are very different from the all-Russian ones. Even if they use nationally recognized names to attract voters, they may well represent broad personal and clan coalitions of local elites.

---

[23] The increase is twofold, from 1 to 2 million rubles per candidate in single-mandate districts, and sixfold (up to 150 million rubles) for parties and electoral blocs.

[24] To avoid direct elections at the subregional level, the administrations there are considered to be units of state power, not of self-administration.

Turnout, even in the most popular regional elections, the gubernatorial contests, is much lower than at the national level: 50–55 percent.[25] Competitiveness is lower as well, with fewer effective candidates and with the winner's margin of victory often reaching 70 or even 80 percentage points. This reflects the desertlike nature of politics in a number of regions, with a lack of potential replacements for the leader. It is especially true with regard to regions where the leader has been ruling since 1990 or even longer (Bashkiriia, Dagestan, Kabardino-Balkariia, and Tatarstan).

Looking at the chain of command – descending from the governor to the deputies to the mayors – makes it clear that cases of total loyalty to, or control by, the governor are rather rare (Tatarstan, Saratov, and Kemerovo). Often, leftist deputies are elected in regions where the rightist governor came to office some time earlier, or vice versa – a phenomenon that can be explained either by a natural disappointment in whoever is in power or by a latent desire to counterbalance one force by the other.

TIMING

Timing is an essential factor that can play a decisive role in an election. In Russia the season is also important. Both bad weather in winter and early spring and good weather in summer can reduce turnout. For example, good weather can provide potential voters with an excuse to take the day off rather than vote. Both situations have disproportionate effects on voters with differing political preferences.[26] Rural regions are different from urban areas. In the more traditional rural areas, religious holidays and the agrarian cycle can be a factor, as the population experiences a contented and plentiful autumn or a troubled spring.[27]

Simultaneous elections make administrative control more complicated. Governors do their best to separate the gubernatorial campaigns

---

[25] This is an average figure, derived from an 85–95 percent or even higher official turnout in some republics in which gubernatorial elections were held simultaneously with national ones and a more usual 40–45 percent turnout in oblasts and krais.

[26] That is why some experts were arguing against December parliamentary elections in 1993 (the same day, December 19, that the first elections to the Supreme Soviet were held in 1936 by Stalin). In 1996, in the presidential elections, the timing of the second round was of vital importance not only because of Yeltsin's bad health but also because the students were on vacation and urban dwellers were away at dachas. This is why the CEC appointed the second round not on Sunday but in the middle of the week, on Wednesday. In order not to violate the law, Wednesday, July 3, was declared a nonworking day. As a result, the official turnout figure showed a drop of less than 1 percentage point.

[27] In 1993, for example, gubernatorial elections were shifted in the Smolensk oblast to avoid coinciding with Easter.

from any others and to ensure that they precede all other regional elections. The governors regard it as even more important to delay elections to local administrative offices than to legislative bodies. In this case, the governor will then be dealing with local heads who know that they are going to be dependent on him, and they are the ones who control the regional electoral machines.[28] By the same logic, Yeltsin allowed extensive gubernatorial elections in 1996 only after the presidential elections. The logic of a governor might be different if he needs to avoid competition with the mayor of a regional center. In such a case, mayoral elections can coincide with gubernatorial ones.[29]

Simultaneous elections to legislatures at all levels took place only once (in 1990). Such elections promote democracy, party development at both national and regional levels, and close working connections between lawmakers at different levels. From the standpoint of democratization, it is regrettable that there are not more such cases.

Early elections give an advantage to incumbents because they can choose a time when competitors will be least prepared. When the federal law restricted changes in electoral terms, epidemics of formal resignations broke out, and in early 2001, the head of the CEC warned that an amendment to the election law was needed to prohibit governors who had resigned from running again in early elections.

The president is, of course, much more powerful than the ordinary governor. Instead of accommodating himself to the political calendar, he can make history by himself. Notably, both wars in Chechnya started on the eve of major electoral cycles and were intensively exploited in the presidential elections of 1996 and 2000.

---

[28] The sequence of the 1996–7 Saratov elections can serve, perhaps, as an almost ideal example of political timing. First, the newly appointed governor cancelled local elections scheduled for April. Then, just before the presidential elections, he appointed new mayors and raion heads. The gubernatorial elections took place two months after the presidential ones. Opening the broad round of gubernatorial elections, they attracted the special attention of the Kremlin. The incumbent won handily on the heels of the presidential campaign. A few months later, at the beginning of the next year, local elections took place; local heads were appointed by the governor not elected by popular vote. Legislative elections took place a year after the gubernatorial ones and coincided with the region's jubilee celebration and Yeltsin's visit. Under the new regional law, the majoritarian system was implemented for the legislative elections instead of the former majoritarian-proportional one, which was less convenient for the authorities.

[29] The analysis of a sequence of gubernatorial, legislative, and mayoral elections in 1996–7 showed that the most widespread option was gubernatorial, mayoral, and legislative in consecutive order; after that came the option of holding the gubernatorial and the mayoral elections at the same time to be followed later by those to the legislature. The most democratic sequence – simultaneous elections – came third, even though it was the least costly (*Political Almanac* 1997, vol. 1, pp. 265–72).

REGIONAL ELECTORAL BEHAVIOR

Models of electoral behavior vary not only according to their timing but also with regard to their geographic location. Regional voting patterns are rather stable and spatially meaningful, which makes it possible to discuss a mature electoral landscape.

Based on voting patterns in the 1995 parliamentary and 1996 presidential elections, five regional types can be distinguished: 1. strongly reformist, 2. moderately reformist, 3. conservative, 4. unstable, and 5. controlled.[30] The two reformist and the unstable groups are almost equal in the support that they receive – approximately 20–25 percent of the voting public. The percentage of the conservatives is approximately 30 percent, and the controlled group is 10 percent. These groups, which are identifiable by a few basic patterns of voting behavior, have distinct social physiognomies. The reformist type is the most urban (the average percentage of city dwellers here is about 80 percent of the regional population), whereas the controlled type is the most rural (more than 50 percent).

In the 1999–2001 electoral cycle, the composition of regional types remained practically the same[31] (Fig. 1).

Types, defined on the basis of the general character of electoral preferences differ by other parameters of electoral behavior as well (see Table 1).

The general character of the electoral landscape can be defined as latitudinal-zonal with a well-pronounced north-south gradient. The most generalized pattern of electoral behavior is represented by five major electoral sectors: the north, the south, the core, the heartland, and the half-moon. The "more developed and progressive" north and the "more conservative and conformist" south can be considered the two poles, with the other three major sectors occupying intermediate positions (Fig. 2).

Variations in electoral behavior within regions can be much larger than between regions. The same two poles can be seen here, with regional centers and cities playing the role of "electoral north" and the

---

[30] See Michael MacFaul and Nikolai Petrov, "Russian Electoral Politics after Transition: Regional and National Assessments," *PSG&E* 38 no. 8, 1997, pp. 507–49.

[31] There were only four regions that changed their types: North Ossetiia and three Far Eastern regions. North Ossetiia left "the controlled" type for "the conservative"; the Amur oblast left the "conservative" type for "the unstable"; Koryak and Chukotka autonomous districts left the "strong reformist" type for the "controlled" type in 1999. (Nikolai Petrov and Aleksei Titkov, "Vybory-99 v regional'nom izmerenii" (Moscow: Carnegie Moscow Center, 2001), pp. 197–224.

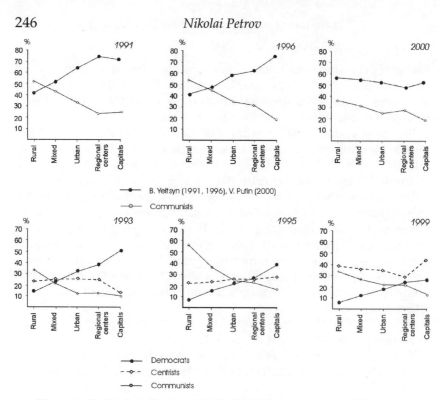

Figure 1. Political preferences, 1991–2000: The rural-urban dichotomy.

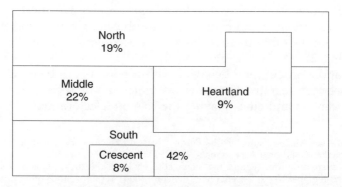

Figure 2. The relative electoral weight of the five macroregions.

periphery the role of "electoral south." The set of graphs (Fig. 1) showing electoral support for "democrats," "communists" and "centrists" by five types of single-mandate electoral districts[32] illustrates this point. The more urban and central the district, the greater the democrats' support and the smaller the support for the communists. However, this distinct regularity was significantly disrupted in the last electoral cycle, which can be explained as one more sign of the decline in polarized politics.[33] The differences in electoral behavior within regions and between regions are eroding.

EXPLANATORY MODELS OF ELECTORAL BEHAVIOR

The following picture emerges concerning the electoral preferences of Russian voters. The basic proportions are rather stable in the majority of oblasts and krais, but erratic with regard to ethnic republics. In the latter units, it is not so easy to distinguish between the changeability of voters and that of regional leaders who control the electorate to varying degrees. In some cases, the evidence of administrative influence is rather clear – for example, when the republics of the North Caucasus almost totally "changed their minds" between June 1991 (the presidential election) and April 1993 (the referendum) or when the Volga republics and Dagestan made a similar turnabout within a few weeks between the first and the second rounds of the presidential election in 1996.

The remarkable stability of certain voting patterns speaks in favor of models that employ the concept of political culture and explain voting behavior by some basic characteristics of the electorate. The primary cleavage is that between the urban and rural (or the industrial and agricultural), taking into account the differences in age, education and economic opportunities. It is reflected in the north-south divide, which appeared in the first elections in 1989 and has reappeared ever since. The urban factor is sometimes sufficient to explain up to 50 percent of the variation in electoral results. Age (especially in regard to pensioners) and education level can be important as well, but these indicators are interrelated.

Different economic indicators such as unemployment, income level, gross domestic product and federal subventions are of much less

---

[32] The same set of 225 single-mandate districts was used both in the 1995 and 1999 Duma elections. We divided them into five groups: capitals (Moscow and St. Petersburg districts, 10.7 million voters in 2000), regional centers (12.1 million), predominantly urban (19.3 million), mixed (53.6 million), and predominantly rural (14.2 million). We then recalculated results of the 1991, 1996, and 2000 presidential and 1993 Duma elections by the same set of districts.

[33] See Michael McFaul, *The Russian 1996 Presidential Election*.

importance in Russia's case. This is rather natural for a transitional period marked by a high level of political and economic instability. Previous attempts to build models suggesting economic determinism have failed.[34] Geographic and political-cultural factors appear to be much more relevant.

BACK TO THE FUTURE

Essentially, the role of elections in Russia can be seen as the legitimization of existing power rather than as providing for the transfer of power. Not the political parties but the authorities and business are the major players in the electoral process. Despite some exceptions in the regions, the attempts to improve elections by means of better electoral laws have failed. Elections have been a pacemaker and catalyst of society's development, but no more than that.

Russian society has become accustomed to elections as a kind of political theater. The revolutionary character of elections, the unpredictability of their results, the sincerity of the nonprofessional actors, the participation of the masses themselves – these are all vestiges of the past. Professionalism, commercialization, and high-quality technical effects have taken over. Elections, which used to be a kind of peoples' theater, have become an academic theater. As in other countries, they have become a necessary attribute of political life and, following the Western fashion, a very expensive attribute.

The elections themselves, their regularity, and habitual character need not evoke either extreme enthusiasm or pessimism. Any election – even if it is controlled, even if it is adapted to the needs of the old nomenklatura system, even if it manipulates public opinion and is accompanied by fraud – is better than none at all. It is an element of public politics that introduces democratic procedures and activates society's development. It provides the ruling class with some feedback from society, and it stimulates the consolidation at least of an elite, if not of society. Finally, it sets a tempo in political developments, expanding current possibilities and formulating tasks for the future.

[34] One of the most serious recent attempts of such a kind was undertaken by Daniel Treisman (*After the Deluge: Regional Crises and Political Consolidation in Russia* [Ann Arbor: University of Michigan Press, 1999]), who tried to build a simple model linking financial aid to the regions' direct and immediate impact on the voting for the "party of power." Effective in his discussion of fiscal federalism, he was less so in using electoral and political statistics and in explaining results of his correlation analysis. I believe that the high degree of political instability and the economic crises shaped campaigns between 1989 and 1996 in a way that made it hardly possible to think about economic determinism. The 1999–2001 cycle might be different.

How stable is the very institution of democratic elections in Russia? Stephen White, Richard Rose, and Ian McAllister are correct in concluding that "before an election, politicians debate not only who should win but also whether an election should be held at all."[35] The political elite needs elections in their present form to legitimize itself, however. Certainly, the huge electoral business is vitally interested in keeping the elections going. Does society need the elections as such? Yes, it does. It needs elections as a pillar of democracy, just as it needed the parliament in 1993, well aware of all its limitations, yet willing to protect it when under threat. Thus, the abolition of elections by some sort of authoritarian regime in Russia seems unlikely. They will rather continue their internal transformation, in the direction that could clearly be seen to emerge during the cycle of 1999–2001.

Elections were then held for the sake of elections, not unlike the carnival in Brazil. They neither brought into existence real political parties nor significantly promoted the building of civil society in the country. They have modified the nomenklatura elite system rather than changed society as a whole. Why was this so? It is like a car engine running in neutral. One needs to get into gear before the car will start moving. Elections are a necessary – but not a sufficient – condition for democratic development.

[35] Stephen White, Richard Rose, and Ian McAllister, *How Russia Votes*, p. xiii.

Leaders, structural conditions, and Russia's foreign policy

RAJAN MENON

AMERICANS' propensity to see politics as an extension of personality is evident in our thinking on Russia, which exalts the importance of leaders, one-to-one relationships, trust, and communication. The erosion of Soviet institutions under Mikhail Gorbachev and the failure of effective governing structures to take root in Russia under Boris Yeltsin reinforced this perspective by making leaders loom large. Yet the wiser course is to understand and anticipate the foreign policy of a state by focusing on "structural conditions," the strategic, economic, and demographic forces that are visible now and can, with reasonable confidence, be expected to frame the context of leaders' decisions in the future.

PUTIN AND THE PAUCITY OF POWER

Unfortunately Vladimir Putin, young, energetic, and sober, and in these respects a stark contrast to his predecessor, feeds the national habit of personalizing politics. Putin is expected to produce big results, although there is disagreement about what precisely they will be. Some fear that he will throttle Russia's fledgling democracy, stoke nationalism, and launch an anti-Western, even neo-imperial foreign policy. Others hope that his youth and forcefulness will energize slothful, sclerotic Russia so that order is created, taxes collected, and corruption curbed.

Whatever Putin's designs, they cannot be separated from the structural conditions created by the legacies of the past and the context of the present. Consider, to begin with, his economic constraints. Russia's gross national product (GNP) is less than that of the Netherlands' ($395 billion vs. $403 billion), and its revenues are smaller than the state of Florida's ($41 million vs. $40 million).[1] Moscow's economic resources will increase if the impressive growth that Russia has experienced since

---

[1] *The New York Times 2000 Almanac* (New York: Penguin, 1999), pp. 219, 524, and 657.

1999 persists, but there are good reasons to doubt that it will. The plummeting in the ruble's value since 1998 has spurred growth by raising the prices of imports and increasing demand for domestically produced goods, but there may not be enough effective demand to sustain the expansion in a country where a third of all people live below the poverty line. Robust investment is critical for long-term increases in growth and productivity; without it, what is in effect an upturn fired by import substitution will stall. Yet, very little foreign investment is coming into Russia, and most of it goes to greater Moscow and a few other areas. In 1999, inflows amounted to a mere $4 billion; on a per capita basis that is a tenth of what Hungary, which has a population less than one-tenth of Russia's, attracted. Per capita foreign investment from 1992 to 1998 was $108; by contrast, Estonia received $1,134; Latvia, $705; Azerbaijan, $408; and Kazakhstan, $325. Russia's share of global foreign direct investment in 1998 amounted to 0.3 percent; Brazil's was 3.8 percent.[2] Portfolio investment, another indicator of investors' confidence, shrank from $681 million in 1997 to $31 million in 1999, although, with inflows amounting to $59 million during the first nine months of 2000, there was a limited recovery.[3]

Anemic foreign investment has not been offset by strong internal investment despite the $60 billion trade surplus amassed in 2000 thanks to the devaluation of the ruble and high oil prices.[4] Investment is critical to Russia's economic recovery, not least because its infrastructure and capital stock, both civilian and military, needs to be modernized or replaced.[5] Unfortunately, investment in critical sectors, such as power generation and telecommunications, is sluggish. The larger view is scarcely more encouraging. Russia's capital investment as a percentage of GNP was 11 percent in 1998, in contrast to 30 percent for Hungary and 25 percent for Mexico.[6] Capital flight, which Russian officials estimate is $18 to $20

---

[2] Richard Ericson, "The Russian Economy: A Turning Point?" paper presented at the Aspen Institute conference, "US-Russia Relations," Prague, August 21–25, 2000; The *Russian Journal*, June 1–7, 2001. Available: http://www.russiajournal.com.

[3] The *Russian Journal*, June 1–7, 2001.

[4] Putin's top economic advisor, Andrei Ilarionov, notes that no more than 15 percent of the gains from rising oil prices and devaluation have been realized by the state and channeled into investment. The rest has been eaten up by imports and capital flight. *The Economist*, January 27, 2001, p. 73.

[5] Richard Ericson notes that "over two-thirds of the equipment in use has been in place over 15 years, and almost one-third is over 20 years old" and estimates that revamping it would require an investment "20 percent larger than GDP in 1997–8." Ericson, "The Russian Economy."

[6] Roughly $7 billion a year in investment is needed to replace aging power generation plants, but a mere $1 billion was mustered in 1999. Likewise, to meet demands for telephones and to digitalize service and modernize long-distance networks, $22 billion in investment is required, but investment in 1999 amounted to $500 million. *The Economist*,

billion a year, is partly to blame.[7] Criminality is deeply embedded in the economy, and bribery is rife. To be sure, there have been positive signs: tax collection has improved, the economy continues to grow at an impressive clip, and oil exports have increased foreign exchange reserves. Only when Russia is able to maintain high growth rates despite a fall in oil prices, however, will we know that there has been a fundamental upturn in the economy that is based on effective reforms and governance rather than contingent circumstances.

Human capital, the second structural constraint, presents an even bleaker picture.[8] Diseases and social ills are pervasive in Russia, with rising rates of HIV/AIDS, tuberculosis, diphtheria, and hepatitis C; substance and alcohol abuse; and poverty and homelessness among children (only 5 to 25 percent of whom are born healthy) are among the signs. The demographic consequence is a rise in mortality rates and a fall in the fertility rates, an imbalance that reduces Russia's population by 750,000 a year. If it continues, Russia's current population of 145 million could fall to 100 million by 2050 and the proportion of citizens in economically productive age groups will shrink while the segment that is retired and depends on social services will increase.[9] These economic and social problems will hobble Russia in the Darwinian age of globalization, particularly if its windfall from oil exports and high economic growth rates should prove short-lived.

Military power, long Russia's strong suit, is also atrophying and is the third constraint. Simply put, the quality and quantity of force available to support Russia's foreign policy will decrease dramatically. Again, the numbers are revealing. Russia's armed forces numbered 2.8 million in 1992; by 1999, they were cut to 1.2 million, and in 2000, officials announced a reduction to 850 thousand by 2003. The military budget, $100 billion in the last year of the Soviet Union, is now $ 7.3 billion, roughly 2 percent of American military spending.[10]

September 2, 2000, p. 58; Yevgeny Gavrilenkov, "Sham Stabilization," in Lawrence Klein and Marshall Pomer, eds., *The New Russia: Transition Gone Awry* (Stanford: Stanford University Press, 2001), p. 193.

[7] The $18 billion estimate is by Mikhail Fradkov, head of the Russian Federal Tax Police; Putin mentioned the $20 billion figure in a speech to a joint session of the legislature in the spring of 2001. *RFE/RL Security Watch* 2, no. 22 (June 4, 2001); *The Economist*, April 7, 2001, p. 57.

[8] The dismal statistics cited later appear, inter alia, in Mark G. Field and Judyth L. Twigg, *Russia's Torn Safety Nets* (New York: St. Martin's Press, 2000); and Murray Feshbach, "Russia's Population Meltdown," *The Wilson Quarterly* XXV, no. 1 (Winter 2001), pp. 15–21; Human Rights Watch, *Abandoned to the State* (New York: Human Rights Watch, 1998).

[9] Feshbach, "Russia's Population Meltdown," pp. 15, 16.

[10] Figures for Russian military manpower and defense spending draw on Russian military expert Alexander Pikaev's presentation, "Ten Years After: Is the Military Reformed?" at the conference "The Fall of Communism in Europe: Ten Years On," the Marjorie

It is sensible to cut defense spending and the size of the military, transforming an unwieldy conscript army into a smaller, well-trained, modern force given Russia's economic problems. What is occurring, however, is not well-conceived military reform but a downsizing driven by economic exigencies resembling a collapse.[11] Because of the lack of money, only 7 percent of the 900,000 men released from the military were retrained for civilian jobs.[12] Nor has a smaller military improved life for those remaining in the ranks, particularly given that, until 2000, the bulk of spending for military procurement went to the nuclear forces. Russia's armed forces have been weakened by obsolescent materiel and reduced training exercises, and, beyond this, they are afflicted by a spreading rot – alcoholism and brutal hazing, rampant in the Soviet army, have been joined by poverty, rising rates of suicide, drug abuse, AIDS, and tuberculosis.[13] Poorly trained, poorly housed, poorly paid, and poorly equipped, Russia's soldiers are thoroughly demoralized. Skills and morale are at a nadir, and the mismatch between the size of the conventional forces and the defense budget is still too large for a turnaround. In a change of policy, it was announced in 2000 that strategic nuclear forces would be cut and their favored budgetary treatment redirected to conventional units.[14] This plan could come to nothing, however, if the war in Chechnya continues to swallow resources, if oil prices fall, or if Russia's growth spurt falters. All three are distinct possibilities.

The war in Chechnya has exposed the plight of the Russian army. Contrary to official bravado, the "bandit formations" (Moscow's dismissive

Mayrock Center for Russian, Eurasian, and East European Studies, Hebrew University of Jerusalem, Jerusalem, Israel, May 14–17, 2001.

[11] Alexander Goltz, "Signals of Reforms but under Soviet Principles," *The Russia Journal*, May 4–10, 2000; idem, "Full Circle for Military Reform," in ibid., September 16–22, 2000; editorial in *Iadernyi kontrol* January–February 2001, translated in *CDI Russia Weekly*, no. 143 (March 5, 2001), pp. 12–13.

[12] Vladimir Mukhin, "Soldiers Worry about Road to Civilian Life," The *Russian Journal* (May 11–17, 2001).

[13] Deborah Yarsike Ball, "The Social Crisis of the Russian Military," in Field and Twigg, eds., *Russia's Torn Safety Nets*, pp. 271–84. According to an Agence France Press report citing "servicemen's support groups," "of the 3,000 noncombatant deaths [in the armed forces] each year, 28 percent are suicides." Reprinted in *CDI Russia Weekly*, no. 147 (April 2, 2001), p. 10. Other sources estimate that between 22.7 and 25 percent of annual military deaths are accounted for by suicide. Rita Bolotskaya, "Military Leaders vs. 'Suicides'," *Podmoskovnye izvestiia*, June 16, 2000, trans. in *Defense and Security* (Moscow) (June 26, 2000) and ITAR-TASS (April 20, 1999). Available www.perso.club-internet.fr/kozlowsk/suicides/html. On the health of conscripts, see Ekho Moskvy Radio, in Russian, 1400 GMT, March 29, 2001, monitored and translated by the BBC, reprinted in *CDI Russia Weekly*, April 2, 2001, p. 10–11.

[14] Fred Weir, "Putin Tries Big Shift in Military Policy," *The Christian Science Monitor*, August 2, 2000.

term for Chechen fighters) remain strong. A small but dispersed, battle-hardened, and motivated array, they continue to kill Russian soldiers (and officials of the pro-Russian Chechen government) using snipers, small-group ambushes, and concealed bombs. The innocuous, weary civilian by day becomes a lethal foe by night.[15] By leveling Grozny, driving some 250,000 Chechens into neighboring Ingushetia (and turning others into internal refugees), Russia has assured Chechen fighters a steady supply of volunteers.

The Chechen government loyal to Moscow is seen as a collection of quislings and will collapse once Russia withdraws.[16] Yet, without a legitimate government that can govern there, Russia must wage an open-ended war, something it cannot afford to do. Already, contract soldiers (*kontraktniki*) lured by (relatively) high salaries are playing a much smaller role because there is no money to pay them, and Russia will have to rely even more on young, inexperienced, summarily trained conscripts. Moscow announced in 2000 that its forces in Chechnya would be reduced by 50 percent to 50,000, but only 5,000 had been withdrawn by May. Further reductions were suspended in the face of increased Chechen attacks.[17] Even a smaller deployment will prove taxing if Chechnya has to be garrisoned for the long haul; pay, construction, and supplies for the war have already consumed a sixth of the 2000 defense budget.[18]

Neither victory nor a negotiated settlement are in the offing, and the 2003 referendum held in Chechnya has made no dramatic change when it comes to the cycle of war and terrorism. Withdrawal under these circumstances would bring disaster, and Russia's leaders have staked

[15] Sixty-two Russian Interior Ministry troops were killed during the first five months of 2001 and since the beginning of Russia's second campaign in Chechnya in 1998, 2,682 soldiers have been killed. See "Russian Troops Killed in Chechnya." Available http://www.cnn.com/2001/world/europe/06/02/chechnya/html. On the melding in Chechnya of civilians and fighters, a Russian officer remarked, "Let's say we are walking down the street and meet a Chechen. Is he a rebel who buried his gun somewhere and who will attack us tonight? Or is he a farmer who wants a peaceful and prosperous Chechnya? We have no way of knowing." David Filipov, "Russia's Hope for Swift Win Dims with Time," *Boston Globe*, May 30, 2001. On the lack of equipment and poor morale, see Vladimir Filichkin, "Apes at War," *Delovoi Ural* (Chelyabinsk), June 20, 2000, p. 6., translated in *Defense and Security* (Moscow), no. 83 (July 19, 2000). Available: http//www.wps.ru/digest/defence.html.

[16] The best Russian analyst of the war in Chechnya is Pavel Felgenhauer. See, for example, "Chechnya: A Vicious Circle," *Moscow Times*, September 21, 2001. Also see Anne Nivot, *Chienne de Guerre: A Woman Reporter Behind the Lines In Chechnya* (New York: Public Affairs, 2001).

[17] *RFE/RL Security Watch* 2, no. 19 (May 14, 2001).

[18] "At What Cost the War in Chechnya?" *Russia Journal*, March 6, 2000; Rajan Menon and Graham D. Fuller, "Russia's Ruinous War in Chechnya," *Foreign Affairs* 79, no. 2 (March/April 2000), pp. 32–44.

too much on victory. The anti-Chechen wave that swept Russia after the mysterious bombings that preceded and facilitated the war helped Putin's political ascent. A continued stalemate in this struggle could be his undoing, especially if the Chechens carry out more audacious terrorist operations along the lines of the 2002 Nord-Ost episode. Moreover, a wholesale withdrawal could risk Russia's hold over the entire North Caucasus, a fragile southern borderland rife with demographic pressures, poverty, unemployment, and conflicts among the bewildering array of ethnic groups over economic and political power, historiography, and the legitimacy of borders.[19] The dogged anti-Russian nationalism evident in Chechnya does not exist elsewhere in the North Caucasus (their neighbors view the Chechens with more than a little ambivalence), but the region is explosive for the other reasons mentioned earlier – and too important to abandon. It is a passageway for oil pipelines; through Dagestan, it gives Russia control over 70 percent of the Caspian Sea coastline; and it is Russia's gateway to the South Caucasus. The end of Russian control could have larger ramifications. Chechnya's instability could infect Stavropol and Krasnodar to the north and even reshape politics in Bashkortostan and Tatarstan, two republics that sit astride the communication routes to Siberia and have Turkic Muslim titular nationalities. True, secessionist movements do not exist in either republic now, but the possibility that they could emerge if chaos in the North Caucasus casts doubt on the Russian Federation's longevity cannot be ruled out.

To overcome the structural problems that encumber it, Russia needs an effective state, one able to keep order, collect taxes, curb corruption, and implement reforms. State-building has historically been a protracted affair, however, and will certainly not be completed in Russia over the next decade. Despite this, Russia will command attention because of its nuclear weapons; it sits on the Security Council, attends the G-8 summits, and makes diplomatic forays into the Middle East. Were it not for its nuclear arsenal, however, Russia would not receive the attention it does. With few other assets, it has a great power's trappings, but few of its substantive attributes. Putin's proclamations about reviving Russia's greatness will merely highlight the gulf between aspirations and abilities in what is now a virtual power. The divorce between

---

[19] Menon and Fuller, "Russia's Ruinous Chechen War"; Anna Matveeva, *The North Caucasus: Russia's Fragile Borderland* (London: Royal Institute of International Affairs, 1999); Yoav Karny, *The Highlanders: A Journey to the Caucasus in Quest of Memory* (New York: Farrar, Strauss & Giroux, 2000); Sebastian Smith, *Allah's Mountains: Politics and War in the Russian Caucasus* (London: IB Tauris, 1998); "Krivoe zerkalo Ingushetii," *Nezavisimaia gazeta*, September 5, 2000, pp. 1, 11; "Dagestan: zhizn' vzaimy," ibid., March 13, 2001, pp. 1, 11.

self-image and efficacy will produce an embittered nationalism marked by finger pointing, victimhood, conspiracy theories, and resentment. The harbingers are visible in Russians' disillusionment and their government's drive to bolster patriotism and reverence for the military and its "information security doctrine."[20]

IN DEFENSE OF STATE INTERESTS

The intellectual fashion of stripping the state of purpose and reducing it to a farrago of contending cliques and cabals has won followers among experts on Russia who, thanks to democratization, can dwell on the domestic sources of Russian foreign policy. Whether the results have been helpful is another matter given that statecraft in Russia is described as a directionless war among special interests. Yet, however weak the Russian state, it is not simply an arena for competition. Nor are its interests either transitory or reflections of deeper power struggles. An obsession with the rivalries among institutions and groups must not obscure the strategic considerations that flow from history, geography, and the nature and extent of national power and that set the context for means and ends. The following will be Russia's most important strategic goals over the next ten years.

First, Russia will maintain a strategic nuclear arsenal (land, air, and sea based) that, although reduced drastically (to fewer than a thousand warheads by 2020) to lighten the economic burden, will suffice to allow retaliation against attacks and thus to deter them. Besides preventing nuclear attacks against Russia (a very unlikely eventuality), such forces will also serve to increase the risks that any state must assume in attacking the Russian homeland with nonnuclear forces. If Russia's conventional military forces remain weak because of its economic problems, nuclear weapons will be relied on to thwart nonnuclear threats. Moscow's renunciation of "no first use," and explorations within the Russian strategic community of ways in which nuclear weapons can, through selective, limited use, compensate for weak conventional forces is a bellwether – a worrisome one, given Russia's aging and poorly maintained nuclear arsenal. Beyond such operational tasks, nuclear weapons will be Russia's ticket to conclaves of the major powers, thus serving a symbolic-political function.

Second, Russia's conventional forces will be reduced below 1 million because of economic pressures and restructured for post–Cold War

---

[20] Fred Weir, "Moscow Pitches Patriot Games," *Christian Science Monitor* (March 22, 2001); *Jamestown Foundation Monitor* (March 1, 2001).

missions. Their main responsibility will obviously be to deter, or, failing that, to repel, attacks on Russian territory, but they will be made smaller and lighter and trained and equipped for broader missions. These will include countering internal secessionist movements, peacekeeping, and coercive diplomacy and deployment abroad, particularly in Central Asia and the South Caucasus. Russia will make a virtue of necessity and re-orient itself as a regional power; doctrines and forces related to the pro-jection of power afar will be scrapped. Creating a new force to replace what is a pared-down version of the Red Army, which was trained and equipped for armored and aerial war in Europe, will require a reallo-cation of resources from nuclear to conventional forces, but even then a revamped military will be slow to emerge given Russia's economic constraints. There will, in short, be a sizeable difference between the planned and the possible.

Third, Russia will try to ensure that, at a minimum, it remains a major power in the "near abroad."[21] This will involve efforts to prevent Turkey, Iran, China, the West, or Western multilateral organizations such as NATO from displacing it or acting in the face of its opposition in the other ex-Soviet republics. Russia will use various means to dissuade states in the near abroad from joining alignments or alliances that it deems unfriendly. It will sign bilateral security treaties (the one with Armenia is an example) and train, equip, and defend regimes against radical religious movements, a growing problem for the Central Asian states. A limited number of bases or installations in Central Asia and the South Caucasus will be maintained, principally to signal to other states (such as Turkey) Russian interests and commitments. Russia will also forge multifaceted, although not multilateral, ties with the other states of the former Soviet Union. The political rationale of these will be to increase their stake in avoiding strategic choices that challenge Russian interests. To this end, Moscow will use their debts to Russia, their dependence on Russian energy, and their reliance on remittances from citizens working in Russia as coercive instruments.

Russia will gradually abandon a multilateral, CIS (Commonwealth of Independent States)–based strategy in favor of a nuanced bilateralism. The CIS has failed as a Russia-led forum for interdependence in eco-nomic and security affairs; it is a talk shop – long on summits, banquets, and proclamations and short on implementation. The division between those members who oppose economic integration and collective defense (Ukraine, Georgia, Azerbaijan, and Uzbekistan) and those who favor it

---

[21] I use this term purely for convenience to refer to the non-Russian republics of the former USSR and not to suggest, as do some Russian writers who use it, that Russia has natural entitlements with respect to its neighbors.

(Belarus, Kazakhstan, Armenia, Kyrgyzstan, and Tajikistan) will only grow. Rivalries and disputes (between Armenia and Azerbaijan, Kazakhstan and Uzbekistan, Uzbekistan and Kyrgyzstan) will doom efforts to move it from cacophony toward cohesion. That will spell the end of Russia's grand but hollow multilateralism. It will be replaced by a bilateral strategy tailored to the circumstances of particular countries and supplemented by agreements with smaller groups of states, agreements that become feasible because they are more manageable and less alarming.

Fourth, Russia will pursue a selective foreign policy outside the near abroad to align means and ends, focusing on the United States, Western Europe (and within it Britain and France, but particularly Germany), Iran, India, China, Japan, Vietnam, and South Korea. Some countries – the United States and Germany are examples – will receive attention by virtue of their overall strategic weight; others (Iran, India, China, and Vietnam) because Russia has convergent interests with them against actual or potential adversaries and because they are major markets for Russian arms; and still others because they offer economic opportunities and assistance (Western Europe, South Korea).

Fifth, Russian policy toward specific countries and regions – particularly the United States, Europe, China, and Japan – will be shaped by diverse motives, some incommensurable. This, rather than institutional rivalries, will be the main source of the ambiguities, inconsistencies, and contradictions. While Russia's foreign policy will not be immune to domestic pressures, its cardinal features will emerge from the encounter between the Russian state, its available power, the nature of that power, and the wider strategic environment or, stated differently, by structural conditions.

THE "NEAR ABROAD": HISTORY'S LEGACIES, GEOGRAPHY'S REALITIES

Russia will consistently oppose the "intrusion" of Western – or what it views as Western-dominated – security organizations into the former Soviet Union. Large countries regard contiguous zones in a near-proprietary manner and seek empire or hegemony, and Russia will be no different. Although it will lack the intent, will, and means to resurrect empire – which is historically passé anyway – it will quite naturally resist what it sees as harmful trends in neighboring areas to which it is linked by geography, history, and culture. The character of Russia's state will not alter this disposition. Russian elites, regardless of political inclination, believe that Russia should at least be *primus inter pares* in the near abroad.[22] This consensus will mean continued opposition to NATO's expansion, particularly its efforts to include Ukraine and Georgia. The OSCE (Organization for Security and Cooperation in Europe) will be handled differently. It is not an alliance, and as a full-fledged member Russia can limit what it does and where it does it. Moscow will not welcome OSCE ventures in the post-Soviet space, but it will assent to them when it can shape the terms of engagement by withholding consent or through direct participation.

NATO will not admit Georgia and Ukraine (despite enthusiasm for admission in the former). The first round of NATO expansion did not have the political consequences within Russia that many feared; Russians overwhelmingly opposed NATO enlargement, but the event had little traction in Russian politics. This pattern will recur in the second round. Russia needs economic cooperation with the West and continuing progress in arms control. It will not risk these important transactions.

The status of ethnic Russians in the near abroad will remain part of Russia's political discourse given nationalism's universal tribalistic allure and its usefulness to demagogues. This issue will be discussed when Russia's leaders meet their counterparts from the other ex-Soviet states, but it will not reach a boiling point. Ukraine and Kazakhstan have long borders with Russia and the largest Russian populations outside the Russian Federation. They have handled what could have been an explosive problem with wisdom and finesse precisely because of these geographic and demographic realities. There have been no civil wars in either country, and Russia has not fostered separatist and irredentist movements. Nor are such dangers likely. The position of ethnic Russians has not been a dominant, let alone incendiary, element in Ukraine and Kazakhstan's dealings with Russia. Part of the explanation lies in the cultural similarities between Russians and Ukrainians, the Russification of Kazakh elites, and the mellow nationalism that prevails in Ukraine and Kazakhstan. The power of pragmatism accounts for the rest. From the outset, Ukraine and Kazakhstan understood that clashes with Russia over the treatment of their ethnic Russian populations would spell disaster. For its part, Russia realized that it would pay a price in the West for brazen intervention; given the size of Ukraine and Kazakhstan, this is a recipe for strategic indigestion in any event. These restraining conditions will remain salient.

Controversies centering on the Russian diaspora have created more friction between Russia and the Baltic states (principally Latvia and

---

[22] Rajan Menon, "After Empire: Russia and the Southern 'Near Abroad'," in Michael Mandelbaum, ed., *The New Russian Foreign Policy* (New York: Council on Foreign Relations, 1998), pp. 100–66.

Estonia) and will continue to do so. The problem thus far has been confined to the political sphere and has not assumed military proportions for several reasons. Russia's leaders knew that attempts to intimidate the Baltic states would mobilize anti-Russian sentiments in the West and strengthen support for bringing them into NATO. Conversely, the leaders of Estonia and Latvia realized that this delicate issue had to be handled in ways that reconciled their projects for nation-building with Russia's interests. Russians in the Baltic countries have adjusted to irksome circumstances even when, as in the case of language and citizenship laws, they resent them. They know that they live better than their ethnic kin in the Russian Federation. This, to use Albert Hirshman's formulation, inclines them to "voice" and, ultimately to loyalty, but not to "exit."[23]

The framework governing interactions between Russia and individual states in the near abroad is already in place and will not change over the next decade. Ukraine's desultory economic reforms, limited economic ties with the West, fruitless quest for NATO membership, energy debt to Moscow (estimated at between $1.4 and $2 billion), and location will ensure its continued and considerable dependence on Russia. Indeed, Russia will increase its economic presence in Ukraine by exchanging Ukraine's energy debt for shares in its industries.[24] Moscow's planned natural gas pipeline from the Yamal peninsula to Germany via Belarus will diminish Ukraine's bargaining power further by reducing both its significance as a corridor for Russian gas exports and the transit fees it receives.[25] So will Ukraine's failure to enter NATO. These asymmetries ensure that Russia will hold the upper hand on other issues, such as the terms of Ukraine's lease of Sevastopol to Russia's Black Sea Fleet.

Georgia, too, will find that Russia is not a spent force, particularly because Tbilisi's hopes for major economic and security ties with the West, let alone admission to NATO, will not be realized. Russia will continue to exert leverage over Georgia by fostering a no-war–no-peace environment in Abkhazia and North Ossetia, regions with which it has what amounts to a direct relationship. Moreover, although Russia agreed (at the November 1999 Istanbul OSCE summit) to relinquish the military bases at Vaziani and Gudauta, it retains two others in Akhalkalaki and

---

[23] Albert O. Hirschman, *Exit, Voice, and Loyalty* (Cambridge: Harvard University Press, 1970).

[24] Anatol Lieven and Celeste Wallander, "Make Russia a Better Neighbor," *New York Times*, March 14, 2001, p. 23.

[25] The fees now amount to 30 billion cubic meters of the 70–80 billion cubic meters Ukraine needs annually.

Batumi.[26] These are areas whose potential disloyalty worries Georgian leaders, and Russian officers have established independent ties with local elites. Concern that a wholesale Russian departure from these regions would aggravate their tensions with Tbililsi is a major reason that Georgia did not press Russia to vacate all bases. Russia also holds economic cards. Georgia depends on Russia for natural gas and owes it $179 million for unpaid deliveries. To drive home the political significance of this dependence, Russia stopped supplies several times in late 1999, and this step was preceded by an imposition of temporary restrictions on Georgians – but tellingly not Abkhazians and North Ossetians – who had hitherto traveled to Russia to work under a CIS visa-free agreement.[27]

Oil revenues will provide Azerbaijan greater leeway vis-à-vis Russia. Yet, it, too, must deal with Russia's alliance with Armenia (symbolized by a defense treaty, arms sales, and military bases), which gives Moscow a decisive role in the future of Nagorno-Karabakh, one that goes far beyond its membership in the OSCE Minsk Group that is working for a solution. As in Abkhazia and North Ossetia, a neither-peace-nor-war stalemate affords Russia leverage over both Azerbaijan and Armenia.[28] Furthermore, Azerbaijan remains economically dependent on Russia despite its energy wealth. Half a million Azerbaijanis work in Russia, and their remittances are critical to a country plagued by high unemployment and widespread poverty. Thus, the significance of Russian warnings in 2000 that it would no longer automatically apply the visa-free regime to all states within the CIS was not lost on Baku.[29] Whether or not it follows through, Moscow made its point.

Russia's record in the South Caucasus and Central Asia is often portrayed as a failure. In fact, it has done rather well – and with a weak hand. Russia's alliance with Armenia defines and limits Azerbaijan's strategic choices. No Georgian official takes seriously the proposition, that appears frequently in Western analysis, that Russia is a bumbling behemoth. Russian companies were included in the Caspian production sharing agreements (PSAs) not because of their technical expertise or wealth, but because Western oil executives appreciated Russia's capacity to act as a spoiler. The government that rules Tajikistan survives because of Russian aid and military backing, and Moscow (along with Iran) was also the moving force behind the precarious peace accord

---

[26] *The New York Times*, November 24, 1999, p. 8.
[27] Lieven and Wallander, "Make Russia a Better Neighbor"; *The New York Times*, January 6, 2001, p. 2.
[28] "The Caucasus: Is a Settlement Possible?" *The Economist*, June 24, 2000, p. 58.
[29] Ibid.; and "Heidar Aliev, Maestro of the Caucasus," ibid., September 2, 2000, p. 48.

of 1997 that put a stop to prolonged and bloody civil war. The fear of radical Islam makes Central Asian states look to Russia as a necessary counterweight.[30] Kazakhstan, Kyrgyzstan, and Tajikistan are particularly inclined to do so, but Uzbekistan, the Central Asian state most eager to reduce Russia's influence, may be forced to rethink its choices, particularly if Washington's unwillingness and Turkey's inability to lend on-the-ground support against the Islamic extremists become evident. In 2001, Uzbekistan agreed to trade natural gas for Russian weapons, and its president, Islam Karimov, described Russia as "not only the guarantor of our security, but also a reliable strategic partner."[31] Although Karimov has responded to the Islamist challenge by forging military ties with Turkey, these are revealing words from a leader prone to warn about the danger of Russian domination.[32]

Despite Russia's weakness, it remains influential in Central Asia and the South Caucasus and will continue to be so. It no longer has an empire in these areas, but neither do competitors overshadow its opportunities and abilities. The United States will not guarantee the security of states in the South Caucasus and Central Asia that face insurgencies. Neither Turkey (whose potential in these regions has been heralded) nor Iran has displaced Russia. There is no sign that China has set that as one of its priorities (although I argue later that it could eventually supplant Russia in Central Asia).

The danger for Russia is not expulsion from Central Asia and the South Caucasus but entanglement. Over time, its strength will be sapped by conflicts that it is pulled into for fear that instability will spread if it desists. Yet, the roots of upheaval there (particularly in Central Asia) will prove long and deep, and intervention will be fruitless – a fool's errand that Russia's citizenry resents because of the blood and treasure it consumes. Propinquity will make prudence difficult, however. Unlike the maritime empires that departed their empires – voluntarily or under duress from nationalist movements – and could do so, Russia is heir to the Romanov and Soviet continental empires and cannot follow their example. The lack of money and public support for a forward policy may force Russia to redraw its defense perimeter at the border with Kazakhstan and at the North Caucasus if it retains that region, or in Stavropol and Krasnodar if it does not. That retrenchment is not at hand.

---

[30] "Putin, Central Asia Leaders Agree to Boost Military Cooperation," CNN.com. Available: http://www.cnn.com/2000/ASIA...al/10/ii/centralasia.russia.ap/index/html.

[31] Michael Lelyveld, "Uzbekistan: Gas for Russian Arms May Be Dangerous Precedent," *RFE/RL Magazine*, May 9, 2001. Available: http://www.rferl.org/nca/features/2001/05/09052001123432.asp.

[32] "A Turkish Move into Central Asia," *The Economist*, November 25, 2000, p. 56.

Russia will find it progressively harder to defend its interest in its southern environs at bearable cost. China, which has been willing to have Russia act as a stabilizer, will then reassess its strategy and assume commitments to maintain stability in Central Asia. Its economic stake there is growing, particularly in the energy sector, and it is increasingly concerned that Turkic nationalism emanating from Central Asia could strengthen Uighur separatism in Xinjiang. A Chinese advance will thus follow a Russian retreat from Central Asia and, in the worst case, from the Far East and Siberia. That will elicit countermoves by India, which now sees Central Asia as an extended economic and strategic sphere and will also heighten competition between Iran and Turkey. Central Asia, weighed down by poverty, demographic pressures, and radical nationalist and religious movements, will not benefit from being the venue for competition. The South Caucasus faces a similar future, although its mix of maladies and rivalries will be different. Russia is blamed for much that is bad in these regions, but its retreat will not improve their lot.

ASIA: NEW ALIGNMENTS, NEW VULNERABILITIES

As the twenty-first century advances, Russia will be on the wrong side of a major shift in the Eurasian balance of power – the acceleration of the already unfavorable trend in its standing with respect to China. This conclusion may appear incongruous given the much-vaunted "strategic partnership" that now binds Beijing and Moscow.[33] Yet, the hyperbole of Russia-China summits with their denunciation of a unipolar (i.e., American-dominated) world must not camouflage the fact that this is a mere marriage of convenience in which one partner increasingly holds the upper hand – something both realize.[34] Russia needs hard currency (arms and energy account for most of its exports); China seeks modern weapons, which no state will give it in the quantity, and with the lethality, firepower, and range, that Russia will; both are multiethnic states battling separatism (Russia in Chechnya, China – to a far lesser degree – in Xinjiang); both oppose freewheeling humanitarian intervention (especially under American auspices) undertaken in the name of self-determination; both worry about the strategic and economic consequences of NMD (national missile defense); and both are ambivalent about globalization, which, despite its many attractions, is also seen as a species of Americanization.

[33] A ten-year treaty of friendship was signed when President Jiang Zemin visited Russia in July 2001. *RFE/RL Security Watch* 2, no. 14 (April 9, 2001), p. 1.
[34] Rajan Menon, "The Strategic Convergence between Russia and China," *Survival* 39, no. 2 (summer 1997), pp. 101–125.

However, no matter their current valence, these shared tactical interests will not produce a durable strategic concord. A rising power, China already operates from a position of advantage against Russia. The margin will increase if its rate of economic growth proceeds apace. Modernization will increase the amount and versatility of China's power, including the capacity to make modern weapons. Its sense of vulnerability will diminish, and its confidence and ambitions will grow. Russia will have little of value to offer it – not capital, not technology, not strategic heft – apart from oil and gas from Siberia and the Russian Far East, and it will become a weak northern neighbor. Russia's vast Far East, rich in resources, poor in people, thinly defended, remote from the centers of Russian power west of the Urals, will slowly become part of an extended Chinese economic system or, in the worst case, metamorphose into a gaggle of statelets under Chinese suzerainty.

The direction and speed of China's transformation, the country's sheer size, the demographic imbalance between its northeastern provinces (Inner Mongolia, Jilin, Liaoning, and Heilongjiang, whose combined population is 129 million) and the Russian Far East (7 million inhabitants) will inexorably work against Russia, with China resorting not to force but to a multifaceted, velvet hegemony. Nor will matters be helped by the troubled legacy of Russo-Chinese relations, which includes Russia's annexation in the 1850s and 1860s (a recent period according to Chinese conceptions of time) of lands that are now part of the Russian Far East. Eurasia's balance of power will feature a Russia under China's shadow, not a Russia in alignment with China.[35] Prominent strategists have been explicit about this scenario in their debates over China's future trajectory and its implications for Russia.[36]

Fortunately for Russia, two other states, India and Japan, are perturbed by China's rise.[37] Even more fortunately, both states – one a major technological power with the capacity to muster far greater military force than it does at present; the other potentially a great power – are located on its flanks. A coalition with them (an outright alliance will be unnecessary and provocative) will force China to spread its resources over three widely separated fronts, thus subjecting it to the classic encirclement maneuver, particularly if Vietnam were to join the lineup.

[35] Rajan Menon and Charles E. Ziegler, "The Balance of Power and US Foreign Policy Interests in the Russian Far East," *NBR Analyses* 11, no. 5 (December 2000).

[36] Dmitri Trenin, "The China Factor: Challenge and Chance for Russia," in Sherman W. Garnett, ed., *Rapprochement or Rivalry?* (Washington, D.C.: Carnegie Endowment for International Peace, 2000), pp. 39–70. For the debate, see Aleksei D. Voskressenski, "Russia's Evolving Grand Strategy toward China," ibid., pp. 117–45.

[37] Rajan Menon and S. Enders Wimbush, "Asia in the 21st Century," *The National Interest*, no. 59 (Spring 2000), pp. 78–86.

The corollary of this prognosis is that Russia will maintain the Soviet-era alignment with India. It is held together by many common interests established during Soviet times and is not threatened by any disputes.[38] In what is a combination of commercial and strategic acumen, India is already the largest destination for Russian arms after China (Vietnam is a major recipient as well). Moscow will also change its approach toward Japan, abandoning what is a relic of the Cold War, but the change will be slow in coming for several reasons. The territorial dispute over the South Kuriles is one. A history of rivalry and conflict and the suspicion and contempt that divides Japanese and Russians is a second. Third, there have to be simultaneous governments in Moscow and Tokyo that have the strength and legitimacy to embrace, and sell to their citizens, a solution in which both countries make big compromises. That said, larger strategic variables, not the territorial dispute, will shape the Russia-Japan relationship. The extent of China's power, how it uses its might (as a revisionist state, or as one that largely works within the existing order), and America's role in the Asian balance of power that forms once Korea is unified are foremost among them.

The Russia-India-Japan-Vietnam coalition will jell if China becomes both stronger and more alienated from the status quo and if the United States reduces its military presence in the North Pacific, whether by choice or out of necessity. In the division of labor, Japan and India will increase their naval forces, while Russia and Vietnam – in what will be an important but subordinate contribution – maintain forces on their border sufficient to necessitate a Chinese counter deployment that disperses its power across widely separate fronts. This military cooperation will be supplemented by an arrangement of geoeconomics in which Russia supplies energy to India and Japan while they invest in Russia (and Vietnam) for pecuniary and strategic reasons. China and the quadripartite coalition will vie for the power and allegiance of a united Korea. Korea's troubled history with Japan and the reality of its border with China – longer than the Russo-Korean border – will dispose it to lean toward China or attempt to squeeze benefits from its pivotal position.

THE WEST: ATTRACTION AND AMBIVALENCE

Russia's future in the near abroad is one of eroding hegemony; in Asia, it will face unfavorable balances of power. The outlook for its dealings with

---

[38] F. N. Iurlov, *Rossiia i Indiia v meniaiushchemsia mire* (Moscow: Institut vostokovedeniia RAN, 1998).

the West is unevenness and ambivalence. The unevenness will stem from converging and conflicting interests: Russia's need for trade, investment, and arms control will necessitate cooperation, and the West will have economic and strategic reasons to reciprocate, but disputes over the size and actions of NATO, humanitarian intervention, globalization, "unipolarity," and "rogue states" will intermittently limit, even imperil, cooperation. Russia's failure to meet the West's expectations and the West's unwillingness to offer the degree of help Russians seek will make for disappointment and resentment on both sides.

The ambivalence arises from the pull of the past – Russia's. In America enthusiasm abounds for a Russia that embraces democracy and markets and joins the Western community; not a few Russians share this vision. Yet, only by distorting Russia's past and present can one assume that Russia has chosen the West and only the details remain to be handled. In fact, Russia has always been ambivalent about the values that typify the West. Consider some towering figures of its history (Miliukov, Chaadaev, Trubetskoi, Gumilev, the later Herzen, Karamzin, Solzhenitsyn) and it is clear that there have been dramatically different visions of what Russia is and should become. Westernizers have been part of the Russian drama since Peter the Great. Others, among them Slavophiles, Eurasianists, and Marxists of various hues, have offered a different plot entirely, rejecting the Western model in favor of a distinct and different path. Russians remain divided about Russia's future – indeed about the nature of its present. A segment of Russian society will reject the view that Russia's only viable path is to accept the end of history and to don Western garb. The view, common in America, that Russia will necessarily and ultimately cast its lot with the West is desire masquerading as thought.

This does not mean that Russia will spurn the West; that is not a realistic choice given its problems at home and abroad. Many Russians will continue to want what the West has (freedom and prosperity); others will regard the West as a monument to shallowness, mindless individualism, and crass materialism – as the embodiment of what Russia must reject. The contention between these views will continue, ensuring that there is no linearity to Russia's attitude and conduct toward the West. Which tendency will prevail? That depends on how long and bumpy Russia's quest for democracy, civil society, and capitalism is – and whether it succeeds. Success, even if slow and punctuated by setbacks, will strengthen Westernizers. If Russia fails and becomes a dysfunctional society of marginal significance in the world, those Russians who oppose Westernization and globalization (a varied lot, to be sure) will prevail.

Russia cannot be counted on to become a partner – not because it is somehow untrustworthy (that adjective is better applied to people, not states), but because of its historical predicament. The Soviet empire collapsed, leaving an economic and social wasteland in most of its remnants. In Russia, the largest remnant, too many protracted and profound changes must take place before something good rises from the rubble. In the West, the consolidation of the territorial state, national identities, markets, and democracy emerged over generations and more or less sequentially, and the process was still wrenching, often violent. Russia is trying to accomplish these complex transformations rapidly, simultaneously, and with little experience with capitalism or democracy. It may succeed, but the voyage will be long and harsh, and the West cannot decide the outcome. By expecting rapid results and a process with no setbacks, the West guarantees that its attitude toward Russia will oscillate between euphoria and despair. Neither emotion supports sound policy.

The West can help Russia create a market economy, but its capacity to do so is limited by what it can spend to this end because the outcome depends overwhelmingly on what happens within Russia and because we have proven to ourselves and to the Russians that we know little about what is proving to be a unique, revolutionary transformation, let alone how to accomplish it successfully. The combination of grand advice (be it shock therapy, a third way, the magic of the marketplace) and limited material help can only breed disillusionment and resentment, now much in evidence in Russia. Assistance must be specific (aid to the educational system, cultural and scientific exchanges, programs that help build Russia's human capital); it must be coordinated with key American allies to make the burden bearable; and it must focus on areas of mutual interest (safe nuclear installations) to garner political support at home. This approach must replace messianic notions of creating democracy and capitalism.

A Russia that fails to create democracy and a market economy need not turn hostile and join the West's adversaries. A failed Russia will be a weak Russia, and its shifting balance of power with China will work to moderate its antagonism toward the West. Scenarios that have Russia leading a civilizational revolt against the West by mobilizing Slavic identity and Orthodox Christianity are creative but fanciful. Ukraine, without which any such coalition would prove hollow, will resist integration, and most of East Central Europe will gravitate toward the West, toward Germany in particular. That leaves the Balkans, which Russia could lead, but to what end? The close of the Cold War has not ended Europe's division, only the nature of the division. Two massive alliances and an Iron Curtain no longer exist, but the European Union's expansion will make for a continent of haves and have nots. Russia's predicament, as represented by its interest in the Balkans, will be that its flock will consist of the latter and that the most important state spurned by the European Union, Turkey, will remain linked to the United States.

The conclusion that Russia will not become an enemy of the West is but a segue to discussing a fundamental change in the nature of the Russian problem. During the Cold War, Russia affected the West by virtue of clarity (an ideological alternative) and strength (the Warsaw Pact). Now Russia's weakness and ambivalence are the problem, and a number of new challenges derive from this change. The safety of Russia's nuclear facilities will remain a continuing problem. Its inability to maintain order in its immediate neighborhood and to balance China could make Eurasia unstable. Because of its penury, it is prone to sell arms and civilian nuclear technology widely and reject the West's calls for restraint (especially if we do not limit our own sales). Globalization will bring recurring shocks to the international order – balance of payments crises in and capital flight from major states; dislocations created by surging energy prices; and instability in important countries – but Russia's periodic economic crises and need for help will strain the capacity of Western-dominated international financial institutions to manage these problems.

Several policy-relevant conclusions follow from the preceding discussion. The West should communicate clearly to Russia what specific aspects of its relationship with China are troublesome and why; however, pumping up this Russo-Chinese duet as a far-reaching realignment is sensationalism that verges on panic. The West should not be surprised by Russia's efforts to retain influence in its immediate neighborhood; it should not consider them a prelude to domination, for which Russia is too weak.

On decisions concerning NATO's expansion or our diplomacy in the Caspian, we should take account of Russia's interests, think of ways to alleviate its anxieties, and offer it incentives to cooperate; this is quite different from giving Russia a veto. NATO should not be enlarged merely because the consequences in Russia might prove to be minimal, short-lived, and confinable. Decisions have to rest on compelling strategic reasons, and those adduced by champions of enlargement are unpersuasive, not least because the putative gains – security and prosperity for Central European and Baltic states – can be attained in other ways. American policy toward the other ex-Soviet republics should not be based on Russia's preferences, but neither should it move forward as if Russia does not exist or matter.

PERSONALITIES VERSUS CONTEXT

Russia's challenge will be to remain whole and to retain the capacity to shape events in its rim lands. Its failure in even these basic endeavors will not be cause for celebration. Russia sprawls across Eurasia, and the effects of its reconfiguration or weakness will spread far and engulf key countries – Ukraine, China, Georgia, Azerbaijan, Kazakhstan most directly, but several others indirectly. Russia's economic or political meltdown could generate refugee flows and illegal migration, cause the failure of nuclear reactors, and increase the chances of fissile material (perhaps even nuclear weapons) being stolen. Rivalries among states seeking primacy in the South Caucasus and Central Asia in the wake of a Russian exit could create new and long-lasting disruptions, including the future threat of interrupting Caspian energy supplies.

These are huge problems, but at least they are knowable and appropriate responses can be prepared. Similarly, even if Putin quits the scene suddenly, the main themes of Russia's strategy are predictable because the factors that set the parameters in which Russian leaders think and act will change but slowly. By focusing on leaders, we observe the texture of the leaves, not the contours of the forest, conflate a diplomacy toward a state and a relationship with a person, and look down at our feet, not out to the horizon. By contrast, structural conditions illuminate the big picture.

POSTSCRIPT

This chapter was completed in 2001, before the attack on the Twin Towers in New York. It therefore has to be asked how far the dramatic events that have taken place over the last two years require a revision of the argument put forward here. After all, since September 11, 2001, the United States has launched two major wars, in Afghanistan and Iraq – a flamboyant and unprecedented assertion of American dominance on the world stage. To illustrate the magnitude of this development, it is sufficient to recall that during the Gulf War of 1991, the United States made a calculated decision not to occupy Iraq, confining itself to the liberation of Kuwait.

Furthermore, the war of 2003 against Iraq (unlike the earlier attack on Taliban-dominated Afghanistan) was launched in the teeth of fierce diplomatic opposition throughout much of the world – an opposition led by a united front of France, Germany, and Russia. It is generally accepted (and there is no reason to doubt) that, in consequence, the hostility toward the United States, which anyway had become deep rooted in

Russian public opinion during the 1990s, has now been significantly enhanced. Speculation also has it that a realignment of alliances could lead to a deep-rooted schism between the United States and Europe, and that the latter, in an effort to counterbalance American power, will embrace Russia – a trend that, in particular could renew the historic bonds between Russia and Germany (or Prussia prior to 1870).

A totally different meaning, though, can legitimately be read into these recent developments. The structural problems examined in the chapter have in fact remained essentially unaltered since 2001 whether reference is made to Russia's economy; the intractable demographic and social problems; the slow pace of military reform; the ongoing armed conflict in Chechnya; or the complex relations with the "near-abroad" and China. Whatever the neo-Slavophile or Eurasian impulses at work within Russian society, Vladimir Putin is hardly going to sacrifice the rapprochement with the United States, which has characterized the country's foreign policy – despite periodic mini-crises – since the era of Gorbachev. The American war in Iraq has made for a rough patch in the relationship between Moscow and Washington, but both sides will place it back on an even keel. And, as argued earlier, even a new leader replacing Putin would find it exceptionally difficult to break out of the framework formed by the existing strategies, which flow from the structural conditions I have identified here.

Index